```
E        March, Allen
715         The history and conquest
.M3      of the Philippines and our
         other island possessions
```

WITHDRAWN

**THE DAVID GLENN HUNT
MEMORIAL LIBRARY
Galveston Community College
Galveston, Texas**

AMERICAN IMPERIALISM
Viewpoints of United States
Foreign Policy, 1898-1941

*Reproduced with the cooperation of the
Hoover Institution of War, Revolution and Peace,
Stanford University, Stanford, California*

THE HISTORY AND CONQUEST OF THE PHILIPPINES AND OUR OTHER ISLAND POSSESSIONS

Alden March

ARNO PRESS & THE NEW YORK TIMES
New York ★ 1970

Collection Created and Selected
by
CHARLES GREGG OF GREGG PRESS

Reprinted from a copy in The Hoover Institution Library

Library of Congress Catalog Card Number: 77-111744
ISBN 0-405-02038-4

ISBN for complete set: 0-405-02000-7

Reprint Edition 1970 by Arno Press Inc.
Manufactured in the United States of America

DAVID GLENN HUNT
MEMORIAL LIBRARY
GALVESTON COLLEGE

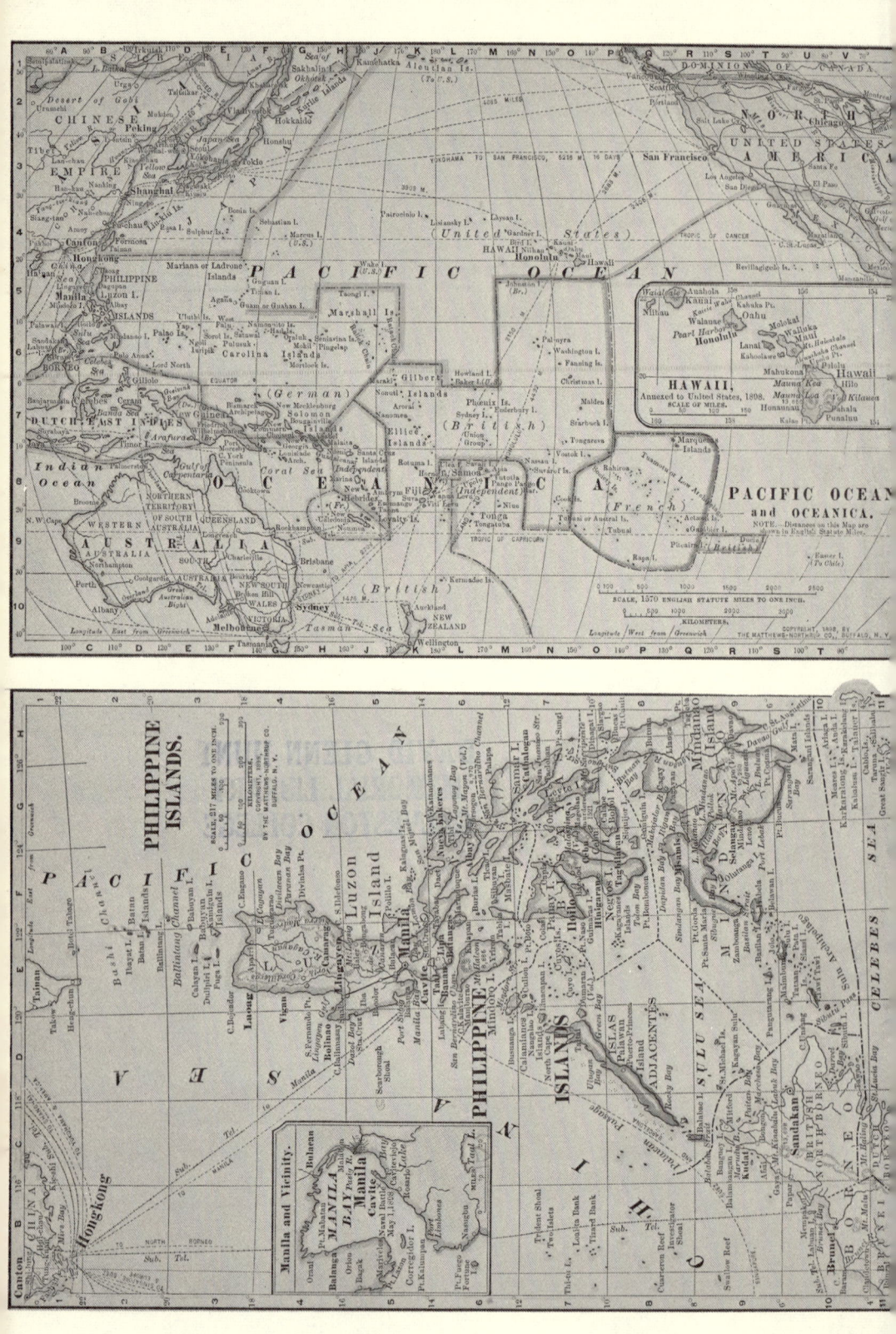

The History and Conquest of the Philippines

AND OUR
OTHER ISLAND POSSESSIONS

By ALDEN MARCH, A. M.

The Noted Journalist and Author

EMBRACING

OUR WAR WITH THE FILIPINOS IN 1899

Together With a Complete History of Those Islands from the Earliest Times to the Present

AN AUTHENTIC HISTORY OF THE SPANISH WAR

PREPARED FROM OFFICIAL GOVERNMENT REPORTS OF OUR ARMY AND NAVY OFFICERS
PRESENTING ALL THE FACTS FOR THE FIRST TIME

THE HISTORY OF CUBA, PORTO RICO,

The Ladrone and the Hawaiian Islands

FROM THEIR DISCOVERY TO THE PRESENT TIME

RICHLY EMBELLISHED WITH OVER ONE HUNDRED FULL PAGE
HALF-TONE AND OTHER ENGRAVINGS

COPYRIGHT, 1899
BY
WM. E. SCULL

ALL RIGHTS RESERVED

INTRODUCTION

THE whole world has turned its eyes upon the Philippine Islands. The nations of Europe and of the far East are anxiously watching their future. The United States stands with that future in its possession. Our country has made itself more vital than ever before in the great brotherhood of nations.

The magnificent victory of Admiral Dewey in the Bay of Manila, when he scorned hidden torpedoes and open foes, and swept the vessels of Montojo's fleet from the face of the waters without the loss of a single man or any considerable damage to his own battleships, not only brought our nation to the very forefront as a naval power, but focused upon the Philippines the eyes of all the world.

Previous to that time nobody knew or cared where the distant archipelago was. To-day there is not a schoolboy who cannot tell you, or a street urchin who does not speak its name as familiarly almost as that of his own city.

Necessarily, however, popular knowledge of the islands is extremely limited. Most persons have read in snatches here and there, of Aguinaldo, of the insurgents, of the famous battle of May 1st, of General Merritt, General Otis, General McArthur and the brave lot of soldiers, volunteers and regulars, who have crossed the 10,000 miles of sea, which leads to this our new possession.

THE PURPOSE OF THIS VOLUME.

It is the purpose of this volume to present a clear, concise, interesting and readable story of the conquest of the Philippines and of our other island possessions.

Now that the smoke of battle has cleared away and we are able to see more distinctly the splendid work of American arms, the valor of the American soldiers, the generalship of the American leaders, and the wise direction of American statesmanship, we are ready and anxious to know not only the story of our march of victory, but also something about the new lands and the new people, which have come under the folds of the flag, and which from now on are likely to be so prominent in the scheme of our national life.

Ever since the beginning of the war an elaborate, careful collection has been made of all books, newspaper and magazine articles, published both in this country and abroad, about the Philippines and about the events which have taken place there since our troops landed on those shores. These have been at the disposal of the writer, and their very possession alone insures the most complete record of the history of the Philippines possible.

This volume aims to bring you in contact with the people of these islands so vividly that you will know their past and their present, and become so interested in their future, that every word spoken for or against them will enlist your attention.

LONG STRUGGLE FOR LIBERTY.

As a people the Filipinos appeal to the American heart through their long years of struggle for liberty,—a struggle that has been marked throughout by a trail of life-blood of patriots,—a struggle that has been waged against unequal odds,—a struggle that was once, years ago, at the verge of successful issue, but was brought to naught at the very hour of victory, by an accident.

As a nation the Filipinos are not strong enough to protect themselves alone against the governments of the world. The United States took them under its protection. It offered to them liberty and civilization under its rule. Unhappily for them the insurgent leaders, whether for motives of personal gain, or from ill-advised sentiments against their protectors, have turned upon the hand that helped them.

The battle which was so costly, both to insurgents and to our own gallant soldiers, has made it impossible for the United States to go back. The demands of civilization hold us to the islands. President McKinley in his speech at Boston in February, 1899, summed up the situation and the duty of the Government as follows:

"The future of the Philippine Islands are now in the hands of the American people, and the Paris Treaty commits the free and

IN THE WAR ROOM AT WASHINGTON

The above illustration shows President McKinley, Secretary Long, Secretary Alger and Major-General Miles consulting the map during the progress of the Spanish-American War. It is in this room that the plans of conducting war by land and sea are formulated and the commands for action are wired to the fleet and the army.

REAR-ADMIRAL WILLIAM T. SAMPSON.

ADMIRAL GEORGE DEWEY.

REAR-ADMIRAL JOHN CRITTENDEN WATSON.

REAR-ADMIRAL WINFIELD SCOTT SCHLEY.

LEADING COMMANDERS OF OUR NAVY IN THE SPANISH-AMERICAN WAR.

franchised Filipinos to the guiding hand and the liberalizing influences, the generous sympathies, the uplifting agitation, not of their American masters, but of their American emancipators.

"No man can tell to-day what is best for them or for us. I know no one at this hour who is wise enough or sufficiently informed to determine what form of government will best subserve their interests and our interests, their and our well-being.

"Until Congress shall direct otherwise, it will be the duty of the Executive to possess and hold the Philippines, giving to the people thereof peace and order and beneficent government, affording them every opportunity to prosecute their lawful pursuits, and encouraging them in thrift and industry; making them feel and know that we are good friends, not their enemies; that their good is our aim, that theirs is our welfare; but that neither their aspirations nor ours can be realized, until our authority is acknowledged and unquestioned; that the inhabitants of the Philippines will be benefited by this Republic is my unshaken belief; that they will have a kindlier government under our guidance, and that they will be aided in every possible way to be a self-respecting and self-governing people, is as true as that the American people love liberty and have abiding faith in their own government and in their own institutions.

"No imperial designs lurk in the American mind. They are alien to American sentiment, thought and purpose. Our priceless principles undergo no change under a tropical sun. They go with a fiat: 'Why read ye not the changeless truth, the free can conquer but to save?'

"If we can benefit these remote peoples, who will object? If in the years of the future they are established in government under law and liberty, who will regret our perils and sacrifices?—who will not rejoice in our heroism and humanity? Always perils, and always after them safety; always darkness and clouds, but always shining through them the light and sunshine; always cost and sacrifice, but always after them the fruition of liberty, education and civilization.

"I have no light or knowledge not common to my countrymen. I do not prophesy. The present is all-absorbing to me, but I cannot bound my visions by the blood-stained trenches around Manila, where every red drop, whether from the veins of an American soldier or a misguided Filipino, is anguish to my heart; but by the broad range of future years, when that group of islands, under the impulse of the year just past, shall have become the gems and glories of those tropical seas, a land of plenty and of increasing possibilities, a people redeemed from savage indolence and habits, devoted to the arts of peace, in touch with the commerce and trade of all nations, enjoying the blessings of freedom, of civil and religious liberty, of education and of homes, and whose children and children's children for ages hence bless the American Republic, because it emancipated and redeemed their fatherland and set them in the pathway of the world's best civilization."

And so the beginning of the new life under the Stars and Stripes at the dawning of the new century will mark an epoch not only in the history of the Philippine Islands, but of the whole world. Upon the people of the United States the future of these new possessions imposes an immense responsibility.

Kipling has written of it as "the White Man's Burden:"

> "Take up the white man's burden—
> Ye dare not stoop to less—
> Nor call too loud on Freedom
> To cloak your weariness.
> By all ye will or whisper,
> By all ye leave to do,
> The silent, sullen peoples
> Shall weigh your God and you."

OUR OTHER ISLAND POSSESSIONS

While the novelty of the islands across the sea draws toward it curious eyes, the American people will never lose sight of the others nearer home, in behalf of which the sons of the flag laid down their lives, and for which the war with Spain was waged.

Cuba, with her historic past, a great drama of war and blood, is and always will be an object of keen interest. Ever since the explosion which blew up the *Maine* and stirred the hot blood of our whole nation beyond control, the past, the present and the future of Cuba have become almost part of our own history. The persecution, enslavement and utter extinction of the native Indians in sixty years

INTRODUCTION

through Spanish cruelty, the new race of Cubans, the feeble insurrection of a hundred years, the more virile Ten Years' War, and, finally, the War of 1895, that last great struggle for liberty, reads like a romance. And at last the terrible oppression and cruelty of Spain brought forth such an agonizing cry for help, that America could no longer resist its appeal, and "for the sake of humanity" took up arms in her behalf.

The campaign in Cuba and Porto Rico was a brilliant one. It was short, decisive, heroic. The deeds that were done, and the victories that were won, rival the greatest stories of valor that the world has ever heard. And now Cuba and Porto Rico are ours,—one temporarily, the other forever. Porto Rico, which Columbus discovered and where he was buried, will be familiar in the future to all the world as a winter resort. Beautiful, fertile and healthful, it will ever be a land of romance and of pleasure and of poetry. Hawaii, too, brought by the new cable in touch with the rest of the world, will be a part of us from this time onward. Their interests and our interests mingle. It is of them, and of Hawaii, "the Paradise of the Pacific," that a fuller knowledge is desired by all persons. And so in this history of our conquest of the Philippines and our other island possessions, they play an important part, and enlist your interest.

ALDEN MARCH.

TABLE OF CONTENTS

CHAPTER I
The Philippines—Past and Present

A Rapid Review of History, Place and People.—The Story of Discovery.—The First World Girdlers.—Another Expedition.—Naming the Islands.—Struggles for Supremacy.—English Take Manila.—Uprisings of the Natives.—The Last Struggle for Liberty.—A Warlike People.—Manila and other Towns.—Industries, Climate, Etc.—Admiral Dewey begins a New Era.

CHAPTER II
Behind Admiral Dewey's Guns

The Magnificent Naval Battle of May 1st Described by an Officer who stood by Dewey during the Fight.—The Personal Side of the Nation's Greatest Hero.—A Brush with German Officers.—The Surrender of Cavite.

CHAPTER III
The Second Battle of Manila

How 8,000 American Soldiers Swept into a Heavily Entrenched City, Garrisoned by Nearly Twice that Number of Spaniards.—Insurgent Army Kept from Plunder.—Rare Bravery and Sacrifice.—What Major-General Wesley Merritt, Commanding the Expedition, General Frank F. Greene, General Arthur McArthur and General Thomas Anderson Said Officially of the Battle.

CHAPTER IV
The Trouble with General Aguinaldo

A Face-to-Face View of the Insurgent Leader.—A Man of Craft and Cunning.—His Rapid Rise to Prominence.—Sold Out His Own People.—The Battle Against the United States.—Insurgents Swept Into the Sea.—Sacrifice of Life and Property.—The Flight of Agoncillo to Canada.—The Battle and the Treaty of Peace in the Senate.—The Oregon Needed "for Political Reasons."

TABLE OF CONTENTS

CHAPTER V

The Men Who Won Fame in Battle

Commanders and Soldiers whose Bravery has Brought them Special Honors.—Intrepid Fighting, Mad Dashes, and Fierce Firing of Boys from Pennsylvania, New York and other States of the East; from Tennessee, Kentucky and the Rest of the South Line; and the Heroic Warriors from Oregon, California, Dakota, Kansas, Iowa and the Middle and Far West.—Individual Deeds of Daring.—Scout Work Outside and Inside of the City.

CHAPTER VI

A Past History Written in Blood

Ever Since their Discovery the Philippines have been the Scene of Terrible Conflicts.—Began with an Alliance of Peace, but soon were Rife with War.—Legaspi Fortified Manila and made it a Stronghold.—The Raid of Limahong, the Chinese Pirate.—A Naval Battle with the Dutch for Half a Century.—England Takes Manila, but Returns It to Spain.

CHAPTER VII

Filipinos' Struggles for Freedom

Periodically the Natives Turned under the Cruel Spanish Heel and Rose up in their Might.—Revolts against the Tyranny of the Church.—How a Flight of Skyrockets once Tore Victory from the Hands of the Natives.—The Last Fight for Freedom.—The Greatest of Insurgent Martyrs, Doctor Rizal.—His Dramatic Execution a Few Years Ago.—Other Fighters for Freedom.

CHAPTER VIII

The Great Value of the Philippines

Why all Nations Covet what the United States has Won.—Importance from a Strategic Standpoint.—Immense Wealth and Resources.—Exports and Imports Amount to over $40,000,000.—Rich in Sugar, Rice, Hemp, Coffee, Cocoa, Spices and a Host of other Things.—Untold and Untried Mineral Wealth.

CHAPTER IX

The People of the Island

Over Eighty Different Tribes, most of whom have never seen a White Man.—Interesting Traits in the Character of the Natives.—Cannibalism in all of its Horrors. Cock Fighting as a Pastime.—How the Better Class Live.—Educational and Social Conditions.—Something about the Aetas, Negritos, Gadanes, Itavis, Igorrotes, Pinguianes and others.

TABLE OF CONTENTS xv

CHAPTER X

Fascinations and Terrors of a New Land

The Awful Wildness of Typhoons.—A Land Ruled by Volcanoes.—Thousands Killed by Earthquakes.—All Business Suspended until Evening, owing to the Heat.—A Glimpse of its Birds, Beasts and Reptiles.

CHAPTER XI

Manila, the Metropolis of the Philippines

A Delightful City which may become a Resort under the Stars and Stripes.—High and Low Life.—Foreigners kept out by the Spanish as much as Possible.—The Chinese Class.—The Splendid Big Convent.—Shops that Delight the Eye.—Rare Fabrics Woven from Plants and Embroidered by Nuns.—A New York Officer's Big Purchase.—A Dress that it took Months to Weave.—Inside of the English Club.—Americans have Started a Splendid Club for the Army and Navy.—The Famous Mestiza Girls.

CHAPTER XII

Other Important Cities of the Islands

A Sight-seeing Trip to Iloilo, Second in Commercial Importance to Manila, Cebu, which once outranked it, Leyte and other Places of Importance.—Scenes and Incidents among the Strange Population.—The Terrible Sultan of Sulu.—Superstitions of the Moros.—Funny Episodes of a very Lively Trip.

CHAPTER XIII

The Future of the Islands

How they will Develop under the Care of the United States.—The Treaty of Peace at Paris and its Effect.—What President McKinley says about the Situation.—Extracts from his Famous Speeches on the Subject.—The views of Anti-Expansionists.—Extracts from Speeches made by Senators and Representatives.—Freedom and Prosperity in Sight for the Long Misgoverned Islands.

CHAPTER XIV

The Ladrone Islands

The Bloodless Battle of Guam.—When the Charleston Opened Fire on the Little City of Agaña, the Governor Thought we were Saluting Him.—A Population which has Twice Disappeared.—Poverty and Laziness on all Sides.—The Value of the Island as a Military Station.

TABLE OF CONTENTS

CHAPTER XV

The Hawaiian Islands, "the Paradise of the Pacific"

Annexed to the United States by Act of Congress, July 7, 1898.—Truly a Paradise in Climate, Fertility and Healthfulness.—Discovery by Captain Cook.—Something about the Inhabitants.—Old Times in Hawaii.—A Pen Sketch of Queen Liliuokalani, the Last of the Royal Line.—The Revolution of 1893.—The Plea for Admission to the United States.—The Mission of Senator Blount.—The Work of American Missionaries.—Some Hawaiian Superstitions and Amusements.—Products and Commerce.—Sugar is to the Islands what Wheat is to our Northwest.—Honolulu, the Capital City.—A Beautiful and Delightful Resort.—On the Threshold of a great Industrial Era.

CHAPTER XVI

Cuba, "the Child of Our Adoption"

The Island whose Cry to Humanity Brought the War of Relief.—How It Received its Name.—The Founding of the Capital, Havana.—A Terrible History of Spanish Cruelty.—The Extermination of a Great People, Beginning in the Time of the Son of Columbus, before 1560 the Whole of the Population had Disappeared from the Island.—The First Cuban Revolt.—The Capture of Havana by the English.—Its Restoration to Spain.—A Long Series of Insurrections.—The Seven Years' War.—The Last and Final Uprising.—The Advent of Weyler, "the Butcher."—Atrocities before which the whole World Stood Aghast.—His Motto was "Subjugation or Death."—American Filibusters Lend a Helping Hand. The Death of General Maceo, through Treachery, a great Blow to the Insurgents.—Weyler and the Reconcentrados.—Two Hundred Thousand Men, Women and Children Die of Disease and Starvation.—Insurgents the Masters of almost the whole Island.—The Fearful Cost of the War.—The Cuban Debt Reached Nearly $300,000,000.

CHAPTER XVII

Possibilities of the Island

Its Possibilities, its Hopes.—The Extent of the Island, its Soil and its vast Products. Rich in Sugar, in Timber and in Minerals, it is a Place Promising Wealth, Rivaling that of the Klondike.—Its Commerce and its Climate.—Havana, the Capital City, and other Ports.

CHAPTER XVIII

The Explosion of the Maine, and War

The Awful Catastrophe to our Battleship in Havana Harbor. A firm Belief that the Vessel was Blown up by Spaniards.—A Naval Board of Inquiry.—A Wave of

THE OREGON.

One of the most renowned ships of the American Navy is the mighty Battleship Oregon. Her famous run from San Francisco around Cape Horn to take part in the Battle of Santiago has never been equalled by any battleship in the world's history. After she won fame in the destruction of Cervera's fleet she was ordered to Manila by Admiral Dewey "for political reasons" and remained there throughout the Philippine War hurling her 13-inch shells into the Insurgent ranks when occasion required.

BATTLE OF MANILA, MAY 1, 1898.

Feeling Sweeps the whole Nation.—McKinley Places the Matter before Congress.
—War is Declared, for the Sake of Humanity.—The First Call for Troops.—All
the States of the Union Respond Immediately with their Quota of Men.—The
Mobilization of the American Army.

CHAPTER XIX

The Campaign in Cuba

close Blockade Established at Havana Harbor.—The First Shot of the War.—The Buena Ventura Captured as the Initial Prize of the Conflict.—Ensign Worth Bagley, of the Torpedo Boat Winslow, Killed, the First Death of the War.— Admiral Cervera's Fleet Leaves Spain for the Cape Verde Islands.—A Period of Search and Apprehension.—The Spanish Vessels Reach Santiago.—Commodore Schley Bottles up the Fleet in Santiago Harbor.—"I've got them and they will never get out alive."—Sampson takes Charge of the Blockade.—Lieutenant Hobson's Daring Deed of Heroism.—The Brilliant Young Naval Officer Sinks the Merrimac at the Mouth of the Harbor so as to Prevent the Enemy from Coming Out.—Afloat on a Raft Amid the Shells of Spanish Forts and Cruisers.— Taken Prisoner and Landed in Morro Castle.—The American Vessels Shelled the Castle, although the Captured Men were Exposed by the Spaniards to the Deadly Fire.—The Magnificent Naval Battle of July 3d.—The Capture of Admiral Cervera and the total Annihilation of the Spanish Fleet.

CHAPTER XX

The Invasion of Cuba by the Army

General Shafter Starts from Tampa with Transports.—The Shutting up of the Spanish Fleet Changes the Campaign from Havana to Santiago.—The Landing of Troops at Baiquiri.—The Brilliant Charge of the "Rough Riders" under Colonel Wood and "Teddy" Roosevelt.—Marvelous Bravery at El Caney and San Juan Hill. The Small American Force though Handicapped on all Sides Wins Victory from the Better Armed and Better Protected Spaniards by Sheer Bravery, and the Mad Rush of their Battle.—Terrible and Costly Hours of Waiting.—Shafter Ill in the Rear, Generals Wheeler, Lawton, Chaffee, Colonels Wood and "Teddy" Roosevelt Lead the Men to a Marvelous Victory.—The Second Day's Fight. —The Spanish Flag of Truce.—Consultation for Surrender.—General Miles, Commander-in-Chief of the Army, Joins Shafter, and Takes Part in the Negotiations.—General Toral Surrenders, after the Destruction of Cervera's Fleet.—Hobson and His Fellow Heroes Exchanged.—A Rousing Reception from the Troops.

TABLE OF CONTENTS

CHAPTER XXI
The Surrender of Santiago

Truce Proclaimed and Prolonged from Day to Day.—Consultation for Surrender of Santiago.—General Miles, Commander-in-Chief of the Army, Joins Shafter and Takes Part in the Negotiations.—General Toral Surrenders.—Terms of Evacuation.—Raising the Stars and Stripes Above the City.—Hobson and His Fellow-Heroes Exchanged.—A Rousing Reception by Land and Sea.

CHAPTER XXII
The Campaign in Porto Rico

General Miles' Plans for the Invasion of the Island.—Preliminary Operations by Sampson's Fleet.—Bombardment of San Juan de Porto Rico.—Miles in Charge of the Army Expedition.—Troops Meet with but Little Resistance.—Capture of Towns, and Movements of the Army.—The First Steps Toward Peace in Washington.—As the Guns of Pennsylvania Troops were Being Placed in Position for a Battle, Word Came from Washington, Announcing that Fighting Must Cease.—The Last Scenes and Shots of the War.

CHAPTER XXIII
Porto Rico—Past, Present and Future

The Island and its Population.—Its Future as a Winter Resort.—Timber in Abundance and Variety.—Minerals and Mining.—Some Facts About its Commerce.—The Chief Cities and Towns of Porto Rico.

CHAPTER XXIV
The Closing Events of the Philippine War

A Proclamation by the Commissioners from the United States.—Dagupan Bombarded.—General Montenegro, One of the Great Insurgent Leaders, Killed.—Lawton's Flying Column Sweeps Down Upon the Province of Laguna.—Santa Cruz Captured.—Lumban and Pagsangan Also Fall Before the American Troops.—Lawton's Expedition Recalled.—MacArthur's Men Gloriously Storm Calumpit's Trenches.

LIST OF ILLUSTRATIONS

	PAGE
Map of the Philippines. *Frontispiece.*	
Map, Hawaiian Islands. *Frontispiece.*	
In the War Room at Washington,	7
Leading Commanders of our Navy in the Spanish-American War,	8
The "Oregon,"	17
The Battle of Manila, May 1, 1898,	18
Typical Group of Negritos, Philippine Islands,	29
Volcano Mayon in Luzon,	30
Church of Cavite, Philippine Islands,	30
Native Boats and Outriggers	39
A Bend in the Pasig River, Manila,	40
The Escolta, Manila,	49
The Barracks at Corregidor After Spanish Withdrawal,	50
Commandante's House, Cavite,	50
Raising the Flag on Fort San Antonio de Abad, Malate,	59
The Beautiful Luneta, Manila's Fashionable Promenade and Drive,	60
A Street Scene in Albay,	69
Sacloban, Island of Leyte,	70
Pampanga, a Village in the Sugar Country,	70
First Battle Between Americans and Filipinos, February 4 and 5, 1899,	79
General Aguinaldo in February, 1899,	80
View Along the Escolta After the Last Great Fire,	89
The Harbor and City of Cebu,	90
Puebla, in the Lake of Bay,	90
Insurgents' Attempt to Burn Manila, February 22, 1899,	99
Café and Chocolate Factory, Manila,	100
Interior View of a Cigar and Cigarette Factory, Manila,	100
Blockhouse Taken by the Astor Battery in Their Famous Revolver Charge,	109
Convent at Malate Showing Effect of Shells,	110
The Philippine Pony and Cart,	110
Saint Ana, a Suburb of Manila,	119
The Cordage Factory of Santa Mesa, a Suburb of Manila,	120
The Famous Spanish Prison, Manila,	120
A Market Man in Manila,	129
Fast Freight of the Philippines,	130
Cockfighting, the Chief Sport of the Natives,	130
The Shipyards and Arsenal at Cavite,	139
The Island of Corregidor, Manila Bay,	140
Native Water Carriers in Iloilo,	165
A Native Filipino Woman,	166
A Spanish Filipino Mestiza,	166
The Mouth of the Pasig River,	175
Young Man of the Upper Class, Philippine Islands,	176
Aguinaldo at the Age of 22,	176
Doing the Family Wash,	176
Native Woman Fruit Seller,	176
Death by the Garrote, Method of Execution in Manila,	185
Savage Negrito Warriors,	186
Tagalog Tribe,	186

LIST OF ILLUSTRATIONS

	PAGE
A Native Residence in the Suburbs of Manila,	195
The Strange Wagons of Albay,	195
Iloilo, Capital of the Province of Panay,	196
A Native Mining Camp in Luzon,	221
A Popular Street Conveyance, Manila,	222
Drying Sugar, Philippine Islands,	222
Bridge Over the Pasig River,	231
A Wedding Procession,	231
All-Chinese-Shop Quarter on the Rosario,	232
Milkmen of Manila at their Dairy,	241
View in Banca, Showing Dutch Fortifications,	242
The Native Farmer and His Faithful Servant,	242
Spaniards Executing Insurgent Chiefs, Manila,	251
Senor Montero Rios, President of the Spanish Peace Commission,	252
General Ramon Blanco, Captain-General of Cuba,	252
Admiral Cervera,	252
Sagasta, Premier of Spain,	252
Royal Palace, Hawaii,	277
Raising the American Flag in Honolulu, August 12, 1898,	277
Church in Honolulu, Hawaiian Islands,	278
Sugar Cane Plantation, Hawaiian Islands,	278
Map of Cuba,	282
Entrance to the Public Grounds, Havana, Cuba,	287
Indian Statue in the Prado, Havana, Cuba,	287
General Antonio Maceo,	288
General Calixto Garcia,	288
General Maximo Gomez,	288
Jose Marti, President of the Cuban Revolutionary Party,	288

	PAGE
The Rough Riders Driving Back the Spaniards, Previous to the Attack on Santiago,	313
Major-General Nelson A. Miles,	314
Major-General Fitzhugh Lee,	314
Major-General Wesley Merritt,	314
Major-General William R. Shafter,	314
Spaniards Repelling the Attack of Cuban Insurgents,	323
United States Battleship "Maine,"	324
Captain Sigsbee,	324
Officers of the "Maine,"	324
The Peace Commissioners,	333
The Fleet of Admiral Cervera at Cape Verde Islands,	334
President McKinley and the War Cabinet,	343
Americans Storming San Juan Hill,	344
City of Havana and Harbor, Showing Wreck of the "Maine,"	369
General Joseph Wheeler,	370
Lieutenant Richmond Pearson Hobson,	370
Governor Theodore Roosevelt,	370
Major-General Elwell S. Otis,	370
Havana Harbor,	379
Landing at Tampa,	379
Camp Scene at Chicamauga,	379
The Surrender of Santiago, July 17, 1899,	380
The Market Place, Ponce, Porto Rico,	421
The Custom House, Ponce, Porto Rico,	421
Native Belles, Porto Rico,	422
Hula Dancing Girls, Hawaii,	422
Sunrise Executions, Outside the Prison Walls, Havana,	431
A Market Girl, Porto Rico,	431
A Volante, the Typical Cuban Conveyance,	431
San Juan, Porto Rico,	432

CHAPTER I
The Philippines—Past and Present

A Rapid Review of History, Place and People.—The Story of Discovery.—The First World Girdlers.—Another Expedition.—Naming the Islands.—Struggles for Supremacy.—English take Manila.—Uprisings of the Natives.—The Last Struggle for Liberty.—A Warlike People.—Manila and other Towns.—Industries, Climate, Etc.—Admiral Dewey begins a New Era.

THE most important, and by far the most interesting, as well as the least known of America's new possessions, gained by her war with Spain, are the Philippine Islands. Comparatively few Americans have ever set foot upon that far-away and semi-civilized land, the possession of which enables America to say with England, "The sun never sets upon our flag."

The Philippines lie almost exactly on the other side of the globe from us. Approximately speaking, our noonday is their midnight; our sunset is their sunrise. There are some 1,800 of these islands, 400 of which are inhabited or capable of supporting a population; they cover about 125,000 square miles; they lie in the tropical seas, generally speaking, from five to eighteen degrees north latitude; and are bounded by the China Sea on the west and the Pacific Ocean on the east; they are about 7,000 miles southwest from San Francisco, a little over 600 miles southeast from Hong Kong, China, and about 1,000 miles almost due north from Australia; they contain between 8,000,000 and 10,000,000 inhabitants, about one-third of whom had prior to Dewey's victory, May 1, 1898, acknowledged Spanish sovereignty to the extent of paying regular tribute to the Spanish crown; the remainder are bound together in tribes under independent native princes or Mohammedan rulers. Perhaps 2,500,000 all told have become nominal Catholics in religion. The rest are Mohammedans and idolaters. There are no Protestant churches in the islands.

THE STORY OF DISCOVERY.

It was twenty-nine years after Columbus discovered America that Magellan saw the Philippines, the largest archipelago in the world, in 1521. The voyage of Magellan was much longer and scarcely less heroic than that of the discoverer of America. Having been provided with a fleet by the Spanish king with which to search for spice islands, but secretly determined to sail round the world, he set out with five vessels on August 10, 1519, crossed the Atlantic to America, and skirted the eastern coast southward in the hope of finding some western passage into the Pacific, which, a few years previous had been discovered by Balboa. It was a year and two months to a day from the time he left Spain until he reached the southern point of the mainland of South America and passed through the straight which has since borne his name. On the way, one of his vessels deserted; another was wrecked in a storm. When he passed through the Straight of Magellan he had remaining but three of his original five ships, and they were the first European vessels that ever breasted the waves of the mighty western ocean. Once upon the unknown but placid sea—which he named the Pacific—the bold navigator steered straight to the northwest. Five months later, about March 1st, he discovered the Ladrone Islands—which name Magellan gave to the group on account of the thieving propensities of the natives—the word *Ladrone* meaning robber.

After a short stay at the islands, he steered southwest, landing on the north coast of Mindanao, the second largest island of the Philippines. The natives were friendly and offered to pilot Magellan to the Island of Cebu, which lay to the north, and which they reported to be very rich. After taking possession of Mindanao in the name of his king, the discoverer proceeded to Cebu, where he gave such descriptions of the glory and power of Spain that he easily formed a treaty with the king of the island, who swore allegiance to his new-found master and had himself and chief advisers baptized in the Catholic faith. Magellan then joined the king in his war against some of the neighboring powers, and on April 26, 1521, was killed in a skirmish. The spot where he fell is now marked by a monument.

FIRST CIRCUMNAVIGATION OF THE GLOBE.

Trouble soon arose between Magellan's sailors and their new-found allies. The Spaniards were invited to a banquet, and twenty-seven of them were treacherously slain. The remainder, fearing for their lives, escaped in their ships and sailed for home. It was soon discovered that they had too few men to manage the three vessels, and one of them was destroyed. The other two proceeded on their voyage and discovered the spice island of Tidor, where they loaded with spices; but a few days later one of the vessels sprang a leak and went down with her freight and crew. The other, after many hardships, reached Spain, thus completing the first circumnavigation of the globe.

SECOND EXPEDITION TO THE PHILIPPINES.

In 1555, Philip II. came to the Spanish throne and determined to send another expedition to the East Indies. His religious zeal inspired him to conquer and christianize the islands. To shorten the long and dangerous voyage, he decided to prepare and start with five ships from the coast of Mexico. Miguel Lopez de Legaspi led the expedition, consisting of four hundred soldiers and sailors and six Augustine monks. In due time the expedition landed at Cebu. The formidable appearance of the ships awed the natives, and on April 27, 1565—forty years after Magellan's remnant had fled from the island—Legaspi landed and took possession. In honor of the Spanish king the archipelago was given the name of the Philippine Islands.

In 1570 Legaspi sent his nephew, Salcedo, to subdue the island of Luzon, the northernmost and the largest of the Philippine group. He landed near the present site of Manila. The trustful natives readily agreed to accept the Spanish king as their master, and to pay tribute. Such slight tribal resistances as were offered were quickly subdued. The next year Legaspi went to Manila to visit his relative; and, seeing the importance of the situation and its fine harbor, declared that city the capital of the whole archipelago, and the king of Spain the sovereign of all the islands. Accordingly, he moved his headquarters to that point, built houses and fortifications, and within a year had the city well organized, when he died, leaving Salcedo as his successor in command. It is remarkable how much these two men accomplished with so small a force; but they did not so much by arms as by cajoling and deceiving the simple natives. Furthermore, they allowed the conquered people to be governed by their own chiefs in their own way, so long as they paid a liberal tribute to the Spanish crown.

The history of the Philippines has been monotonous from their discovery until the present, a monotony broken at times by periods of adventures in which Manila has generally been the central scene.

STRUGGLES FOR SUPREMACY.

About 1580, Limahong a Chinese pirate, took the city with an rmed fleet of sixty-two vessels, bearing 4,000 men and 1,500 women. The met with stubborn resistance, but succeeded in scaling the walls and entering the city. The Spanish forces were driven into a fort, which the Chinese stormed. A bloody hand-to-hand conflict followed, and the Chinese were finally repulsed.

Early in the seventeenth century the Dutch attempted to obtain possession of the Philippines. They captured scores of Spanish merchantmen and treasure ships. Many naval engagements followed, the details of which read like the thrilling records of buccaneers and pirates, rather than the wars between two civil powers. Finally, after half a century of warfare, the Dutch were decisively beaten, and abandoned their efforts to capture the Spanish islands, much to the disadvantage of the Filipinos, for the islands of Java, Sumatra and other Dutch possessions to the south of the Philippines have been remarkably prosperous under the mild rule of the Netherlands.

MANILA TAKEN BY THE ENGLISH.

In 1662, the Chinese planned a revolution against the Spanish authorities. The governor heard of it, and a general massacre of the Mongolians followed. It was even planned to destroy every Chinaman on the islands, and they were in a fair way to do it, when, at length, the Spaniards bethought themselves that by so doing they would practically depopulate the islands of tradesmen and mechanics. Accordingly, they offered pardon to those who would surrender and swear allegiance. In the year 1762, England sent a fleet under Admiral Cornish, with General Draper commanding the troops, against Manila. After a desperate battle the city fell, and the terms of surrender incorporated provisions for free trade, freedom of speech, and, best of all, freedom in religion to the inhabitants of the islands, and required Spain to pay England about $4,000,000 indemnity. By the Peace of Paris, in 1763, however, the war between England and

TYPICAL GROUP OF NEGRITOS

Throughout the Philippine Islands are found mountain tribes known as Negritos. They are the aborigines, and are doubtless of African descent. They are black with kinky hair. About forty or fifty families of them usually live together. Their weapons are of bamboo, and they poison their arrows and spears. There are over 600,000 of them in the islands.

VOLCANO "MAYON," IN THE HEMP-PRODUCING DISTRICT OF LUZON.

This is said to be the most beautiful volcano in the world. It is 8,233 feet high, its shape is a perfect cone and its crest is always fiery. It has indulged in several destructive eruptions. In 1814 many houses were destroyed and 2500 people were killed and wounded. At its base are famous hot springs of great medicinal virtue.

CHURCH OF CAVITE.

It was in this church that many devout Catholics took refuge when Admiral Dewey was bombarding the forts and Spanish forces at Cavite.

Spain was terminated, and one of the conditions was that Spain should retain the sovereignty of the Philippines. The English troops were withdrawn, and the unfortunate islands were again placed (as Cuba was by the same treaty) under the domination of their tyrannical mistress, and remained under Spanish rule from that time until the Americans freed them in 1898.

UPRISING OF THE NATIVES.

In nearly all the uprisings of the natives, the tyranny of the Church, as conducted by the friars and priests, was the cause. Such was the case in 1622, in 1649 and in 1660. The occasion of the revolt of 1744 is a fair example of the provocations leading to all. A Jesuit priest ordered all his parishioners arrested as criminals when they failed to attend mass. One of the unfortunates died, and the priests denied him rights of burial, ordering that his body be thrown upon the ground and left to rot in the sun before his dwelling. The brother of the man in his exasperation organized a mob, captured the priest, killed him, and exposed his body for four days. Thus was formed the nucleus of a rebel army. The insurgents in their mountain fastnesses gained their independence and maintained it for thirty-five years, until they secured from Spain a promise of the expulsion of the Jesuit priests from the colony.

Other revolutions followed in 1823, 1827 and 1844, but all were suppressed. In 1842, the most formidable outbreak up to that time occurred at Cavite. Hatred of the Spanish friars was the cause of this uprising also. Spain had promised in the Council of Trent to prohibit friars from holding parishes. The promises were never carried out, and the friars grew continually richer and more powerful and oppressive. Had the plan of the insurgents not been balked by a mistaken signal, no doubt they would have destroyed the Spanish garrison at Manila, but a misunderstanding caused their defeat. The friars insisted that the captured leaders should be executed, and it was done.

THE LATEST STRUGGLE FOR LIBERTY.

In 1896, the insurrection broke out again. Its causes were the old oppressions: unbearable taxes, and imprisonment or banishment, with the complete confiscation of property of those who could not pay; no justice except for those who could buy it; extortion by the friars; marriage ceremony so costly that a poor man could not pay the fee; homes and families broken up and ruined; burial refused to the dead, unless a large sum was paid in advance; no provision and no chance for education. Such were some of the causes that again goaded the natives to revolution and nerved them with courage to achieve victory after victory over their enemies until they were promised most of the reforms which they demanded. Then they laid down their arms, and, as usual, the Governor-General failed to carry out a single pledge.

Such was the condition, and another revolt, more formidable than any of the past, was forming, when Commodore Dewey with his American fleet entered Manila Bay, May 1, 1898, and by a victory unparalleled in naval warfare, sunk the Spanish ships, silenced the forts, and dethroned the power of Spain forever in a land which her tyranny had blighted for more than three hundred years.

THE PEOPLE—THEIR MANNERS AND CUSTOMS.

It is impossible within the scope of this article to give details concerning all the inhabitants of this far-away archipelago. Professor Worcester, of the University of Michigan, tells us that the population comprises more than eighty distinct tribes, with individual peculiarities. They are scattered over hundreds of islands, and one who really wants to know these peoples must leave cities and towns far behind, and, at the risk of his life, through pathless forests, amid volcanic mountains, at the mercy of savages, penetrate to the innermost wilds. Notwithstanding the fact that for hundreds of years bold men, led by the love of science or by the spirit of adventure, have continued to penetrate these dark regions, there are many sections where the foot of civilized man has never trod; or, if so, he came not back to tell of the lands and peoples which his eyes beheld.

DIFFICULTIES OF EXPLORING THE COUNTRY.

There have been great obstacles in the way of a thorough exploration of these islands. Spain persistently opposed the representatives of any other nation entering the country. She suspected every man, with a gun, of designing to raise an insurrection or make mischief among the natives. The account of red tape necessary to secure guns and ammunition for a little party of four or five explorers admitted through the customs at Manila is one of the most significant, as well as one of the most humorous, passages in Professor Worcester's story of his several years' sojourn while exploring the archipelago.

In the second place, the savage tribes in the interior had no respect for Spain's authority, and will have none for ours for years to come. Two-thirds of them paid no tribute, and many of them never heard of Spain, or, if so, only remembered that a long time ago white men came and cruelly persecuted the natives along the shore. These wild tribes think themselves still the owners of the land. Some of them go naked and practice cannibalism and other horrible savage customs. Any explorer's life is in danger among them; consequently most tourists to the Philippines see Manila and make short excursions around that city. The more ambitious run down to the cities of Iloilo and Cebu, making short excursions into the country from those points, and then return, thinking they have seen the Philippines. Nothing could be further from the truth. Such travelers no more see the Philippine Islands than Columbus explored America.

Even near the coast there are savages who are almost as ignorant as their brethren in the interior. Mr. Stevens tells us that only "thirty miles from Manila is a race of dwarfs that go without clothes, wear knee-bracelets of horsehair, and respect nothing but the jungle in which they live." The principal native peoples are of Malayan origin. Of these, to the north of Manila are the Igorrotes, to the south of Manila are the semi-civilized Visayas, and below them in Mindanao and the Sulu Archipelago are the fierce Moros, who originally came from the island of Borneo, settling in the Philippines a short time before the Spanish discovery. They are Mohammedans in religion, and as fanatical and as fearless fighters as the Turks themselves. For three hundred years the Spaniards have been fighting these savages, and while they have overcome them in nearly all the coast towns, they have expended, it is said, upward of $100,-000,000 and sacrificed more than one hundred thousand lives in doing so.

The fierce Moro warriors keep the Spanish settlers along their coasts in a constant state of alarm, and the visitor to the towns feels as if he were at an Indian outpost in early American history, because of the constant state of apprehension that prevails. Fortunately, however, the Moros along the coast have learned to distinguish between the Spaniard and the Englishman or American, and through them the generosity of the *Englese*, as they call all Anglo-Saxons, has spread to their brethren in the interior. Therefore, American and English explorers have been enabled to go into sections where the Spanish friars and monks, who have been practically the only Spanish explorers, would meet with certain death. The Mohammedan fanaticism of the Moros, and that of the Catholic friars and Jesuits, absolutely refuse compromise.

The Negritos (little Negroes) and the Mangyans are the principal representatives of the aboriginal inhabitants before the Malayan tribes came. There are supposed to be, collectively, almost 1,000,000 of them, and they are almost as destitute of clothing and as uncivilized as the savages whom Columbus found in America, and far more degenerate and loathsome in habits.

THE CITY OF MANILA.

The Island of Luzon, on which the city of Manila stands, is about as large as the State of New York, its area being variously estimated at from 43,000 to 47,000 square miles. It is the largest island in the Philippine group, comprising perhaps one-third of the area of the entire archipelago. Its inhabitants are the most civilized, and its territory the most thoroughly explored. The city of Manila is the metropolis of the Philippines. The population of the city proper and its environs is considered to be some 300,000 souls, of whom 200,000 are natives, 40,000 full-blooded Chinese, 50,000 Chinese half-castes, 5,000 Spanish, mostly soldiers, 4,000 Spanish half-castes and 300 white foreigners other than Spaniards. Mr. Joseph Earle Stevens, already referred to, who represented the only American firm in the city of Manila, under Spanish rule (which finally had to turn its business over to the English and leave the island a few years since), informs us that he and three others were the only representatives of the United States in Manila as late as 1893.

The city is built on a beautiful bay from twenty-five to thirty miles across, and on both shores of the Pasig River. On the right bank of the river, going up from the bay, is the old walled town, and around the walls are the weedy moats or ditches. The heavy guns and frowning cannon from the walls suggest a troubled past. This old city is built in triangular form, about a mile on each side, and is regarded as very unhealthful, for the walls both keep out the breeze and keep in the foul air and odors. The principal buildings in the old part of the city are the cathedral, many parish churches, a few schoolhouses and the official buildings. The population in the walled city is given at 20,000. Up to a few years ago, no foreigner was permitted to sleep within its walls on account of the Spaniards' fear of a conspiracy. A bridge across the Pasig connects old Manila with the new or unwalled city, where nearly all of the business is done and the native and foreign residents live. This section of the city is known as Binondo and its chief street is the Escolta.

EARTHQUAKES AND TYPHOONS.

It does not take one long to exhaust the sights of Manila, if the people, who are always interesting, are excepted. Aside from the cathedral and a few of the churches, the buildings of the city are anything but imposing. In fact, there is little encouragement to construct fine edifices because of the danger from earthquakes and typhoons. It is said that not a year passes without a number of slight earthquake shocks, and very serious ones have occurred. In 1645 nearly all of the public buildings were wrecked and 600 persons killed. A very destructive earthquake was that of 1863, when 400 people were killed, 2,000 wounded and 46 public buildings and 1,100 private houses were badly injured or completely destroyed. In 1874 earthquakes were again very numerous throughout the islands, shocks being felt at intervals in certain sections for several weeks. But the most violent convulsion of modern times occurred in 1880 when even greater destruction than in 1863 visited Manila and other towns of Luzon. Consequently there are very few buildings to be found more than two stories high; and the heavy tile roofs formerly in use have, for the most part, been replaced by lighter coverings of galvanized iron.

These light roofs, however, are in constant danger of being stripped off by the typhoons, terrible storms which come with a twisting motion as if rising from the earth or the sea, fairly pulling everything detachable with them. Masts of ships and roofs of houses are frequently carried by these hurricanes miles distant. The better to resist the typhoons, most of the light native houses are built on bamboo poles, which allow the wind to pass freely under them, and sway and bend in the storm like a tree; whereas, if they were set solidly on the earth, they would be lifted up bodily and carried away. Glass windows being too frail to resist the shaking of the earthquakes and the typhoons, small, translucent oyster shells are used instead. The light thus admitted resembles that passing through ground glass, or, rather, stained glass, for the coloring in the shells imparts a mellow tinted radiance like the windows of a cathedral.

MANILA AS A BUSINESS CENTER.

The streets of Manila are wretchedly paved or not paved at all, and, as late as 1893, were lighted by kerosene lamps or by wicks suspended in dishes of cocoanut oil. Lately an electric plant has been introduced, and parts of the city are lighted in this manner. There are two lines of street cars in Manila. The motive power for a car is a single small pony, and foreigners marvel to see one of those little animals drawing thirty-odd people.

The retail trade and petty banking of Manila is almost entirely in the hands of the half-castes and Chinese, and many of them have grown immensely wealthy. There are only about three hundred Europeans in business in the whole Philippine group, and they conduct the bulk of the importing and exporting trade. Manila contains a number of large cigarette factories, two of which employ 4,000 and one 10,000 hands. There is also a sugar refinery, a steam rice mill, and a rope factory worked partly by men and partly by oxen, a Spanish brewery and a German cement factory, a Swiss umbrella factory and a Swiss hat factory. The single cotton mill, in which $200,000 of English capital is invested, runs 6,000 spindles.

The statistics of 1897 show that the whole trade of Manilla comprised only forty-five Spanish, nineteen German, and seventeen English firms, with six Swiss brokers and two French storekeepers having large establishments. One of the most profitable businesses is said to be that of selling cheap jewelry to the natives. Breastpins which dealers buy in Europe for twelve cents each are readily sold for from $1.50 to $2.00 each to the simple Filipinos. Almost everything that is manufactured abroad has a fine prospective market in the Philippines, when the condition of the people permits them to buy.

A certain charm attaches to many specimens of native handiwork. The women weave exquisitely beautiful fabrics from the fiber of plants. The floors of Manila houses are admired by all foreigners. They are made of hard wood and polished with banana leaves and greasy cloths until they shine brightly and give a cool airiness to the room.

Any kind of amusement is popular with the Filipinos—with so much leisure on their hands—provided it does not require too great exertion on their part. They are fond of the theatre, and, up to a few years ago, bullfighting was a favorite pastime; but the most prominent of modern amusements for the natives and half castes is cockfighting. It is said that every native has his fighting cock, which is reared and trained with the greatest care until he shows sufficient skill to entitle him to an entrance into the public cockpit where he will fight for a prize. The chickens occupy the family residence, roosting overhead; and, in case of fire, it is said that the game "rooster" is saved before the babies. Professor Worcester tells an amusing story of the annoyance of the crowing cocks above his head in the morning and the devices and tricks he and his companions employed to quiet them. The Manila lottery is another institution which intensely excites the sluggish native, and takes from him the money which he does not lose on the cockfights. Under the United States Government this lottery will, no doubt, be abolished in time. It formerly belonged to the Spanish Government, and Spain derived an annual profit of half a million dollars from it.

GENERAL COMMERCE OF THE PHILIPPINES.

It is hardly necessary, so far as the commercial world is concerned, to mention any other locality outside of the city of Manila. To commerce, this city (whose total imports in 1897, were only $10,000,000, and its exports $20,000,000) is the Philippine Islands. Its present meagre foreign trade represents only an average purchase of about one dollar per inhabitant, and an average sale of two dollars per inhabitant for the largest archipelago in the world, and one of the richest in soil and natural resources. The bulk of these exports was hemp, sugar, and tobacco; and, strange as it may seem, the United States received 41 per cent. of her hemp and 55 per cent. of her sugar for the year 1897, notwithstanding the fact that we had not one commercial firm doing business in that whole vast domain.

The city of Iloilo is on the southern coast of the fertile island of Panay, and, next to Manila, the chief port of the Philippines. It has an excellent harbor, and the surrounding country is very productive, having extensive plantations of sugar, rice and tobacco. The population of Iloilo is only 12,000, but there are a few larger towns in the district, of which it is the seaport. Though the city at springtides is covered with water, it is said to be a very healthful place, and much cooler than Manila.

The other open port, Cebu, on the eastern coast of the island of the same name, is a well-built town, and has a population of about 13,000. From this point the bulk of the hemp for export comes.

GENERAL CHARACTER OF THE ISLANDS.

It is impossible to speak of the other islands in detail. Seven of the group average larger than the State of New Jersey; Luzon is as extensive as Ohio, Mindanao equals Indiana; and, as we have stated before, about four hundred of the islands are inhabitable, and, like Java, Borneo, and the Spice Islands, all are rich in natural resources, They are of a volcanic origin, and may be described in general as rugged and mountainous. The coasts of most of the islands are deeply indented by the sea, and the larger ones are well watered by streams, the mouths of which afford good harbors. Many of the mountainous parts abound in minerals. Mr. Karuph, President of the Philippine Mineral Syndicate, in May, 1898, addressed a letter to Hon. John Hay, at that time our ambassador to England, in which he declares that the Philippines will soon come prominently forward as a new center of the world's gold production. "There is not a brook," said Mr. Karuph, "that finds its way into the Pacific Ocean whose sands and gravel do not pan the color of gold. Many valuable

NATIVE BOATS AND OUTRIGGERS

Boats of the upper type were used to land the U. S. troops at Manila. One of those in which the Astor Battery landed sank in the surf just before reaching shore. The natives carried the men ashore on their shoulders. The lower boat is a fisherman's craft used by the Negritos, who shoot fish in the clear water with bows and arrows.

A BEND IN THE PASIG RIVER, MANILA

In the foreground is an old cigar and cigarette factory. Farther up is a sugar house, where a poor grade of refining is done. The cathedral spire and dome of the Church of San Francisco, the oldest church in Manila, rise in the distance.

deposits are close to deep water. I know of no other part of the world, the Alaskan Treadwell mines alone excepted, where pay ore is found within a few hundred yards of the anchorage of sea-going vessels." In addition to gold, iron, copper, lead, sulphur, and other minerals are found, and are believed to exist in paying quantities. The numerous mineral springs attest their presence in almost every part of the principal islands.

FORESTS AND TIMBER.

The forest products of the islands are perhaps of greater value than their mineral resources. Timber not only exists in almost exhaustless quantity, but—considering the whole group, which extends nearly a thousand miles from north to south—in unprecedented diversity, embracing sixty varieties of the most valuable woods, several of which are so hard that they cannot be cut with ordinary saws, some so heavy that they sink in water, and two or three so durable as to afford ground for the claim that they outlast iron and steel when placed in the ground or under water. Several of these woods are unknown elsewhere, and, altogether, they are admirably suited for various decorative purposes and for the manufacture of fine implements and furniture.

Here also are pepper, cinnamon, wax, and gums of various sorts, cloves, tea, and vanilla, while all tropical fruits, such as cocoanuts, bananas, lemons, limes, oranges of several varieties, pineapples, citrons, bread-fruits, custard apples, pawpaws, and mangroves flourish and most of them grow wild, though, of course, they are not equal to the cultivated fruit. There are fifty odd varieties of the banana in the archipelago, from the midget, which makes but a single mouthful, to the huge fruit eighteen inches long. There seems to be no limit to which tropical fruits and farm products can be cultivated.

The animal and bird life of the Philippines offer a field of interesting research to naturalists. There are no important carnivorous animals. A small wild cat and two species of civet cats constitute about all that belong to that class. The house cats of the Philippines have curious fishhook crooks in the ends of their tails. There are several species of deer in the archipelago. Hogs run wild in large numbers. The large water buffalo (*carabao*) has been domesticated and is the chief beast of burden with the natives. The *timarau* is another small species of buffalo, very wild and entirely untamable; and, though numerous in certain places, is hard to find, and when brought to bay dies fighting.

Birds abound in all of the islands; nearly six hundred species have been found, over fifty of which exist nowhere else in the world. One of these species builds a nest which is highly prized by Chinese epicures as an article of diet. Prof. Worcester tells us "the best quality of them sometimes bring more than their weight in gold." Crocodiles are numerous in fresh-water lakes and streams, attaining enormous size, and in certain places causing much loss of life among stock and men as well. Snakes also abound, and some of them are very venomous. Cobras are found in the southern islands. Pythons are numerous, some of the smaller sizes being sold in the towns and kept in houses to catch rats, at which they are said to be more expert than house cats.

All the domestic animals, aside from the *carabao*, have been introduced from abroad. Cattle are extensively raised, and in some of the islands run wild. The horses are a small Spanish breed, but are very strong and have great endurance. Large European horses do not stand the climate well.

CLIMATE, VOLCANOES, ETC.

The mean annual temperature of Manila is 80 degrees F. The thermometer seldom rises above 100 degrees or falls below 60 degrees anywhere in the archipelago. There is no month in the year during which it does not rise as high as 91 degrees. January and December are the coldest months, the average temperature being 70 to 73 degrees. May is the warmest, the average being 84 degrees. April is the next warmest, with an average of 83 degrees; but the weather is generally very moist and humid, which makes the heat more trying. The three winter months have cool nights. Malaria is prevalent, but contagious diseases are comparatively few. Yellow fever and cholera are seldom heard of.

The Philippines are the home of many volcanoes, a number of them still active. Mayon, in the island of Luzon, is one of the most remarkable volcanic mountains on the globe. It is a perfect cone, rising to the height of 8,900 feet, and is in constant activity; its latest destructive eruption took place in 1888. Apo, in the island of Mindanao, 10,312 feet high, is the largest of the Philippine volcanoes. Next is Canloon in Negros, which rises 8,192 feet above the sea. Taal is in a lake, with a height of 900 feet, and is noteworthy as being the lowest volcano in the world. To those not accustomed to volcanoes, these great fire-spouting mountains, which are but prominent representatives of many lesser ones in the islands, seem to be an ever-present danger to the inhabitants; but the natives and those who live there manifest little or no fear of them. In fact, they rather pride themselves in their possession of such terrifying neighbors.

Such is an outline view of the Philippine Archipelago of the present day. A new era has opened up in the history of that wonderful land with its liberation from the Spanish yoke. The dense ignorance and semi-savage barbarities which exist there must not be expected to yield too rapidly to the touch of human kindness and brotherly love with which the Christian world will now visit those semi-civilized and untamed children of nature. Nevertheless, western civilization and western progress will undoubtedly work mighty changes in the lives of those people, in the development of that country, during the first quarter of the twentieth century, which ushers in the dawn of its freedom.

THE BATTLE OF MANILA.

In all the annals of naval warfare there is no engagement, terminating in so signal a victory with so little damage to the victors, as that which made the name of George Dewey immortal on the memorable Sunday morning of May 1, 1898, in Manila Bay. The world knows the story of that battle, for it has been told hundreds of times in the thousands of newspapers and magazines and scores of books throughout the civilized world. But few, perhaps, who peruse these pages have read the simple details of the fight as narrated by that most modest of men, Admiral Dewey himself. We cannot better close this chapter on the Philippines than by inserting Admiral Dewey's official report of the battle which wrested the Filipinos from Spanish tyranny and placed nearly ten millions of oppressed people under the protecting care of the United States.

ADMIRAL DEWEY'S STORY OF MANILA.

"UNITED STATES FLAGSHIP OLYMPIA, CAVITE, May 4, 1898.

"The squadron left Mirs Bay on April 27th, arrived off Bolinao on the morning of April 30th, and, finding no vessels there, proceeded down the coast and arrived off the entrance to Manila Bay on the same afternoon. The Boston and the Concord were sent to reconnoitre Port Subic. A thorough search was made of the port by the Boston and the Concord, but the Spanish fleet was not found. Entered the south channel at 11.30 P.M., steaming in column at eight knots. After half the squadron had passed, a battery on the south side of the channel opened fire, none of the shots taking effect. The Boston and McCulloch returned the fire. The squadron proceeded across the bay at slow speed and arrived off Manila at daybreak, and was fired upon at 5.15 A.M. by three batteries at Manila and two near Cavite, and by the Spanish fleet anchored in an approximately east and west line across the mouth of Bakor Bay, with their left in shoal water in Canacao Bay.

"The squadron then proceeded to the attack, the flagship Olympia, under my personal direction, leading, followed at a distance by the Baltimore, Raleigh, Petrel, Concord and Boston in the order named, which formation was maintained throughout the action. The squadron opened fire at 5.41 A.M. While advancing to the attack, two mines were exploded ahead of the flagship, too far to be effective. The squadron maintained a continuous and precise fire at ranges varying from 5,000 to 2,000 yards, countermarching in a line approximately parallel to that of the Spanish fleet. The enemy's fire was vigorous, but generally ineffective. Early in the engagement two launches put out toward the Olympia with the apparent intention of using torpedoes. One was sunk and the other disabled by our fire and beached before they were able to fire their torpedoes.

"At 7 A.M. the Spanish flagship Reina Christina made a desperate attempt to leave the line and come out to engage at short range, but was received with such a galling fire, the entire battery of the Olympia being concentrated upon her, that she was barely able to return to the shelter of the point. The fires started in her by our shells at the time were not extinguished until she sank. The three batteries at Manila had kept up a continuous fire from the beginning of the engagement, which fire was not returned by my squadron. The first of these batteries was situated on the south mole-head at the entrance of the Pasig River, the second on the south position of the walled city of Manila, and the third at Malate, about one-half mile further south. At this point I sent a message to the Governor-General to the effect that if the batteries did not cease firing the city would be shelled. This had the effect of silencing them.

"At 7.35 A.M. I ceased firing and withdrew the squadron for breakfast. At 11.16 I returned to the attack. By this time the Spanish flagship and almost all the Spanish fleet were in flames. At 12.30 the squadron ceased firing, the batteries being silenced and the ships sunk, burned and deserted.

"At 12.40 the squadron returned and anchored off Manila, the Petrel being left behind to complete the destruction of the smaller gunboats, which were behind the point of Cavite. This duty was performed by Commander E. P. Wood in the most expeditious and complete manner possible. The Spanish lost the following vessels: Sunk, Reina Christina, Bastilla, Don Antonio de Ulloa; burned, Don Juan de Austria, Isla de Luzon, Isla de Cuba, General Lezo, Marquis del Duero, El Correo, Velasco, and Isla de Mindanao (transport); captured, Rapido and Hercules (tugs), and several small launches.

"I am unable to obtain complete accounts of the enemy's killed and wounded, but believe their losses to be very heavy. The Reina Christina alone had 150 killed, including the captain, and ninety wounded. I am happy to report that the damage done to the squadron under my command was inconsiderable. There were none killed, and only seven in the squadron were slightly wounded. Several of the vessels were struck and even penetrated, but the damage was of the slightest, and the squadron is in as good condition now as before the battle.

"I beg to state to the department that I doubt if any commander-in-chief was ever served by more loyal, efficient and gallant captains than those of the squadron now under my command. Captain Frank Wildes, commanding the Boston, volunteered to remain in command of his vessel, although his relief arrived before leaving Hong Kong. Assistant Surgeon Kindelberger, of the Olympia, and Gunner J. C. Evans, of the Boston, also volunteered to remain, after orders detaching them had arrived. The conduct of my personal staff was excellent. Commander B. P. Lamberton, chief of staff, was a volunteer for that position, and gave me most efficient aid. Lieutenant Brumby, Flag Lieutenant, and Ensign E. P. Scott, aide, performed their duties as signal officers in a highly creditable manner; Caldwell, Flag Secretary, volunteered for and was assigned to a subdivision of the five-inch battery. Mr. J. L. Stickney, formerly an officer in the United States Navy, and now correspondent for the New York *Herald*, volunteered for duty as my aide, and rendered valuable service. I desire especially to mention the coolness of Lieutenant C. G. Calkins, the navigator of the Olympia, who came under my personal observation, being on the bridge with me throughout the entire action, and giving the ranges to the guns with an accuracy that was proven by the excellence of the firing.

"On May 2d, the day following the engagement, the squadron again went to Cavite, where it remains. On the 3d the military forces evacuated the Cavite arsenal, which was taken possession of by a landing party. On the same day the Raleigh and the Baltimore secured the surrender of the batteries on Corregidor Island, paroling the garrison and destroying the guns. On the morning of May 4th. the transport Manila, which had been aground in Bakor Bay, was towed off and made a prize."

CHAPTER II
Behind Admiral Dewey's Guns

The Magnificent Naval Battle of May 1st Described by an Officer who stood by Dewey during the Fight.—The Personal Side of the Nation's Greatest Hero.—A Brush with German Officers.—The Surrender of Cavite.

MAY 1, 1898, will go down in history as the date of the greatest naval battle the world has ever seen. Farragut made himself immortal by his famous order, "Damn the torpedoes; go ahead." Commodore George Dewey, taught in the school of Farragut, went ahead in Manila Bay, regardless of torpedoes or glowering forts.

On the night of April 30th the United States squadron was off Manila Bay. Darkness came on, and all aboard the vessels were in a state of keen expectancy. At 10 o'clock all hands were piped to fighting quarters, and all lights were "doused." No one knew what the next few hours would bring.

Commodore Dewey had been warned that Spanish mines and torpedoes had been sunk at the mouth of the bay. Balloon-shaped, with the island of Corregidor across the neck, the bay lent itself naturally to defence. The path to Manila was a narrow and dangerous one, but Dewey, fearless and confident, decided to make the dash, and either win or lose all in one stroke.

What a picture the scene conjures up to one's mind! The inky blackness of the night, the ships themselves lightless, the men keyed to a state of excitement, anxious as to what their fate would be, their Commodore calm as though there was no enemy ahead or danger beneath. All is silence except the swish of the waters as the fighters ploughed through. Then a spark or two blown from the funnel of the *McCulloch* against the black sky betrays to the sentinels on the forts at the harbor the presence of the fleet. The sharp boom of a gun, another, and still another, echo across the bay. They give to the Spanish forces the first inkling of the approaching battle.

The story of that battle, so modestly and simply told in the report of Commodore Dewey, has already been given. At his side on the flagship *Olympia* all through the engagement stood a young naval officer, Ensign W. Pitt Scott. His name was mentioned by Commodore Dewey in the report to the War Department, and he was specially commended for bravery in the battle.

ENSIGN SCOTT'S STORY OF THE BATTLE.

It is stated by Colonel George A. Loud, who witnessed the battle from the Revenue Cutter *McCulloch*, that a six-pound shell cut the rigging four feet over Commodore Dewey's head just as Ensign Scott was raising a signal flag and the halyards were shot away. Ensign Scott has told the story of the battle, which is given herewith. He writes:

"The Spaniards had ten ships fighting to our six, and, in addition, had five or six shore batteries, some of which bothered us a great deal. We steamed by their line and fired some deadly shot at them. We had anticipated that once across their line would be sufficient to silence them, but they did not yield, and so, when we got to the end of the line, we turned and went back at them again. It was getting really interesting now, for many of their shots were coming close to us, and the screech of the missiles as they whistled over our heads was anything but pleasant. Now and then we would see a shot strike in the water ahead of us and explode and the pieces of it come at us. I will never forget it.

"I was surprised to find how little it disturbed us. I never believed I would ever feel so unconcerned while the shots were falling around us. No one seemed to care an iota whether the shells dropped on us, or fell a distance away, and in the intervals, between which we were making signals, the most commonplace remarks were made.

"We passed across the enemy's line the second time; but that did not seem to silence them any more than the first, and we had to try it a third time, with no better result, although perhaps their fire was not so heavy as at first. A small torpedo boat came out and attempted to get within striking distance of the *Olympia*, but our secondary battery drove her in; a second time she came out and at

THE ESCOLTA, LOOKING SOUTH

This is the Broadway of Manila. Along this famous street the principal retail shops of the city are situated. Chinese and half-castes are the principal retail merchants. At the time of the capture of the city by Admiral Dewey and General Merritt there were not over one dozen European merchants in Manila. Not one American firm was there; the last one, a Boston hemp dealer, having been driven out some years before.

THE BARRACKS AT CORREGIDOR AFTER SPANISH WITHDRAWAL.

The two American newspaper correspondents, while touring the island, were guided by six Igorrote warriors from Aguinaldo's army. Notice they are armed with primitive savage weapons.

COMMANDANTE'S HOUSE, CAVITE.

The largest arsenal in the Philippines is at Cavite. It is now being used to manufacture and store ammunition for the U. S. troops.

us, but again our fire was too much for her, and some of our shots striking her, she had barely time to get back to the beach, or she would have sunk.

THE FLAGSHIP BORE THE BRUNT OF THE FIRE.

"It soon became apparent that the Spaniards were concentrating their fire on the *Olympia* (as flagship), and we then received the brunt of the fight. At one time the *Reina Christina*, the Spanish flagship, attempted to come out from her position and engage us at closer distance, but we turned our fire on her and drove her back.

"A fourth time we steamed across their line, and a fifth, and it began to look as if they were not going to give in until after all our ammunition would be exhausted, which would leave us in a very serious predicament, in the midst of the enemy and in one of their ports, 7,000 miles from supplies; so after the fifth time across their line we withdrew to count up our ammunition, to see how we stood, and get breakfast.

"It was only 7.30 A.M., but it seemed to us as if it were the middle of the day. Then we began to count our casualties, and found that no one had been killed and no one injured, with a few slight exceptions.

"But it was the dirtiest-looking crowd I have ever seen, and by far the oddest. It was so hot that nearly all of the men had stripped off all their clothes,—in fact, in the turrets they did strip off about everything but their shoes, which they kept on to protect their feet from the hot floor. Commodore Dewey himself, the most dressed man in the battle, was in white duck; the rest of us appeared without collars and some without shirts, an undershirt and white blouse being more than sufficient for our needs, and, if our blouses were not off, they certainly were not buttoned.

STANDING UNDER SHARP FIRE.

"We were a mighty dirty crowd. Our faces and clothes were full of smoke and powder and saltpetre, and the perspiration rolling around in that made us picturesquely handsome. I would have given a good deal for a picture of the ship's company, men and officers.

"Then we looked around to see where the ship had been

injured, and found that she had been struck several times, none of which materially hurt her. On the bridge where we stood was, perhaps, the hottest place of all, for at least four shots struck within thirty or forty feet of it. One of the ugly shots flew over our heads with a screech, but its cry was a little different from most of the others, and several of us said, 'That hit something', and we looked aloft to see if it had, and found the halyards on which we had a signal flying cut in two, and the signal out to the leeward. Another shot cut the wire-rigging ten feet over our heads, while any number flew close over us without striking anything.

"About halfpast ten we returned to the attack, and gave the *Baltimore* the post of honor in leading, as we were very short of 5-inch ammunition, and the way that the *Baltimore* did fire into the Spanish batteries was a caution. It was not long before the enemy was completely silenced and the white flag run up. Two of their ships were on fire and burning fiercely, and one was sinking. The *Don Antonio de Ulloa* was the last to give in, and after she was abandoned by her crew, she still kept her flag flying, which necessitated our firing at her until it was lowered; but as no one was left on board to lower it, we kept firing at her until she slowly began to sink. It was a grand sight to see her settle aft, with the flag of Spain upon her.

"Then we sent one of the smaller ships in to destroy those that were still afloat, and the *Petrel* burned and sunk four or five of them, while the *Concord* fired a large transport, which, we afterward learned, was quite full of coal and stuff for the Spaniards. Altogether our six ships, the *Olympia, Baltimore, Raleigh, Boston, Concord,* and *Petrel,* burned and sunk almost the entire Spanish fleet that is in the East, as follows, viz.: Sunk, the *Reina Christina* (flagship), *Castilla* and *Antonio de Austria,* the *Isla de Cuba,* the *Isla de Luzon,* the *Marques del Duero,* the *Velasco,* the *General Lezo,* the *El Correo,* and the transport *Isla de Mindanao*. There is still one small vessel, the *Argus,* on the ways, but she is so badly damaged by shot that I doubt if she would float if we tried to put her into the water. Besides, we captured the *Manila,* a splendid 1900-ton vessel, which they used as transport, and on which we expect to send home our trophies in the way of captured guns, etc. We also captured any number of tugs and steam launches, some of which we are now using. Some of them were very fine tugboats.

ALL WERE PROUD OF THE SHIPS' WOUNDS.

"Everyone seemed proud of the wounds to the ships. The evening of the fight I had to go around to the different ships on an errand for Commodore Dewey, and on each one all hands made it a point to take me around and show me where each shot hit them.

"The harbor presents quite an unusual appearance with eight or nine ships showing just above water, the masts charred, and their upper works (those that can be seen) nothing but a twisted mass of iron. It looks as if we had done something to pay for the *Maine*.

"I got ashore several days after the engagement and walked through the navy yard. It presents a woeful sight. The barracks had any number of holes in the sides, and things were strewn all over. In one room of the the commandant's house we saw where a large 8-inch shell had gone through the roof, and after carrying away the thick planking had exploded, knocking down the side of the room and wrecking everything in it. In another building I saw where a shell had gone through the side of it, and had scattered the bricks all over the room."

In this remarkable battle, Admiral Montojo, the Spanish Commander, fought with the bravery that won from Admiral Dewey compliments and congratulations. His flagship, the *Reina Maria Christina*, the best of his fleet, dashed bravely towards the long line of belching vessels of Dewey's squadron, hoping to cripple at least one of the warships, that was pouring such an awful fire into his fleet. It was the madness of despair.

Dewey signalled for a concentration of fire upon the on-coming vessel, and as she neared the *Olympia*, the latter discharged her 8-inch guns both fore and aft, killing sixty of the Spaniard's crew, including her captain, chaplain and a lieutenant, and causing her boilers to explode. The flagship was a burning wreck, and was forced to retire. Admiral Montojo transferred his flag to the *Isla de Cuba*, which maintained a vigorous fire until she too sank at her moorings.

Admiral Montojo's own account of the fight is interesting as giving a Spanish view of the greatest of naval encounters. The

Admiral is a spare man, of small stature, about 65 years old, with an air of an old Spanish Grandee. He speaks English fluently, but with a slight accent, and the following are his own words in describing the battle:

THE SPANISH ADMIRAL'S ACCOUNT OF HIS DEFEAT.

"About 5 o'clock on Sunday morning I observed the American squadron coming in line straight across the bay towards Cavite. We prepared to receive them. A few minutes after 5 o'clock the engagement opened, the battery on Pont Sangley (Cavite) firing on each ship as she came within range. The American ships did not reply. All the Spanish ships were in Cavite Bay at anchor—the *Reina Christina* (my flagship), *Castilla, Don Juan de Austria, Ulloa, Isla de Cuba, Isla de Luzon, Marques del Duero,* and some small gunboats. The *Reina Christina* and the *Don Juan,* as you know, were old cruisers; the *Castilla* was a wooden cruiser, but was unable to steam owing to the breakdown of her engines; the *Ulloa* and *Velasco* were helpless, and were undergoing repairs off the arsenal.

"The *Olympia, Baltimore, Raleigh,* and *Boston* engaged my flagship in turn about 5.30, attracted by my flag. I recognized the necessity of getting under way, and accordingly slipped both anchors, ordering the other ships to follow my example. Although we recognized the hopelessness of fighting the American ships, we were busy returning their fire. The *Reina Christina* was hit repeatedly. Shortly after 6.30 I observed fire forward. Our steering gear was damaged, rendering the vessel unmanageable, and we were being subjected to a terrific hail of shell and shot. The engines were struck, and we estimated that we had 70 hits about our hull and superstructure. The boilers were not hit, but the pipe to the condenser was destroyed. A few moments later I observed the afterpart on fire. A shell from the Americans had penetrated and burst with deadly effect, killing many of our men.

"My flag lieutenant said to me, 'The ship is in flames. It is impossible to stay on the *Christina* any longer.' He signalled to the gunboat *Isla de Cuba,* and I and my staff transferred to her, and my flag was hoisted on her. Before leaving the *Christina* my flag was hauled down. My flagship was now one mass of flame. I ordered away all the boats I could to save the crew. Many of the men jumped overboard without clothing and succeeded in reaching the shore, several hundreds of yards away. Only a few men were drowned, the majority being picked up by the boats.

"Before jumping overboard, Captain Cadarso's son, a lieutenant on board the *Christina*, saw his father alive on deck, but others state that as the Captain was about to leave a shell burst overhead and killed him. We estimate that 52 men were killed on board the *Christina* and about 150 wounded. The chaplain was killed. The assistant physician, the chief engineer, and three officers were wounded. The boatswain and chief gunner were both killed. In the *Castilla* only about 15 men were killed, but there were many wounded, both on the *Castilla* and the *Don Juan*, on which 13 men were killed. Altogether, so far as we know at present, 400 men were killed and wounded in our ships.

"As soon as I translated myself from the *Reina Christina* to the *Isla de Cuba* all the shots were directed upon the *Cuba*, following my flag. We sought shelter behind the pier at Cavite, and, recognizing the futility of fighting more, I prepared to disembark, and gave orders for the evacuation of the remainder of our ships. The *Castilla* had been on fire from end to end for some time, and was, of course, already abandoned. The *Ulloa* was also burning.

THE LAST SPANISH SIGNAL.

"My last signal to the Captains of all vessels was—'Scuttle and abandon your ships.'

"This was about 7.30. The *Reina Christina, Castilla, Don Juan de Austria, Velasco,* and *Ulloa* were all destroyed in this engagement. To prevent the guns being of use to the Americans, the Captains, on abandoning, brought away portions of the mechanism, and also succeeded in saving all the ships' papers and treasure. At this point there was a cessation of firing. The *Boston* sent ashore a boat with an officer carrying a white flag, and parleyed with the Chief of the Arsenal. He asked permission to destroy the vessels completely without interference from the shore. After consultation with me, the Chief of the Arsenal replied that it was not competent on my part to give any pledge; the ships were at his mercy and he could do with them as he liked. While the parleying was proceeding, the *Petrel* and *Concord* went across the bay, and fired a large number of shots into the *Isla de Mindanao*, which was lying ashore near Bacoor, and she soon caught fire. Her captain had run her ashore when the American squadron was observed making for Cavite Bay. She never fired a shot.

"I was wounded in the left leg by an iron splinter, and my son, a lieutenant, was wounded in the hand by a shell splinter. We were both wounded on the *Reina Christina*. I directed the movements of my squadron from the bridge. There was no conning tower. The Captain of the *Boston* said to my chief of staff, Captain Boado, 'You have combated with us with four very bad ships, not warships. There was never seen before braver fighting under such unequal conditions. It is a great pity that you exposed your lives in vessels not fit for fighting'. Commodore Dewey also sent me a message by the British Consul, saying that, peace or war, he would have great pleasure in clasping me by the hand, and congratulating me on the gallant manner in which we fought."

A WILD EXULTANT CHEER OF VICTORY.

And so the great fight ended. When the little *Petrel* announced that the Spanish fleet had scuttled their vessels and fled, a great cheer went up from all the men who had braved the perils of the Spanish fire, and that cheer was doubled and redoubled when, later on, it was announced that not one man of the American fleet had lost his life. The only death was due to apoplexy brought on by the intense heat. The Chief Engineer of the *McCulloch* was the victim; he suddenly expired, not in the battle, but just as the fleet was entering the mouth of the bay.

Fighting ceased about 12.15 P. M., by which time all the Spanish ships were sunk or burned. The arsenal was ablaze, and throughout the night explosions were occurring in Cavite Bay—an alluring spectacle of destruction.

It was in the smaller incidents of this great battle that Commodore (thereafter to be known as Admiral) Dewey showed to his men, and to the whole world, what manner of man he was. The withdrawal of his fleet so that his men, exhausted by the severe work of battle, might have breakfast has thrilled every heart. His kindness and courtesy in complimenting a defeated foe for personal bravery, proved him a gentleman even in war. His cablegrams to the Navy Department show him a man of rare modesty. One sentence in the second of his dispatches, harmonizing as it does with the keynote of the whole war—"humanity"—will live in history with the sayings of the greatest men the world has had. Let us repeat his own words: "I am assisting in protecting the Spanish sick and wounded. Two hundred and fifty sick and wounded in hospital within our line." That was humanity's own voice. When in naval history had such a spectacle ever been witnessed. Before the smoke of battle had even cleared away, the victorious commander was plying the hand of brotherly charity to stay the sufferings of the men with whom he had been engaged in deadly combat.

GEORGE DEWEY, ADMIRAL, HERO, STATESMAN, GENTLEMAN.

The United States Navy has never had, perhaps, as remarkable a figure as George Dewey. From Maine to Mexico, from the Atlantic to the Pacific, his name is as familiar, and he is as beloved, as any of the great figures of the nation's history.

Admiral Dewey is not only a great fighter, but has proved himself a great statesman. The situation after the downfall of Cavite was a perplexing one; immediately after the battle, Dewey had cut the cable that connected Manila with the rest of the world and he was, therefore, thrown upon his own resources as to what to do in an emergency. He could not be directed by the government at Washington. He had gone to the islands seeking only the Spanish fleet, and determined to carry out the cabled instructions he had received at Hong-Kong, ordering him to "find the Spanish fleet and capture or utterly destroy it." How well he did this has already been told. But now the question of holding an arsenal, captured by him, without having at his disposal any considerable force of armed soldiers confronted him.

The insurgent forces under General Aguinaldo had moved upon Manila, when the attack had been made upon the fleet in the bay. After the withdrawal of the Spanish forces from Cavite the insurgents were eager to plunder the houses left by the terror-stricken people.

They did not hesitate to rob even the dead. But Admiral Dewey determined not to allow such things, and immediately he had his hands full.

DEWEY HAS NEED FOR FIRMNESS.

To add to his troubles the German Emperor sent to Manila Bay several of his mighty battleships in command of Admiral von Diedrich. The sympathies of Germany were apparently with Spain, and the German Admiral let no opportunity go by without showing his feelings in the matter. An incident occurred when the insurgents were making an attack upon the Spanish outposts which is worth recording. The fighting between the Spaniards and insurgents was always done under cover of darkness, partly because of the extreme heat, and partly because of the guerrilla style of warfare which was carried on. When the battle was begun the German vessels in the harbor turned their powerful search-lights upon the places where the insurgent army was concealed, thus putting them in the glare of the light and rendering them an easy mark for the Spaniards who were hidden effectually by the darkness. But the light rested there only for a moment. Admiral Dewey sent peremptory orders to the German Admiral that if the lights were not extinguished immediately, or if the action were repeated, he would consider it an act of war against the United States, and take steps accordingly. The lights were never again flashed upon the struggling insurgents.

When Admiral Dewey was ready to shell the Spanish forces, he ordered all of the vessels of the foreign powers then in the harbor to remove to a distance of three miles from his fleet. The attitude of the German fleet, though not openly hostile, had been significantly unfriendly. When the German Admiral received Dewey's order he removed to the required distance, but lined up his vessels in such a way that they bore directly upon the American fleet so that in case there was a display of open partisanship on the part of Germany, Dewey's fleet would be between two fires,—the fires of the forts on the one hand, and the fires of the German warships on the other.

A FRIENDLY ACT BY THE BRITISH ADMIRAL.

It was then that the British friendliness, which had been such a prominent feature at home, displayed itself as a reality. The British

RAISING THE FLAG ON FORT SAN ANTONIO DE ABAD, MALATE

This old fort was silenced by Dewey's guns August 13, 1898, with the assistance of land forces under General Anderson. The Astor Battery on shore under Captain March, supported General McArthur's forces on the right wing. It was the California and Colorado Volunteer Regiments, with the Eighteenth Regulars, who finally drove out the Spaniards and occupied the position, where the Californians at once raised the Stars and Stripes. The marks of Dewey's shells are seen on the side of the fort.

THE BEAUTIFUL LUNETA, MANILA'S FASHIONABLE PROMENADE AND DRIVE

This most celebrated drive and promenade in the city of Manila is by the old sea wall. The Governor and Archbishop, with their escorts and striking equipages came every afternoon to air themselves, and in the cool of every summer evening, when the fine military band of the Spanish army used to play. The whole population apparently came out to listen. This was also the place of all great processions, executions, etc.

Admiral moved his warships and came at anchor in a position immediately between the vessels of Germany and those of the United States. If Germany, therefore, had fired a shot, it would have fired through the warships of England. The trouble ended then and there, although the German Admiral kept up petty annoyances for some time. Finally, Admiral Dewey turned to one of the German Admiral's Lieutenants and said to him, "If Germany wants war with my country, it can have it in five minutes." The invitation, it is needless to say, was not accepted.

It was thus that Admiral Dewey met emergencies—ever polite, ever the cultured man of the world, but ever the firm, fearless officer, ready to fight if need be to uphold the dignity and honor of his nation and himself. It is fitting that the nation has especially singled out such a man for the highest office that can be given to men of the navy. The President personally tendered him the thanks of the people; Congress made him Rear Admiral, and revived for him the grade of Admiral, which went out of existence many years ago with Admiral Porter. Although his personal history has already been given, it may be well to recall the leading facts in his career.

Admiral Dewey is a man to admire at close range. Many heroes lose their gloss on close acquaintance. With Dewey this is not so. Through a long line of sturdy stock he has inherited a culture, an integrity, and a force of character that make him a man to honor. He was born in a fine old Colonial mansion in Montpelier, Vt., sixty years ago. He was a young man when he first fell in love with his life work. He wanted to go to sea, but his father did not take kindly to the idea. A compromise was effected. The boy at 14 left the Montpelier public school to enter the Norwich University at Northfield, Vt., a military school, where his useful enthusiasm was temporarily appeased by musket practice and drills. But the craving for the sea life was still strong with Dewey.

THE EARLY CAREER OF DEWEY.

So his father secured for him an appointment to the Naval Academy at Annapolis in 1854; he graduated in 1858. When Fort Sumter was fired on in 1861, Dewey received his commission as a Lieutenant on the seventeen-gun steam sloop *Mississippi*. His

Yankee blood was hot for fight, and he and his vessel participated in the terrific actions of the West Gulf squadron. History tells how young Dewey received the baptism of battle, and how owing to the terrible fire of the shore batteries on the Mississippi River the crew were forced to abandon their vessel. The last to leave the ship were the Captain and his First Lieutenant, George Dewey. Again and again through the war he showed his metal. He served on the famous *Kearsarge* and afterward on the flagship *Colorado*. He received his first command in 1870, the *Narragansett*. Passing through various years of service, Dewey became, in 1884, a Captain and Commander of the *Dolphin*, one of the first craft of the new navy. His promotion continued rapidly. From 1885 to 1888 he commanded the *Pensacola*, flagship of the European squadron.

On account of his devotion to method, his close application to detail and his wide knowledge of naval science he was elevated, in 1888, to the head of the Bureau of Equipment and Recruiting, with the rank of Commodore. In 1893 he served as a member of the Lighthouse Board, and three years later, having reached the actual rank of Commodore, he became President of the Board of Inspection and Survey. He left that important post to take command of the Asiatic squadron.

His son, George Dewey, speaking of his father a few days after the great victory, said: "When I said good-bye to him at the station I told him, 'I hope you will have a most pleasant and successful cruise.' He said with a laugh, 'Well, I guess I will, I am the first Commodore to go out there since Perry, and that ought to mean something?' All the others have been Admirals since Perry, and that rather seemed at the moment to have attached some significance to the fact that he was the first Commodore on the Asiatic squadron since then."

THE MAN IN WHITE IN A PERSONAL WAY.

Admiral Dewey is known as the Man in White in the Philippines. He is a stickler for dress, is himself always immaculate, and insists that those around him shall be careful about their personal appearance. Those who think, from his photograph, that he is a small man, are mistaken. He weighs fully 185 pounds, and is so near 6 feet in height, that he gives one the impression of being fully that. He carries himself well, is graceful, though somewhat quick and nervous in his movements, and his face reflects keenness, cleverness, and an appreciation of good humor. He has a quick temper which sometimes leads him to say stinging things, but his self-control is so excellent, that one cannot but admire how well he holds himself in check. He is the idol of every man in his command, and what is more to his credit, he was their idol before he became the victor at Manila Bay.

When ashore, he is a great club man, a fine horseman, and an expert gunner. His wife died many years ago, shortly after the birth of their only son, George. Dewey is an early riser when on shore, temperate to the degree of abstemiousness. He enjoys a good table, but eats sparingly; he is fond of a good cigar after dinner, and occasionally smokes between times. He is methodical, business-like, cool and very deliberate; he does his own work well, and expects everybody else to do the same. He is very fond of children, and in his younger days, when he visited his native town, it was very often a familiar spectacle to see him on the piazza of the old Dewey home surrounded by a group of wide-eyed youngsters, telling them stories about daring men-of-warsmen and sea battles.

Eugene Field's verse is not a bad description, in many respects of George Dewey:

> " A single man, perhaps, but good ez gold and true ez steel,
> He could whip his weight in wild cats and you never heard him squeel,
> Good to the helpless and the weak; a brave an' manly heart,
> A cyclone couldn't phase, but any child could rend apart;
> So like the mountain pine that dares the storm which sweeps along,
> But rocks the wind in summertime, an' sings a soothin' song."

CHAPTER III

The Second Battle of Manila

How 8,000 American Soldiers Swept into a Heavily Entrenched City, Garrisoned by Nearly Twice that Number of Spaniards.—Insurgent Army Kept from Plunder. —Rare Bravery and Sacrifice.—What Major-General Wesley Merritt, Commanding the Expedition, General Frank V. Greene, General Arthur McArthur and General Thomas Anderson Said Officially of the Battle.—The Peace Protocol.

AFTER the occupation of the arsenal at Cavite by Admiral Dewey that officer waited without further fighting until he could receive reinforcements from the United States sufficient to enable him to take and hold Manila. The insurgents, however, kept up a continuous fighting in the region around Manila until they practically held all of the territory except that city in their grasp. They fought with great bravery, and, although checked by Admiral Dewey at the outskirts of the city, they managed to drive the Spanish behind their fortifications and force them to the wall. They held Malabon, Tarlac, and Bakkoor, Aguinaldo establishing a provisional government at the latter place and announcing himself dictator of the islands. The insurgents were eager to rush upon the city, but Dewey refused to allow "Hordes of passionate semi-savages to storm a civilized metropolis." He forbade them to cross the Malate River, seven miles south of Manila, threatening to bombard them with the *Petrel*.

In a campaign of two weeks the insurgents took 3,000 prisoners, including 2,000 soldiers of the regular Spanish army. On July 13th Dewey sent the following cablegram to the Naval Department: "Aguinaldo informs me his troops have taken all of Subic Bay except Isla Grande, which he was prevented from taking by the German man-of-war *Irene*. On July 7th the *Raleigh* and *Concord* went there; they took the island and about 1,300 men with arms and ammunition. No resistance. The *Irene* retired from the bay on their arrival."

This last sentence contains in a nutshell one of the most exciting incidents in the history of the war, an incident which almost involved our nation in a war with Germany. This was the first open action of the German Admiral against the United States. When the insurgents were about to take the island, the German warship *Irene* appeared on the scene and protected the Spaniards there from attack. Dewey, when informed of the matter, sent the *Boston* and *Raleigh* to the island, and the *Irene* slunk away. One shot from the *Raleigh* caused the Spaniards to raise the white flag. The captain of the *Irene* explained that he interfered "in the cause of humanity," and for a time it seemed as though the German meddling would prove a serious matter. The German government, however, repudiated the incident, and that, together with Dewey's splendid handling of the situation, prevented the affair from assuming the proportion it threatened.

In the meantime three expeditions were on their way across the ocean to take charge of matters, and reinforce Admiral Dewey. General Wesley Merritt was appointed Commander-in-Chief of all the forces in the Philippines, and arrived at Cavite July 25th. Some days before, on June 30th, the first expedition under General Thomas Anderson had landed. Another expedition under General Frank V. Greene arrived on July 17th, and the third, under General McArthur, arrived July 30th, five days later than General Merritt.

Immediately upon the arrival of General Merritt it was decided, after a conference with Admiral Dewey, to attack and take Manila. No time was lost. General Merritt stated in his dispatch that "to gain approach to the city Greene's outposts were advanced to continue a line from Camino Real to the beach. On the night of July 31st, Spanish attacked sharply. Artillery outposts behaved well. Held position. Necessary to call out brigade. Spanish loss rumored heavy." Our loss was 9 killed, 9 seriously wounded and 38 slightly wounded.

This plain statement of facts gives no idea, however, of the real battle which initiated our soldiers into the warfare of the Philippine Islands. The fighting took place amid a terrible rainstorm, a rainstorm such as we are not familiar with in the United States; 3,000 Spanish troops made a concerted sortie from Manila on the outposts and trenches of Camp Dewey, near Malate. The attack was directed at the American right flank held by the Tenth Pennsylvania troops. The trenches of the Americans extended from the beach to the left flank of the insurgents. Sunday was the insurgent feast day, and their left flank withdrew, leaving the American right flank exposed. Companies A and E of the Tenth Pennsylvania and Utah Battery were ordered to reinforce the right flank; it was there that the attack was made. The brave Pennsylvania men never flinched, but stood their ground under a withering fire. The alarm spread and the First California Regiment with two companies of the Third Artillery who fight with rifles were sent as reinforcements.

The Utah battery covered itself with glory, and all the men showed the greatest pluck under the trying deluge of nature and of the Spaniards. The enemy was repulsed and retreated in disorder. The Spanish loss was about 350 killed and 900 wounded. On the night of August 1st the fighting was renewed, but the enemy had been taught a lesson and made the attack at long range with heavy artillery. The Utah Battery replied, and the artillery duel lasted about an hour.

General Greene, in his report of the battle, says: " Major Cuthbertson, Tenth Pennsylvania, reports that the Spaniards left their trenches in force and attempted to turn our right flank, coming within 200 yards of his position. But as the night was intensely dark, with incessant and heavy rain, and as no dead or wounded were found in front of his position at daylight, it is possible that he was mistaken, and that the heavy fire to which he was subjected came from the trenches near Block House 14, beyond his right flank, at a distance of about 700 yards. The Spaniards used smokeless powder, the thickets obscured the flash of their guns, and the Mauser bullet penetrating a bamboo pole makes a noise very similar to the crack of the rifle itself; hence, the difficulty of locating the enemy.

" This attack demonstrated the immediate necessity of extending our intrenchments to the right, and, although not covered by my instructions (which were to occupy the trenches from the bay to Calle Real, and to avoid precipitating an engagement), I ordered the First Colorado and one battalion of the First California, which occupied trenches at 9 A.M., August 1st, to extend the line of trenches to the Pasay Road. The work was begun by these troops, and continued every day by the troops occupying the trenches in turn, until a strong line was completed by August 12th, about 1,200 yards in length, extending from the bay to the east side of the Pasay Road. Its left rested on the bay, and its right on an extensive rice swamp, practically impassable."

The right flank was refused, because the only way to cross a smaller rice swamp, crossing the line about 700 yards from the beach, was along a crossroad in rear of the general line. As finally completed the works were very strong in profile, being five or six feet in height and eight to ten feet in thickness at the base, strengthened by bags filled with earth.

"The only material available was black soil saturated with water, and without the bags this was washed down and ruined in a day by the heavy and almost incessant rains. The construction of these trenches was constantly interrupted by the enemy's fire. They were occupied by the troops in succession, four battalions being usually sent out for a service of twenty-four hours, and posted with three battalions in the trenches and one battalion in reserve along the crossroad to Pasay; Cossack posts being sent out from the latter to guard the camp against any possible surprise from the northeast and east.

TERRIBLE SERVICE IN THE TRENCHES.

"The service in the trenches was of the most arduous character, the rain being almost incessant, and the men having no protection against it; they were wet during the entire twenty-four hours, and the mud was so deep that the shoes were ruined and a considerable number of men rendered barefooted. Until the notice of bombardment was given on August 7th, any exposure above or behind the trenches promptly brought the enemy's fire, so that the men had to sit in the mud under cover and keep awake, prepared to resist an attack, during the entire tour of twenty-four hours.

"After one particularly heavy rain a portion of the trench contained two feet of water, in which the men had to remain. It could not be drained, as it was lower than an adjoining rice swamp, in which the water had risen nearly two feet, the rainfall being more than four inches in twenty-four hours. These hardships were all endured by the men of the different regiments in turn, with the finest possible spirit and without a murmur of complaint.

"August 7th the notice of bombardment, after forty-eight hours, or sooner if the Spanish fire continued, was served, and after that date not a shot was fired on either side until the assault was made on August 13th. It was with great difficulty, and in some cases not without force, that the insurgents were restrained from opening fire and thus drawing the fire of the Spaniards during this period.

"Owing to the heavy storm and high surf it was impossible to communicate promptly with the division commander at Cavite, and I received my instructions direct from the Major-General commanding, or his staff officers, one of whom visited my camp every day, and I reported direct to him in the same manner. My instructions were to occupy the insurgent trenches near the beach, so as to be in good position to advance on Manila when ordered, but meanwhile to avoid precipitating an engagement, not to waste ammunition, and (after August 1st) not to return the enemy's fire unless convinced that he had left his trenches and was making an attack in force. These instructions were given daily in the most positive terms to the officer commanding in the trenches, and in the main they were faithfully carried out.

AMMUNITION WAS WASTED.

"More ammunition than necessary was expended on the nights of August 2d and 5th, but in both cases the trenches were occupied by troops under fire for the first time, and in the darkness and rain there was ground to believe that the heavy fire indicated a real attack from outside the enemy's trenches. The total expenditure of ammunition on our side in the four engagements was about 150,000 rounds, and by the enemy very much more.

"After the attack of July 31st, August 1st I communicated by signal with the captain of the United States steamship *Raleigh*, anchored about 3,000 yards southwest of my camp, asking if he had received orders in regard to the action of his ship in case of another attack on my troops. He replied:

"'Both Admiral Dewey and General Merritt desire to avoid general action at present. If attack too strong for you, we will assist you, and another vessel will come and offer help.'

A STREET SCENE IN ALBAY

Albay is the principal sugar district of Luzon island. Notice how the native houses are set upon bamboo poles, high from the ground; the entrance is effected by means of ladders reaching to the floors. At night the ladder is pulled up and the native feels safe from intrusion. The bamboo and the palm leaf and bark are about all the material the Filipino needs to build his house.

SACLOBAN, ISLAND OF LEYTE.

The island of Leyte belongs to the Visayan group, and contains about 3,000 square miles, being the eighth in size in the Philippine Archipelago. The finest quality of hemp comes from this island.

PAMPANGA, A VILLAGE IN THE SUGAR COUNTRY.

This historic village, on the island of Luzon, is memorable for the terrible massacre of the Chinese by the Spaniards at this point in the early history of the islands.

"In repeating this message, Lieutenant Tappan, commanding United States steamship *Callao*, anchored nearer the beach, sent me a box of blue lights, and it was agreed that if I burned one of these on the beach the *Raleigh* would at once open fire on the Spanish fort."

General Greene issued this address to the troops : "Camp Dewey, near Manila. The Brigadier-General commanding desires to thank the troops engaged last night for gallantry and skill displayed by them in repelling such a vigorous attack by largely superior forces of Spaniards. Not an inch of ground was yielded by the Tenth Pennsylvania Infantry and Utah Artillery stationed in the trenches. A battalion of the Third Artillery and First Regiment California Infantry moved forward to their support through a galling fire with the utmost intrepidity. The courage and steadiness shown by all in their first engagement is worthy of the highest commendation."

THE DOWNFALL OF MANILA.

Manila fell before American arms on August 13th. The combined land and naval forces took the city with little or no opposition. The official story of its downfall is told in the following dispatch sent by General Merritt to the War Department:

"MANILA, August 13th.—On the 7th instant Admiral Dewey joined me in forty-eight-hour notification to Spanish commander to remove non-combatants from city. Same date reply received, expressing thanks for humane sentiments, and stating Spanish without places for refuge for non-combatants now within walled towns.

"On 9th instant sent joint note, inviting attention to suffering in store for sick and non-combatants in case it became our duty to reduce the defences, also setting forth hopeless condition of Spanish forces, surrounded on all sides, fleet in front, no prospect of reinforcements, and demanded surrender as due to every consideration of humanity. Same date received reply, admitting their situation, but stating Council of Defence declares request for surrender cannot be granted, but offered to consult government, if time was granted necessary for communication via Hong Kong. Joint note in reply declining.

"On the 13th joined with navy in attack with following results : After about half hour's accurate shelling of Spanish lines, McArthur's

Brigade on right and Greene's on left center under Anderson made vigorous attack and carried Spanish works. Loss not accurately known—about 50 in all. Behavior of troops excellent; co-operation of the navy most valuable. Troops advanced rapidly on walled city, upon which white flag shown and town capitulated. Troops occupy Malate, Bynondo, walled city San Miguel. All important centers protected. Insurgents kept out. No disorder or pillage."

The fleet under Admiral Dewey opened the engagement at 9.30 o'clock in the morning. A sudden cloud of smoke, green and white, against the stormy sky completely hid the *Olympia*, and a shell screamed across two miles of turbulent water, and burst near the Spanish fort at Malate. Then the *Petrel* and *Raleigh* and the active little *Callao* opened a rapid fire directed toward the shore end of the intrenchments. The Spaniards replied feebly.

Less than half an hour after the bombardment began, General Greene reported that it was possible to advance. Thereupon six companies of the Colorado regiment leaped over their breastwork, dashed into the swamp and opened volleys within 300 yards of the Spanish lines. The land forces under General Anderson advanced from the South, General Greene in command of the First Brigade held the left wing, General McArthur of the Second Brigade was on the right of the line and covered two miles.

The Spanish made a hard fight against the right and left wings, but after a while were forced to retreat inside the Malate fort, from which they were driven by the fire from the ships. The American troops speedily captured the fort. Our land forces followed closely upon the retreating Spaniards. The Second Battalion of the First California headed the advance on the city. A company of the First Nebraska did effective work with Gatling guns.

TOOK A BLOCKHOUSE AT PISTOL'S POINT.

The Astor Battery gave a splendid example of daring in this assault. At the call of General McArthur, Captain Peyton C. March volunteered to dislodge some Spanish soldiers occupying a blockhouse which controlled the roads at Passay. Fifteen or more of his men accompanied him, armed only with pistols, in the rush up the hill in the face of deadly Spanish fire. Of these fifteen but three, including Captain March, remained when the Spaniards fled from the blockhouse. All the others had been either killed or wounded in the charge. It was a costly and magnificent show of bravery, but it served the purpose, and practically ended the fighting for the day.

General Greene, in his report of the battle, says:

"Captain Grove and Lieutenant Means, of the First Colorado, had been particularly active in this work and fearless in penetrating beyond our lines and close to those of the enemy. As the time for attack approached, these officers made a careful examination of the ground between our trenches and Fort San Antonio de Abad, and, finally, on August 11th, Major J. F. Bell, United States Volunteer Engineers, tested the creek in front of this fort and ascertained not only that it was fordable, but the exact width of the ford at the beach, and actually swam in the bay to a point from which he could examine the Spanish line from the rear. With the information thus obtained it was possible to plan the attack intelligently. The position assigned to my brigade extended from the beach to the small rice swamp, a front of about 700 yards.

"After the sharp skirmish on the second line of defence of the Spaniards, and after Greene's brigade moved through Malate, meeting a shuffling foe, the open space at the Luneta, just south of the walled city, was reached about 1 P.M. A white flag was flying at the southwest bastion, and I rode forward to meet it under a heavy fire from out right and rear on the Paco Road.

KEPT THE INSURGENTS OUT.

"At the bastion I was informed that officers representing General Merritt and Admiral Dewey were on their way ashore to receive the surrender, and I therefore turned back to the Paco Road. The firing ceased at this time, and on reaching this road I found nearly 1,000 Spanish troops who had retreated from Santa Ana through Paco, and coming up the Paco Road had been firing on our flank. I held the commanding officers, but ordered these troops to march into the walled city. At this point the California regiment a short time before had met some insurgents who had fired at the Spaniards on the walls, and the latter in returning the fire had caused a loss in the California regiment of 1 killed and 2 wounded.

"My instructions were to march past the walled city on its surrender, cross the bridge, occupy the city on the north side of the Pasig, and protect lives and property there. While the white flag was flying on the walls yet, very sharp firing had just taken place outside, and there were from 5,000 to 6,000 men on the walls, with arms in their hands, only a few yards from us. I did not feel justified in leaving this force in my rear until the surrender was clearly established, and I therefore halted and assembled my force, prepared to force the gates if there was any more firing. The Eighteenth Infantry and First California were sent forward to hold the bridges, a few yards ahead, but the Second Battalion, Third Artillery, First Nebraska, Tenth Pennsylvania and First Colorado were all assembled at this point. While this was being done, I received a note from Lieutenant-Colonel Whittier, of General Merritt's staff, written from the Captain-General's office within the walls, asking me to stop the firing outside, as negotiations for surrender were in progress.

"I then returned to the troops outside the walls and sent Captain Birkhimer's battalion of the Third Artillery down the Paco road to prevent any insurgents from entering. Feeling satisfied that there would be no attack from the Spanish troops lining the walls, I put the regiments in motion toward the bridges, brushing aside a considerable force of insurgents who had penetrated the city from the direction of Paco, and were in the main street with their flag, expecting to march into the walled city and plant it on the walls. After crossing the bridges the Eighteenth United States Infantry was posted to patrol the principal streets near the bridge, the First California was sent up the Pasig to occupy Quiapo, San Miguel and Malacanan, and with the First Nebraska I marched down the river to the captain of the Port's office, where I ordered the Spanish flag hauled down and the American flag raised in its place.

"The resistance encountered on the 13th was much less than anticipated and planned for, but had the resistance been greater, the result would have been the same, only the loss would have been greater. Fortunately, the great result of capturing this city, the seat of Spanish power in the East for more than three hundred years, was accomplished with a loss of life comparatively insignificant."

General McArthur is strong in his expression of approval of heroic work. In his report he says:

"The combat of Singalong can hardly be classified as a great military event, but the involved terrene and the prolonged resistance created a very trying situation, and afforded an unusual scope for the display of military qualities by a large number of individuals.

"The invincible composure of Colonel Ovenshine, during an exposure in dangerous space for more than an hour, was conspicuous and very inspiring to the troops; and the efficient manner in which he took advantage of opportunities as they arose during the varying aspects of the fight was of great practical value in determining the result.

"The cool, determined and sustained efforts of Colonel Reeve, of the Thirteenth Minnesota, contributed very materially to the maintenance of the discipline and marked efficiency of his regiment.

"The brilliant manner in which Lieutenant March accepted and discharged the responsible and dangerous duties of the day, and the pertinacity with which, assisted by his officers and men, he carried his guns over all obstacles to the very front of the firing line, was an exceptional display of warlike skill and judgment, indicating the existence of many of the best qualifications for high command in battle.

"The gallant manner in which Captain Sawtelle, brigade quartermaster, volunteered to join the advance party in the rush, volunteered to command a firing line, for a time without an officer, and again volunteered to lead a scout to ascertain the presence or absence of the enemy in the blockhouse, was a fine display of personal intrepidity.

"The efficient, fearless, and intelligent manner in which Lieutenant Kernan, Twenty-first United States Infantry, Acting Assistant Adjutant-General of the brigade and Second Lieutenant Whitworth, Eighteenth United States Infantry, aid, executed a series of dangerous and difficult orders, was a fine exemplification of stall work under fire.

"The splendid bravery of Captains Bjornstad and Seebach, and Lieutenant Lackore, of the Thirteenth Minnesota, all wounded, and, finally, the work of the soldiers of the first firing line, too, all went to make up a rapid succession of individual actions of unusual merit."

THE SPANIARDS HOIST THE WHITE FLAG.

At 11.30 A.M. the Spaniards hoisted the white flag. A conference to arrange the terms of surrender was held at the palace of the Governor-General at 4 P.M. General Jandenes agreed to surrender, and the American flag was raised at 5.30 P.M. by Lieutenant Brumby, of the *Olympia*. The total number of Spanish soldiers who surrendered exceeded 8,000, and there was an unlimited supply of arms and ammunition. In the attack 5 were killed and 43 injured.

The terms of capitulation, as given in General Merritt's report, were as follows :

"The undersigned having been appointed a commission to determine the details of the capitulation of the city and defences of Manila and its suburbs and the Spanish forces stationed therein, in accordance with the agreement entered into the previous day by General Wesley Merritt, United States Army, American Commander-in-Chief in the Philippines, and His Excellency Don Fermin Jandenes, acting General-in-Chief of the Spanish Army in the Philippines, have agreed upon the following :

"1. The Spanish troops, European and native, capitulate with the city and its defences, with all the honors of war, depositing their arms in the places designed by the authorities of the United States, and remaining in the quarters designated and under the orders of their officers, and subject to the control of the aforesaid United States authorities, until the conclusion of a treaty of peace between the two belligerent nations. All persons included in the capitulation remain at liberty, the officers remaining in their respective homes, which shall be respected as long as they observe the regulations prescribed for their government and the laws in force.

"2. Officers shall retain their side arms, horses and private property. All public horses and public property of all kinds shall be turned over to staff officers designated by the United States.

"3. Complete returns in duplicate of men by organization, and full lists of public property and stores shall be rendered to the United States within ten days from this date.

"4. All questions relating to the repatriation of officers and men of the Spanish forces and of their families, and of the expenses which said repatriation may occasion, shall be referred to the Government of the United States at Washington.

"Spanish families may leave Manila at any time convenient to them.

"The return of the arms surrendered by the Spanish forces shall take place when they evacuate the city, or when the American army evacuates.

"5. Officers and men included in the capitulation shall be supplied by the United States, according to their rank, with rations and necessary aid as though they were prisoners of war, until the conclusion of a treaty of peace between the United States and Spain. All the funds in the Spanish treasury and all other public funds shall be turned over to the authorities of the United States.

"6. This city, its inhabitants, its churches and religious worship, its educational establishments, and its private property of all descriptions are placed under the special safeguard of the faith and honor of the American Army.

F. V. GREENE,
Brigadier-General of Volunteers, U. S. A.

B. P. LAMBERTON,
Captain, United States Navy.

CHARLES A. WHITTIER,
Lieut.-Colonel and Inspector-General.

E. H. CROWDER,
Lieut.-Colonel and Judge-Advocate.

NICHOLAS DE LA PETRA,
Auditor-General Excmo.

CARLOS,
Coronel de Ingenieros.

JOSE,
Coronel de Estado Major."

PEACE.

While the battle was planned, overtures had been made through the mediation of the French Ambassador at Washington, on behalf of the Spanish Government for a cessation of hostilities, to culminate in a treaty of peace. The peace protocol was signed at 4.23 P.M. on Friday, August 12th. The sixth article of the protocol was as follows: "On the signing of the protocol hostilities will be suspended, and notice to that effect will be given as soon as possible by each government to the commander of its military and naval forces."

As the Manila cable had been cut and was not in use, it was impossible to communicate the news of peace to Admiral Dewey or General Merritt. Consequently they were ignorant of the fact that peace had been declared when they assailed and took Manila. Allowing for difference in time, the surrender of Manila took place a few hours after the signing of the peace protocol. This proved the turning point of most of the arguments which took place later, when the Peace Commissioners met together at Paris to discuss the conditions of the treaty.

In the meantime, however, General Merritt ruled supreme in the captured city, keeping out insurgents and protecting people and property.

FIRST BATTLE BETWEEN AMERICANS AND FILIPINOS, FEBRUARY 4 AND 5, 1899

Sunday, February 5, 1899, our first battle with the Filipinos occurred. This battle began between the outposts the night before, but it was the next day that it raged in its fury, and the Americans closed the day with less than fifty killed and less than 300 wounded, while the Filipinos lost over 3,000 killed and wounded, and more than 4,000 prisoners.

GENERAL AGUINALDO
This is the Philippine chief as he appeared in military uniform in February, 1899.

CHAPTER IV

The Trouble With Aguinaldo

A Face-to-Face View of the Insurgent Leader.—A Man of Craft and Cunning.—Sold out His Own People.—Fought against Uncle Sam.—Insurgents Swept into the Sea.—Immense Sacrifice of Life and Property.—The Flight of Agoncillo to Canada.—The Oregon Sent for by Dewey "for Political Reasons."—Germany Takes a Friendly Step.—Emperor William Removes All His Warships from Manila Bay, and Places German Interests in American Hands.

THE fighting in the Philippines did not end with the downfall of Manila or the signing of the Peace treaty. The insurgents had to be reckoned with. From the beginning they proved even harder to handle than the Spanish. Inflated with victory, General Aguinaldo, the insurgent leader, proclaimed himself Dictator of the islands, and it was with difficulty that his followers were held in check by the American forces without open hostility. It became evident that we should have trouble with the insurgents. That it would be as serious as after-events proved, was not imagined.

On June 13th Aguinaldo issued a "declaration of independence," of which the following is a rough translation:

"To the district headmen and village headmen of the province of Bulacan, from the Political Military Governor of this province, whose headquarters are now transferred to the town of San Francisco de Malabon, and combined with the section under his orders at Bacoor, Binacayan, Imus, Novaleta, Salinas and Cavite Viejo. They only require to be combined with the other forces in Indiang and Silang, near by, and then our troops will be sent forward, and within a few days will be found in possession of almost the whole province, which, being maritime, will be found in a position to proclaim effectively our independence. This proclamation will not be long deferred, because the ultimate object of this government will thus be best attained notwithstanding the suggestions of some of our principal associates. It is better and more convenient to select as the place on account of its being near the sea, the township of Cavite Viejo, which is an old port, originally the town of Cavite.

"Wherefore I decree as follows:

"The 12th day of this month is fixed for the declaration of the independence of this our beloved country, in this township of Cavite Viejo, for the due and proper solemnization of which auspicious event there should be on the day named an assemblage of all district headmen and commanders of our forces, and through the proper representatives there should be a notification issued for the purpose of inviting the attendance of all who have in any way assisted in the good work, such, for example, as the distinguished Admiral of the American squadron and his commanders and officers, to all of whom, as having lent invaluable aid in the glorious work, a courteous invitation will be sent. After the formal reading of the declaration, the same will be signed by all who wish to give support thereto.

"Given under our hand and seal at Cavite this 9th day of June, 1898. EMILIO AGUINALDO,
Dictator of the Philippines."

Various congresses were convened within the succeeding months, and Aguinaldo thought it wiser to change his title from that of Dictator to President of the Revolutionary Government of the Filipinos. He experienced some trouble in securing a suitable cabinet, and the list was changed several times. The following is the latest make-up of the Cabinet: President of the Cabinet and Minister of Foreign Affairs, Mabini; Minister of the Interior, Teodoro Sandica, civil engineer, educated in England and Belgium, and taken to Manila from Hong Kong by Admiral Dewey; Minister of War, General Baldomero Aguinaldo, a cousin of Aguinaldo, the President of the so-called Filipino Government, and a leader of the insurrection from the beginning, said to be a large landowner of Cavite; Minister of Finance, General Trias, a close ally of Aguinaldo; Minister of Public Works, Gregorio Gonzaga, a lawyer, formerly the Filipino Agent at Hong Kong, and formerly Spanish Attorney-General in Visayas.

The following description of Aguinaldo by Joseph L. Stickney, who was with Admiral Dewey during the battle of May 1st and landed later, gives a good view of the insurgent leader and his character. He says:

"Having been on terms of friendly association with General Aguinaldo and his staff during the last half of May and the whole of June, I had an opportunity to get some idea of the man who is to-day one of the most important individual factors in our dealings with the Filipinos.

"Emilio Aguinaldo, now about 29 years old, is a man of an intelligence far beyond that of most of his people. He comes of a good family in the province of Cavite, near Manila, where he was educated and where he entered the bar. He joined the insurgents immediately after the outbreak of the rebellion in the latter part of 1896, but it was not until after the execution of Dr. Rizal that he became one of the leaders of the revolt.

"The blockade maintained by the Spanish squadron in Philippine waters against the importation of arms for the insurgents gradually drove the Filipinos to the wall, and in December, 1897, the celebrated 'pacification' of the islands was negotiated, the go-between being Senor Pedro Paterno, director of the Manila museum, a Filipino, who had remained at least passively loyal to the Spaniards. The Filipino junta at this time was composed of Emilio Aguinaldo, who exercised such executive powers as were possible to so feeble an organization; Senor Artacho, Home Secretary; Senor Montenogro, Foreign Secretary; Vito Bilarmino, War Secretary; and Baldomero Aguinaldo, Secretary of the Treasury.

"The so-called 'pacification' consisted in a purchase of the insurgent leaders for the sum of $800,000 (Mexican), equal to about $400,000 in gold. Aguinaldo and his associates agreed to surrender all the arms in the possession of the natives and to quit the archipelago, remaining away at the pleasure of the Spanish government, and to use their utmost influence to disband and disarm all the insurgent forces.

"Aguinaldo was to go to Hong Kong to receive the first installment of the Spanish money, amounting to $400,000 (Mexican), and he was then to cable to Artacho, who surrendered himself to the Captain-General as a hostage. On receiving Aguinaldo's cable message that the money had been paid, Artacho was to dissolve the insurgent organization, disband the troops and give up their arms. This part of the programme was carried out in December, 1897, or the early part of January, 1898.

"The cash payment was divided among the junta and Aguinaldo started for Paris. He had gone no farther than Singapore, however, when the destruction of the *Maine* in Havana harbor brought on an acute tension of the relations between the United States and Spain and he remained in Singapore to see whether the Filipinos might not profit by Spain's difficulties.

"General Aguinaldo sailed from Hong Kong for Manila Bay in the dispatch boat *McCulloch*, May 17, 1898. He landed in Cavite on the 19th. As I accompanied him from Hong Kong, and was able to be of some service to him, I was received at his headquarters with great cordiality until after the arrival of the first detachment of troops. About that time Aguinaldo began to think he was a great man, and as he was tiresome and often ridiculous when trying to live up to his own estimate of himself, I saw less and less of him.

"He took possession of one of the numerous abandoned houses in Cavite, and at first he acted with good judgment and simplicity. In a day or two the natives flocked into Cavite in droves, and as a small steamer arrived from Hong Kong, laden with arms and ammunition, in a week there were more than 1,000 men ready to take the field against the Spaniards in Cavite Province.

"On the night of May 26th Aguinaldo sent 600 men across the Bay of Bacoor in canoes. This force was attacked by 300 Spaniards on the morning of the 28th, and all the latter were captured. Sharp and continuous fighting occurred for a week, during which—after having succeeded in witnessing the fighting for two days without Aguinaldo's consent or assistance—I obtained from him a guide and a passport which enabled me to go into battle with more comfort and less risk.

"When Manila was fairly invested by the insurgents, Aguinaldo's ideas of his own importance and power underwent a very apparent expansion. He had been obliged to quit Cavite, as our troops needed the town; but he moved his headquarters to Bacoor, and there he was as inaccessible to ordinary mortals as if he had been the Emperor of China.

"Anyone who expects Aguinaldo to make gross blunders in dealing with our people will probably be disappointed. He is an exceptionally shrewd man. He is of the distinctly Japanese type in appearance, having the broad, square forehead, which betokens intellect, re-enforced by the bumps in the back of his head, which indicate the endurance and persistence of a strong animalism.

"He has rather large eyes, set wide apart, and a straight but sensual nose. His lips are full, and his chin round and not determined. His height is about 5 feet 4 inches, and he carries himself very erect. His color is a light chocolate. He speaks and writes Spanish and Tagalog, the native language of the island of Luzon. He understands English fairly well, though he always made a pretense of not being able to speak or comprehend it. I had reason for believing that he could have held all his conversation with us in English without an interpreter if he had wished to do so."

BELIEVED TO BEAR A CHARMED LIFE.

One of Aguinaldo's great holds over the insurgents was through their superstition. They believed that he bore a charmed life. The Spaniards had often placed large sums on his head, at one time $25,000 having been offered for him dead or alive. He managed, however, to escape both capture from the Spanish and treachery from his own men. At one time some of the insurgents, who were envious of his power, poisoned the food which was to have been given him at dinner. In some lucky way, however, Aguinaldo happened not to taste the meal, and he escaped what would have otherwise been certain death.

The following interesting account of a visit to Aguinaldo's headquarters at Cavite, once the home of a rich native, is given: "The house is broad, low, roomy, and typically Spanish. There is a paved court at the street entrance, and, while Aguinaldo occupied it, a guard of insurgents lined it on either side. They would come to present arms as you passed by, and good form called for a salute in return. A stairway leads from the court, and the landing at the top is large, and makes a good ante-chamber.

Here stand guards in uniforms of blue. There is little delay, and the summons to enter the reception-room comes quickly. Aguinaldo comes in, extends his hand, and then motions the visitor to a seat. He wears a spotless suit of white linen, a white shirt with well-polished front, a high collar and a black cravat tied in a bow, and red velvet slippers embroidered in gold. At first sight you would take him for a Japanese student. It takes a long stretch of the imagination to believe that this youthful-looking man in white is a leader of a large force of warlike people.

In his office he has a modern desk, backed with a beveled edge mirror that came from Europe, a couple of large, strong iron boxes, an abundance of easy chairs, an old grand piano, and a large hat-rack of fanciful design. The only signs of war were the ends of sword chains that peeped through holes in the coats of the officers who were with him.

Such was the man with whom the American commanders had to deal,—a man who sold out his own countrymen, and, because the full price of their slavery had not been paid to him, he returned from his voluntary exile and again placed himself at the head of the people he had betrayed. There is little wonder that the American commanders viewed him with suspicion and checked his onward march.

While the peace conference was being held at Paris to discuss the terms of a treaty, General Merritt was present to consult with the American members of the commission on the subject of the situation in the Philippines. General Otis was ordered to replace him in control of the island. The situation which confronted General Otis was not a pleasant one, but no serious outbreak occurred for some time.

Toward the end of December, however, Aguinaldo assumed an attitude of open defiance against American arms. He ensconsced himself at Malloas, about twenty miles from Manila, and made that the seat of the so-called Revolutionary Government. He began to run things in a high-handed manner, and became even more despotic and overbearing toward his own people than the Spaniards ever were. In the interior cities, controlled by the insurgents, he levied taxes upon the natives much more excessive than any exacted by the old rulers of the islands.

It became evident to General Otis that something had to be done. The insurgents were inflamed by reports sent to them from the United States by Agoncillo, who had been sent to this country by the Junta of the Filipinos to keep an eye on the legislation here. The behavior of this envoy of the Philippine insurgents was such that it was deemed wise to place secret service agents on his track. It was found that he and other Filipinos in this country were plotting against our Government, consequently the watch kept upon him was made so keen that Agoncillo fled for Canada, fearing arrest.

THE ATTACK OF THE INSURGENTS.

About the same time that he fled, the news was cabled across the sea that the Filipinos had attacked Manila, and that on the 5th of February a desperate battle had been waged, in which the insurgents were utterly routed and lost nearly 2,000 men.

The story of the battle, as briefly told in the official cablegram of General Otis, is as follows :—"Adjutant-General : Insurgents in large force opened attack on our outer lines at 8.45 last evening; renewed attack several times during night; at 4 o'clock this morning entire line engaged; all attacks repulsed; at daybreak advanced against insurgents, and have driven them beyond the lines they formerly occupied, capturing several villages and their defence works; insurgents' loss in dead and wounded large ; our own casualties thus far estimated at 175 ; very few fatal. Troops enthusiastic and acting fearlessly. Very splendid execution on flanks of enemy ; city held in check, and absolute quiet prevails; insurgents have secured a good many Mauser rifles, a few field pieces, and quick-firing guns, with ammunition, during last month."

In another dispatch General Otis states that our casualities aggregate 250. He buried 500 of insurgent dead and held 500 prisoners. Their total loss was 4,000.

The fighting was not the result of the aggression on the part of the Americans, but was precipitated by the action of two native soldiers who refused to obey the order of a sentry who challenged them as they attempted to pass his post. These two natives advanced to the outpost of the First Nebraska Regiment, stationed to the northeast of Manila. The sentry ordered them to halt, but they insolently refused to do so. He called upon them again, and as they paid no attention to his order, he leveled his rifle and fired upon them.

No sooner had the shot been fired than the Filipinos, who were occupying block-house No. 7, fired a signal for a general attack upon the Americans. Immediately the insurgents moved against the American troops, the Nebraska Regiment being the first to meet the attack. It was evident that the insurgents expected to take our troops by surprise, consequently they were not prepared for the vigorous reception which they received. The Nebraska, Montana, and North Dakota outposts replied briskly until reinforcements arrived. The Filipinos concentrated at three points, Caloocan, Gagalangin, and Santa Mesa. At about 1 o'clock the insurgents opened fire simultaneously from all three places, supplementing the attack by the fire of two seige guns at Balik-Balik, and advancing their skirmishes at Paco. The Utah Light Artillery and the Third Artillery did splendid work. The engagement lasted over an hour. The United States cruiser *Charleston* and the gunboat *Concord*, stationed off Malabon, opened fire, and did great damage to the insurgents.

At 2.45 A.M. there was a fusilade along the entire line, and the monitor *Monadnock* opened fire from off Malate. With daylight the Americans advanced. The California and Washington regiments made a splendid charge and drove the Filipinos from the villages of Paco and Santa Mesa. The Nebraska regiment also distinguished itself, capturing a very strong position at the reservoir, which is connected with the waterworks. The Kansas and Dakota regiments compelled the enemy's right flank to retire to Caloocan.

FILIPINOS DROWNED LIKE RATS.

The brigade under General King charged upon a strong force of the enemy, and, yelling wildly, drove them helter-skelter into the Pasig River, where, in a frenzy of terror, they were drowned like rats.

The utter fearlessness of the American soldiers was never better demonstrated than in this onward charge. The Ygorates, armed with bows and arrows, made a very determined stand, in the face of the fire of artillery, and left many dead upon the field. Evidently they did not know what guns were, for they stood in the face of the fire without realizing that they were at a disadvantage, and were mowed down like wheat. One of the chiefs, who was captured, said he had never seen a modern field piece before.

VIEW ALONG THE ESCOLTA AFTER THE LAST GREAT FIRE

The city of Manila is in constant danger of destruction by fire and many serious conflagrations have occurred. The native houses are built almost entirely of bamboo frames and covered with palm leaves, and the stone and brick business structures are much surrounded with awnings and porches. Hence the fire department of Manila, which is poorly equipped, has little chance to check a fire once it gains headway.

GEN. ARTHUR MacARTHUR. GEN. CHARLES KING.

GEN. HENRY W. LAWTON. GEN. FRED. FUNSTON.

POPULAR COMMANDERS IN THE FILIPINO WAR.

The next day General Hale's brigade advanced and took the waterworks outside of the city. They had a sharp skirmish with the enemy, which made no determined stand. The pumps were damaged, but the missing parts were found later, and the works were soon placed in good order.

The terrible loss of the rebels may be gained from the fact that one hundred and sixty of them were buried in one field on one day, and eighty-seven in another. The Americans worked hard to bring hundreds of the suffering insurgents to the hospital for treatment. The character of the insurgents may be judged from the fact that they used the flag of truce as a defence for their own fire. All through Manila white flags were shown from the houses of the natives, and, as the soldiers passed by, they were shot at from these very windows.

A Filipino Colonel went out from his line under a flag of truce. Several American officers promptly went to meet him, but when the parties met the concealed insurgents opened fire, whereupon the Colonel apologized for the barbarous conduct of his troops and returned to his lines.

On February 10th an advance was made upon Caloocan, the stronghold of the insurgents. It was taken after some brisk fighting, and with slight loss on our part; but General Otis was not satisfied. He pushed on to Malabon, to which the insurgents had retreated, and soon was in possession of the town. Before leaving, however, Aguinaldo's savage hordes set fire to the town, and much damage was done to property.

The trouble was not confined to the Island of Luzon. Brigadier General M. D. Miller sent an ultimatum on February 10th to the commander of the rebels at Iloilo, notifying him that it was his intention to take the town by force, if necessary.

WARNING NON-COMBATANTS TO LEAVE.

The warships began to shell the town at eight o'clock the next morning, and soon cleared the trenches of the insurgent force. A detachment from the cruiser *Boston* and the *Petrel* were landed and marched into the town, hoisting the Stars and Stripes over the fort. Not a single man on the American side was injured.

After the taking of Caloocan, General Otis pressed the advantage, and Haytay and Canita were taken by the American advance guard without a shot having been fired. While this was going on, the insurgents inside of Manila made determined efforts to burn down the city. Buildings were fired in three different sections at the same time, and the flames were controlled by the troops only after severe labor. A considerable number of the incendiaries were shot, and a few of our soldiers were wounded. The fire was most successful at Tongo, the northernmost suburb of the city, which lies on the shore of the bay. The rebels in hiding were very active while the Americans were fighting the fire and caused a great deal of annoyance. For a time business was suspended in this district, and many suspects were placed under arrest. The *Monadnock*, of Dewey's fleet, joined in the work of dispersing the Filipinos, effectively shelling the rebel lines under the direction of the signal corps on shore. In the skirmish a surprising discovery was made, that many of the insurgents were armed with dummy rifles, there being about three of these to one of the Mausers, which explained in part the secret of the apparently good equipment of the Filipinos.

While the skirmishing was going on, Admiral Dewey telegraphed the Naval Department as follows:

"MANILA, February 24th.

For political reasons, the *Oregon* should be sent here at once.

DEWEY."

This dispatch was made public by an accident. Secretary Long inadvertently handed it with a number of others to some newspaper men, and for a time the department was kept busy, trying to explain exactly what Dewey meant. The general opinion was that the Admiral wanted the famous vessel, not for any effect on the insurgents, but as a notice to foreigners to keep hands off. The *Oregon* was promptly dispatched to Manila. Not long after this the German war vessels at Manila were withdrawn, and the interests of German residents were placed in the hands of the American officials there. Admiral von Diederichs, who had proved so offensive to Dewey, was withdrawn by his Government, and in his place Prince Henry of Germany was sent to take charge of the German squadron which had been sent to Hong Kong. It was stated at the time of the change that Admiral von Diederichs had shown a lack of tact in the management of affairs at Manila Bay, and consequently the trouble which had hampered Dewey at first disappeared, and the Germans apparently assumed a friendly attitude toward our Government.

CEBU IS TAKEN.

The United States gunboat *Petrel*, commanded by C. Cornwell, visited Cebu, the most important of the Visayas group, on February 22d. The Commander sent an ultimatum ashore declaring the intention of the Americans to take possession peaceably, if possible, by force if necessary. The rebels immediately vacated, taking their guns to the hills. A party of marines was landed, and the American flag soon floated over the Government building there.

For some time the fighting was confined to the region around Caloocan, and this was not aggressive, but defensive. The insurgents, kept up a guerilla warfare at night, which proved rather troublesome, but, as usual, not serious. On March 3d General Otis stated that he had captured 1,500 insurgents since February 4th.

March 3d was a red-letter day among both the army and navy people in the island. President McKinley sent to the Senate the name of George Dewey to be an Admiral of the Navy under the act approved the day before, and Brigadier-General Elwell S. Otis, United States Army, to be Major-General by brevet to rank from February 4th, and the Senate confirmed both nominations. Secretary Long and Secretary Alger cabled congratulations for themselves and for the President, and the news was received with great enthusiasm everywhere in the Philippines where American soldiers or sailors were stationed. Admiral Dewey raised his four-starred flag on the *Olympia*, and was saluted by the guns of the forts, the foreign warships, the British cruiser *Narcissus* and the German cruiser *Kaiserin Augusta*, and all the American ships in port.

On March 4th the United States cruiser *Baltimore* arrived at Manila from Hong Kong, having on board Professor J. G. Shurman and Professor Dean C. Worcester, the two of the civil members of the United States Philippine Commission. The transport *Senator* arrived on the same day with six companies of the Twenty-second Infantry as reinforcements to Otis' command. Reinforcements, aggregating 4,800 men, were hurried forward as fast as possible, bringing the total number of officers and men up to 41,800. The force then there consisted of twenty regiments of infantry, one engineer battalion, seven troops of cavalry and eleven batteries of artillery. Nineteen vessels with an aggregate of 297 officers, 2,990 men and 253 marines made up the naval contingent, which did not include the transport *Solace* with 162 officers and men which was constantly passing back and forth from Manila.

On March 10th the United States transport *Grant* arrived, having on board Major-General Henry W. Lawton, who had so distinguished himself in Cuba and was an old Indian fighter, together with the Fourth United States Infantry and a battalion of the Seventeenth United States Infantry.

WHEATON'S FLYING COLUMN.

General Wheaton was put in charge of a new divisional brigade and advanced on March 13th from San Pedro Macati for the purpose of corralling the enemy. He moved on Pasig, meeting with slight resistance, as the enemy was in full retreat. His Flying Column sought to cut off communication between the south and north insurgents' armies. Guadalupe and the city of Pasig were quickly captured. The enemy fought furiously under a heavy fire and were caught in a trap with the Flying Column on one side and the Pasig River on the other. They made a stand for an hour and were finally forced into the jungle in full retreat.

The American advance began at daybreak, the cavalry leading at a sharp trot. A dash across the open brought the column to a clump of timber commanding the rear of Guadalupe. The advance, supported by the Oregon troops, opened a heavy fire on the insurgents, and then the column divided, the right swinging towards the town of Pasig, and the left advancing with a telling fire into the brush where the insurgents were concealed.

At Guadalupe church a handful of the rebels made a sullen stand, but finally broke and ran. The rebels who had taken refuge in the jungle were discovered by river gunboats, which poured a disastrous fire into them. Everywhere the followers of Aguinaldo fled for safety, and for a time the troops were ordered to cease firing to get some rest before attacking Pasig itself. When the attack was finally begun, a heavy rain was falling. After a vigorous fight, the Filipinos finding themselves outwitted and defeated fled to the northward, and by 5 o'clock the whole American line bivouaced around the city. The next day the column advanced beyond Pasig to the shore of Laguna Bay, sweeping everything before it. The enemy made a running fight and suffered severe loss. Their avenues of communication north and south were effectively closed.

A BRUSH WITH THE ENEMY.

Between Pateros and Taguig General Wheaton with the Twentieth and Twenty-second Infantry, the Oregon and Washington troops, section six of the Sixth Artillery, and a squad of the Fourth Cavalry came upon the enemy massed in such a force as to cause an unusually heavy fight. The enemy was driven back with great loss.

On March 16th the First Battalion of the Twentieth United States Infantry advanced from Pasig, clearing the country to Caintia, a well-defended village of seven hundred inhabitants. The enemy was dislodged after a half-hour's fighting, during which the American troops advanced in splendid order under heavy fire, charging across the rice fields against overwhelming odds.

General Otis sent the following cablegram on March 15th: "Three thousand insurgents moved down last night to the towns of Pasig and Pateros, on shore of Laguna Bay, fronting Wheaton's troops on Pasig River line; by heavy fighting Wheaton has dislodged and driven them back, taking 400 prisoners and inflicting heavy loss in killed and wounded; he reports his loss as very moderate; he now occupies these towns with sufficient force to hold them."

Our troops found 106 dead Filipinos and 100 new graves near Pasig. The prisoners were unarmed, and, it is presumed, they executed their threat of throwing their arms into the river.

In the meantime a number of the Filipinos had grown tired of the continuous victories of our troops, and some of the prominent leaders among the insurgents advised surrender to the United States and an acceptance of our terms of government. Twelve adherents of the plan of independence were sentenced to death by Aguinaldo, because they wrote, advising surrender, and General Legarda, who visited Malolos for the purpose of advising Aguinaldo to give up the unequal struggle, was executed on the spot by orders of the rebel leader.

ON TOWARD MALOLOS.

It was decided to make a concentrated effort to capture Malolos, the capital of the insurgent temporary government and the headquarters of the insurgent leader. Here the Filipinos had massed their forces, and here, too, they had thrown out protection and trenches, and had prepared themselves for a fierce fight. It was hoped that, by taking this place, the backbone of the insurgent struggles would be broken. In order to meet the American advance, Aguinaldo's forces concentrated in large number about Malabon, which lies to the north of Manila, on the railway and on the shore of the bay. They had constructed several lines of trenches around Malabon, and there they awaited the onward movement of our army.

The fighting began when, on March 25th, General MacArthurs' division, consisting of the brigades of General Harrison Gray Otis, General Hale and General Hall, supplemented by General Wheaton's brigade, advanced and captured the towns of Novaliches on the left, and San Francisco del Monte and Mariquina on the right, clearing the rebel trenches in front of the line north from the river to Caloocan. They also secured possession of the railroad, practically cornering the flower of Aguinaldo's army at Malabon and in the foothills of Singalon, twenty miles apart. The plan was to strike north of Polo.

The attack was begun at 6 o'clock in the morning. The Nebraska and Colorado Volunteer Regiments encountered the first strong resistance. This was at San Francisco del Monte, and in the surrounding trenches. The Cavalry outflanked the enemy, who broke and ran, but later made a stubborn stand in the woods north of the Laloma church

The rebels adopted the American tactics of holding their fire until the enemy were about 1,000 yards away, and they fired lower than usual; but the boys from the United States fired volleys with terrible effect, and then rushed forward, cheering and sweeping everything before them. The Twentieth Kansas and Tenth Pennsylvania, with the Montana Volunteers on the left, protected by the Utah Battery, advanced over the open rice fields on the double-quick, yelling fiercely and occasionally dropping in the grass and firing by volley. The enemy, strongly entrenched in the woods, kept up a steady fire until the Americans were in close quarters, and then they broke and fled. The bodies of 125 of their dead were found in the trenches and many more in the woods.

Within ninety minutes after the advance was made, the whole front, for a distance of three miles to the north, had been cleared. General Hale's brigade had simultaneously swept in a northwesterly direction, routing the enemy. Our advance was over open ground for a mile and a half. The Third Artillery, under command of Major William A. Kobbe, at the apex upon which the line was to turn, got the hardest fighting and lost nine per cent. of its men.

BRAVERY OF THE KANSAS TROOPS.

As the line swung northwest, and came to the Tuliahan River, General Wheaton's brigade moved out from Caloocan, where it had been held in the trenches, and swept the insurgents directly in front, making the American line stretch along six miles of the south bank of the river. The bridge at Caloocan had been destroyed, and there were solid lines of insurgents in trenches across the river. Bullets were flying all around, but the Third Kansas Artillery boldly waded across the stream, and fiercely stormed the blockhouse which commanded the approach. They were forced almost to swim owing to the depth of the water, but, soaking wet, they charged the trenches and the blockhouse with the wildest cheers, and the Filipinos, who had never heard of such fighting, fled at their approach. It was a most inspiring spectacle of heroism to all who saw it,—a spectacle that shall ever live in history.

In this fight General MacArthur and General Hale, with their staffs, were frequently under heavy fire. The heat was terrific, and at times all of the officers, except the two Generals, were forced to dismount, overcome by the heat. The next day MacArthur dashed beyond Polo and to the northeast, and captured Meycauavan, two miles from Polo. It is at the base of the rough hills and the jungles, and the whole way is lined with trenches. The fight here was a brisk one, and among those who fell was Captain Krayenbuhl, who had been promoted for individual bravery at the battle of Manila, as described in another chapter. He was one of the most popular and efficient young men of the campaign, and his death was deplored by everybody who knew him.

General MacArthurs' plan was to cut off the 5,000 insurgents in Malolos from the rest of the insurgents, but he was unable to carry it out, owing to the roughness of the ground and the thickness of the jungle, which prevented him from getting far enough around to the north of Polo to shut the enemy in.

THE TRAGIC DEATH OF COLONEL EGBERT.

In this engagement Wheaton's brigade figured almost exclusively. There were engaged the Fourth, Twenty-second, and Twenty-third Infantry, the Utah Troop, the Third Artillery, and the Oregon troops. These were stretched out along the railroad from Caloocan to the Tuliahan River. The rebels had destroyed the bridge over the river, and on the further side made their stand, while the engineers were trying to replace the floor of the bridge on the iron girders. The Second Oregon Regiment dashed across the river, wading and swimming. The Twenty-second and four companies of the Twenty-third gained the west bank of the river about the same time. From the river the land rose steadily for half a mile to Malinta, which stands at the summit of the hill. The crest was torn up with intrenchments, but the Americans moved steadily forward, yet no reply came from the hidden foe. They waited until our troops were within 300 yards of them, and then the seemingly deserted trenches belched forth a deadly fire.

The Twenty-second, which was in the advance, with gallant Colonel Harry C. Egbert at their head, dashed at the entrenchments. The Oregon and Kansas troops at the right and left were fighting with great gallantry, but they were in the woods, while the men of the Twenty-second were in the open, and as these heroes of Santiago made that magnificent charge up the hill in the face of the deadly fire of the insurgents, Colonel Egbert fell forward in his saddle mortally wounded.

Close behind him struggling through the grass came General Wheaton and his staff. The soldiers bore the litter with the dying Colonel back, and, as they passed the General, he bared his head and

INSURGENTS' ATTEMPT TO BURN MANILA, FEBRUARY 22, 1899

On the night of February 22nd, in spite of the watchfulness of General Otis, the insurgents set fire to Manila in the three quarters of the city known as Santa Cruz, San Nicolas and Tondo. Nearly 1000 houses were burned, and the flames spread so rapidly that a destruction of the whole city was threatened. The firemen in attempting to extinguish the flames were fired upon and the hose was cut repeatedly; but the Americans finally extinguished the flames and quelled the uprising within the city.

CAFÉ AND CHOCOLATE FACTORY, MANILA
Chocolate and cocoa are the products of the cocoa tree, which was introduced early in the history of the islands by missionaries from Mexico.

INTERIOR VIEW OF A CIGAR AND CIGARETTE FACTORY, MANILA
The chief manufacturing industry in Manila is that of making cigars and cigarettes. The Spanish Government made this a State Monopoly during their ownership of the islands. The growth and manufacture of tobacco is destined to be one of the greatest industries of the Philippines.

gave a soldier's greeting to the dying officer. "It was done nobly," said the General. "I am done for, I am too old," gasped Egbert; and his words proved only too true, for the gallant hero of two wars was dead before they got him to the rear. Thus ended a record of continuous service as a line officer for nearly forty years.

Colonel Egbert was appointed a first lieutenant in the army from civil life in 1861. He was taken prisoner at the Battle of Gettysburg, but escaped and rejoined his command. He was severely wounded in 1864 in the Battle of Bethesda Church, Va. In the Santiago campaign he commanded the Sixth Infantry until shot through the body on July 1, 1898, when he was disabled. For his distinguished service in this battle he was appointed a Brigadier-General of volunteers, which grade he held until December 1, 1898, when, in the reduction of volunteers, he was honorably discharged. He had been promoted Colonel in the regular army on July 1, 1898, and was assigned to the Twenty-second Infantry, whose Colonel, Charles A. Wikoff, was killed at San Juan. The Twenty-second sailed for Manila February 1st, and in this great charge, so similar to that up the hill at Santiago, it again sacrificed its commanding officer to the bullets of the foe.

The advance to Malinta was made over the Nivalichaes Rial. The Filipinos fled along the railroad, burning rice mills, tearing up the tracks and obstructing everywhere. They took refuge in the church of Malinta and made a stand there, but the American troops came on a run and took the place by assault.

MALABON IS TAKEN.

General MacArthur's division pressed on along the torn up rail roads toward Malabon, and at his near approach the insurgents set fire to that place and fled back to Malolos as fast as they could. The condition of the country was such that rapid progress was not possible, but with every step of the advance the Americans carried victory with them. Try as they would, the American forces were unable to carry out their plan of catching Aguinaldo and his whole army between the two advancing lines. The Filipinos were able to make more rapid progress than the American troops, owing to their familiarity with the country.

On March 27th, the American forces advanced from Meycauavan, General Harrison Gray Otis leading his brigade on the left of the railroad track and General Hale's brigade taking the right of the track. The resistance was small until the Americans approached the Marilao River within sight of Marilao itself. Again the Filipinos made a stand on the river bank, and when the Americans came near they delivered an effective fire. The river was too deep to ford, and the infranty consequently could not accomplish much. The fire of the Filipinos was such as to lead to the opinion that they were well trained soldiers, probably members of the Milita which the Spaniards organized. The entrenchments of the Filipinos were a revelation to our troops, and were found to have been designed by capable engineers and constructed with care and thoroughness.

A BOLD CHARGE BY COLONEL FUNSTON.

Behind them the Filipinos did effective work, but when the American field artillery came into action it put a dramatic end to the battle. Approaching under cover of the bushes to a clear space not more than sixty yards from the trenches, the artillerymen dashed into plain view, shouting as though in full charge and prepared to fire. Knowing the effect of our artillery the Filipinos were eager to quit before they received a rain of shell. A hundred or more fled from their trenches, while others remaining displayed a white flag and shouted, "Amigos," (meaning friends). The infantry had been chafing at not getting into action, and Colonel Funston with twenty of his Kansas followers again jumped into the river and swam across to the opposite side. They forthwith made a charge and captured 80 prisoners with all their arms. It was a foolhardy act according to the books, but it made the name of Colonel Funston and his Kansas Regiment famous all over the world. A lot of men from the Tenth Pennsylvania also crossed the river and captured 40 prisoners. Finally the town fell before the Americans. They were now but eight miles away from Malolos, the insurgent capital, and everybody was eager to press on to what they thought would be the final contest of the war. But General MacArthur thought it best to give the men a rest for a little while. Early on the 29th, he advanced rapidly to Bocave, and at 11.45 he advanced toward Bigaa, and at 3.15 in the afternoon he turned toward Guiguinto, 3½ miles from Malolos. There was some fierce fighting in the afternoon. Troops crossed the river at Guiguinto by working artillery over the railroad bridge by hand and swimming mules against fierce resistance.

AGUINALDO IN COMMAND.

During the fight Aguinaldo commanded his troops in person for the first time since the war against our troops began. Prisoners who were captured, say that officers stood behind the Filipino soldiers with whips instead of swords and lashed the men to keep their position. As the enemy fled they tore up the tracks of the railroad, making the progress of our troops very slow.

During the approach to Malolos, General MacArthur and his staff, while walking abreast of the line, came near losing their lives. Everything was quiet when suddenly a shower of bullets came on all sides from sharp shooters in trees and on house tops. These were speedily dislodged. The march towards Malolos was rapidly accomplished.

ENTERING THE INSURGENT CAPITAL.

As the troops neared the outskirts of the city, General Hale's and H. G. Otis' brigades were stretched between the sea and the mountains. The scene was a magnificent one; the splendid line with its waiving colors looked like a rainbow, and as it neared the outskirts of the city a number of Filipinos bearing a flag of truce came out to meet it. At the sight of the white signal of surrender, our troops broke into cheers and song, but when our messengers approached, the bearers of the flag of truce turned and ran back to their capital. An instant pursuit was begun and our troops were received with heavy volleys from the outskirts of the town. On the right the jungle swarmed with little blue figures. It was the rear guard, protecting the retreat of the rebel army and destroying the railroad track as they swept on.

The Americans camped all night outside the city. The Generals held a council of war, for they believed that, on the morrow, they might have to fight 20.000 men. The battle opened at daybreak with the bombardment of the trenches in front, and for half an hour the shells fell in a shower. From the huts natives threw knives at Kansas men, while showers of arrows flew on all sides. The right wing unbroken advanced over fields and through streams, taking the main trenches south of the city. They found them deserted. A few men came out to meet the advancing line and informed the soldiers that the army had gone by railway toward the interior.

The Kansas men led the left, and at the end of the main street of the city they were met by a barricade of stones from which a hot fire was poured by a few insurgents, but Colonel Funston leaping from his horse and swinging his hat led the Kansas men over the barricade and down the street with terrific yells, firing volleys as they ran. But the town was deserted and there the victorious American army rested and feasted, while the American flag flew over the Government building of Aguinaldo's capital. The shattered army had fled for its life into the interior, and Aguinaldo and his cabinet had left two days before, and could not be found.

And for a time, at least, the backbone of the rebellion was broken.

A FEW PROCLAMATIONS BY AGUINALDO.

It was evident, from later information, that Aguinaldo had determined to stake all in an attack upon the American forces. He issued several proclamations defining his position, on February 2d, 3rd and 5th.

The first declares the Americans opened the fight, and calls upon the Filipino Congress to sustain the Constitution. The second says:

"We have fought our ancient oppressors without arms, and we now trust to God to defend us against the foreign invaders."

His proclamation of February 3rd says:

"I order and command:

"First—That peace and friendly relations with the Americans be broken and that the latter be treated as enemies, within the limits prescribed by the laws of the war.

"Second—That the Americans captured be held as prisoners of war.

"Third—That this proclamation be communicated to the Consul, and that Congress order and accord a suspension of the constitutional guarantee, resulting from the declaration of war."

Aguinaldo's proclamation of February 5th says the outbreak of hostilities was "unjustly and unexpectedly provoked by the Americans," and refers to his manifesto of January 8th, publishing the alleged grievances of the Filipinos at the hands of the army of occupation, and the "constant outrages and taunts which have been causing misery to the Manilians," and refers to the "useless conference" and "contempt shown for the Filipino Government" as proving a "premeditated transgression of justice and liberty."

The rebel leader also refers to the former losses of the Filipinos, but says "slavery is bitter," and calls upon them to "sacrifice all upon the altar of honor and national integrity."

He insists that he tried to avoid, as far as possible, an armed conflict, but claims that all his efforts were "useless before the unmeasured pride of the American representatives" whom he charges with having treated him as a rebel "because I defended the interests of my country, and would not become the instrument of their dastardly intentions."

Aguinaldo concludes with saying:

"Be not discouraged. Our independence was watered freely by the blood of martyrs, and more will be shed in the future to strengthen it. Remember, that efforts are not to be wasted that ends may be gained. It is indispensable to adjust our actions to the rules of law and right, and to learn to triumph over our enemies."

The attack upon Manila by the insurgents was made at a time when the country was watching expectantly to see what the Senate would do in the ratification of the Peace Treaty, which had been framed in Paris. The day preceding the rebel uprising it looked as though the treaty would not be ratified. The news of the slaughter of our troops reached this country the day before the vote was to be taken in the Senate. Immediately the whole nation was swept with feeling. Everybody deplored the sacrifice of life, and everybody looked to the Senate to see what the effect of the news would be. When a vote was taken the Paris Peace Treaty was ratified by a vote of 57 to 27, amid the greatest excitement.

The Peace Treaty was ratified by Spain, and, on April 11th, the last act in the Spanish-American drama was played. This formal and final scene took place at the White House, and, curiously enough, it happened on the anniversary of the day on which President McKinley, in a Message to Congress, asked for authority to intervene in the Cuban situation.

The final scene was the exchange of the ratifications of the Peace Treaty. The French Ambassador, M. Cambon, handed President McKinley the Spanish copy of the treaty, handsomely engrossed and bound in morocco. The President took from his desk and handed to the Ambassador, who represented the Government of Spain, the American copy of the treaty, also engrossed and bound in dark blue morocco. Each bowed as the exchange took place, and the ceremony so simple, yet so full of meaning, was over.

After the exchange of the ratifications, President McKinley issued his proclamation, which reads:—

"WHEREAS, A Treaty of Peace between the United States of America and Her Majesty, the Queen Regent of Spain, in the name of her august son, Don Alfonso XIII., was concluded and signed by their respective plenipotentiaries at Paris on the 10th day of December, 1898, the original of which convention being in the English and Spanish languages, is word for word as follows:

(Here the full text of the treaty is given.)

AND WHEREAS, The said convention has been duly ratified on both parts, and the ratifications of the two Governments were exchanged in the city of Washington, on the eleventh day of April, one thousand eight hundred and ninety-nine.

"Now, THEREFORE, Be it known that I, William McKinley, President of the United States of America, have caused the said convention to be made public to the end that the same and every article and clause thereof may be observed and fulfilled with good faith by the United States and the citizens thereof.

"IN WITNESS WHEREOF, I have hereunto set my hand and caused the seal of the United States to be affixed.

"Done at the city of Washington this eleventh day of April, in the year of our Lord, one thousand eight hundred and ninety-nine, and of the Independence of the United States, the one hundred and twenty-third. "WILLIAM McKINLEY.

[SEAL] "By the President.
"JOHN HAY, Secretary of State."

CHAPTER V

The Men Who Won Fame in Battle.

Commanders and Soldiers whose Bravery has Brought them Special Honors.—Intrepid Fighting, Mad Dashes, and Fierce Firing of Boys from Pennsylvania, New York and other States of the East ; from Tennessee, Kentucky and the Rest of the South Line ; and the Heroic Warriors from Oregon, California, Dakota, Kansas, Iowa and the Middle and Far West.—Individual Deeds of Daring.—Scout Work Outside and Inside of the City.

NOWHERE throughout the war was the valor of volunteers or the heroism of regulars more strikingly shown, than in our conquest of the Philippines. Far away from home, in a strange land, among a strange people, cut off even from communication by any regular channel, these brave sons of the Stars and Stripes faced heat and fever and finally the bullets of their foes to bring victory to American arms both by land and sea. So striking was their conduct in facing the rough chapters of a soldier's life, that Major-General Merritt comments, in his report, of "the exemplary spirit of patient, even cheerful endurance shown by the officers and men, and this feeling of admiration for the manner in which the American soldiers, volunteers and regulars alike, accept the necessary hardships of the work they have undertaken to do, has grown and increased with every phase of the difficult and trying campaign which the troops of the Philippine expedition have brought to such a brilliant and successful conclusion."

He was particularly struck by the fortitude of General Greene's command just after landing. It was encamped on a strip of sand near the shore where "the greater portion of the force had sheltered tents only and were suffering many discomforts, the camp being in a low flat place, without shelter from the heat of the tropical sun, or adequate protection during the terrific downpours of rain so frequent at that season." As was usually the case, the hardships of inactivity were much more trying than the dangers of battle. Men were willing to face bullets who found it difficult and irksome to bear up under the routine work of camp in the hot tropical sun, with the food which a soldier has to put up with, especially in a tropical land with the nearest place of supply many miles away. But everywhere the gallant boys of the United States showed their true metal, whether it was before the raking fire of the Spanish, the treacherous bullets of the insurgents or the blazing heat and terrible storms of the Philippines.

The force which occupied Manila consisted of 470 officers and 10,464 men. These were drawn from all over the Union—the east, north, south, and west joined hands and gave up the flower of their men to champion the American corps. The troops were under Major-General Wesley Merritt, and were made up in three expeditions, the first of which left California on May 25, 1898, under control of General Thomas Anderson. It consisted of 115 officers and 2,386 men, the first United States troops to land. They arrived sixty days after Dewey's famous victory of May 1st.

The second expedition left San Francisco on June 15th, and had on board 158 officers and 3,428 men, in command of General Frank V. Greene. The transports bearing this expedition arrived on July 17th, and the wild shouts of those who had landed over two weeks before, and those on board Admiral Dewey's fleet who were impatiently waiting so that the decisive blow might be struck, greeted the incoming vessels, and drove away any feelings of homesickness which might have seized the boys on their way across the long stretch of ocean.

The last of the transports to arrive was those leaving June 27th, and reaching Manila on July 30th, in command of General Arthur McArthur. He had with him 197 officers and 4,650 men. Five days before this, General Merritt had reached Manila on the transport *Newport*, which had on board the Astor Battery and others, and the commander of all the forces had taken charge of affairs on the island. Immediately upon his arrival, he was closeted with Admiral Dewey, and the two went over the situation thoroughly and discussed plans for the future. The landing of the troops was the first difficulty encountered on the island, everything had to be taken in in cascoes and dug-outs, and some of the boys had interesting experiences while the operation was going on

BLOCKHOUSE TAKEN BY THE ASTOR BATTERY IN THEIR FAMOUS REVOLVER CHARGE

On August 13th, while the United States troops were advancing on the city, General McArthur called for volunteers to storm blockhouse No. 14 on the Spanish entrenchments. Captain Peyton C. March, of the Astor Battery, led the charge with twenty-six men armed only with 38 calibre revolvers. Twenty three of the men were shot down; but the Spaniards fled, and Captain March took the blockhouse This photograph was taken after the capture and furnished us by one of the soldiers engaged in the assault

CONVENT AT MALATE SHOWING EFFECT OF SHELLS
This convent stands in front of Fort San Antonio de Abad, and was wrecked by shells in the battle of August 13th. The hottest fighting was done around it.

THE PHILIPPINE PONY AND CART
Large European and American horses are not found in the Philippines. The climate seems to be fatal to them. The small native pony, however, is remarkably strong for its size and has wonderful endurance.

For instance, on the day the Astor Battery landed, it stormed incessantly, and to add to the gayety of the occasion, one of the cascoes containing the special ammunition for the handsome guns with which Colonel Astor had equipped them, sunk before it reached land. Consequently the battery was forced to remain out of action on the first days' fight, and most of them had to swim in to reach shore.

Many were the deeds of daring done in the fighting which followed the landing of the American troops,—deeds which called forth commendations for special distinction from those in command. Many more were the deeds which history will never record, and which never will be known except among a few of those who witnessed them. General Merritt, in his report of the attack upon Manila, when the city was so easily taken, and the loss was so comparatively small, comments especially upon the valuable work of his own staff and his personal aids. He says: "Brigadier-General R. P. Hughes, my Inspector-General at San Francisco, was especially noticeable in accomplishing the instruction of green troops that came to the city, many of them without arms, clothing or equipment of any kind.

"I desire especially to express my acknowledgments to Brigadier-General Babcock, my Adjutant-General and Chief of Staff, for his most valuable services from the inception of the campaign in San Francisco to the close of the work at the present time. This officer is too well known to require special mention of his services in any one direction. He was at my right arm, not in the office, but in the field, and much of the success that has attended the expedition is due to his individual efforts.

"I desire especially to mention Major McClure and Major Whipple of the pay department, who volunteered their services after they had completed their legitimate duties, and performed excellent service whenever called upon. Major McClure was especially important in his services immediately after the surrender, taking long rides under my orders to the Spanish lines and bearing instructions to them which resulted in effecting their withdrawal in such manner as to prevent the insurgents from pillage in the northern part of the city.

"I especially call attention to the services of Captain Mott, as mentioned in the report of Brigadier-General Greene. He was cheerful, willing, intelligent and energetic in the discharge of the multifarious duties imposed upon him in connection with our troops and trenches during the rainy season, and in the final action showed those rare characteristics which stamp him as a very superior soldier." In speaking of the landing of reinforcements to General Greene's troops, he says: "The landing was finally accomplished after days of hard work and hardships, and I desire here to express again my admiration for the fortitude and cheerful willingness of the men of all commands engaged in this operation."

Too much cannot be said in praise of the bravery and skill as commanders, of General Arthur McArthur, whose forces really bore the great brunt of the battle upon the city, of General Greene and of General Anderson. They in turn each commend those of their commands who came under their individual notice for conspicuous bravery. General Merritt tells of the work of the Colorado skirmishers who left the shelter of their breastworks on August 13th, and advanced rapidly toward the Spanish line. They found that the Spanish trenches were deserted, "but as they passed over the Spanish works, they were met by a sharp fire from a second line situated in the streets of Malate, by which a number of the men were killed and wounded, among others the soldier who pulled down the Spanish colors, still flying on the fort, and raised our own." Thus died a hero, who is not even known by name in this report, and thus died many others who faced the bullets of the Spanish guns for the sake of the flag which this man raised.

General Anderson pays this tribute to his men: "The opposition we met in battle was not sufficient to test the bravery of our soldiers, but all showed bravery and dash. The losses show that the leading regiments of the First Brigade—Thirteenth Minnesota, Twenty-third Infantry, and the Astor Battery—met the most serious opposition and deserve credit for their success. The Colorado, California and Oregon regiments, the Regulars and all the batteries of the Second Brigade showed such zeal that it seems a pity that they did not meet foemen worthy of their steel."

Major-General Merritt pays particular tribute to the work of General McArthur. He says, in his report: "The works of the second line soon gave way before the determined advance of Greene's troops, and that officer pushed his brigade rapidly through Malate and over the bridges to occupy Binondo and San Miguel, as contemplated in his instructions. In the meantime the brigade of General McArthur, advancing simultaneously on the Pasay Road, encountered a very sharp fire, coming from the blockhouses, trenches and works in his front, positions which it was very difficult to carry, owing to the swampy condition of the ground on both sides of the roads, and the heavy undergrowth concealing the enemy. With much gallantry and excellent judgment on the part of the brigade commander and the troops engaged these difficulties were overcome with a minimum loss, and McArthur advanced and held the bridges and the town of Malate, as was contemplated in his instructions."

One of the instances, which has probably never before been recorded, of individual bravery and sacrifice of life, is that of the two sergeants of the Astor Battery, who met death in the splendid and heroic charge upon the blockhouse just outside of Manila. Sergeant Holmes was charging up the hill, with Sergeant Crinnims at his side. A bullet struck the latter, and he fell mortally wounded. As Holmes bent over him to help him and was speaking to him, a bullet entered Holmes' open mouth and with terrible force blew out the back of his head completely. There was no mark at all where the bullet entered, and the brave soldier fell dead at the feet of a comrade whom he had stopped to assist.

On the night of July 31st, when the Spaniards, to the number of 3,000, made their first attack on the American troops, the Tenth Pennsylvania Volunteers, Battery K, of the Third Artillery Regulars, and Battery A, of Utah, displayed bravery that called forth the highest plaudits of all who were in command. It was a magnificent exhibition of what volunteers could do. The brave men from Pennsylvania and the First California Regiment never flinched under the most glittering fire. The Utah Battery, under Captain Young, covered itself with glory. The men pulled their guns through mud, axle deep. After the battle, General Greene issued this address to the troops:

"The Brigadier-General commanding desires to thank the troops engaged last night for gallantry and skill displayed by them in repelling such a vigorous attack by largely superior forces of Spaniards. Not an inch of ground was yielded by the Tenth Pennsylvania Infantry and Utah Artillery, stationed in the trenches. A battalion of the Third Artillery and First Regiment California Infantry, moved forward to their support through a galling fire with the utmost intrepidity. The courage and steadiness shown by all in their first engagement is worthy of the highest commendation."

The attack of the insurgents upon our troops brought forth more heroism and splendid behavior under fire. Captain Charles King, who himself stands high on the rolls of valor, says, in describing the battle of his own men: "Let no man say the Filipinos cannot fight; they are brave and skillful. As for the California, Idaho and Washington Regiments, and Dwyer's and Hawthorne's gunners, words are inadequate." He also speaks of the gallantry of Captain Otis, of Company A, First Washington, who "lost much of his ear, but none of his nerve." In describing the death of one of the gallant old heroes of the fight, he says: "General Anderson in person led the attack in the direction of San Pedro, while the brigade commander, with the Washington and Idaho Regiments, made the dash on Santa Ana. It was about 8 o'clock. The fields toward San Pedro were open and lightly held, but to the left of the road to Santa Ana the insurgents had strong redoubts, earthworks and Krupp guns. They fought with obstinate courage and no little skill, but their valor was of no avail against the determined rush of the Washingtons and Idahos. Gallant old Major McConville, of the Idaho, got his last order from the lips of the brigade commander as together they rode across the bridge, and his death wound was received leading his men into the attack. The fight was fierce in front of the left wing. The insurgents held on to a redoubt in front of Pandacan until our line had swept beyond the other flank. In the dash upon this earthwork, Captain Fortman, First Washington, led two companies across the stream, fording the Concordia, as almost all the brigade had to, waist or breast deep. One of McConville's companies attacked at the same moment from the right, and between them the insurgents were driven into the Pasig, leaving forty dead and many wounded."

The American troops seemed to enjoy the dangers of the contest. They drove the insurgents before them like a flock of sheep, or as one burly Colorado fighter, who was discussing the capture of the waterworks, put it: "It reminded me of a rabbit-drive on the Colorado plains."

One of the things which caused the American troops to give no quarter to their foes in one of the fights, was the trip in which Dr. Young, formerly Quartermaster-Sergeant of the Third Artillery, lost his life. He was scouting and was captured by the insurgents, who hacked his body to pieces and left it mutilated on the ground. The sight of it aroused all of the fighting blood in the troops, and they pressed forward to avenge his death with great zeal.

In the taking of Caloocan, a small town just north of Manila, the Filipinos were routed with the most vigorous advance by the American troops. One eyewitness of the fighting has this to say about it : "Brigadier-General H. G. Otis holds the extreme left of the American line from the bay near Cakiican. The regiments on the line and in support are : the Twentieth Kansas, Colonel Funston, eleven companies; First Montana, Colonel Kerster, nine companies ; Third Artillery, Major Kobbs, four batteries as infantry, and the Tenth Pennsylvania, Colonel Hawkins, four companies. Two companies of the Tenth Pennsylvania are behind the walls of the De la Loma churchyard. Across the ravine from the Montana regiment is Captain Jensen's company, holding the stone fort supporting Grant's Battery of four Utah guns ; a fifth gun is to the left and on the railroad, supporting the Kansas troops.

"To reach its present position the brigade has advanced four times since Saturday in a series of brilliant combats on different parts of the line of action, especially so on the 4th, 5th and 7th.

"Several bayonet charges were made on the 7th during the advance of the right and centre. The taking of the Chinese cemetery on the 5th by the Montana and Pennsylvania regiments was a superb piece of work. A brilliantly executed advance up the slope in the open made a battle picture that would delight any veteran."

An individual exhibition of bravery has brought the name of Major J. F. Bell, of the Volunteer Engineer Corps, to the front and caused him to be particularly noticed in the report of General Greene to the War Department. Just before the attack was made upon Manila General Greene found it necessary to know the exact condition of the territory lying between the trenches of his troops and Fort

San Antonio de Abad. The Americans, of course, were practically unfamiliar with the ground around the city, and the only method of finding out exactly the lay of the land was through the work of expert scouts. Owing to the comparatively open nature of the land. This work was more than usually dangerous, and every man who started out on it expected to sacrifice his life to the cause.

Major Bell, whose skill as an engineer, as well as his coolness and bravery made him a valuable man in such an emergency, was delegated to report to the General the exact condition of things between the two opposing lines. Between our trenches and the fort was a creek, the depth of which was a matter of doubt, and it was debated whether it was necessary to build a bridge across the stream or not. Under cover of the darkness, with Spanish sharp-shooters lurking all about so that any false step might have caused the crack of a rifle, Major Bell tested the creek right in front of the frowning fort, and discovered that it was of such a depth that it could easily be forded by the troops. He crossed the river, found out its exact width, and then with audacity and bravery which showed the metal of the man, he swam up the river to the bay and around in the very rear of the Spanish troops, where he secured invaluable details which led to an intelligent attack upon the stronghold of the Spanish.

This was but one of the numerous similar feats performed which the demands of the situation called for. The low walls of the rice fields, hardly more than a foot high, were sometimes the only things that stood between the scout and discovery and certain death. Men went for miles almost flat upon their stomachs, crawling like snakes through the marshy rice fields, raising their heads just enough to note the condition of things around them, ready for any emergency or any danger.

One of the New York men, who was a member of the volunteers, swam for miles around the forts of the enemy, facing what was almost certain death, if discovered, with a zeal and cheerfulness that was inspiring to all who heard of the deed.

The influence of the bravery of one man in command is illustrated by the following incident in which a captain turned what looked like defeat into a splendid victory. While the first day's fight was going on, Captain O'Hara, in command of the Battalion of the Third

Artillery, was lying in his tent trying to get a little rest. He was unable to get to sleep, however, and he found himself involuntarily keeping track of the firing of the men. He knew that they had but fifty rounds of ammunition with them, and he realized that, at the rate they were firing, this would soon be used up. He did not know what the trouble was; but he did know that if these men, who were shooting from the trenches into the dark were attacked, they would want help when their ammunition was gone, and they would want it pretty badly, too.

As he lay in his tent, thinking over the situation, he counted the volleys one by one, as they pealed on the night air, until they became indiscriminate, and then he knew that the boys were getting rattled. He had no orders, but he took a chance, and he took it just in time. He sounded the assembly, and, as the bugle-call rang out over the camp, the men of Battery H tumbled out of their tents and formed into line, rifles in hand, and one hundred and fifty rounds of ammunition at their belts. Down in the camp below, where the Third Artillery was, a bugler heard the call and took it up. The First Colorado men heard it and swarmed out with their guns. Nebraska followed suit, and soon half of the camp was in arms. Leaving Captain Hobbs in command of Battery H, with orders to be ready to advance at the bugle call and to bring ten thousand rounds of extra ammunition, Captain O'Hara, with his orderly and his bugler, started up the road toward the front. A little beyond the corner of the camp he met another orderly coming on the dead run. The man was blown and frightened. He had run through a rain of bullets on his way back for help, and it had increased his excitement and enlarged his notion of what had happened. "We are whipped," he shouted to Captain O'Hara; "we're—" But O'Hara didn't care to hear any more. His bugler was already blaring out the command, "Forward!" Back in the camp the bugler of the waiting Captain Hobbs answered the call, and all pressed up the road as hard as they could go. All along the road the bugler sounded the cry of "Forward," and the men of Battery H, crawling up through the dreadful mud, answered with a cheer and a fresh spurt.

Somewhere ahead O'Hara knew that his lieutenant, Krayenbuhl, and his own battery were either waiting or already in action.

He met men coming to the rear with the wounded, and some, too, coming without wounded. "We're beaten," they shouted, but the only response they got was the call of the bugler, "Forward." These shame-faced stragglers fell in with the Captain, his orderly, and the bugler, and little by little they gained in numbers as they went along. Up the Camino Real they went with mud, ankle-deep, and the rain pouring down in torrents, and all the time the bugle kept singing out the single word, "Forward", and every time it sounded the answer came sharp and clear from Battery H, which was coming behind.

At the cross-roads and the first barricade, where Krayenbuhl had been posted, there were only a few stragglers, and Captain O'Hara knew that his lieutenant had swung into the rescue of his own accord. Here they were overtaken by Battery H, and all together lifted up their voices in a cheer that was carried down to the trenches. There the hard-pressed Pennsylvanians heard it and it gave them new strength. As the reinforcements were going along, Captain Hobbs felt a sudden sharp sting on his right thigh. He put his hand down and felt blood, and knew that he was hit, but he did not stop.

As the Captain surmised, Krayenbuhl, who had been keeping a sharp watch out, had been impressed with the indiscriminate firing at the front and knew that help was needed. So he piled in to give them that help, sending a message over to Battery K, on his right, to join in, in a hurry. They reached the Pennsylvania boys just in time, for their ammunition had just about given out. Krayenbuhl, realizing that the boys were a little bit rattled, jumped among the excited men, who were firing at will, and shouted to them to get together. He threatened to shoot the first man who fired without orders. His own men swung into action like clockwork, and this, with his personal bravery, had the desired effect. The Pennsylvanians steadied down as the first volley of these regulars, fired as though it was one charge, rang out. That volley, too, reached the ears of O'Hara and Hobbs as they were puffing along with their men. They recognized the roar of the Krag-Jorgensen rifles, and they knew from the way they were fired that the men behind them were regulars, and that they were their own men in action. But O'Hara did not slack up, and his men went right on, stimulated with the knowledge that they would be able to snatch victory from the jaws of defeat.

SAINT ANA, A SUBURB OF MANILA

Among the most interesting of the many sights to the visitor are the native suburbs around the city of Manila, devoted to the homes of the laboring classes. Many of these plain little houses have pianos and other musical instruments. The air is full of song and music every night in native quarters.

THE CORDAGE FACTORY OF SANTA MESA, A SUBURB OF MANILA.

One of the great industries of the Philippines is hemp-raising, but almost the entire product has been shipped to the United States and England for manufacture. Many cordage factories will no doubt be built in the islands under America's progressive rule.

THE FAMOUS SPANISH PRISON, MANILA.

What the Cubans suffered in Morro Prison, Havana, was fully equaled by the tortures of the Filipinos in the above landmark of Spanish cruelty in the East Indies.

In the meantime the frightened courier had stumbled through the camp and finally, almost exhausted, cried out, "Somebody take my gun! Help me to General Greene! We are whipped! Oh! its awful!" They almost dragged him over to General Greene's quarters in a native hut just in front of the camp. The General was up expecting a message from the front. "General," said the wretched courier, "send reinforcements, send every man, send every company. We are whipped; the whole battery is wiped off the earth, and we are out of ammunition." General Greene put his hand on the frightened messenger's shoulder and said steadily, "keep cool young man; it's all right; we will send you help;" and after a while he was able to get a more explicit account of what had happened and sent plenty of aid. But O'Hara's men had already turned defeat to victory.

Here is how one fellow faced death. Private McIlrath, of Battery H, who was acting Sergeant in command of 20 men, was a first class soldier and had been in the army for fifteen years. There was a good deal of confusion when his men jumped in the trenches to help the Pennsylvanians, and so McIlrath stood up on a parapet and said, "We have got them, now boys, get together and give it to them in volleys," and while he was walking back and forth on top of the parapet steadying the men in the trenches, and getting them to fire together, he was hit in the head by a Mauser bullet, and fell back among his comrades, to die in the hospital the next day.

Private J. F. Finlay, of Company C, First California, especially distinguished himself. For such work as his, Englishmen get the Victoria Cross. Finlay is detailed to Major Jones' transportation department as interpreter His mother was a Mexican, and he learned Spanish before he did English. When ammunition was sent forward Finlay was in charge of the train. He had eight carromatta loads of it, each carromatta with a native driver. He started when the Spanish fire was hottest and went straight up through the open fields. The bullets buzzed and whistled all about him. They ripped through the tops of his carts, and one of them hit one of the drivers in the leg. Finlay kept on as if he were going after corn on a pleasant afternoon, until he reached the old insurgent trench. Then he halted his train and went forward along to find some one from the Tenth

Pennsylvania, to whom he could deliver the ammunition. That last hundred yards into our trench was what Captain O'Hara, who has seen plenty of hot work, called a "very hot place." It was swept incessantly by Spanish bullets. But Finlay hunted around until he found his man, went back and got his carromattas, and started forward. One of his ponies was shot just in the rear of our trench. Finlay took it out of the cart, and with a native driver, hauled the cart along to its place, delivered his cartridges, and started back.

On the way he found Captain Richter lying in the field where he had fallen. He jumped out of his carromatta, put the Captain in, and started on. Pretty soon he found another wounded man. That one was picked up too, and back he went to camp. Then he turned the wounded over to the surgeons and got orders to take ten carromattas to the front and bring back the wounded. Back over that bullet-swept field he went again, as cool and unconcerned as if on a drive through Golden Gate Park, did his work, brought in the wounded, and turned in to get what sleep he could before the hard day's work began soon after daylight.

These are but a few of the heroic deeds which have reached the ears of the public mainly through the reports of Commanders of the Army. The list of dead and wounded upon the battlefields tells its own story of the heroism of those who accepted death as payment for their loyalty to their country. That list is growing day by day, so that the number of graves of the soldier dead is becoming so large that their more fortunate companions have started a movement for the erection of a monument to commemorate their valor. The special burying grounds at Camp Dewey, and the portions of the cemeteries in Manila which have been given over to the soldiers who fell in battle are pathetic commentaries upon the courage with which our men faced the Spanish and insurgent fire and disease. Even though it is probable that the bodies of our dead will be removed to the United States at some time, nevertheless, the movement for the erection of a monument in Manila to commemorate their deeds is being vigorously pushed. It has been suggested that this monument be erected on the Luneta, the great military parade ground. It is hoped that the sum of $50,000 will eventually be raised.

CHAPTER VI

A Past History Written in Blood

Ever Since their Discovery the Philippines have been the Scene of Terrible Conflicts.—They Began with Peace, but soon were Rife with War.—Legaspi Fortified Manila and made it a Stronghold.—The Raid of Limahong, the Chinese Pirate.—Naval Battles with the Dutch for Half a Century.—England Takes Manila, but Returns It to Spain.

THE history of the Philippine Islands is a history of bloodshed. Their discovery followed close upon the discovery of America by Columbus. The Spanish government, in order to stimulate the search for unknown lands, published a general concession to all who wished to search for them. Many were the expeditions fitted out, but few were successful.

The chief search was for rich spice islands which had hitherto been undiscovered. A contract was made between King Charles of Spain and Magalhaens, who is familiarly known as Magellan, by virtue of which the latter started out on a voyage of discovery. On the 10th of August, 1519, the expedition started in the direction of the Canary Islands. Magellan had many adventures, including mutiny of his own men, before he finally reached and passed through the seaway, which now bears his name, Strait of Magellan, dividing the island of Tierra del Fuego from the mainland of Patagonia. This notable event took place on the 28th day of October, 1520. The expedition, which had formerly consisted of five vessels, dwindled down to three, and these three, to their great satisfaction, found themselves on the Pacific Ocean, the first mariners to find that the Atlantic and the Pacific were joined together.

THE DISCOVERY OF THE PHILIPPINES.

Cheerfully they kept on their voyage of discovery. On the 16th of March, 1521, the Ladrone Islands were reached. Here they had trouble with the natives, who stole one of the ships' boats,—so

Magellan named it "Robber Island,"—and a bloody battle was necessary before the boat could be regained. The fleet then continued its course westward, and finally arrived at the mouth of the Buttean River, on the island of Mindanao, and landed the first white man upon the Philippines.

It was Easter week, and there, on the shore of this new land which was to figure so largely in the history of their country, these men of chance, who sailed in the hope of discovery without definite knowledge as to what the day would bring forth, knelt down upon the shore and celebrated the first mass of the land over which the Church was thereafter to rule.

The natives were friendly, and did everything possible for Magellan. He took formal possession of the territory in the name of Charles the First, and then sought other islands nearby, to which he was directed by the Chief of the tribes of Mindanao. So the expedition arrived on the 7th of April at Cebu, where they were met on the beach by 2,000 men in battle array. The reception, however, was one of peace rather than that of war, and it was not long before a compact had been made, in which the king of the island and all his men swore fealty and obedience to the king of Spain.

The people of Cebu were at war with the tribes on the opposite coast, so Magellan sided with his new allies, and went to war with them. On the 25th of April, 1521, he was shot by an arrow and killed. Three monuments, one opposite the city of Manila, another on the spot where he was killed, and the third at the city of Cebu, where he landed, commemorate the three great events in his life in the Philippines.

A MASSACRE OF SPANIARDS AT A BANQUET.

Thus the Philippines came under the rule of Spain. The command of the islands was assumed by Duarte de Barbosa, one of Magellan's followers. Barbosa, with twenty-six of his companions, was invited to a banquet by Hamabar, king of the island. At this banquet the king killed all of his guests except one, and that one was held for ransom from the other members of the expedition. The exploring party, however, pulled up anchor and departed, leaving him to his fate. They had been reduced to one hundred persons, all told, and found that they were unable to manage all of the three vessels, so one of them was burned at sea.

The expedition touched at Borneo, and finally reached the Island of Tidor, which had already been discovered by the Portuguese. From there the explorers returned home, where they were received with great honor.

Several other expeditions were sent out by the king, but none of them were successful, until 1543, when an expedition reached the islands which they named Philippines, in honor of Philip, the son of King Charles, heir apparent to the throne.

When, a few years later, King Charles abdicated in favor of his son, that ruler determined to follow in his father's footsteps, and annex territory by discovery, and inspired further by religious sentiment, he ordered an expedition to go to the Philippine Islands to conquer and christianize its people.

TO CONQUER AND CHRISTIANIZE THE ISLANDS.

Urdaneta, one of the brave and fearless captains of a former expedition, and a man who had fought under King Charles, but had taken the habit of an Augustine monk, was entrusted with the spiritual care of the races to be subdued. He was accompanied by five priests of his order. The whole expedition, consisting of four ships and one armed frigate, carried four hundred soldiers and sailors under the command of General Miguel Lopez de Lagaspi. This general was of noble birth, and had a reputation for piety, justice and loyalty to the Crown.

The expedition reached the Philippines in the latter part of January, 1565. It was resolved to land at Cebu, which was a safe port. The vessels anchored off the port of Dapatan on Mindanao Island, to the great astonishment of the ruler there. He sent one of his subjects to investigate the vessels, and the man returned with such an extraordinary account of how the men ate stones (hard biscuits), drank fire and blew smoke out of their mouths, that the prince thought it wise to be friendly.

From him Legaspi learned that Cebu was a powerful kingdom, and considered rich by the neighboring states, consequently he resolved to take possession of it. He landed there on the 27th of

April, 1565, and, as the natives opposed his entrance, he took the town by force and sacked it. It was no easy matter, however, to continue there, for the surrounding tribes harrassed the newcomers continuously, and finally a council was held to discuss the advisability of leaving. General Legaspi decided to remain, and so the first days of contest against the natives began, and from that time to this the island has been a constant scene of trouble.

The work of pacification not only of Cebu, but of the islands nearby, was steadily pushed forward by Legaspi. He was a man of strength, and little by little he won the confidence of the natives, their dethroned king accepted baptism, and his daughter married a Spaniard.

AN ATTACK BY PORTUGUESE.

Then, in the midst of Legaspi's success, the rival Portuguese sent an expedition to dispute possession of the territory. They were compelled to retire, but Legaspi learned through that experience the necessity of being prepared for any emergency. He accordingly built a fortress, marked out plots of land for Spanish residences, and finally, in 1570, Cebu was declared a city, and Legaspi was made Governor-General of all the lands that he could conquer by royal grant from King Philip.

Legaspi sent his grandson, Captain Juan Salcedo, to the island of Luzon to bring it under Spanish dominion. He went to the north and was received with extraordinary friendliness by the chiefs of Tondo and of Manila. They yielded up their territory, paid tribute and became allies of the Spaniards, against their own people, and apparently were not given anything at all in return. A treaty of peace was signed and ratified by the exchange of drops of blood, as was the custom in those lands.

Later on, one of these friendly young chiefs, whose name was Soliman, ruler of Manila, repented of his bad bargain and led his tribes in revolt. He set fire to his capital to prevent its falling into the hands of the invaders, and was completely routed in battle by the Spaniards. Salcedo pardoned him afterward, on his taking the oath of allegiance to the King of Spain.

News of the trouble at Manila reached Genèral Legaspi, and he proceeded at once to that place. He took formal possession of the

THE INVASION OF THE CHINESE PIRATE 127

whole territory, declared Manila to be the capital of the Philippine Islands, and proclaimed the sovereignty of Spain over the whole archipelago. He set the natives to work to fortify the place and to build a large residence for himself and a church for the priests. He also built one hundred and fifty smaller dwellings for the other Spaniards who were with him. The City Council of Manila was organized on the 24th of June, 1571, and on the 20th of August of the next year, Legaspi died, leaving a name which will always live in Spanish history. In the meantime Salcedo continued his task of subjugation, and during the next few years most of the nearby tribes were made subject to the domination of Spain. General Legaspi's formal successor, as Governor, was Guido de Lavezares, who was appointed in accordance with sealed instructions from the Supreme Court of Mexico. During Lavezares' rule the Chinese pirate Limahong tried to land upon the Philippines and conquer them. His acts against traders caused him to be outlawed by the Chinese Emperor, and for a long time he had been the terror of the Chinese coast. He happened to fall in with a trading junk, which had just returned from Manila, and in his usual way he took possession of her, and forced the captain and his crew to take him back to the capital of Luzon.

Visions of wealth and pictures of how easily the islands might be captured were before him. He got together a fleet of 62 armed junks, having on board 2,000 sailors, 2,000 soldiers and 1,500 women and sailed forth to capture and establish a new kingdom.

THE INVASION OF THE CHINESE PIRATE.

On the 29th of November, 1574 he arrived with his squadron at the Bay of Manila, and sent a lieutenant at the head of 600 fighting men to demand the surrender of the place. But a strong gale, probably one of the terrible typhoons, sprang up and destroyed several of his junks and about 200 of his men. He was forced by the storm to Paranque, a village a few miles south of Manila. There he landed and had no resistance until he came fairly to the gates of the city. The marauders burned the residence of Martin de Goiti, second in command to the Governor, and killed him, and the flames and smoke which arose gave the first sign which the Governor had of the approach of the enemy.

The Spaniards took refuge in the fort of Santiago, and just as the Chinese were on the point of taking it by storm, some fresh troops arrived, led by a Spanish sub-lieutenant. The Chinese, though they were the vanguard of a large body of men, sounded a retreat. A bloody hand-to-hand combat followed, and the Chinese fled to their ships. In the meantime Limahong with reserve forces went off to the capital by sea and attempted to take it. The city was set on fire and a band of chosen men under Sioco, a lieutenant, advanced toward the fort, and then a desperate contest began. Limahong supported the attack with his vessels' cannons.

After prolonged fighting the Spaniards finally gained the victory, and the followers of the pirate fled, demoralized. Although foiled in his attempt to take Manila, Limahong determined to set up a capital for himself at the mouth of the Agono River, in the province of Pangasinan. He announced to the natives that he had just conquered the Spaniards, and they received him cordially, so that he founded his new capital there and fortified it. The Spaniards soon sought him out, however, and, as luck would have it, a force of Chinese arrived, also seeking to discover the whereabouts of the pirate. They united their forces, and Limahong, seeing that he was destined to get himself into trouble, cleverly slipped away from his enemies and fled. Thus ended the invasion of the Chinese pirate, and the day of his flight is kept as a public holiday and gala day still.

The conquest of the natives was continued until the death of Salcedo from the fever, on the 11th of March, 1576.

THE BATTLES BY SEA WITH THE DUTCH.

Following upon some internal trouble as to the question of prestige of Governor, Supreme Court, and Church in the civil affairs of the colony, came the conflict with the Dutch. The latter sent vessels which hovered about the waters of Moluccas Islands to take any trading vessels which they could run across. In roving around, these Dutch vessels were able to take many prizes, and the Philippine colony lost large sums by the seizure of vessels sent to them by the Mexican colony, upon which it was almost entirely dependent for troops and European articles. So the Spaniards in the Philippines began fitting out vessels to protect themselves against this naval

A MARKET MAN IN MANILA

This type of enterprising huckster marches up and down the streets and alleys of Philippine cities crying his vegetables (very much as the familiar "*Old iron, rags, copper, bones and brass!*" collectors traverse the streets of American cities) stopping at the doorways from which he may be hailed.

FAST FREIGHT LINE OF THE PHILIPPINES.

This is the craft in which the country farmer conveys his product to market. The enormous size of the faithful water Buffalo may be judged by comparing it with the master who sits upon his back.

COCK FIGHTING, THE CHIEF SPORT OF THE NATIVES.

Every native has his fighting cock, which lives and sleeps in his house with him, and is loved by the owner as much as his own children. The Filipino will bet his last dollar on the issue of a battle between his own and another's game-cock.

enemy. A fleet composed of several frigates, 1 ship, 6 galleys and 100 smaller vessels, all well armed, was brought together. The fighting men upon them numbered 100 Spaniards, 400 Arquebusiers, 1,000 Archers and Lancers, besides 100 Chinese to row the galleys. The Chinese turned out to be a very important part of the expedition. They formed a conspiracy to exterminate the Spaniards. They fell upon them while they were asleep and massacred them. Eighteen of the troops escaped by jumping into the sea. The Governor awoke, and, hearing the noise, ran up on deck, where a Chinaman chopped his head open with a cutlass, so that he died in a few hours. The Chinese were afraid to venture below where the priests and armed soldiers were, so they fastened up the hatches and escaped to Cochin China, where the King and Mandarins seized the vessel and all that she carried. This proved a crushing blow for the time, but other expeditions against the Dutch were more successful, the most notable one being that under Juan de Silva, the Governor.

He sent out a fleet, comprising 6 ships carrying 70 guns and 2 galleys, and a number of smaller vessels, having on board over 1,000 Spaniards. They met the Dutch, and after a fierce struggle lasting 6 hours, they won a splendid victory, recovering plundered merchandise to the value of $300,000.

In various years subsequently the Spanish of the Philippines and these warlike Dutch vessels met on the seas and fought. The battles continued for over 50 years, during which time the Dutch did not attempt to take possession of the islands themselves or their government, but contented themselves with naval attacks, and with plundering the vessels which brought supplies to the Spaniards.

For some years the inhabitants of the Philippines were not annoyed by foes from without, but the dissensions which arose between Church and State kept their history from being commonplace.

In the middle of the seventeenth century an event that proved of importance to the Spanish in the archipelago occurred. The Tartars invaded China and overthrew the Min Dynasty, the Chinese Emperor being succeeded by the Tartar Emperor Kungchi, who had brought nearly all the Chinese Empire under his control. There was one Mandarin, however, who held out against him. His name was

Keuseng. He boldly asserted his independence, and flung defiance in the teeth of the victorious Tartar.

He retired to the island of Kinmuen, where he fortified himself as strongly as possible, and held out an offer of protection to any Chinese who desired to help him in his fight against the Tartar rule. So the Emperor issued an edict that no man should inhabit China within 4 leagues of the coast, except in those provinces which were known to be loyal to him. This, of course, played havoc with the coast, and all of the Chinese who had lived for generations by the sea and earned a living by fishing, etc., were forced to flee to the interior.

But the valiant Keuseng was not at all daunted. He turned his attention to the Formosa Island, which was nearby, and at that time in control of the Dutch. He had little trouble in taking the island, which at that time had about 600 European settlers and a garrison of 2,200. The artillery stores and merchandise there were valued at about $8,000,000. Keuseng had a force of 100,000, and after taking the Dutch stronghold he announced himself as King of Formosa. He sent Riccio, an Italian Dominican missionary, as an ambassador to the Governor of the Philippines, ordering the latter to pay tribute to, him or he would attack Manila.

The Spaniards, however, had no idea of yielding to the demands of Keuseng. So they decided to concentrate all of their forces in Manila, and in order to do that they demolished the forts on the other islands and transferred their garrisons to the capital. That brought the troops in Manila up to 100 cavalry and 8,000 infantry.

THE MASSACRE OF THE CHINESE OF MANILLA.

Everything was placed in readiness for the proposed attack, and then the Spaniards began to suspect that the Chinese residents of the city were getting up a rebellion, Therefore they did the best they could to incite them to some overt act, so that they might have a pretext for their massacre.

The Chinese population prepared for self-defence, and finally one of them killed a Spaniard in the market place, The Government took this for an excuse, and suddenly opened up a terrible fire on the people. Many of the peaceful Chinese traders hung themselves through fear; others were drowned in their attempt to escape by sea; while still others fled and were able to reach Formosa, where they joined Keuseng's army. About eight or nine thousand, however, remained in the city and held their ground. On these the Spaniards turned their wrath, and for a time desperate fighting was general.

It looked as though the Chinese were going to win the victory, so the Governor sent ambassadors to offer terms. One of these ambassadors came back to tell the Governor on what terms the Chinese would return, leaving the other behind, who in his absence was beheaded. This started a general extermination of the Chinese, and the Spaniards swore they would kill every Chinaman on the island. But as all the tradesmen and mechanics were of that race, the Spaniards found that they were inconveniencing themselves, so finally they desisted in their general slaughter and pardoned all who laid down their arms.

While this was going on in the Philippines, Keuseng was preparing himself to sweep down on Manila and capture it. He died, however, before he could carry out his campaign. His successor was more peacefully inclined, and he entered into a treaty with the Governor of Manila by which they renewed their old commercial relations. Not long after, a rebellion arose among the former followers of Keuseng, which resulted in the Tartar party obtaining possession of the island and annexing it to China.

It was then that Riccio, the ambassador to the dead King, was called upon to explain the result of his mission to the Philippines, and he so presented things that the Chinese governmeat was satisfied, and did not take up the cause of their subjects, otherwise the history of the Philippines might have been radically different.

ENGLAND'S FLEET REACHES THE PHILIPPINES.

On the 1st of May, 1762, Spain agreed to unite her forces with those of France against England, and war was declared shortly after. England pushed her conquest of island territory with great strength and rapidity, and among other things sent a fleet to the Philippine Islands with orders to capture Manila.

The fleet arrived there on the 22d of September, and was made up of thirteen ships in command of Captain-Admiral Cornish. They demanded the surrender of the city, which was refused, whereupon Brigadier-General Draper disembarked his troops and a bombardment and attack was begun. The whole force in Manila was about 600 men and eighty pieces of artillery, while the British forces consisted of 1,500 men, 3,000 seamen, 800 Sepoy fusileers and 1,400 Sepoy prisoners, a total of 6,700.

The office of Governor-General was being filled at the time by Archbishop Manuel Antonio Rojo, who was temporarily acting in that capacity. He was willing to yield the city, but a war party under the leadership of a magistrate of the Supreme Court named Salazar swept aside his authority and declined to surrender. Salazar, however, instead of bravely leading his men to battle, fled from the city, leaving the war party to struggle along as best it could.

Two rich vessels which were about entering the port of Manila from Mexico, laden with goods valued at $2,500,000, were captured by the British. The fight began and was kept up in a lively way by artillery for some time. The Archbishop's nephew was taken prisoner, and an officer was sent by the British General with a small force to return the young man to his uncle. Some of the natives fell upon the party and murdered them all. The officer's head was cut off and the savage natives refused to give it up. Consequently General Draper, inflamed by this act, redoubled his efforts to prosecute a merciless campaign against Manila.

BRITISH TAKE MANILA.

After a fierce struggle, in which defeat and victory alternately perched upon the banners of the British, General Draper and his troops entered the city on the 5th of October, demolished the forts and overturned the artillery.

Terms of capitulation were offered and accepted. The fort was delivered up to the British, and the British flag floated above the walls. The natives, who had been imported by General Draper, were plundering the city, so he had them all driven out, as it proved, so that his own soldiers might pillage the place. He placed a guard at the doors of the nunneries and convents to protect the inmates, and then gave up the whole place to the victorious troops to plunder for three hours.

It was an awful scene, and the atrocities and bloodshed and murder which took place then will forever blot the name of Draper in history. The following day a similar scene was allowed, and it was only when the Archbishop besought the General to have compassion on the city that that officer restored order.

Draper then demanded the surrender of Cavite, which was agreed to by the Archbishop and the magistrates, but the officer in command of that place refused to comply. Later, however, he left the garrison, and the natives plundered it.

When the city capitulated it was agreed that an indemnity of $4,000,000 should be paid to the British, one-half in money and valuables, the other half in treasury bills on Madrid. In order to raise this amount heavy contributions were levied upon the inhabitants, and, although the Archbishop gave up his rings and the cross which he wore around his neck, and the Church gave up its silver plate and ornaments, the amount raised only reached $546,000. The British proposed to accept $1,000,000 in cash, and take the rest from the cargo of an expected vessel, the *Philipino*, if she had not been seized previous to the day of capitulation. Then every effort was made to raise this million, but it proved unsuccessful. The day before the city surrendered, a messenger had been sent away with $111,000 with orders to hide it. An effort was made to get the money back, but it had been placed in the hands of Franciscan friars, who refused to give it up, and removed it from place to place. The British insisted upon their claim, and sent troops to intercept the landing of the cargo of the expected *Philipino*. These troops overran the country, but were unable to secure the treasure.

GENERAL DRAPER ADOPTS A NEW POLICY.

Draper adopted a policy of kindness to secure himself in power. He made a tool of the Archbishop, and issued a friendly proclamation to the natives, saying that the King of England would not exact tribute from them as the Spaniards had done. The Archbishop, at his instance, convened a council of native headmen and of representative families, and proposed the cession of all the islands to the King of England.

There was one man, however, Simon De Anda, who determined to take up arms rather than yield to the British yoke. He declared himself Governor-General of the island, and a number of his countrymen upheld him, together with the Austin friars, who joined the rebel party, and were a power in the land. A number of expeditions were sent against Anda, but he managed to avoid any open contact with them. It was decided to send an expedition out to Bulacan to capture it. The convent there was fortified with three small cannons, and when the British vanguard came up it opened fire and caused great havoc. When the British returned the fire, the natives fled panic-stricken, and when an assault was made upon the convent there was a terrible fight and great slaughter, and finally the invading troops proved victorious and took the place.

Occasionally the Lieutenant-General of Anda, whose name was Bustos, appeared and manœuvred about the convent, but did not dare to make an attack. Finally, however, the British made a sally upon him, and routed him completely.

A conspiracy was then organized among the Chinese in the province of Pampanga against Anda, and the Chinese entrenched themselves for slaughter. The clash finally came between the two, with the result that Anda won the victory, and large numbers of the Chinese were slain. Anda issued a general decree declaring all the Chinese to be traitors to the Spanish flag, and ordered them to be hanged wherever they were found. In consequence of this order thousands were executed who had nothing at all to do with the war.

A PRICE PLACED ON ANDA'S HEAD.

The British, harassed by Anda's troops without, were compelled to take precautions against an uprising of the natives within the walls of the city. Anda in the meantime, having obtained the treasure from the long-expected *Philipino* was able to organize quite a respectable army. He harassed the British right and left, and a price was placed upon his head by the British commander. In the meantime Anda had been officially acknowledged by the King of Spain, and therefore was given legal right to the position that he had usurped, so that the British commander had to communicate with him officially whenever occasion demanded.

The friars were busy inoculating the ignorant natives with the idea that the British were infidels, and so persuaded the people that this was a holy war. They abandoned their mission of peace for that of the sword, and once thereafter the British met with their reverse in battle, having been caught in ambush.

TREATY OF PEACE.

While all this was going on news came from Europe that the preliminaries of peace were going on, under the terms of which Manila was to be evacuated by the British and given back to Spain. Anda claimed that he was the proper person to assume control of things, and one of his friends, named Villa Corta, sought the same honor. The Archbishop who had surrendered the city died, and Anda was acknowledged by the British as Governor. The other rival factions, however, were not so easily set aside, and fierce quarrels ensued, which were happily ended by the arrival of a newly appointed Attorney-General from Spain, Don Francisco de la Torre.

After the signing of the treaty of peace in Paris the British evacuated the city, and the Spanish flag was once more hoisted over the fort of Santiago, and the day was made a day of general rejoicing.

THE SHIPYARDS AND ARSENAL AT CAVITE

Cavite is a city of about 5000 inhabitants, ten miles from Manila. The Spanish arsenal and the only shipyards in the colony are located here. It is the chief naval station of the islands and has always been considered the key to Manila from the sea. It was seized by the insurgents in 1872 and again in 1896, and it was its forts that so harassed Dewey with their bombardment, and it was one of the first places occupied by the Americans after the fall of Manila.

THE ISLAND OF CORREGIDOR, MANILA BAY.

This fortified island rises up 640 feet high in the channel entrance to the Bay of Manila. The lighthouse on the hill is the point from which the signal rocket was sent up announcing Dewey's approach, and at 14 minutes past eleven, on the night of April 30, 1898, the first shots were fired at his vessels from these forts. The Raleigh, Boston and Concord returned the fire and silenced the enemy.

CHAPTER VII
Filipinos' Struggles for Freedom.

Periodically the Natives Turned under the Cruel Spanish Heel and Rose up in their Might.—Revolts against the Tyranny of the Church.—How a Flight of Skyrockets Tore Victory from the Hands of the Natives.—The Last Fight for Freedom.—The Greatest of Insurgent Martyrs, Doctor Rizal.—His Dramatic Execution a Few Years Ago.—Other Great Fighters for Freedom.

THE struggles for liberty of the natives form a most romantic chapter in the history of the Philippines. Conquered by a foreign foe whose civilization and power were such as to enable them to hold these barbarians in check, time and again they rose up in their might to regain the liberty they had lost. Patriots, men of finer mould than most of the natives, men who had a little learning which enabled them to hold a place of influence among their own people, inspired now and then ineffectual attempts to break the shackles of subjection.

Philippine history is blotted with the blood of martyrs and patriots who have sacrificed their lives in the feeble hope that their country might be free. These uprisings began from the very first, for although in the time of Legaspi the great chiefs of Manila and Tondo submitted to the Spanish yoke, this did not imply a total surrender of all of the islands of the archipelago—at least it did not render them passive to the rule of the foreigners. Each separate island, and each separate chief had to be brought into subjection, and this kept the European forces busy from the moment they entered into possession of the Philippines, up to the present day.

THE FIRST GREAT UPRISING.

In 1622, a great uprising and struggle for freedom took place on Bojol Island. This was largely a struggle against the Church. The Jesuit missionaries had taxed the islanders beyond their power to pay, and had insisted upon their accepting forms of worship which they did not understand, and in which they did not believe. Their own Pagan form of worship was more to their liking, and so one day they rebelled and proclaimed their intention of regaining their liberty of government, and especially of Church.

Then followed wild times of plunder, of fire and of battle. Towns and churches became heaps of smouldering ashes, the images within the sanctuary were defiled, destroyed and the remnants scattered; but the rebels could not win. The Governor of Cebu gathered a large number of troops, who with superior arms and superior knowledge of warfare, drove the insurgents like sheep into the interior of the island, where they took refuge and fought in the manner of insurgents of later years.

BRUTALITY OF A PRIEST BRINGS REBELLION.

For over a century their attacks upon the Government were spasmodic and disorganized, but in 1744 there was a more serious rising of the natives, brought on by the high-handed acts of a Jesuit priest named Morales. He was in the habit of arresting natives who did not attend mass, and of punishing them as he saw fit. He also exercised his functions as a priest as it pleased him, and once he left the body of one of the natives to decompose, refusing to allow it to be buried. In doing this he made an enemy of the dead man's brother named Dagohoy, who organized a party for revenge. He swore that he would pay the priest back in his own coin or lose his life in the attempt, and what he swore to he did, for not long afterward Morales, the priest, was captured and executed, and for four days his body was allowed to rot in the tropical sun.

Not satisfied with that, Dagohoy pushed forward his fight into an organized struggle for freedom. Great numbers of the natives flocked to his standard, and for thirty-five years this army of insurgents harassed the government troops constantly, so that it was necessary to always be on the alert against their incursions. The expulsion of the Jesuits from the colony alone ended the uprisings, and after that Dagohoy and his army submitted to the Spaniards, and were pardoned.

Simultaneously with the uprising of the natives on Bojol Island in 1622, there was an insurrection in Leyte, and the Governor of

Cebu was forced to go to the assistance of the governor of that island. The united armies forced the insurgent leader to the wall; he was captured and executed, and his head was placed at the top of a high pole in the market place, as a warning to those who aspired to break away from the Spanish rule. Some of the prisoners were garroted, others were publicly executed with arrows, and still another was horribly tortured by being burned to death.

Seven years later the province of Surigao in the East of Mindanao Island turned against their conquerors. They burned churches, killed priests and laid waste the territory for the space of three years before they could be suppressed. Twenty years later, in 1649, an attempt was made by the Spanish to secure troops for the arsenal at Cavite, from the natives of Samar Island. This did not seem to please the tribes there, so they rebelled, sacked and burned the churches along the coast, and gradually increased in number and power, until it was found necessary to send not only large forces of troops, but armed vessels after them.

KILLED THE MOTHER OF THE REBEL LEADER.

The leader of the insurrection, a native headman named Sumoroy, fled to the hills to escape capture. Not being able to lay their hands upon him, the Spaniards captured his aged mother and literally tore her to pieces in their fiendish desire to revenge themselves upon the insurgent chief. It sounds like the stories made so familiar in later years in Cuba, where thousands of women and children were sacrificed to awful atrocities, because members of their families had dared to take up arms against the rule of Spain. But Sumoroy reached his limit at last. He was able to withstand or evade the attacks of his enemies, but like all such leaders he could not avoid the treachery of his own people. He was betrayed and captured, and in the manner of the Spanish at that time, was beheaded, and his head placed upon a pole as a horrible example.

This, too, was the fate of another rebel chieftain ten years later, who surrendered on promise of pardon, only to find himself a martyr. These riots of 1649, as the insurgents uprisings were then termed by the Spanish, extended to other provinces. In Albay, in Masbate Island, in Zamboanga, in Cebu, in Caraga and Butuan, many Europeans fell victims of the fury of the insurgents. In the latter place the Spanish method of dealing with the rebels was well illustrated.

The captain there offered pardon to all who would yield to the rule of Spain, and the insurgent army, poor, half-starved and homeless, as most of such armies must naturally be, came in large numbers to accept the proffered friendship and pardon of the authorities. The result is an old story in these days, when the Spanish idea of honor is so well understood. Most of those who surrendered were killed; others were made slaves, and still others were sent to the galleys for life.

In 1660 one of the most notable of all the native uprisings took place. It seems that the people had been very much harassed by the Spanish authorities, and placed in a condition which was little better than slavery, though not actually such in name. They were forced to do work without recompense, and finally they rebelled in Pampanga. The revolt spread all through the country, and a certain Andres Malong declared himself King. Word was sent right and left to the adjacent countries that the natives must revolt against the Spanish, or incur the new King's displeasure. Consequently three good-sized armies were formed—one of 6,000, another of 3,000, and another, commanded by King Malong himself, of 2,000 followers. As they moved on, they gradually increased in strength and equipment, until finally they reached a total of 40,000 men. But again history repeated itself, and a much smaller force of Spaniards, better trained and better armed, routed them completely, and the rebel leaders eventually suffered the same penalty of patriotism—death. And so the roll of insurgent uprisings goes on from generation to generation, each decade furnishing its new leaders and new struggles for freedom, all ending in the same way, in annihilation and death.

FIREWORKS MISTAKEN FOR SIGNAL.

Coming down to the end of the present century, we find daring efforts still going on to win back freedom to the natives. The nearest approach to success probably the insurgents ever had was in 1872. Cavite, the stronghold guarding the city of Manila, was the centre of the plot. Some of the native soldiers in the arsenal there were in the conspiracy, and it was arranged that when everything was ready for them to strike the decisive blow on which they had staked their all, a flight of rockets at night should announce the fact to all of the tribes. But fate played a strong hand against the fighting people. Nearby the arsenal of Cavite a throng of people gathered on that day to celebrate one of the many feasts which mark the life of the people. At this feast, as a sort of parting entertainment, fireworks were sent off. The waiting tribes in and near Cavite, mistook these fireworks for a signal that the time was ready to strike, and so they unwittingly began the revolt without the support of their comrades across the bay. They succeeded in taking possession of the arsenal, and made an attack upon many of the influential Spaniards in the city; but before they could get any further, and before the other troops could reach them, the government army had been called out and soon retook the arsenal and made the struggling insurgents prisoners.

This ended the best organized and the most successful struggle ever made by the Filipinos, up to the time of the latest struggle, begun in 1896. It was due, as indeed was all of the other uprisings, largely to the oppressions of the friars, and to the taxes which were laid upon the people by the Spanish.

THE EXECUTION OF DR. RIZAL.

This final struggle for liberty left a pathetic record of martyrdom, heroism and sacrifice. One of the central figures of its martyrs was Dr. Jose Rizal.

Dr. Rizal was perhaps the greatest man that the native uprisings have ever known. Had he lived, he would to-day be the man of power among the insurgents; and had he lived, it is quite probable that the natives would never have fought against the United States and taken up arms against the people who offered them a new lease of life, under new and free institutions, and, at the same time, the protection of the greatest nation in the world.

The story of Dr. Rizal is, in the main, the story of every Filipino patriot, and yet there is an added pathos in his romance, because here was a man educated far above the rank and file of any nation; a poet, whose works will live forever in Philippine literature; a man of personal force and magnetism; an orator, an essayist, a historian of no ordinary ability; a man, whose crime was patriotism, whose only offence was the outpouring of a pent-up soul against the cruel wrongs and the barbaric indignities which were inflicted, not especially upon himself, but upon his countrymen, who were dearer to him than self.

This talented man, who is known among the Filipinos as "the Talego Martyr," belonged to the tribe of that name. While still young, he showed extraordinary gifts, and it was decided to send him to Europe to receive his education. He went to Spain and to France, and for some years studied hard and trained himself up, not only as a physician, but for the position which he afterwards took as the leader of his people and the foremost literary man that his island has given to the world.

Burning beneath the treatment which his people received, he turned his keen pen to writing essays against Spanish oppression. He did not spare either priests, or officials, and for this he was exiled to the island of Dapitan. But even in exile he did not cease his writings in behalf of his countrymen. While there he met a woman of Irish parentage, a Miss Taufer, with whom he fell desperately in love. She, in turn, reciprocated the affection of this brilliant young Filipino, and they were engaged to be married. Before the ceremony took place, however, Dr. Rizal was re-arrested and brought back to Manila. From then on he was a prisoner, never knowing liberty again. He was sent to Madrid and then brought back to Manila, where he was sentenced to death. He was charged with conspiracy against the government of Spain.

When it was announced that this brave young patriot was to give up his life, Miss Taufer went to the Spanish officials and begged that she might be allowed to wed Dr. Rizal, even though he had but a few days to live. The officials granted her request, perhaps thinking that it would be little comfort to the man, and might add to the terrors of death.

What a tragic scene was there, as the two young lovers stood together and were wedded in the little cell, the barred windows of which barely admitted light enough to show the features of the priest who performed the ceremony! The solemn words of the rites, which seemed more like those of a funeral than of a wedding, almost stuck in the throat of the priest as he proceeded. Together the bride and groom waited for the summons to come. It came all too soon. Dr. Rizal was led away to the execution, which was to take place on the Luneta, the chief promenade of the city. Like all of the executions, it was a great public event—almost a festival. Thousands of people gathered around to see this frail young man, whose courage was great and whose conviction and patriotism were strong, stand up before his executioners and give his life, a martyr to his cause and to his people.

Rizal displayed great fortitude to the end. He dressed with care, and walked composedly between two priests to the place where he was to be shot. Upon his arrival in the centre of the plaza, he recognized several of his friends in the vast crowd of people and spoke to them cheerfully. Eight native soldiers made up the firing party. Rizal looked at them carefully, and seemed to take a farewell gaze at the sky and the familiar scenes around him, before he knelt down, about ten feet from the muzzles of the rifles. He kissed the crucifix, and, with his eyes fixed upon the rippling, sunlit waters of the bay, he received the volley of eight bullets in his back, dying instantly.

Another bullet was put into his body, to make sure that life was extinct, and then the band struck up a lively air, and the crowd, some with curiosity, others with veneration and sadness, passed by the prostrate figure, and the romance of the life of Jose Rizal was ended.

His widow, fired with revenge, set off on foot to the rebel camp at Imus, where she was hailed as a modern Joan of Arc. She assumed command of a company of insurgents and took the field, winning more than one splendid victory. Later she determined that she could be of more assistance to the cause by personally appealing for financial aid among sympathizers. She came to this country, and appeared in leading circles at Philadelphia, New York, Chicago and other places.

The farewell thoughts of this hero and martyr, Dr. Rizal, are interesting. The night before his execution he wrote them down in a poem on Spain, which is still preserved in the insurgent archives. The translation is as follows:

Farewell, adored fatherland! Our Eden lost, farewell!
Farewell, O sun-lov'd region, pearl of the Eastern sea!
Gladly I die for thy dear sake; yea, thou knowest well
Were my sad life more radiant far than mortal tongue could tell
Yet would I give it gladly, joyously for thee.

On blood-stained fields of battle, fast locked in madd'ning strife,
Thy sons have dying blest thee, untouched by doubt or fear.
No matter wreaths of laurel; no matter where our life
Ebbs out, on scaffold, or in combat, or under torturer's knife,
We welcome Death, if for our hearths, or for our country dear.

I die while dawn's rich Iris-hues are staining yet the sky,
Heralds of the freer day still hidden from our view
Behind the night's dark mantle. And should the morning nigh
Need crimson, shed my heart's blood quickly, freely, let it dye
The new-born light with th' glory of its ensanguined hue.

My dreams when yet were ling'ring my childhood's careless years,
My dreams, my hopes, when vigor pulsed in my youthful heart,
Were that one day, gem of the East, thine eyes, undimmed with tears,
Might darkly glow, that I might see unwrinkled, free from fears
Thy lofty brow wherefrom for aye all blushes should depart.

Hail unto thee, dreams of my life! My dying soul doth cry
All hail to thee! And ye I hail, my aspirations deep
And ardent! Oh, how sweet it is to fall beneath thy sky,
To die that thou mayst live, and, for thy welfare high,
In thine enchanted bosom eternally to sleep!

If on my grave, midst the thick grass, thou shouldst see spring one day
A simple, humble flow'ret, Life victor over Death,
Sweet symbol of my loving soul, ah, kiss the dew away.
Approach to it thy gentle lips, that in my tomb I may
Feel on my brow thy tender sigh, the soft warmth of thy breath.

Let o'er my grave the placid moon shed its soft tranquil light;
Let cool dawn's fleeting splendor shine on my resting place;
Let the deep murmur of the wind caress it in the night;
And if above my lonely cross it stay its restless flight,
'Twill breathe a prayer of peace and chant a canticle of grace.

THE FAREWELL THOUGHTS OF DR. RIZAL

Oh, let the rain rise pure to Heav'n beneath the sun's hot rays
And carry to the throne of God my loving, lasting request.
Let friendly soul's weep for my end, and in the after days,
On evenings clear, when o'er my tomb some gentle being prays,
Pray also thou, O Fatherland, for my eternal rest.

Pray for all those who died alone, betrayed, in wretchedness,
For those who suffered for thy sake torments and misery,
For our poor, loving mothers' hearts, who weep in bitternes,
For widows, tortured captives and orphans in distress,
And pray for thy dear self that thou may'st finally be free.

And when dark night enshrouds in gloom the silent cemetery,
When but the lonely dead are left watching by the sea,
Disturb not their repose, nor dispel the mystery,
Perchance then shalt thou hear cither or psaltery
Well tuned, 'tis I, my country dear, 'tis I singing to thee.

And when the memory of my grave has faded from the mind,
When my tomb bears no cross nor stone to mark where I lie dead,
Plough o'er the spot, turn up the earth, and scatter to the wind
My ashes ere they turn to naught; let them go unconfined
To form thy rolling meadows and flower-covered glade.

No matter, then, if all forget; still, still shall I be near;
Still shall I breathe thy od'rous air, still wander in thy ways,
And dwell in space, a thrilling note loud-sounding in thine ear;
I shall be perfume, light and shade, sound, color, refrain clear,
Telling forever of my faith and singing thy dear praise.

Farewell, adored country! I leave my all with thee,
Beloved Filipinos, whose soil my feet have trod,
I leave with thee my life's loves deep. I go where all are free;
I go where are no tortures, where th' oppressor's power shall be
Destroyed, where faith kills not, where He who reigns is God.

Farewell, my parents, brothers, all friends of my infancy,
Dear fragments of my heart, once to my bosom pressed
Round our lost hearth. Give thanks to God in glad tranquillity
That after day's long, weary hours I sleep eternally;
Farewell lov'd beings, stranger sweet; to die is but to rest.

JOSE RIZAL.

Another insurgent leader, who was executed in Manila for the part he took in this same uprising, was Francesco Venezuela. He was a mestizo (half-caste) by birth, but educated himself far beyond the others of his class. He became one of the great factors in the struggle, and in his house the great uprising was planned. He made one fatal error, however. He wrote to the Premier of Japan, knowing that that nation had long coveted the Philippines, and asked for aid against the Spanish, at the same time disclosing the plans of organization, and promising rich spoils in the division of territory. This communication somehow or other found its way back to the Spanish Governor, and it is said that the aid of the Church was sought, and that Venezuela's wife was so influenced by the priests at confessional that she finally told the secrets of the insurgents and betrayed her own husband.

Venezuela was taken prisoner with three others, who were with him in his home. They were tried, condemned, and executed. Just before the fatal volley was fired, the secretary of one of the officers of Spain approached Venezuela, and, holding a paper before his eyes so that he might read it, said: "Sign this and your life shall be spared, with safe conduct to any foreign country you may wish." The paper was a promise to disclose the names of the leaders who were associated with him in the uprising, their source of supplies and their plans. Venezuela drew himself up and said, "Was it for this that you have postponed your holiday? You need not have done so; you may kill me now, for you will have many more to deal with. This is but just the beginning," and so he and his three silent comrades, to each of whom this offer of life was made, turned to death like brave men.

The first volley did not kill Venezuela, and so volley after volley was ordered, until all of the bodies were filled with bullets. Then, as if to clinch the horrors of the whole spectacle, one of the soldiers advanced, and placing the muzzle of his gun against Venezuela's head, literally blew his brains over the ground.

HORRIBLE ATROCITIES OF THE SPANISH.

The atrocities of the Spanish during this last terrible struggle for independence are too horrible to contemplate. The instruments of torture used during the Spanish Inquisition three centuries ago, which had been kept in the monasteries of Manila, were brought out and used to extort confession from insurgent prisoners. More than 3,000 suspects were maltreated or hurled into the famous "Black Hole" of Manila.

An eyewitness described the treatment of prisoners, as follows: "The prisoner is taken before the military court, bound with cords that cut into the flesh, and subjected to examination. If his answers are not satisfactory—and they ordinarily are not, unless guilt is confessed—he is taken to the torture chamber. After being stripped, he is first subjected to whipping with rattans, two hundred blows or more if the victim is especially obstinate. If this is not successful, thumb-screws are brought into play, and the poor wretch, already half dead from the beating, is obliged to undergo the exquisite pain of these little instruments. These torturing machines are the same as actually used in the days of the Inquisition. This programme of torture is well known to be a fact; the natives add more tortures to it. They say prisoners are placed against a board wall and small nails are driven through each finger, holding the arms out as in a crucifixion, until the suffering man cries out a "confession." In other cases the suspects are so bound as to be unable to move from one position. Water is so arranged above them that drop after drop falls on their heads, causing great torture."

THE TERRIBLE "BLACK HOLE" OF MANILA.

Another of the leaders of the insurrection tells of the awful "Black Hole" of Manila, which was a small dungeon under the bastions of San Sebastian Intra Muros. The room was forty feet square, sloping steeply towards the sea. At the time he was in it there were one hundred and sixty-nine prisoners in that little place, huddled together like rats. In the roof was a grated hole three feet square; on the floor, on the lowest side next to the sea, there was another hole. These were the only means of ventilation. The prisoners nearest the grating could barely breathe, and the others panted like dogs and tore their clothes in the effort to keep from falling dead under the smothering heat. Every once in a while the grating in the ceiling above would be opened and a man, more dead than alive, would be hurled in upon the living mass below. The Spaniards seemed to enjoy watching these human rats sway and crush each other beneath the grating, and they came, now and then, to watch them, laughing at their death struggles.

During the day one of the men was taken out, only to be thrust back sometime afterward with his eyes gouged out and his feet gashed and burned with fire. His brother, who was also a prisoner there, looked at him in frenzy, and the next time the grating was opened he sprang up on the backs of the other prisoners and grabbed the neck of a Spanish lieutenant who was peering in. Several Spanish soldiers came running to the help of their comrade. They used their swords freely, but the man hung to the officer like a demon, and then finally they thrust their swords deep into the prisoner's chest and, as he fell back on his horror-stricken fellows below, the lieutenant whom he had seized, groaned and expired. He had been choked to death. As the day wore on, the men became crazed and trampled on each other in their effort to get air. When night fell, the tide of the ocean rose inch by inch until it reached the grating down at the end of the room. The sea-water began coming in, and those who had not been suffocated now faced the terrors of drowning. It was a night of awful torture. In the morning it was found that fifty-four men had been smothered to death or drowned; twenty others were so far gone that they could not recover. The prisoner who tells this story of horror feigned death and was taken out with the others, and managed eventually to make his escape.

But still the revolution went on, under the leadership of Emilio Aguinaldo. The method of fighting which the insurgents adopted was such that it was possible for the contest to be continued indefinitely and at great cost to the Spaniards. The insurgents had no money and needed little. They had sympathizers all over the country and lived from hand to mouth, half starved, half clothed and almost without ammunition, but in their guerilla warfare they were able to keep the Spaniards constantly harassed. Several important battles were fought, and many of the insurgents met the fate of Dr. Rizal through execution. Finally, the Governor-General of the islands decided that it was cheaper to buy out the insurgents than to fight against them, and so Aguinaldo and his fellow leaders of the insurrection sold out their countrymen for $800,000, $400,000 of which was deposited in a bank in Hong Kong in cash, and the remainder was to be given to Aguinaldo later.

This ended the war—not a very creditable or honorable ending to a struggle for liberty, but one which shows some of the insurgent leaders in their true light as men who are willing to barter away anything for gold, and men who are in insurrection for business purposes. Aguinaldo and his fellow, under the terms of the sale of their coutrymen's freedom, promised to leave the country and return no more. They went to China and there got into a wrangle about the division of the spoils, which almost got into court, but was finally settled outside.

The remaining $400,000 was not paid up at the time of the advance of Admiral Dewey upon Manila, so Aguinaldo, notwithstanding the fact that he had already received half of the amount specified, thought he was absolved from the terms of the contract calling for his staying out of the country, and, hoping that by following in the wake of Dewey's guns he might profit in some way, he returned to Manila, was placed at the head of the insurgent army once more, and to-day is a great figure in the insurgent life of the Philippines, a traitor to his own countrymen, a traitor to the Americans, who befriended him, a soldier of fortune without honor.

OTHER INSURGENT LEADERS.

The insurgents of to-day have among their rank a number of young natives who have had the benefit of a good education and who, consequently, are able to handle their ignorant brethren with much skill. Tedoro Sandica, who has been made the Minister of Interior of the so-called Revolutionary Government, is a civil engineer, who learned his profession in England and studied for some time in Belgium. He was staying in Hong Kong, an exile from his country, when Dewey landed there, and he was allowed to return to Manila on one of Dewey's vessels. A cousin of Aguinaldo, by the name of Baldomero Aguinaldo, is one of the prominent leaders of the insurrection, and has been since its beginning. He has the rank of general, and has recently been made Minister of War in the new government. He is said to be a large landowner at Cavite. Gregorico

Gonzaga is another well-known patriot, a lawyer of some ability, who used to have charge of Filipino affairs at Hong Kong, and before that occupied a position of trust under the Spanish government, having been Attorney-General for the Spanish in Visayas. Other leaders among the insurgents are Leandro Ibarra, who is Secretary of the Interior, and Mariano Trias, who is Secretary of Agriculture, under Aguinaldo.

Senor Felipe Agoncillo, whose unsavory career in the United States brought him into much prominence, is another of the leading lights connected with the last uprising and now influential in the new government. He, too, has a good European education, was in control of the Junta at Hong Kong for some time, and then was given the important mission of coming to America and trying to look after the affairs of the Filipinos in this country. He is a man of strong individuality and much ability in many ways.

Such, briefly, are some of the men who have been closely identified with the efforts of the Filipinos to regain the liberty which they lost so long ago, and which will never be theirs as a self-ruling, independent nation. To them has come a new liberty, a liberty of which they know nothing, a liberty that is personal freedom under staple government without oppression and without disgrace, a liberty which America alone could give.

CHAPTER VIII

The Great Value of the Philippines

Why all Nations Yearn for what the United States has Won.—Importance from the Strategic Standpoint.—Immense Wealth and Resources.—Exports amounting to over $20,000,000.—Rich in Sugar, Rice, Hemp, Coffee, and Cocoa, Spices, and a Host of other Things.—Untold and Untried Mineral Resources.

EVERY nation in the world envies the United States its possession of the Philippines. There is no power in the eastern hemisphere, which would not jump at the opportunity to possess this land of wealth, which, besides its intrinsic value, is tenfold more precious because of its situation. It is the key to the great commerce of the far East, which is slowly opening up, year by year, and which, in the future of the new China, will become a great factor in the commercial life of every country of the globe.

As a station in time of war it is unsurpassed—perhaps the best in the Pacific Ocean—and fortified and guarded, it will be invaluable to the United States as long as she possess it.

The islands themselves are filled to overflowing with riches, the full extent of which is little dreamed of to-day.

Spain has always kept her colonies from improving their natural resources and turning them into gold, except inasmuch as they happened to personally enrich the Governor-General and other Spanish officials. There was little chance for energetic foreigners who were willing to put capital into business to gain a foothold there. Spain met them at the gate, and when it found what their intentions were it slammed the gate in their face. However some large firms managed to establish places of business at Manila and in some of the other larger towns, and these, mostly Englishmen, are a great power in the city.

THE TRADE OF THE ISLANDS EXCEEDED $44,000,000.

Notwithstanding the embargo placed upon the trade of the Philippines with other nations, the statistics show that at high-water mark, which was in 1880, their exports and imports amounted to $44,042,815. Official statistics in regard to the foreign commerce of the islands are not available for the years subsequent to 1894, and estimates since that time are based on reports of other countries in Bata, procured by consular officers and merchants of Manila.

In 1894 the total trade was worth $30,792,559, of which $14,250,717 were imports and $16,541,842 exports. These figures are unusually small compared with the official values of preceding years. In the period between 1880 and 1894 the average annual value of commerce was as high as $37,566,005. Many fluctuations occurred within this time, but taken as a whole there was a noticeable decline in trade. It is probable, however, that this decline was not a decrease in the quantity of the merchandise handled, but in the price, which fell off considerably.

The distribution of the Philippine commerce among the various foreign countries of the world is a matter of great interest. Taking the year 1893, which is the last year in which there are official statistics available, it is shown that nearly 85 per cent. of the entire import and export trade of the islands was divided among four countries, England, China, Spain and the United States. Out of a total of $38,073,725 England had $14,207,832, or 37.32 per cent. of the total; China is credited with 18.66 per cent., the value being $7,104,111, most of which went to Hong Kong; Spain had $7,024,128, or 18.45 per cent., while the United States had $3,951,603, or 10.38 per cent.; Germany only had 3.32 per cent. and France 1.89 per cent.

Manila is rich in agricultural products. Hemp and sugar form the leading staples of the island, and these are the principal factors in their trade; in fact together they make up 75 per cent. of the total export valuation. After these are leaf tobacco, cigars and cigarettes. At one time coffee was also one of the leading exports, but there has been a great decline in its production, because of the ravages of an insect which laid waste the coffee groves. But these are not all. Rich woods, oils, rice, cocoa, spices, indigo and many other things flourish on the island, and if properly encouraged would yield rich returns to the investor.

Recognizing what a splendid field the Philippines offer in the line of agriculture, the Secretary of Agriculture, James W. Wilson, on behalf of the Government of the United States, sent commissioners over there to see what the future promised for the agriculture of the islands. The commissioners returned enthusiastic for the new land and talked of it as though it were a veritable Klondike, as yet undeveloped, but having hidden in it fortunes for those who know how to bring them forth.

In the years before so many colonies were opened up in all parts of the world, there were a few who went to the Philippines and made large fortunes out of sugar and hemp, but more recently there were hundreds of people who started out to make money with only one-tenth of the capital necessary to run the places which they had. Consequently they soon fell into the hands of money lenders, so that they barely were able to earn an honest living from large estates which were mortgaged up to the hilt, and were really owned by the men who advanced money on them.

The value of sugar cane land depends largely on its nearness to a port, on the condition of the sugar market, on the quality of the soil, on its situation in the island, and on a thousand and one other things. For instance, in the province of Bulacan, which is near Manila, land which yields on an average of twenty-one tons an acre is worth $115, because of its nearness to the capital. In Pampanja province, which is not very much farther away, better land, yielding about thirty tons an acre, is worth only $75; still further north, in the province of Neuva Ecija, where it is difficult to get the sugar to market, land which will yield thirty-five tons of sugar to the acre can be bought for about $30. This gives an indication of how money might be made by the introduction of railroad and other facilities for transportation.

The finest sugar cane producing island in the Philippines is Negros, in the Visaya district. In size it is equal to Porto Rico, but only half of it is opened up, simply for want of capital. Some appreciation may be had of exactly what that means, when it is known that this island, handicapped as it is, produced in 1889 about 80,000 tons of raw sugar. The yield of sugar cane may be estimated roughly at from thirty to forty tons an acre, and the price varies from $35 to $70 an acre. The sugar from Iloilo is chiefly exported to the United States, where there is demand for raw material only, while from

Manila a certain quantity of refined sugar ready for consumption is sent to Spain. Consequently they have some high-class European machinery in the latter place, while in the former many rough mills, such as were introduced by the Chinese, are still in use.

According to those who have carefully looked into the matter, the output of sugar could be very largely increased if intelligent care were directed to the seasons. A great deal of sugar is lost by delay in various branches of cutting and milling and planting. An estate turning out five hundred tons of sugar is considered a large one. In the northern Philippines the plantations are worked on the co-operative principle. The landowner divides up his estate and sublets it to a tenant on shares; in the southern plantations the system is different —men are paid by the day for their work. The total export of sugar between 1886 and 1890 averaged 381,068,699 pounds a year. The topnotch was 444,626,218 pounds in 1889.

Next to sugar, rice is most generally cultivated, although not so largely exported. It is the staple article of diet of the native, and is grown everywhere. Notwithstanding this fact, however, the supply is very much smaller than the demand, and large quantities have to be imported to supply the natives with sufficient for food. This is due partly to the fact that it pays better to use the land for sugar cane than for raising rice, and many of the owners of plantations have converted their property, formerly used for rice, into the raising of sugar. There are very few machines for successfully cleaning the rice, owing to the fact that any machinery which is good for one variety of rice would not be suitable for another, and there are so many different varieties, that the loss in the end would be greater than the gain.

The number of different kinds of rice paddy is estimated at twenty. The Macan or low land rice is much finer in quality than the others, and usually very white. There is rarely more than one crop a year obtained of this rice, while of the poorer qualities as many as three crops can be secured. The seed of the lowland rice is planted in June on what is called the "seeding plot." It is allowed to grow for about six weeks and reaches the height of about a foot. Then it is pulled up by the roots and transplanted in flooded fields. Little banks of earth are placed all around the fields, so that the water cannot run off, and just before the plants are placed in them the fields are plowed up. Then the planters go along with their bundles of plants, and, picking them out one by one, stick them into the mud. This to the ordinary mind seems like a very long and laborious operation, but the natives are experts in the transplanting, and it does not take them as long as one would think to get over a large field.

It takes about four months for the rice to ripen. Harvest is usually begun at the end of November. The paddy is made into stacks at the end of January, and about the middle of April the rice is separated from the straw. This is done in a good many ways. Some flail it, others beat it out with their feet, while still others, particularly around Cavite, spread the sheaves out and trot a number of ponies around over it. There is not much money in rice-raising, as it is carried on at present, but it is probable with the introduction of new ideas and machinery instead of human hands, a rice farm might be made to pay a good dividend.

THE TERRIBLE PLAGUES OF LOCUSTS.

One of the great troubles with which planters both of rice and of sugar have to contend is the plague of locusts. They come in swarms of millions at a time, and travellers state that they are so thick that while the locusts are passing by, the trees on the other side are not visible. Mr. Foreman, one of the most intelligent observers who has ever written about the Philippines, describes one experience that he had, as follows: "Sailing along the antique coast one evening, I observed on the fertile shore a large, brown colored plateau. For the moment I thought it was a tract of land which had been cleared by fire, but on nearing it I perceived that countless numbers of locusts had settled on several fields. We put in quite close to them, and I fired off a revolver, the noise of which caused them to move off slowly in a column."

These locusts increase and multiply rapidly. The new-born insects are not able to fly until they are about ten days old, so they devastate the fields and practically clean them of their crop. A large mass of locusts will destroy the crop for miles and miles in a single night. The way to get rid of them is a problem. The method employed for the young locusts is to build a barrier at one side of the field, dig a pit in front of it, and then put a small army of men around the other three sides and let them beat around until they scare the young locusts into jumping in heaps in the pit. Sometimes twenty tons of locusts are destroyed on one plantation in one season. Noise is the great aid in ridding a place of the winged pests; the natives take tin cans and drums and anything else that makes a sound and scare the locusts so that they fly away. Other natives light fires to smoke them out. Some of the natives use the locusts as food, frying them into what they call a very delicious dish.

A GREAT TRADE IN MANILA HEMP.

Next to the trade in sugar, the most money has been made up to the present time in hemp, which is a wild species of plantain found in many parts of the island. It is something like the banana plant, and only experts can tell the difference. The hemp grows best on sloping land. The tree in the islands reaches an average height of ten feet, from which the fine fibre is drawn out by hand with a knife, and without killing the tree Many attempts have been made to do this by machinery, but so far nothing satisfactory has been produced. The plant requires three years to arrive to a state in which the fibre can be taken out. One of the advantages in the raising of hemp is that the clearing of other trees from the plantations is not necessary, inasmuch as the plants thrive best in the shade. The great drawback in hemp plantation is the fact that the planter has to wait three years at least before he can get his money back or reap any profit from it. The risk after that period is comparatively small.

One of the great difficulties in the handling of a hemp plantation by the European is due to the laziness of the native. If left to himself he cuts the plant at any period during its maturity, although he is perfectly aware that there are certain periods at which, if cut, the fibre is much more valuable than at others. The native, when he is hard up, strips a few of the trees, leaving them exposed to the rain and air to soften, as the fibre may be more easily withdrawn then. It is no loss to him that the fibre discolors, and is therefore not so valuable. He has tricks of the trade, which the European soon becomes used to. He delivers this colored fibre at night instead of in daytime, first to conceal the fact that it is colored, and secondly so that the fibre may absorb the dew at night, and consequently weigh more. One advantage which the Manila hemp has is that it is a monopoly, for no other place produces it, consequently there is no competition in the trade except with other fibres of a somewhat similar nature. Statistics show that the average annual export of Manila hemp was 66,508 tons between 1886 and 1890, the highest being in 1888, when 80,400 tons were exported. Measured in value, the Manila hemp imported into the United States between 1888 and 1897 formed about 55 per cent. of our total imports from the Philippine Islands. During 1897 the hemp brought from Manila was valued at $2,701,651; and in 1889, owing to the high value of the product, the amount imported was worth $6,436,750.

ON A COFFEE PLANTATION.

Coffee is another industry which may be developed greatly in the future. The chief value of a coffee plantation is that the trees bear profitably for twenty-five years before they become practically useless, and some even longer than that. The best coffee comes from the provinces of Batangas, Cavite, and La Laguna. The report of the United States Government shows that the average annual export of coffee from the islands between 1886 and 1890 amounted to 12,752,-228 pounds. The price of a good plantation is about $180 per acre. Four years after the trees are planted they begin to give coffee that is salable. The trees flourish best on high land and in hilly districts, and care is needed to keep the trees shaded from the hot rays of the sun. In Batangas great pains are taken in this matter, and consequently the coffee is very good. The cost to the owner of having the plantation looked after is about one-half of the produce, so supposing the selling price is up to the average, the grower makes about 18 per cent. upon his invested capital. One year out of every five is sure to give a short crop, consequently it pays better to buy from the small growers than to envolve a great deal of capital in one large estate.

The berries from the tree are picked by the women and children, and then washed; afterward they are dried and pounded until they are perfectly clean. The plantations give only one crop a year.

The tobacco industry was introduced into the islands from Mexico, and has grown so large that it has become one of the great industries of the place. The tobacco trade was in charge of the government for a long time, until it led to so many dishonorable acts on the part of officials that the monopoly was abolished. In 1890, 20,102,387 pounds of leaf tobacco and 3,027,384 pounds of cigars and cigarettes were exported. The quality of the tobacco grown there cannot compare with that of the best Cuban plant according to experts, but is still of such a high grade as to make it capable of becoming a large factor in the export trade. The best quality is produced in the northern parts of Luzon, the choicest being from Cagayan and La Isabella.

Some of the southern districts raise maize or Indian-corn in place of rice. It is pulverized between stone or hard wood slabs, and then eaten. Cocoa trees are plentiful, growing readily in damp or hot districts. The quality is very good, but the occupation is decidedly risky, as a single storm will throw down almost ripen fruit and ruin a man in a day, and disease attacks the plants. If it were not for this a cocoa planter would make handsome profits.

VALUABLE TRACTS OF TIMBER TREES.

The Philippines are remarkably rich in valuable timber trees. Sapan wood is found in most of the islands. It is crocked and hard, and so heavy that it sinks in water, but is susceptible of a very fine polish. The heart of the branches is used to make a dye known in the trade as "false crimson." There were 15,438,072 pounds of sapan wood exported in 1888. Many other fine woods are produced and offer a good field for exports. Among them is what is called "narra," the mahogany of the Philippines. It is always employed in Manila in the manufacture of furniture. It runs in a variety of shades from straw colored to blood red. The former is more common, but a llare equally valuable. The Filipinos presented Consul Williams, who took such a great interest in their welfare, with a splendid piece of this mahogany as a gift.

The fruits of the island are not very fine, compared with those of America. The mango is most abundant, and is very good. People eat as many as a dozen a day without harm, and they are very cheap. The banana is plentiful all the year round. It grows wild, but is also largely cultivated. The islands also yield oranges, lemons, and plenty of pineapple.

The Philippines contain vast tracts of mineral land, filled with gold, copper and iron, which some day will yield untold wealth to the world. It is confidently predicted, by many who have looked into the matter, that the gold fields of the archipelago will some day yield an output greater even than that of the Klondike, and we all may live to see a wild rush to the Philippines similar to that to Australia years ago, to California in '59, and to the Klondike in the last few years. All of the streams on the eastern side of Luzon carry gold down from the mountains, and there is no little brook which does not pan at least a little yellow color.

FORTUNES IN GOLD WAITING FOR DISCOVERY.

The overgrowth of the islands is so dense that ordinary prospecting for gold is out of the question, but as the country becomes opened up, there is no doubt but that fortunes will be found waiting for discovery. When the Dons first landed in the Philippines they found gold an article of traffic among the natives, and to-day, outside of the large towns, uncoined gold is used extensively as a medium of exchange. It is weighed on small scales, and its value is estimated at about $11 per ounce, owing to its impurities. It is known that there is a good deal of gold in the province of Benguet, central Luzon, and also in the northeastern part of the Island of Mindanao, the streams there are particularly rich.

The people of this island carry gold around and use it as money Their method of obtaining the precious metal is, of course, very primitive. They wash the sand and gravel of the streams in wooden bowls, seeking the golden specks which fall to the bottom. In other places they crush the rock to powder and then treat that in the same way. The gold occurs about three feet from the surface of the ground, and increases in quantity to a depth of eighteen feet. The pieces of rock are carried out of the pits in baskets, up ladders of bamboo. They are crushed by what is known as the "errastra," an apparatus consisting of a block of rock, which is moved like a millstone on another rock by means of buffalo power. Water is added, and the result is a fine mud, which is washed by the women, who kneel before a wooden gutter filled with water. Each woman has a washing board, over which water from the gutter flows through a small outlet. The water washes away most of the light sand and other matter, and what is left is treated in a wooden bowl and finally in a cocoanut shell. A small quantity of slimy juice of the gogo is mixed in with the water to keep the sand suspended. Of course, most of the gold is lost during this process, but that which is secured in the shape of dust is put into a small shell and covered with a little charcoal. This is placed in a fragment of a broken pot and the charcoal is lighted. Then a woman blows gently through a little bamboo tube upon it, melting the gold into a small lump. One of the nuggets thus secured was tested and was found to contain 77 per cent. of gold, 19 per cent. of silver, 3 per. cent. of earth and 1 per cent. of iron.

COAL BARONS LOOK TO THE PHILIPPINES.

There is plenty of coal in the archipelago, and yet a large part of the mineral in use there is imported from other countries. This is due largely to the fact that the mining of coal is extremely difficult and expensive. The only means of transport are buffalo carts, and these are neither efficient, quick or cheap. The island of Cebu contains large beds of coal, and the mines of Compostella are said to be very rich, the lodes averaging a thickness of two miles; but they have never been fully opened for want of capital. The coal is of medium class, still the Spanish naval authorities were willing to contract for large quantities of it; but it was impossible to make it pay under the present method of cart transportation.

In Aplaco Mountain, in Cebu, the coal is said to be of good quality; but not to contain much heating power. In the province of Albay, collieries were begun, and after awhile were abandoned, handicapped as usual by failure of transportation. It is calculated that, up to the year 1876, $1,300,000 was spent on the mines in the Philippines without any apparent return.

IRON IS PLENTIFUL AND ALMOST PURE.

There is plenty of iron, in which the ore is said to yield 75 per cent. of pure metal, yet it is impossible to mine it at a profit, owing to the lack of railways. It has frequently been tried, but never with success.

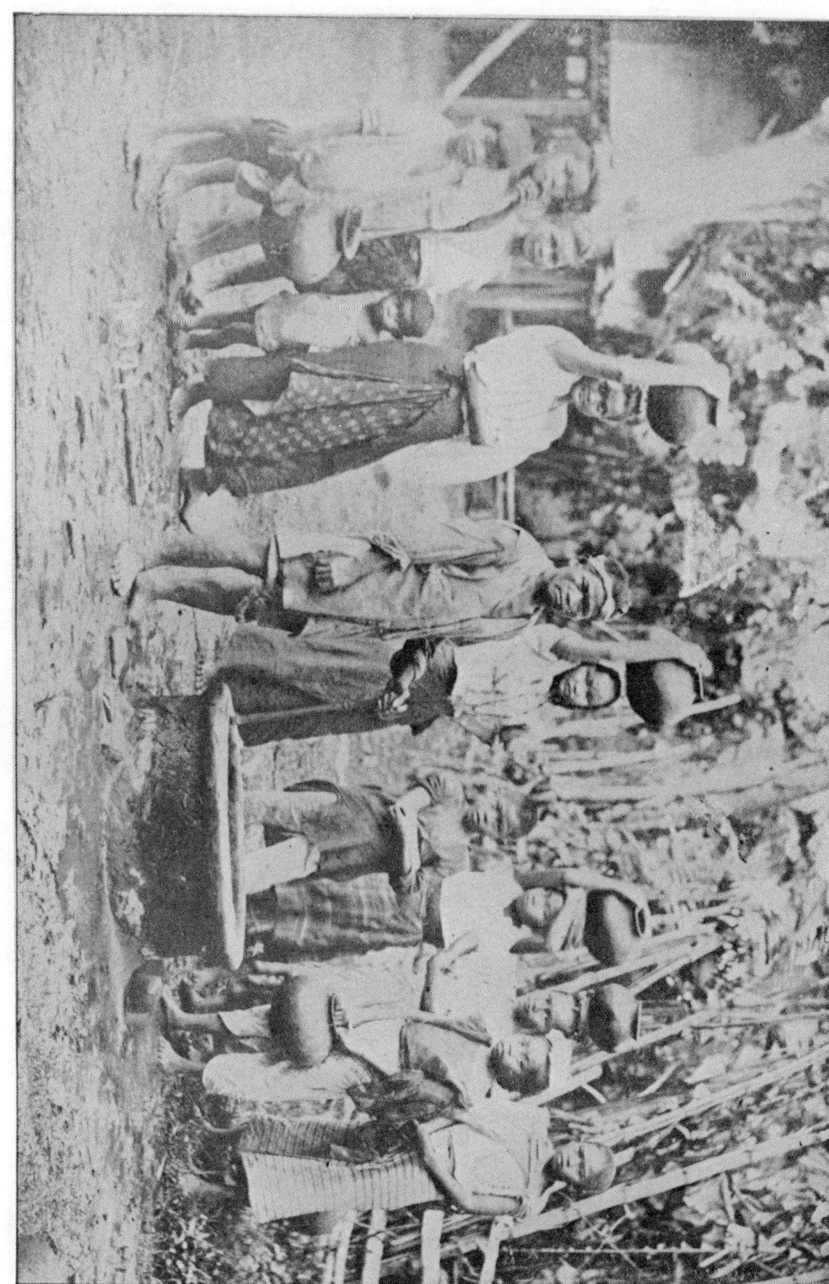

NATIVE WATER CARRIERS IN ILOILO

In the Philippine Islands, as in all other countries of the Orient, it is customary for the natives to carry their drinking water from public wells. More than three thousand years ago Moses met his future wife at the well. The servants of Abraham made the bargain with Rebecca to marry Isaac at the well. Christ met the woman of Samaria at Jacob's well. The women and the children of the East still keep up the ancient custom, in semi-savage as well as civilized lands.

A SPANISH PHILIPINO MESTIZA

Upper garments of costly Piña cloth, and skirt of richly embroidered silk. The mestizas are the offspring of foreigners and the natives. There are many Chinese and Spanish half-castes. The latter are generally very handsome.

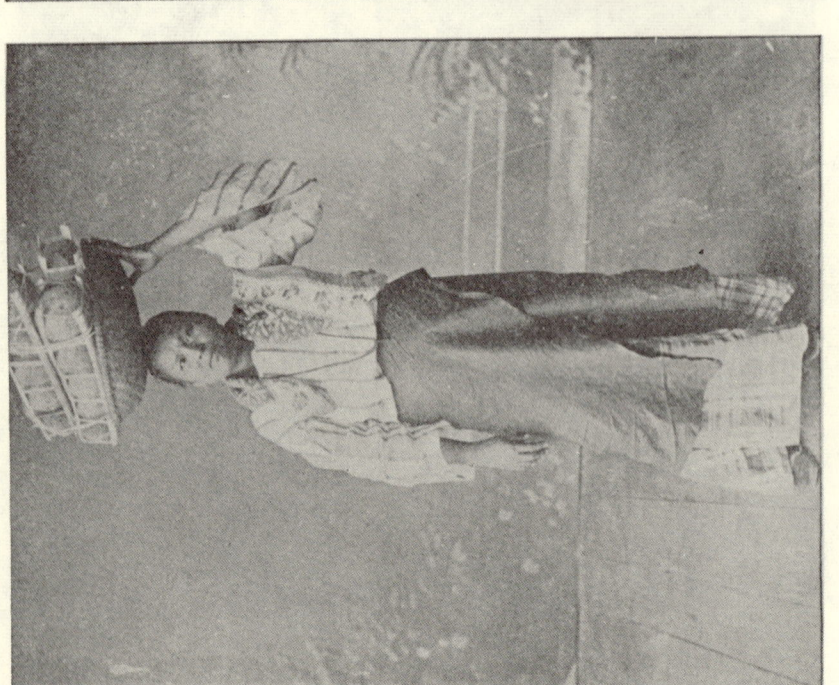

A NATIVE PHILIPINO WOMAN

Women peddlers upon the streets of Manila are common sights. They sell bread, milk, fruits, flowers, water, etc., and carry their heavy burdens always upon their heads.

There are rich mines near Manila, and others at Angat, in Bulacan province, the latter giving undoubtedly a very rich ore. The mines there are still being worked, though on a very small scale.

One of the important items of wealth in the Philippines is copper, of which there are great deposits. The natives use copper utensils, and the Igorrotes have carried on copper mining for centuries. The ore found at Mancayan contains 16 per cent. of copper. In the interior of the island of Luzon, copper occurs in large masses, and as yet the great extent of the commercial value of that deo sit is unknown. The natives get the copper by placing fragments of rock in a round hollow in clayed ground, with which a conical funnel of stone is connected; a fire is lighted, and blowers with bamboo are worked with plungers to make a draft.

These, with the deposits of sulphur, marble and gypsum, and with the addition of the valuable pearl fisheries of Sulu, make the man who yearns for fields where wealth can be had for the finding, turn his eyes towards these our new possessions, which hold in their hearts fortunes that, if uncovered, would show riches beyond the wildest imagination.

CHAPTER IX

The People of the Islands

More than Eighty Different Tribes on the Islands.—Interesting Traits of Character of the Natives, both Half-Civilized and Barbarous.—Cannibalism and its Horrors.—Something about the Curious Peoples—The Aetas, Negritos, Gadanes, Itavis, Igorrotes, Tinguianes and many others.

BUT what of these people, whom we have placed beneath the Stars and Stripes, both by the right of capture and purchase of their land? Who are they? What are they? How do they live? These are questions which everybody asks, when the thought of the Philippines is presented. Most persons know very little of them, except that they are a half-civilized lot of people, at best, and the lowest order of barbarians, at worst.

And this general impression is almost correct; civilization is at a very low ebb in the Philippines. Of course, the Spaniards who have settled there, the Europeans who carry on business dealings on the islands, some of the Chinese merchants, and even some of the high-caste natives, are people of culture; but the great overwhelming mass of residents on the island are in low stages of savagery.

Let us look for a minute at some of the tribes outside of the capital of Manila and the region round about. The recent attack by insurgent forces upon the American troops has made most people familiar with the name at least of the Igorrotes, whose chief was captured in the fight, and whose tribesmen stood before the awful fire of our guns, wondering what on earth they were and why their ranks were thinned out, as if by some mysterious force.

The chief admitted, as has been stated, that he never saw firearms before, and this may well be believed, for he himself and all his men went into the conflict armed with bows and arrows. These Igorrotes occupy a very considerable portion of the island of Luzon, of which Manila is the capital. From a physical standpoint, they are about as fine a race of people as one would wish to see. They wear their hair long, almost down to their shoulders; they have flat noses and high cheek bones, and are broad-shouldered and strong of limb.

Like most of the people of this sub-tropical isle, they are exceedingly lazy, and do very little except prey upon nearby tribes. Murder is so common as to be almost a pastime, and they have a way of avenging murders on the murderer's family, if they cannot lay hands upon the culprit himself.

They have given the government of Spain as much trouble as any of the tribes on the island. The task of civilizing them has been absolutely abandoned by the Spanish, and the occasional expeditions to place them under subjection have been so weak as to encourage these native sons of the isle in the belief that the power of Spain is not very much of a thing to dread. The expeditions, moreover, seem to have given the Spanish officers an opportunity for license, which so prejudiced these savages against Europeans, that all overtures, either of Church or State, were scorned as being beneath contempt by these islanders. They refused absolutely to receive baptism or accept Christianity, basing their feelings in the matter upon the actions of the only representatives of Christian races which they knew, and who proved themselves immoral and untrustworthy.

DESCENDED FROM THE FOLLOWERS OF THE PIRATE.

There is a half-caste tribe, called the Igorrote-Chinese, which is supposed to have come down through the generations from the Chinese followers of the terrible pirate, Limahong. They have intermarried with the original tribe, and the result is a very individual class of islanders, who combine the fierceness and strength of the Igorrotes and the cunning and cleverness of the Chinamen.

Among the best known of the wilder tribes are the Aetas, or Negritos, who are found here and there in almost all of the islands. They are supposed to be the original inhabitants. In color they are almost as black as African negroes; they have short, curly hair, something like Astrakhan fur. They are, perhaps, the most cowardly people extant, and have no idea of facing the Spaniards in a fair fight. They are not habitually overburdened with clothing, and are usually armed with a lance and with bow and arrow, the latter of which is tipped with poison. Their agility is their chief characteristic. They run with great speed and climb trees almost as easily as monkeys. They have, apparently, no mentality or stability, and even those brought under the influences of civilization have lapses, during which they go back to their native customs and native haunts.

Their religion is a religion of superstition. They are too lazy to work, and live principally on fish, roots and the rice common to the mountains. Spasmodically they rush down upon nearby tribes and settlements which have made some progress under civilization, and carry off anything they lay their hands on. The government was kept busy protecting property against such raids for some years, but recently this people have been driven so far into the interior that their visitations for plunder are becoming less and less frequent. Their idea of plowing the earth and making it yield forth fruit in its season, seems to be to scratch up the surface of the ground slightly, without clearing it of shrubs or trees, and then sprinkling it with seed and trusting to luck for something to grow.

A WEDDING CEREMONY AMONG THE SAVAGES.

Mr. John Foreman, who traveled through their country, describes an interesting and typical wedding ceremony which he witnessed there, as follows: "The young bride, who might have been thirteen years of age, was being pursued by her future spouse, as she pretended to run away, and it need hardly be said that he succeeded in bringing her in by feigned force. She struggled and again got away, but a second time she was caught. Then an old man with gray hair came forward and dragged the young man up a bamboo ladder. An old woman grasped the bride, and both followed the bridegroom. The aged sire then gave them a ducking with a cocoanut shell full of water, and they all descended. The happy pair knelt down, and the elder, having placed their heads together, they were man and wife. We endeavored to find out which hut was alotted to the newly married couple, but we were given to understand that, until the sun had reappeared five times, they would spend their honeymoon in the mountains. After the ceremony was concluded, several present began to make their usual mountain call. In the lowlands, the same peculiar cry serves to bring home straggling domestic animals to their nocturnal resting place."

The Gadanes occupy the extreme northwest of Luzon, and have so far removed from the centre of civilization that comparatively little is known about them. They possess many of the attributes of the other tribes, are very dark in color and live chiefly on fish and vegetables. Their chief pride is their warlike record, so much so, in fact, that when a young man makes up his mind to assume the bonds of matrimony, he usually starts out on the warpath, in order to dangle before his prospective father-in-law enough scalps to make himself worthy of notice. If one or two young warriors happen to be paying attention to the same dusky maiden, the hunt for scalps becomes a contest, and the man who kills the most people is likely to win the prize.

THE FIRE-TREE STIRS THE NATIVES TO WAR.

This practice of proving courage at the expense of their enemies, breaks out in a marked degree when the flowers of what the Spaniards call the fire-tree are in bloom. The fire-tree is covered with brilliant red blossoms, and their appearance is regarded as a signal to the members of this race to count up scalps and celebrate victory with weird rites.

The Gadanes go about armed in such a way that they can get a breakfast or kill a man with equal ease. Their lances are long, with tridented tips with which they both fish and kill, and their arrows carry at the point two rows of teeth made out of flint or seashells.

To the south of them live the Itavas, who are much similar to them, but neither as fierce or as brave. They are ready to protect themselves against assault, but are not very eager to go into war for the savage love of the sport. Their skin is lighter and their hair is shorter than their neighbors'.

The Tinguianes, who occupy the district of Elabra, are pretty well under control of the Spanish government; physically they are fine specimens. They wear their hair in a tuft on the top of the head, like the Japanese, and their nose is aquiline, but the rest of their features are much like that of the ordinary lowland native.

They are not very warlike, and have been kept pretty well in hand by the government troops. The Spaniards appoint their petty governors, as they do in all of the subdued districts, and when that governor assumes his office, it is related that he takes the following picturesque oath: "May a pernicious wind touch me, may a flash of lightning kill me, and may the alligator catch me asleep, if I fail to fulfill my duties."

Picturesqueness seems to be the vogue in oaths. When a man is brought up to the bar of justice on any accusation, he has the right to plead guilty or not guilty. If he denies the accusation, a handful of straw is burnt in his presence, and he is made to hold up an earthen-ware vessel and say: "May my belly be converted into a pot like this, if I have committed the deed attributed to me." If the transformation does not take place immediately, that is considered proof positive that he is innocent, and he is allowed to go free.

They have no temples, but they worship gods who are hidden in mountain cavities. They have priests, supposed to be in touch with these gods, and they are appealed to on all occasions. For instance, when a child is to be named it is carried into the woods and the pagan priest is sought. He stands over the new-born babe with a knife in his hand. He pronounces a name and, at the same time, sticks the knife into a tree nearby. If sap runs out of the tree, the name is adopted; if not, he tries another name, changing it each time until the sap oozing out of the wound in the tree tells the waiting people that the deity has decided upon that name.

These people build their houses in trees or on posts, sixty or seventy feet from the ground. In these houses they keep a goodly supply of large rocks, so that when their enemies come around and try to climb up to their dwellings, they drop a stone on their heads. They hang skulls of horses and buffaloes out of their windows for luck. Some of the families of El Abra and Ilocos, which are descended from the Tinguianes, have become so civilized that they are considered valuable as workmen and servants and are sought in preference to any of the others. There is another race of people supposed to have descended from Hindoo soldiers who formed part of the British troops which occupied Manila in 1763. These people are very decidedly different from the ordinary native. They occupy the Morong district. They are Christians, hard working and law abiding. They are the only people who voluntarily pay their taxes.

There are in the Philippines a few types of that tropical curiosity known as albinos, who have pure white skin and light, sometimes red hair, with pink eyes. They become almost blind in the daytime, owing to the glare of the tropical sun.

SIXTY LANGUAGES AMONG EIGHTY TRIBES.

There are sixty distinct languages spoken in the eighty tribes of the islands, and out of 9,000,000 people not more than a quarter of a million can read and write Spanish, the only language whereby, up to this time, they could be instructed. Almost all of the education seems to have been among the Tagalos, not because they are mentally superior to the other races, but because they happen to occupy the region round about Manila. The Tagolos form about one-sixth of the population of Luzon, yet the casual visitor to the Philippines, or even those who reside in Manila, naturally know more about this race than any other. The other races have been rather jealous of the Tagalos, and dislike them, which made the prospects of civilization through these nations even harder than by direct education of the other tribes.

Long and careful study of the Filipino shows that in many respects his character is a mystery. A native may run along for years in a normal way, exhibiting fairly good sense and obeying the law, and then, all of a sudden, he will break out into theft or murder or some other crime, just because, as he puts it, "his head is hot." For instance, there was a native who served with one of the members of the Spanish colony for forty years without getting himself into any very great trouble. One day a son of his master came back from a trip bringing with him a $1,000. The old servant got hold of the bag containing the money, ripped it open, and took out about $30, leaving the rest untouched. He was charged with the crime and calmly admitted it, although he could not offer any reason for not taking the whole sum while he was about it.

CHARACTERISTICS OF THE FILIPINO.

The ordinary native is fond of gambling and passionately devoted to cockfighting. He is ready to make all kinds of promises, but is rarely ready to carry them out. If he commits a

THE MOUTH OF THE PASIG RIVER

The city of Old Manila is surrounded by water. On the west is the sea, to the north is the Pasig River, while moats, connected with the river by sluices, flank the other two sides. All the principal warehouses of the city are on the Pasig, and ships deliver and receive their cargoes direct, without the necessity of cartage.

YOUNG MAN OF THE UPPER CLASS
White duck or crash trousers and a silk or piña shirt make a fashionable suit.

AGUINALDO AT THE AGE OF 22
Dressed in fine Piña cloth shirt.

DOING THE FAMILY WASH
The glory of all Philippine women is their long and beautiful hair.

NATIVE WOMAN FRUIT SELLER
And customers, Manila.

fault, or breaks anything by accident, he rarely comes forward and admits it, but tries to hide it until it is found out. The natives are quick to pounce upon any sign of leniency on the part of their European employers. If a foreigner tries to do them a good turn, they will impose upon him ever afterward, thinking that it is the sign of weakness on his part, which, as might be imagined, has resulted in the European residents of the place adopting an atmosphere of authority and harshness more pronounced than might have been the case under different circumstances. If a man pays a native twenty cents for something that he has done, and that is the regular price, he takes it and is glad to get it, but if he gives him thirty cents, the native will raise a storm of protest and grumble, because he didn't get fifty cents.

The American troops are responsible for a great deal of trouble among the native servants and tradespeople from this very mistaken kindness. When the troops first landed, and there was any work to be done which had to be done by the natives, they paid them a dollar a day for what they were ordinarily receiving twenty-five cents, and thought they were getting off cheaply, according to American prices. And so, after a while, there was a pronounced exodus of native servants from the houses of the residents of Manila and Cavite, because they could get four times as much pay from the Americans as from the residents. After a while the Americans became aware of the fact that they had been too generous and tried to reduce prices for work, but then the natives showed that singular characteristic referred to, and declined to take less than the Americans had originally paid. For sometime there was a good deal of disorder and discomfort resulting from this, but recently things have quieted down, but wages and prices have gone up all over the civilized parts of the islands.

GRATITUDE A THING UNKNOWN.

Gratitude is a thing almost unknown to the native Filipino; he does not seem to understand the feeling which prompts one person to give another a gift of any kind. It is a remarkable fact that in the southern islands of the Philippines there is no word or phrase to express thanks for a gift. This would tend to show that the idea of gratitude was wanting, and consequently there was no need of words to express that idea. The native has a funny way of asking for anything. He never comes straight out with his request, but starts a long tale of woe, probably beginning with an elaborate lie, which you can see through at a glance, and finally coming to the point, with a very beseeching voice, and a face as innocent as though he had never told a lie in his life.

He never voluntarily returns anything that he borrows. If you speak to him about it, he calmly tells you that he did not return your loan because you never asked him for it. When a European does make a loan of money to a native, it behooves him to parley a little with the borrower, and finally compromise by lending him a little less than he asks, otherwise he would be a target for requests for the next six months.

The natives are, like most Orientals, good imitators, but not inventors. No matter what you give them, they will sit down and make a copy of it. A native has no idea of sticking to one trade; he will be a servant one week, go out as a sailor the next, and probably wind up as a lawyer or a bandit the week following. He regards the European as an awful being, and the farther away from the centers of civilization that one goes in the islands the more awful one finds the conception of Europeans. The name is much like that of our "Bogy-man," who will "ketch you if you don't look out!" The women scare their children into submission with the awful word "Castila" (European). If a baby cries, it is hushed by this magic word; if a white man comes near a hut in the less civilized parts of the islands, the same word is used as a cry of caution to all who may be within.

These people are a people of superstition and without humor. A joke is taken with the utmost seriousness, and is sometimes enlarged upon by the natives until its consequences are serious. They rarely show anger, and receive everything without a change of a muscle of the face; but they store up their wrath for future use, and patiently wait until the opportunity comes for them to plunge a knife into their enemy. A native never can keep a secret, but he is silent in service, with sometimes the most extraordinary results. He will let your horse die for want of food, and tell you afterward it is because the animal had nothing to eat.

He never comes when first called, and, sometimes, when one native wants another, he has to call him five or six times before the other responds, although he has heard the summons from the very first. The native does not hesitate to steal, but he usually confines himself to things he wants, and does not take things merely because they are valuable.

One of the peculiar traits of the Filipinos is that they will never step over a person who is asleep on the floor, and they will not wake anybody, except on the utmost provocation. Their argument in the matter is that the soul is absent from the body while one is asleep, and if it went very far away, it would not have time to get back, if the man were suddenly awakened. If you go to call on a native and are told he is asleep, you might as well turn around and go away again until he wakes up.

The average Filipino is a good father and a good husband in many ways, although he thinks more of his game cock than his family. In cases of fire, natives have been known to pick up their fighting birds and flee, leaving their wives and children to take care of themselves, and get out as best they could.

If you put a question suddenly to a native he apparently loses his presence of mind, and gives any reply that happens to come to him, no matter whether it is true or not. Then, as you ply him with questions, he will amend his statement little by little, until finally the truth comes out. He is not ashamed of lying, but is chagrined if his lie fails in its purpose.

The Tagalog is quite sociable, and if you visit him, he receives you very hospitably. The Visaya, who lives in the south of the island, and is as much civilized as the Tagalog, is not so friendly. He seldom smiles before a stranger, has as little conversation with them as possible, and puts on a great deal of airs.

There is one thing about these half-civilized islanders that gives hope that some day they may be governed successfully, and that is their sense of justice. Once convinced that they are being justly treated, they are perfectly satisfied. If you beat a man when he knows he has done wrong, he will never say a word; but if he thinks he is being unjustly chastised, he will carry a grudge against you for years.

The colleges at Manila have done much to educate the brighter natives. The people have very little idea of art, but all of them are musicians of more or less ability. Native orchestras can be procured for almost nothing, and they will play the most difficult music at a moment's notice. The American soldiers used to hire an orchestra to play during meals and all evening for twenty-five cents.

When I asked a prominent army man, who had just returned from Manila, what struck him as the most remarkable thing that he came across during his visit to the island, he replied without hesitation, "A native orchestra playing Sousa's 'Stars and Stripes Forever', and 'A Hot Time in the Old Town To-night'. Since the advent of the American soldiers the musical repertoire of the native musicians has undergone a decided change. They have adopted almost all of the popular songs of this country, and play them apparently in preference to anything else. One American officer, who received a large roll of music from friends in the United States, untied the package, called the leader of the native orchestra which was to play at a little dinner that he was giving, and, sitting down at the piano, played a dozen of the selections. That evening the whole orchestra rendered these selections one after the other, without notes, to the amazement of the assembled guests.

These musicians think nothing of trying the most difficult German and Italian operas, and almost any native orchestra in Manila can give you the overture to "Tannhæuser" in first-rate style, or anything else that you wish of a similar nature. There is little native music of any sweetness or value, and the natives seem to avoid playing what they have. They never get tired of music, and they will play for hours at a time practically for nothing.

THE NATIVE DANCE.

Their dancing is interesting, and, if well executed, is very graceful. One of their typical dances, known as the Comitan, is that of a girl rising and dancing a pas seul with a glass of water on her head. Another popular dance is accompanied by a song which is an alternate diminishing and raising of the voice, with slow movement suggesting sorrow and then coy, and rapid and energetic steps to show elation.

The native costumes are very interesting. In a city like Manila, and in its surroundings many varieties of attire may be seen upon the streets at the same time. The Spaniards wear the ordinary European costumes, the British generally dress in white, and the Chinese have their peculiar national dress. The pure natives and many half-breeds wear a shirt which falls outside of the trousers. It is usually white, with a long, stiff front, cut after the European fashion, but some of the well-to-do natives wear the beautiful pina cloth, an extremely fine, yellow-tinted material, woven from fibres of the pineapple-tree.

A native woman wears a flowing skirt of bright colors—red and green and white, the length of her train and the material depending entirely upon her pocket-book. They wear chemisettes, and cover their shoulders and neck with a starched neckcloth of pina. To the chemisette are added wide, short sleeves. The hair is brushed up from the forehead without a part, and coiled tightly. The native woman is very fond of jewelry. She always carries a fan, without which she would feel ill at ease. She wears no stockings, and the feet are covered with a kind of slipper which has no heel, and just enough upper in front to put two or three toes in. She holds herself badly, and is not prepossessing. The ordinary peasant woman is very much more picturesque. She wears a short skirt, which is made up of a rectangular piece of stuff, folded around her, and tucked in at the waist. She is very erect in her walk, due probably to the fact that she has balanced jars of water or baskets of fruit on her head since infancy. Sometimes the better class natives wear shirt skirts of silk or satin, with gold lace or embroidery, which is very becoming.

WHAT THE VISAYA WOMEN WEAR.

The Visaya woman wears a robe like that of the Javanese, which is kept in place by being drawn tightly around the body, reaches to the feet, and is tucked in at the waist. Sometimes she will put another piece of cloth over this.

The costume of the native men, who have attended the colleges in the city, are amusingly like those of the college student of Europe. They dress their hair fantastically, wear patent leather shoes, and felt hats carefully tilted to one side.

The native has a decided dislike of being pressed into military service. He is brave if led by his superiors, or if fighting against his equals; but when he becomes convinced that his antagonist is his superior, it has a depressing effect upon him. He admires bravery, and has a great contempt for cowardice. Whenever he is in service he is a good soldier until his leader is shot. After that he simply becomes demoralized.

The Filipinos delight in pillage and destruction, and whenever they are victors in a battle there is no holding them in. They resort to all sorts of tricks to escape military service. For instance, a deed of property showed the names of two brothers on it exactly alike. Inquiry disclosed the fact that it was not a mistake, but that the two brothers were given the same name for the purpose of evading military service. One of them had to serve, but the other escaped because the Spaniards never suspected that there were two brothers of the same name in the same family. This was quite a common trick among the poor natives.

Such are Uncle Sam's new people. Little is known of most of them; a large proportion of them have never been seen, and perhaps will never be for many years. In some of the smaller islands the natives are so uncivilized that cannibalism in all its horrors is still rife; and in all of the islands brigandage and piracy are common. What to do with these people is a serious question. Shall we suffer the fate which Kipling so vigorously expresses—

> "And when your goal is nearest
> (The end for others sought),
> Watch sloth and heathen folly
> Bring all your hope to naught."

CHAPTER X.

Fascinations and Terrors of a New Land.

The Awful Wildness of Typhoons.—A Land Ruled by Volcanoes.—Thousands Killed by Earthquakes.—All Business Suspended until Evening, owing to the Heat.—A Glimpse of its Birds, Beasts and Reptiles.

THE Philippines would be a delightful place to live in, were it not for two things—the terrible typhoons, which sweep the country from time to time, and the equally terrible though less frequent earthquakes, which carry death and destruction to the people of the islands. One can get used to the heat in the Philippines, and live a fairly comfortable and peaceful existence, if that were all, but the typhoons and the earthquakes are not pleasant to even think of.

As might be imagined, the temperature on the islands is not very low, but then it has the advantage of not being very variable, and consequently when one gets used to the heat and accustomed to the method of living there, he begins to think that after all the Philippines are a pretty pleasant place to live in. The climate is very healthy, and aside from the diseases which are common in all tropical places, and which to a great extent can be prevented by personal carefulness, the residents there are able to keep in very good physical condition and enjoy life thoroughly.

FOUR PERIODS OF WEATHER IN THE PHILIPPINES.

The maximum temperature is about 98, and the minimum 75 degrees, both records being based on calculations made at noon in the shade. There are four periods in Manila weather, with which everybody is probably familiar. Spring begins in December and continues in January and February, and these three months form about as delightful a period of existence as it is possible to contemplate. March and April and May are months of intense heat, in which the people work only in the early morning and in the evening, all of the central portion of the day being devoted to the difficult task of keeping cool and taking life easy. Then begins the period of heavy rain, which continues for four months, June, July, August and September. The remaining two months, October and November, are doubtful. Sometimes they are quite as wet as the preceding months, and at other times they are dry and delightful.

Very low temperature, or sudden change of temperature, is practically unknown, and one is able to calculate pretty well what kind of weather he may expect, barring the typhoons. These terrible storms which lay waste the country far and wide are expected at least once a year. Sometimes they are not as severe as others, and sometimes they carry in their wake death and destruction incredible to the people of the United States. The typhoons come in the rainy season, between April and the middle of December. Houses are made roofless, and some of them are blown down, ships are torn from their anchorage in the harbor and sometimes blown for miles to be dashed upon the shore and destroyed.

THOUSANDS KILLED BY TERRIBLE TYPHOONS.

In 1882 a great typhoon swept Manila accompanied with torrents of rain, which added to the damag . A number of houses were unroofed, and two Chinamen who went out in the storm for the purpose of helping themselves to a new corrugated iron roof with the assistance of the storm, were found on the streets the next day with their heads almost cut off, On the 6th of October, 1897, one of the most disastrous typhoons ever reported visited the Philippines. Thousands of lives were lost, including many Europeans, and damage to property was something appalling. The typhoon struck first at the Bay of Santa Paula, in the province of Samar. Fully four hundred Europeans were drowned, and it is estimated that six thousand natives perished. The entire southern part of the island was devastated.

The typhoon reached Leyte and struck the capital of Taclobam with great fury. In less than half an hour the town was filled with ruins, the natives were panic-stricken and fled to reach clear ground so they could lie down and let the storm pass over them. Four hundred were buried beneath the debris of wrecked buildings, and one hundred and twenty-six bodies of Europeans were picked up by the authorities when the search for the dead was made.

DEATH BY THE GARROTE METHOD OF EXECUTION IN MANILA.
Everybody turns out to see a public execution in Manila. The victim rides to the place of death sitting on his coffin. On the scaffold he is seated against a post; a brass collar—the Garrote—is placed around his neck; the priests hold up a crucifix in front of him; the executioner suddenly twists a screw from behind which touches the base of the brain: a convulsive shudder and the victim is dead.

TAGALOG TRIBE.

The above "snap shot" exhibits the every-day working costume in the country, the tribe to which General Aguinaldo belongs. Strange as it seems many of these people have pianos in their houses.

SAVAGE NEGRITO WARRIORS.

These natives fight with bows and arrows, some of them were engaged in the battle of Manila, February 4th and 5th, 1899.

During these typhoons rivers often overflow their banks and extensive areas are submerged. The approach of the wind is usually known through the sudden effect which its proximity has on the barometer. Hours before its arrival there will be a sudden fall, while if the center of the storm is near the barometer varies quickly up and down, so that the observer knows what to expect. The terrible winds of the typhoon are usually accompanied by tidal waves, which are quite as destructive. They sweep over the land in the most unexpected fashion, and a vessel which before the approach of a tidal wave was calmly moored in the harbor will, after it subsides, find itself resting upon the top of a building some distance away.

EARTHQUAKES WORK HAVOC TO LIFE AND PROPERTY.

But even more terrible in its effects than the typhoon is the earthquake, which is not at all a stranger to the Philippines. One of the greatest curiosities to the American soldiers who visited Manila was the ruins of a building which had been rent and destroyed by the force of an earthquake.

The most serious shock, next to the war, which occurred in this century, was in June, 1863. It lasted half a minute, and yet in that little space of time over $8,000,000 worth of property was wrecked beyond recovery, and the falling buildings rolled up a death list of four hundred, while over two thousand people were injured. This was in Manila alone, for Manila has, so to speak, a corner on earthquakes.

The official records made at that time show that forty-six public edifices were thrown down, twenty-eight were nearly destroyed, five hundred and seventy private buildings were wrecked and five hundred and twenty-eight were so badly damaged as to be almost a total loss. In 1880 there was an earthquake which did a great deal of damage, but which caused no loss of life, and in 1881 the records show twenty-three slight quakes, but the natives and even foreigners get so used to these little shocks that they hardly notice them.

This upheaval of 1880 had a permanent effect upon the architecture of the city of Manila. Up to that time the larger and more extensive buildings had heavy tiled roofs which caused great damage and were easily destroyed. After that galvanized corrugated iron came into general use for roofing, and now none of the larger buildings in the civilized parts of the Philippines are covered with anything else. Owing to the combination of heavy winds and earthquake shocks the poorer natives cover their houses with "*nipa*," a long, broad, flat leaf of the nipa-tree, a gigantic fern found almost everywhere in the Philippines. The thick, pithy texture of its leaves yields sufficient protection against the sun and also sheds the rain. Its drawback is its liability to catch fire, and sometimes the destruction of entire towns is due to the fact that the houses are roofed in nipa.

In getting possession of the Philippines the United States secured the finest volcano from the standpoint of beauty in the world, as well as the most active one. The former is the Mayon Volcano, in the province of Albay, in the extreme east of Luzon Island; the latter is the Taal Volcano, in the center of Bombon Lake, only thirty-four miles due south from Manila.

THE ERUPTION OF A VOLCANO.

Clustered around the bottom of the Mayon Volcano are several towns and villages, including the capital of the province Albay. In 1814, on February 1st, this volcano burst forth in all its power. Five towns were totally demolished, and the inhabitants fled into caves to shelter themselves, but many were overtaken by the stones ejected from the bowels of the earth, and some even by the lava which flowed down the side of the mountain. Father Francisco Aragoneses, who was in charge of the church there, estimated that twenty-Two hundred people were killed, to say nothing of the large number who were injured in this eruption.

There were other eruptions in 1887 at which only a small quantity of volcanic matter was thrown out, doing little damage. On the 9th of July, 1888, there was one which was much more destructive. Two towns were damaged greatly, several nearby plantations were destroyed, many cattle were killed and fifteen of the natives lost their lives.

This beautiful mountain forms almost a perfect cone and rises in the air to a distance of 8,200 feet. But the best known volcano in the Philippines is the Taal, which stretches its snowy peak into the air quite near to the City of Manila. It is on a little island in the centre of Bombon Lake, and it has been in an active condition since the mind of man runneth not to the contrary. This, too, was in the shape of a beautiful cone, up to the year 1749, when there was a great outburst, which rent it in two, leaving the crater exposed to sight, as it remains to-day.

In 1754 one of the most notable of the terrible eruptions of this volcano took place, destroying the towns of Taal, Tanauan, Sala and Lipa, and seriously damaging Balayan, fifteen miles distant.

The cinders from this eruption are said to have reached Manila, thirty-four miles distant, as a bird flies, and one writer, in speaking of this eruption thirty-six years after its occurrence, said that the people in Manila were forced to light their candles at midday, and walked around the streets thunderstruck for eight days during which the baptism of fire was visible. The smell of the sulphur lasted for six months after it was all over, and the lake waters gave up thousands of dead fish and alligators.

DRAMATIC SCENE AT THE UPHEAVAL OF THE EARTH.

There is still extant a description of the priest, Francisco Vencuchillo, preserved in the archives of the corporation of St. Augustine in Manila. He tells, in detail, all about the great calamity of 1749, as well as that of 1754. He noticed a strong light on the top of Volcano Island about 11 o'clock at night on the 11th of August, 1749, but paid little attention to it. While he was asleep, however, a noise like that of artillery firing awoke him. He thought it come from the guns of a vessel expected from Mexico, but when the shots continued rapidly, one after the other until he counted a hundred or more, he became alarmed and imagined that some naval engagement was taking place off the coast. Some of the natives ran to him and begged him to flee, telling him that the island had burst, and when daylight came an immense volume of smoke could be seen coming from the top of the volcano, and here and there smaller streams of smoke rose like plumes. It was a magnificent sight to see great mountains of sand hurled from the lake, in the form of pyramids, and then fall back again like the water from a fountain, and while he was watching this spellbound, a tremor of the earth shook the convent, in which he was standing, to its very foundations.

Pillars of sand rose out of the water near to the shore, and then a second shock caught them before they had fallen and they, with the trees on the island, were thrown down and submerged into the lake. The land shifted, so that houses which were formerly on an elevation were placed in a valley, and vice versa. The activity continued for three weeks, and for the first three days ashes fell like rain. The eruption of 1754, as this same priest chronicles it, was even more terrifying to witness. It began between 9 and 10 o'clock at night on May 15th. Lava poured forth from the volcano in such quantities that only the water of the lake kept the people from being burned to death. Soon stones were hurled as far as the shore and fell upon the villages there. The eruptions continued incessantly, until the 10th of July, when a heavy shower of mud, black as ink, fell on the country round about. A suburb of Sala was swamped with mud. During this phenomenon a constant noise was kept up, which lasted only for a short time, but the fire still continued to belch forth from the mouth of the volcano until the 25th of September. On that night stones fell, and the people of Taal left their houses, fearing lest the weight of these stones would crush them in.

PANIC AND RUIN FOLLOW IN THE WAKE.

On the 29th of November, beginning at 7 o'clock in the evening, the eruption was at its worst and the volcano threw up more fire than during all the preceding seven months put together. The whole of the island seemed to be a mass of molten metal, and the lava hurled up seemed to reach to the very clouds. A strong wind was blowing, and with the terrible noise which appeared to come from the bowels of the earth, a huge mass of stones was thrown up with great violence, and nearly all of the people fell prostrate and began to pray. The waters of the lake rose and crept toward the houses, and the frightened inhabitants, laying hands upon whatever property they could, fled for their lives, terror-stricken. Panic ruled everywhere; people wept and prayed and confessed their sins; shouting and lamentations were heard on all sides; and then when the night was spent, and the next day began, no one could tell whether the sun shone or not, for darkness ruled for forty-eight hours. When light reappeared the whole village of Taal had been abandoned. In some of the villages nearby the people climbed upon the house tops to throw down the cinders which were threatening to crush the structure under their weight.

On the 30th of November the smoke and noise seemed greater than ever. The lightning flashed, and the end of the world seemed to have arrived. For a day afterward there was a period of comparative calm, and then followed a hurricane which lasted for two days. The government house and stores, the prison, the state warehouses and the royal rope wharf, together with the church and the convent at Taal and many private houses, were completely destroyed in this upheaval.

The road from Taal to Balayan was impassable for some time, because of the lava. This ended the life of Taal, once the capital and the greatest city of that province, and forever after it was deserted, and Batangas on the coast took its place as the chief town of importance and became the capital.

This volcano of Taal can be reached easily, the ascent occupying about half an hour. The crater is 4,500 feet wide, and in it are three separate lakes of boiling liquid, which change color from time to time. At periods there appears also a lava chimney from which smoke is emitted. All of the islands are of more or less volcanic origin. In Negros Island, the Canlauan Volcano sometimes can be seen to be in a state of eruption, and on the island of Camiguin the inhabitants awoke one morning to find that the territory which was the previous day a plain had become a volcanic mountain.

TERRORS OF PHILIPPINE JUNGLES.

Ordinarily, when one thinks of tropical lands, he pictures to himself visions of poisonous reptiles and beasts of prey which render life unsafe. The Philippines offer little to fear from either beast or reptile. The only beast of prey, known in the islands, is the wild cat, and the only wild animal which is greatly to be feared is the buffalo. The jungles and swamp' re filled with snakes and lizards, centipedes, spiders and tarantulas, but deaths resulting from poisonous contact with any of these are comparatively few.

The natives cure the bite of a centipede with a plaster of garlic crushed until the juice flows, which is renewed every hour. Rarely one comes across boa constrictors, which sound very terrible, but which really are the most harmless of all the snakes on the islands. The most fatal of the snakes are called by the natives *alupong* and *daghong palay*. Their bite is fatal if not cauterized at once. The latter is found in the deep mud of the rice fields and among the tall rice plants. Everywhere the stagnant waters are infested with leeches, and there is a small specimen of the same family which jumps into one's face in the dense forest, which, to say the least, is very annoying. Perhaps the greatest nuisances on the islands are the ants. They overrun everything, and are all shapes and sizes, consequently most of the furniture in one's house in Manila has to be protected by bowls of water to keep the ants from climbing up. The ant eats its way through most of the wood, and sometimes renders it necessary to pull down and rebuild great warehouses, owing to their inroads. Mosquitoes are troublesome, and rats and mice are very plentiful. There are plenty of bats, which afford a variety of sport, which is much indulged in by those who enjoy shooting. Deer and wild boar are also plentiful, and monkeys can be found in the forests. The great plague of locusts has already been referred to. In the mud of stagnant waters there is a kind of beetle called the *Tanga*, which the natives relish greatly as an article of food, and they bring as high as fifty cents a dozen.

The wild buffalo enables those who are anxious to look for dangerous sport to enjoy a buffalo hunt. The tame buffalo, however, is the great beast of burden of the Philippines. Everywhere one goes he sees this plodding and awkward beast, and the native regards him with the same affection that a man has in America for a horse. When a tame buffalo is six years old he is considered in the prime of life for hard work, and for another six years, if he is well taken care of, he will be able to continue doing just as hard labor. Then for five years after that, providing that he has always been very well treated, he will be able to do light labor and earn his keep.

It is a common sight to see the natives in Manila down at the riverside letting their buffaloes take a bath. It is an amphibious animal, and if it had its own way would pass one-third of its time in water or mud, and it is impossible to keep them healthy without bathing them at least once a day. The buffaloes are very strong and slow, but very easy to train. The people ride them without a saddle, and a child is able to guide them by means of a piece of split rattan attached to a string in the nostrils of the animal. They recognize the voices of different members of the families to which they belong, and will obey the command to come or stand still when spoken to.

Singularly enough the Europeans do not seem to be able to manage these buffaloes, as they have neither the patience, the voice or the peculiar movement which the natives use to handle them. The buffalo has not much endurance, and is unable to work more than a couple of hours during the hot part of the day without rest and a bath. If it receives a strain of any kind, or a broken leg, it rarely recovers, and it is subject to an affection of the throat and diseases of the blood which are sometimes epidemic and kill them off in great numbers. These buffaloes are worth from $10 to $30, according to the province, and to the use to which they are put.

The Philippines also have a small pony which is not indigenous, and which is a fairly good little animal. Pony races take place near Manila every spring, and while the meet lasts, it is a great occasion, being attended by the Governor-General and all of the better-class Spaniards of the city. The Philippines are filled with birds of beautiful plumage and rare coloring. Pheasants, snipe, wild ducks, wild pigeons and water fowl are common; parroquets, parrots, humming birds and dozens of others abound everywhere.

ILOILO, CAPITAL OF THE PROVINCE OF PANAY.

This city, on the Island of Panay, is next to Manila the most important seaport of the Philippines. It is built on a low marshy plain, but owing to surroundings enjoys an almost constant sea breeze, which makes it much cooler and healthier than Manila. It surrendered to the American forces February 11, 1899.

A NATIVE RESIDENCE IN THE SUBURBS OF MANILA.

Every cottage, however humble, is surrounded by tropical trees and flowers. The interiors are remarkably clean and cheerful. Bamboo enters largely into the construction of all native houses and they are generally covered with thatch.

THE STRANGE WAGONS OF ALBAY.

The eighty-odd different tribes who inhabit the Philippines have varying dialects, manners, and customs. The peculiar house-roofed wagons, shown in the above illustration, are found in only one locality.

CHAPTER XI

Manila, the Metropolis of the Philippines

A Delightful City which may become a Resort under the Stars and Stripes.—High and Low Life.—Foreigners kept out by the Spanish as much as Possible.—The Chinese Class.—The Splendid Big Convent.—Shops that Delight the Eye.—Rare Fabrics Woven from Plants and Embroidered by Nuns.—A New York Officer's Big Purchase.—A Dress that it took Months to Weave.—Inside of the English Club.—Americans have Started a Splendid Club for the Army and Navy.—The Famous Mestiza Girls.

WHEN, after valiant battle, the American troops entered the City of Manila, they found a curious but delightful old place without any sign of having been in touch with advanced civilization as it exists to-day, and bearing the ear marks of a land that had come down the years holding fast to the traditions of centuries ago, and not yielding to the touch of progress.

But there is something decidedly interesting in this capital city of Luzon, and a visit to it is well worth while, for the old city and the new, the odd people, the curious little houses, the estates of the rich, the hovels of the poor, and the customs, which are such a remarkable blending of Spanish and native, all contribute to make Manila an attractive temporary, if not permanent residence.

Coming up the muddy Pasig River and wending one's way through cascoes and dug-outs, the traveller comes to this old fortified city with its bastioned and battlement walls built way back in 1598. These walls are about two miles and a quarter long, and make the city a stronghold. All around the outer wall is water—on one side of it the Pasig River, on the other the sea, and around the rest the remnants, of an old moat, which has long ago gone into disuse, and which is now filled with stagnant slime and offensive water.

There are eight drawbridge entrances to the city proper, which up to 1852, were always raised at night closing the city effectually. But the earthquake in that year caused a change, and thereafter these ancient drawbridges were kept down. On the south side of the river, which is the city proper, are situated some government offices, branch post and telegraph offices, the colleges, convents, meteorological observatory, and artillery depot, a cathedral and eleven churches; on the other side of the river or rather on the island of Binondo, all of the business houses are situated, and this is the lively part of the city.

As you enter the bay you find two passages by the little island of Corregidor, on which is a light house, a signal station and the fort which sent the first shot to announce the fact that Dewey's vessels had entered the harbor.

ON THE STREETS OF MANILA.

The streets of the city are badly paved and badly lighted; petroleum lamps and cocoanut oil are largely used, although in later years electricity has been introduced in the more favored avenues and along the docks. The first thing which impresses one on entering the city is the lowness of the buildings. Hardly any of the residences are more than two stories in height and even in these the lower story is not used for living purposes, and is either uninhabited or used as servants' quarters on account of the dampness. The upper story usually has a very large hall, dining and reception rooms and sleeping rooms adjoining. The kitchen is often separate from the rest of the house being connected by a roofed passage. The ground floor is usually of stone or brick but the upper story is almost entirely made of wood, with sliding windows all around. These windows are filled with opaque oyster shells, instead of glass, as they admit the light but not the heat of the sun's rays.

There are no very high buildings in the city owing to the earthquakes. One of the interesting places is the great cathedral which is probably its most imposing building, although most of the churches stand out prominently because of the low structures which prevail on all sides. The City Hall, a number of government buildings, the palace of the Archbishop, and the Jesuit and Dominican colleges are also prominent features of the city's architecture.

The city has two lines of street cars, one of which runs through the Escolta which is the principal high-class business street and on through that portion of the city which is devoted to the residences of the Spanish; the other crosses the bridge and goes on up the Rosario, and out to the suburbs. It is funny in this out of the way land beyond the sea to come across street cars made in Philadelphia. They are very small and are drawn by single ponies of the diminutive Philippine pattern. The approach of the car is announced by the tooting of the horn of the driver.

ON THE LUNETA—THE GREAT DRIVE AND PROMENADE.

Old Manila is a very quiet happy-go-lucky sort of a place, without many attractions. The theatres do not amount to anything and rarely have performances worth going to. Were it not for occasional cockfights and for the numerous religious processions which bring out large crowds, and for the drives in the afternoon, the place would be very dull indeed. The great drive and promenade of the city is the Luneta, which is an oval piece of ground on which have been placed one or two stands for bands and chairs and benches for the crowd to sit around and listen to the music. In the evening the place is constantly thronged and the native bands, which are splendid organizations with skilled musicians, render programmes which delight the listener, and round and round this place in an apparently endless stream drive the carriages of the well-to-do people of the city, and the social rulers, going all the time in the same direction, for it is forbidden for anybody, except the Governor or Archbishop to drive in the opposite direction.

Here, on the Luneta, many a tragic scene has been enacted, for this ground of pleasure was also the execution place of the Spanish. Here they mowed down, before the gaze of a motley crowd of onlookers, the insurgents who had been condemned to death, and here, on the sea-wall, hundreds of poor unfortunates gave up their lives for their country.

On the Escolta, the chief business street, are the high-class stores of the city, that is the stores which keep European and American goods, which are very expensive owing to the high tax that is put on them when they are brought in. In these, very tempting things are displayed more for the Spanish residents and other foreigners, than for the natives.

The latter deal almost entirely with Chinese merchants, who occupy the nearby streets and especially the Rosario across the river which is lined from one end to the other with Chinese stores. They sell everything on earth that could be desired by the native and here the common people jostle each other and shop and enjoy themselves.

The sights in this quarter of the city are very interesting. The gay colors of the native costumes, mixing with those of the Chinamen, here and there the uniform of a Spanish soldier, occasionally a fair senorita driving by in her carriage, now and then some man wearing the garb of a religious order, and at the present time the ever-present uniform of the American soldier who has found in this quarter of the city the most attractive place for buying and for mingling with the natives and learning their curious habits.

The whole of Binondo across the river is usually pretty active. It is there that the British merchants have their import and export headquarters and a large part of the trade passes through their hands. It is a funny experience to go through these Chinese Bazaars or stores to buy. One proprietor probably owns three or four stores and sometimes ten or twelve, consequently if a customer does not like the price asked for an article he goes on to the next place and does no better, because the first man has run around the back way and told the other man how much he has asked for the article and so, being under one management, this one charges the same, so finally the customer pays the price asked.

The Chinese control such things as bootmaking, furniture making casting, painting, dyeing, while the natives are the silversmiths, the furniture polishers, the bookbinders, etc. The Germans had a monopoly of the drug stores not long ago, but the educated natives and half-castes have entered the field and are now largely controlling the business.

HACKMEN WHO DO NOT IMPOSE ON TRAVELERS.

When one wants to go around the city, he hires a carriage and Filipino pony, at a very moderate rate, and wonderful to relate, the driver will not try to cheat you. He charges you so much a mile, and very rarely overcharges.

During Holy Thursday and Good Friday of Easter week, the whole business of the town is absolutely suspended. Carriages, or any other vehicles are not allowed on the streets; the shops are closed and the whole city is still. Even the soldiers who are on duty are forced to point the muzzles of their guns to the ground as they walk along. All of the people who appear on the streets wear black, even the natives. There is an imposing religious procession on Good Friday afternoon, which winds through the city and out into the suburbs. All the church-bells are tolled with muffled hammers until after the following Saturday morning's mass. It is a curious sight to see the expectant throng of people waiting for the signal of unmuffled bells to announce that the feast is over. In all the alleys and by-ways, public and private vehicles are ready, and the minute the bells are rung, the streets become an active, shouting, jumbled mass of humanity, trying to make up for lost time in their business.

WHERE HOLIDAYS ARE PLENTIFUL.

The religious feasts and processions are so common that I have heard it stated that out of the 365 days in the year, 160 are holidays of some sort or other, chiefly Saints' days. Each village and each suburb, both in the capital and outside of it, is supposed to be looked after by some patron Saint, which has his special day, and every annual feast is taken as an excuse for a big procession.

IN A MANILA HOTEL—A MANILA BED.

There are in Manila two hotels, which are considered very good as hotels go. It takes a European some time to get used to the cooking of native dishes, and it takes him still longer to get used to the Philippine idea of comfort while asleep. It is no small task to wrestle with a Philippine bed, which is springless, unyielding and anything but comfortable. It has four high posts covered with lace curtains, and usually a mosquito bar. Where an American bed boasts springs, it has a rattan surface, similar to that of a rattan chair, which is extremely hard, and the thin mat which is placed over it and the hard pillow and almost as hard bolster which are given one to sleep on are not conducive to rest. It is rather a serious task to get into one of these beds without allowing the mosquitoes to precede you, but one gets the hang of it after awhile and manages to get to sleep. From 1 to 3 o'clock in the afternoon most people are asleep. Lunch hour all over the colony is noon, and the visiting hours are from 5 till 7 in the evening. Dinner is served at about 8 o'clock, and after that the more formal functions take place.

The social class distinction is not as rigidly carried out in Manila as it is in some of the British Colonies, India for example. The Spaniards exchange visits with some of the Mestiza class, and even with some of the wealthier of the natives. Everybody is hospitable as a rule to visitors. The government officials, however, have never encouraged the visits of foreigners to Manila; in fact, they have done their best to discourage them. Nevertheless there is quite a large colony of foreigners, all of them representatives of business firms, who do heavy trade with the islands.

Everywhere you go in Manila (or at least this was true during the Spanish regime), one would have a lottery ticket poked in his face. The lotteries were in control of the Spanish government, and they made a revenue amounting to half a million dollars annually from the sale of tickets.

COCKFIGHTING IN MANILA.

The Filipinos have a great passion for cockfighting, and this too was in control of the government, which received from it a very large return. Cockfighting is allowed only on Sundays and feast days, and, by special permission in Manila alone, on Thursdays. The tax for a pit is rented out to the highest bidder for a fixed sum. The laws in regard to this sport are very strict. The maximum amount which may be staked by any one person in one contest is $50, and it is regulated that the bird shall wear but one metal spur. The sport causes the same enthusiasm among the natives as horse racing does in England, and they will spend years training a bird which perhaps might be killed in the very first fight.

Much has been written about bullfights, which always took place at Placo. They were very mild affairs, at worst, and attracted a very inferior quality of the natives. Most of the fights were ludicrous instead of interesting, in which the fighters would go up and twist the tail of the bull or vault over his head as he came toward them in a mad rush, amid the hoots of the crowd.

There are five daily papers in Manila, three of which are considered good. This does not include the new paper which has just been founded by the army boys from the United States, which is a lively little sheet devoted to American interests.

One of the places which the American officers found open to them, and in which they have enjoyed many a pleasant evening, was the European Club, which occupies a very handsome place on the right bank of the Pasig River, about twenty minutes' drive from Manila. The controlling spirits in this organization are the English-speaking people employed in the big commercial houses, but a number of the prominent Spanish residents are also members of the club. As soon as the American troops landed on the island and took possession of Manila, the first thing the army men decided to do was to establish an American club, and negotiations were entered into for a splendid property in the residence section of the city, which doubtless by this time have been completed and the first steps taken for the introduction of American club life into the Philippines.

WEAVING PINA CLOTH IN THE CONVENTS.

There is more curiosity on the part of American soldiers in the weaving of the Filipinos than in anything else. The beautiful pina cloth, which is woven from the pineapple fibre, is a fabric which arouses the envy of every man who has a wife, sister or sweetheart in America. The weaving is done in the convents, and there hundreds of the natives, guarded by the nuns, work from morn until dewy eve, turning out the finest fabric and the most beautiful embroidery possible.

They embroider birds in natural plumage, flowers so natural that one thinks the odor will come from them, and fanciful designs that would cause the average American girl to catch her breath and break the commandment which forbids covetousness. One rich New York man, who is a volunteer officer, ordered a magnificently embroidered gown for his daughter. It cost a fortune, and people came from far and near to look at the material while it was being made, and for the two months during which these convent workers toiled over that beautiful fabric, it was the show piece of the whole city and one of the great attractions to all who were there.

The dainty handkerchiefs, embroidered with a skill that is wonderful; the magnificent screens of sandalwood, carved by native artists and containing fabric woven with the hands of experts; the equally dainty fans of sandalwood, covered with cloth and embroidered true to nature; the curious spoons wrought by the native workers, the magnificent silks offered at low prices by the Chinese merchants, all were tempting inducements to the army boys, and thousands of dollars were given in exchange for these gifts to be sent home.

Perhaps more is known of the Mestiza girls than of any other inhabitants of the island. They are the half-caste people, who are really the prettiest types of women on the island. They have long flowing hair which reaches almost to the ground, and its shiny blackness makes it beautiful to see. They too are the most graceful and noted of the dancers of the island, and there is scarcely a social function in which they do not figure conspicuously.

Such is the life in this, the leading city of our new possession. It is the abiding place of about 300,000 people, of which 200,000 are natives, 90,000 are Chinese and Chinese half-castes, 5,000 are Spanish and 3,000 white foreigners other than Spaniards.

It is the nearest mart to the civilized world outside. From it run the monthly Spanish mail steamers and the smaller boats which go to Hong Kong. Who knows what the future may bring forth for this, the chief town of the Philippines, in its ripe old age? Who knows how many ships will come and go under the policy of the open door? Who can tell what wealth will sail from out her ports now that above the arsenal, there flies the Stars and Stripes?

CHAPTER XII

Other Important Cities of the Islands

A Sight-seeing Trip to Iloilo, Second in Commercial Importance to Manila—Cebu, which once Outranked it, Leyte and other Places of Importance.—Scenes and Incidents among the Strange Population.—The Terrible Sultan of Sulu.—Superstitions of the Moros.—Funny Episodes of a very Lively Trip.

A VISIT to Iloilo, the second city of importance in the Philippines is extremely disappointing after one has been to Manila. The little mail steamer that takes you to the island of Panay, of which Iloilo is the capital, is a dingy little affair, but even it seems out of place as it comes to anchor in front of the shabby-looking creek on which Iloilo is situated. The shore is almost as nature made it, except for slight embankments of soil which have been thrown up to protect some of the produce houses against the water.

There is neither wharf nor improvements, and the steamers get as near the shore as it is possible for them to go, and then land their passengers over a plank which extends from the deck to the shore itself. It is a low, forbidding-looking place, this Iloilo. It is hot all of the time, and in addition to this it is dirty and badly cared for. From the point where the creek enters into the sea up to the square in the centre of the city there is a series of sheds, used to store sugar in, punctuated here and there by offices of commercial firms. The largest buildings in the place are the headquarters of the various tradespeople who have made Iloilo what it is. Not many years ago this town was unknown to the commercial world, and the annual crop of sugar which it drew from the island was practically allowed to go to waste because the expense of carrying it up to Manila left little profit for the owners of plantations, and did not encourage them to engage largely in business.

Then came the change. A number of English and German business men saw the opportunity for reaping a rich harvest from this very fruitful little isle, and they established headquarters there and

205

had direct communication with foreign ports. The result was that the unknown village of Iloilo soon surpassed Cebu in trade and became a town second only to Manila in size and in business importance.

IN THE ILL-KEPT SQUARE OF ILOILO.

In the square, which is, like most of the city, in a perpetually bad condition, are the church, the tribunal, the convent and a few small houses. At one side of this square is a new block of buildings made of brick, stone and wood, with iron roof, really the most respectable part of the city in appearance. The main street is the Calle Real, which does not run in a straight line, but winds its way out into the country. The houses make no pretence to beauty. They are of all shapes and sizes, and as for a building line on the streets such a thing is comparatively unknown, and in some places one has to walk off the pavement out into the middle of the road to pass a house.

All around are rows of dirty-looking little houses which are inhabited by the poorer class. Perhaps the most striking building in the place is the Government house, which is made of stone and wood. In front of it is a little garden in the shape of a semicircle, and in front of this is a little round fenced-in piece of ground, in the middle of which is a flag-pole. About one-third of the business quarter of the town is built on land which some years before was nothing but a swamp, and has been reclaimed by being filled up with earth.

All during the wet season the place is a mass of shallow pools and mud. It is a pretty expensive place to live in, and there is little to do after one gets there. One cannot hire any conveyance of any kind, and there are no theatres or places of amusement, unless a bowling alley may be classed under the latter head. The streets are practically deserted, except for bullock-carts filled with sugar cane.

Sugar is the chief stimulus to the life of the city. One can guess that readily, because the odor of it pervades the whole place. After the insurgents obtained possession of Iloilo, ruin and devastation played havoc with the town. It became more unkempt and uninviting than before, and when the American troops captured it, it was reeking with filth. At the other end of the island is the town of Concepcion, near which there are many exceedingly fertile sugar plantations. It is even a more despondent-looking place than the capital city. The whole place is dilapidated, the people are poverty-stricken, and, altogether, it is neither convenient nor pleasant to live in. From Concepcion it is but a short journey to Cebu, on the east coast of the island of the same name. Years ago this was a flourishing and important commercial center. It possesses considerable interests, inasmuch as it was the first place upon which the Spanish settled in the Philippines, and from 1565 to 1571 it was the capital of the whole colony.

Now it has a population of about 10,000. It forms quite a contrast to its rival, Iloilo, in that it is clean and well kept, and the roads which lead from it are in a very good condition for some miles. The city has a customhouse and is open to trade with the foreign countries. It has a cathedral, the Church of St. Nicholas, the chapels of the Paulist Fathers and the Jesuits and the Church of the Santo Nino, "the Holy Child of Cebu."

THE FAMOUS "HOLY CHILD OF CEBU."

This church is perhaps the most famous of all the religious places in the whole archipelago. It was on this spot that an image of the Christ Child was alleged to have been found in July, 1565, by a soldier named Juan de Camus. This image was venerated and kept by the Austin friars as though it were a sacred gift direct from Heaven. A fire occurred in the church in which the image stood in 1627, but the image itself was saved, and has been ever since considered the most wonderful of all the sacred relics of the island.

It is made of wood, is black, and is about fifteen inches in height. As it exists to-day, it is almost covered with valuable trinkets which have been presented to it. When it is shown to the public the occasion is always one of great festivity, and the image is worshiped with a fervor that is almost incredible. In fact, during the feasts held in its honor, natives come from all parts of the island to prostrate themselves before it.

In this city, too, is the spot where the first cross was erected upon the island on the day when Legaspi landed. This sacred relic also has the reputation of having been miraculously preserved. It is made of bamboo, and although the edifice in which it was placed was once burned to the ground, this cross rose unscathed from the flames, according to tradition, and is still worshiped second only to the wonderful image.

The channel which leads up to the city is marked by buoys, and there are four lighthouses which show the entrance to the port. Right in front of the city is Magtan Island, on which has been erected a monument to show the spot where Magellan, the discoverer of the Philippines, met his death by being mixed up with a conflict between two of the native chiefs.

Not far back of the city is a range of hills, from the top of which the view is extremely beautiful. In the ward of Pampango there still remains the old fortress of San Vidal, which was built when the Spanish first formed a settlement there. The Chinese shops are in the Lutao district, and the half-caste shops are chiefly grouped in the Parian, which was at one time the most important part of the city, but which has lately fallen in decay.

At Guadaloupe and Mabolo are the big cemeteries of the city, and at the end of the road leading to the former is the place where shooting contests and the annual pony races take place. On the way to Mabolo there is the hospital for lepers, those poor unfortunates, who sent over, sarcastically no doubt, as a gift from the Emperor of China, are still to be found both in Manila and in this, the original settlement of the Spanish, living out their loathsome lives, confined rigorously under the law, and a public charge until death comes to their relief.

The city has vice-consulates representing America, Great Britain, Italy and Germany, and there is quite a little colony of foreign residents there who are engaged in commerce. It is the residence of the Brigadier-Governor of the Visayas and of the Governor of the island.

The climate of the island is very healthy, and altogether it is a delightful place to live in. The whole population of the island is about 600,000.

But by far the most interesting, and, it may be added, the most troublesome of the residents of the archipelago, are those in the domain of the Sultan of Sulu. Since the Spaniards first landed on the Philippine Islands there has been more slaughter and more trouble from this little group of islands than from any of the larger islands, excepting perhaps Luzon. The very first overtures made to the ruler of the region round about Sulu resulted in the decapitation of the General who was sent to make the overtures, and the return of his body to the Governor at Manila, and that seemed to be the fate of all the first emissaries of the Spanish Government to this terrible Sultan.

And not only was he a terror to the Spanish, but he ruled over a people famous far and near as brigands and pirates. These natives, who call themselves Moros, but whom the Spanish call Mussulmans, are still as wild as they were in the old days, for civilization has had apparently no effect on them.

For over two centuries and a half their war junks visited every part of the adjoining islands and laid waste the territory. Thousands of the colonists were murdered, and others suffered a fate worse than death by being kept as slaves and made to serve the caprices of their captors. Villages and churches were destroyed, and for many years nothing was safe in the archipelago. They did not even stop at Luzon; and it is still in the minds of some who are alive how the approach of the pirates in the Bay of Manila struck terror into the hearts of the people. It was not until 1860 that any check at all could be put upon this reign of terror, but in that year eighteen steam gunboats, which cruised around the waters in the neighborhood, brought some degree of safety to the colonists, and piracy, as a wholesale business, became a thing of the past.

AN AGREEMENT WITH THE SULTAN OF SULU.

Many years before this occurred, the Sultan of Sulu entered into a compact with the Spanish authorities by which he acknowledged the sovereignty of the King of Spain, but this amounted only to as much as the parchment it was written on, for the Sultan of Sulu did as he pleased; and even if he personally were disposed to be friendly to the Spaniards, there was always a rival willing to take up the lance against him and oust him from his throne.

And so things went on until 1876, when the uprisings of the people attained such proportions that an expedition was necessary to enforce submission. A large body of troops, headed by Vice-Admiral

Malcampo, went to the islands, marched into the interior and incidentally into ambush, so that sacrifice of life was great. It, however, accomplished a little, and the Spanish flag was raised in several places, where it was still flying, before the United States came into possession of the islands.

RULER OVER ONE HUNDRED AND FORTY ISLANDS.

The domain under the rule of the Sultan comprises Sulu Island, which is about thirty-four miles long and twelve miles wide, and one hundred and forty smaller islands, half or more of which are not inhabited. The number of people embraced in the Sultan's dominion is about 107,000. Besides these, there is a half-caste branch of Mussulmans, nominally under this Sultan's rule, who inhabit the southern half of Palauan Island.

The present Sultan did not inherit the throne, but was practically elected by his own people. In 1885, when the rightful heir to the Sultanate was sent for to come to Manila to receive his investiture, he declined to comply, probably having in mind the fate of his predecessors who went to Manila for the same purpose and were made prisoners, and finally lost their lives. So the Spanish authorities announced that they would confer the Sultanate upon anybody the people elected.

An election was held, and when the throne was offered to the man chosen, he accepted and took the oath of allegiance to the King of Spain on the 24th of September, 1886. He was then given the title of His Excellency Paduca Majasari Malauna Amiril Mauminin Sultan Harun Narrasid. In addition to this he was given the rank and grade of a Spanish Lieutenant-General. The Sultan had hardly become settled in his new office before the leaders of what is called the National party, which is a party opposed to the acknowledgment of the dominion of Spain over the islands, rose up in arms against him. The insurrection spread to the adjoining islands of Siassi and Bongao. The chief of the latter island, whose name was Pandan, was arrested, and the garrison of Sulu was greatly reinforced and strengthened in the great expectation of a general uprising. In the meantime one of the most cruel of the Mussulman chiefs named Utto openly defied Spanish authority. Consequently an expedition was sent out against him, and after two months of vigorous fighting, peace was declared between the two, and the event was the sign for a great celebration at Manila, the feast lasting for some days.

Yet, notwithstanding the fact that, whatever expedition is sent against these savage tribes is successful, as far as victory in conflict is concerned, it is still true that little effect has been made upon the Mussulmans from the standpoint of civilization. They decline to learn either civilized religion or civilized ways, and, although kept down in places by force of arms, nevertheless, the moment the back of authority is turned, they instinctively turn to their weapons and savagery wins the day.

A FORTUNE SPENT IN SUBJUGATION.

It has cost a fortune for the Spaniards to gain the little foothold which they have had; and yet, even then, it was not safe for Spanish officers to wander very far out of town without a strong body-guard.

Under the present state of things, that is, the state of things that existed before the possession of the islands by the United States, the Sultan of Sulu received a salary of $2,400 from the Government of Spain. He was practically the lord and master of all his subjects and all that they owned. He was supported by three ministers, a Minister of War, a Minister of Justice, and another one who acts in his capacity when he leaves.

John Foreman tells of a very interesting trip which he made in 1881 to the Sultan of Sulu. The danger of such a trip may be imagined when it is stated that a young officer had been sent on some mission just outside of the town accompanied by two guards, and had returned with one of his hands cut off as a souvenir of a brush with the Mussulmans; a number of military officers were sitting in a cafe in the town when a number of Mussulmans came up behind them and cut their throats. Both of these events took place a day or two before Mr. Foreman's trip. Describing his visit, Mr. Foreman said:

"On our arrival at Maybun, we went first to the bungalow of a Chinaman—the Sultan's brother-in-law—where we refreshed ourselves with our own provisions and learned the gossip of the place. On inquiry, we were told that the Sultan was sleeping, so we waited at the Chinaman's. I understood this man was a trader, but there were no visible signs of his doing any business. Most of our party slept the siesta, and at about 4 o'clock we called at the palace. It was a very large building, well constructed, and appeared to be built almost entirely of materials of his country. A deal of bamboo and wood were used in it, and even the roof was made of split bamboo, although I am told that this was replaced by sheet iron when the young Sultan came to the throne. The vestibule was very spacious, and all around pleasantly decorated with lovely shrubs and plants peculiar to most mid-tropical regions. The entrance to the palace is always open, and we were received by three *Dattos*, who saluted us in a formal way, and, without needing to ask us any question, invited us, with a wave of the hand, to follow into the throne-room.

IN THE PRESENCE OF THE SULTAN.

"The Sultan was seated, on our entering, but when the bearer of the despatches approached with the official interpreter by his side, and with us following, he rose in his place to greet us.

"His Excellency was dressed in very tight silk trousers, fastened partly up the sides with showy chased gold or gilt buttons, a short Eton-cut olive green jacket, with an infinity of buttons, white socks, ornamented slippers, a red sash around his waist, a kind of turban, and a kris at his side. One could almost have imagined him to be a Spanish bullfighter with an Oriental finish-off.

"We all bowed low, and the Sultan, surrounded by his Sultanas, put his hands to his temples, and, on lowering them, he bowed at the same time. We remained standing, whilst some papers were handed to him. He looked at them—a few words were said in Spanish, to the effect that the bearers saluted His Excellency in the name of the Governor of Sulu. The Sultan passed the documents to the official interpreter, who read or explained them in Sulu language; then a brief conversation ensued, through the interpreter, and the business was really over. There was a pause, and the Sultan motioned to us to repose on cushions on the floor, and we did so. The cushions, covered with rich silks, were very comfortable. Servants, in fantastic costumes, were constantly in attendance, serving betel nut to those who cared to chew it.

"One Sultana was fairly pretty, or had been so, but the remainder were heavy, languid and lazy in their movements; and their teeth, dyed black, did not embellish their personal appearance. The Sultan made various inquiries, and passed many compliments on us, the Governor, Governor-General and others, which were conveyed to us through the interpreter. Meanwhile, the Sultanas chatted amongst themselves, and I guessed they must have been criticizing us as much as we were observing their guise, features, attire, etc. They all wore light colored "dual garments" of great width and tight bodices. Their coiffure was carefully finished, but unfortunately a part of the forehead was hidden by an ugly fringe of hair—a disfigurement which, however, is common among Hongkong Eurasians and some European ladies.

"We had so little in common to converse on, and that little had to be said through an interpeter, that we were rather glad when we were asked to take refreshments. They at least served to relieve the awkward feeling of looking at each other in silence. Chocolate and ornamental sweetmeats were brought to us, but what frightful mixture the chocolate was, I could not tell, I believe it was made with cocoanut oil, and to avoid a scene consequent on an indisposition, I elected to leave it.

"We were about to take our departure, when the Sultan invited us to remain all night in the palace. The leader of our party caused to be explained to him that we were thankful for his gracious offer, but that being so numerous, we feared to disturb His Excellency by intruding so far on his hospitality. Still the Sultan politely insisted, and whilst the interpretation was being transmitted, I found an opportunity to let our chief know that I had a burning anxiety to stay at the palace for the curiosity. In any case, we were a large number to go anywhere, so our leader, in reply to the Sultan, said, that he and four of his accompaniment would take advantage of His Excellency's kindness.

"We withdrew from the Sultan's presence, and walked through the town in company with some functionaries of the Royal household. There was nothing very striking in the town; it was like most others. There were some good bungalows of bamboo and thatching. I noticed that men, women and children were smoking tobacco or chewing and had no visible occupation. Many of the smaller dwellings were built on piles out to the sea. We saw a number of divers preparing to go off to get pearls, mother-of-pearl, etc. They are very expert in the occupation, and dive as deep as one hundred feet. Prior to the plunge, they go to a grotesque performance of waving their arms in the air and twisting their bodies in order—as they say—to frighten away the sharks; then with a whoop, they leap over the edge of the prahu, and continue to throw their arms and legs about for the purpose mentioned. They often dive for the shark and rip it up with a kris.

A NIGHT IN THE SULTAN'S PALACE.

"Five of us retired to the palace that night, and were at once conducted to our rooms. There was no door to my room; it was, strictly speaking, an alcove. During the night, at intervals of about every hour, as it seemed to me, a palace servant or guard came to inquire how the senor was sleeping, and if I were comfortable, 'duerme el senor?' (does the gentleman sleep?) was apparently the limit of his knowledge of Spanish. I did not clearly understand more than the fact that the man was a nuisance, and I regretted there was no door with which to shut him out. The next morning we paid our respects to His Highness, who furnished us with an escort—more as a compliment than a necessity—and we reached Sulu town again, after a very enjoyable ride through a superb country."

"These Sulu Islanders have no compunctions of conscience about killing people, and the habit seems to be so deeply rooted in them, that it cannot be eradicated. Mr. Foreman illustrates this as follows: 'In 1884, a Mussulman was found on a desolate isle lying off the Antigue coast (Panay Island), and of course, had no documents of identity, so he was arrested and confined in the jail of San Jose de Buenavista. It was rather a rough way of treating any unfortunate castaway. From prison he was eventually taken to the residence of the Spanish Governor, a very humane gentleman, and a personal friend of mine. There he worked for some little time among the other domestics.

"In the study of Don Manuel, the Governor, there was a collection of native arms, which took the fancy of the Mussulman. One morning he seized a kris and lance, and, bounding into the breakfast room, capered about, gesticulated and brandished the lance in the air much to the amusement of the Governor, and his guests. But in an instant the fellow (hitherto a mystery, but undoubtedly a *juramentado*), hurled the lance with great force towards the public prosecutor, and the missile, after severing his watch-chain, lodged in the side of the table. The Governor and the public prosecutor at once closed with the would-be assassin, whilst the Governor's wife, with great presence of mind, thrust a table knife into the culprit's body between the shoulder blade and the collar bone. The man fell as if dead, and, when all supposed that he was so, he suddenly jumped up. No one had thought of taking the kris out of his grasp, and he rushed around the apartment, severely cut two of the servants, but was ultimately despatched by the bayonets of the guards who arrived on hearing the scuffle. The Governor showed me his wounds, which were slight, but his life was saved by the valor of his wife—Dona Justa."

"The costumes worn by the Sulu Islanders are very original and striking. The women wear gay colors, with a preference for green and scarlet. Their skirt, if such it may be called, or double lower garment, is very loose, and their upper clothing is extremely tight. Their hair is worn in a coil on the top of the head, and they are very much better looking than most of the people of the Philippines. They are extremely fond of jewelry, and their hands and ears are filled with rings, sometimes of metal, but more often of sea-shells.

The men wear costumes which are equally as bright as those of the women, but the fit of the costume is reversed, that is, their upper garment is very loose, while their lower ones are as tight as a gymnast's. Their whole attire is plentifully sprinkled with buttons, and to crown it all, they add a turban, which is very picturesque, and which tells their rank by the way in which it is tied. They are strong, agile, and rather attractive looking savages, and extremely brave. For weapons they have daggers, lance-heads, and so on, manufactured on the anvil, showing a certain knowledge of the arts, and an expertness of workmanship. The most curious thing they use, is a coat of mail, made of buffalo horn and wire, the latter probably obtained from Singapore. It protects splendidly against arrows or sword thrusts but not bullets. They are great pearl fishers, and the Sultan claims a right to all of the pearls which are of an unusually large size. They are very devout according to their own ideas of religion, and their priests are usually the most influential men in the various tribes. They have one day in the week devoted absolutely to worship, in which they all go to their temples and listen to the prayers and recitations of their priests.

A NATIVE FUNERAL.

On the birth or death of a child or some other important event they have a very solemn ceremonial. They keep a New Year's feast and during the year they have several days of fasting. All of the young men above fifteen years of age are supposed to be enrolled in the service of the Sultan, and are forced to carry arms. The priests are the doctors as well. Whenever a chief dies they chant a funeral hymn, and the bereaved family goes about lamenting, accompanied by the noise of symbals and gongs. The neighbors rush in and join in the general lament, and as soon as that is over, they all sit down to a feast. The body is sprinkled with salt and camphor, but is buried with very little ceremony. The grave is marked by a stone or wooden tablet, and a slip of board of bamboo is placed around it, and a piece of wood carved like the bows of a canoe is stuck in the earth nearby, with a cocoanut shell full of water in front of it.

The town of Sulu proper is built on the plain not very much above sea level. Its barracks are as fine as those in Manila. There are some houses of stone and brick, and others of wood, with corrugated iron roofs. The church is impretentious. There are tasteful gardens and squares around, and the whole city is well laid out and well drained.

"It is supplied with water conducted in pipes from a spring about a mile and a quarter away. By this, and the excellent drainage, the place has become very healthful, although once it was a hot bed of fever. Around the town is a wall, constructed for defence, with two forts outside and three inside. It is a lively, interesting town, and a nice place to live in as long as one remains inside of the fortifications.

The inhabitants of the Sulu Islands are exceedingly superstitious. They are naturally afraid of anything they do not know all about, and consequently all travelers in that country report that it is exceedingly difficult to get photographs of them, as they turn and flee whenever the camera is pointed at them. They think, according to some of the travelers, that they would die in a short time if photographed.

A NATIVE WEDDING.

Dean C. Worcester, in his excellent work on the Philippine Islands, describes a native wedding, which is exceedingly interesting. He says:

"By exercising considerable diplomacy we contrived to get admission. We were shown into a large, poorly-lighted room, which had a good floor of hewn timber. The well-to-do Moros of the whole region round were assembled. Such gaudy costumes we had never seen. They were silk, for the most part, and the pinks, purples, scarlets, blues and greens were simply gorgeous. At one side of the room was an 'orchestra.' The chief musical instrument consisted of a wooden frame over which were strung cords that supported nine small kettledrums, tuned to the notes of the scale. A woman, kneeling before this affair, beat out rude airs on it with a pair of sticks. Large kettledrums were suspended from the ceiling, and on the floor were several double-ended wooden drums with heads of python skin.

"The kettledrums were made of bell metal, and the combination of sounds produced by the various instruments was by no means unpleasant at first, though its monotony wearied one in time.

"On one side of the room the floor was strewn with mattresses and cushions, among which lounged the prospective bridegroom surrounded by friends. The centre of the floor was cleared for dancing; in fact, dancing was going on when we entered. The performers came out one at a time, and their movements were critically watched and freely commented on by the spectators. Moro dancing consists chiefly of contortions of the body above the waist, and movements of the arms, wrists, and hands. The feet are used comparatively little.

"Some of the attitudes assumed by the dancers were very graceful; others were decidedly grotesque, and interesting only as they showed into what remarkable shapes human forms could be twisted. Tiny children executed timid steps, and an old woman, white-haired, toothless, and nearly bent double, took her turn with the rest, winning great applause.

"The bride, meanwhile, was in a small side room making her toilet. We inferred from the sounds we heard that she had plenty of help. The bridegroom donned his costume in public, putting it on over the handsome Moro suit that he already wore. First came a pair of gauze trousers several sizes too large, then a shirt of similar material, quite too small; next his companions produced a skirt of rich silk, into which he climbed with great difficulty. He evidently was not accustomed to skirts. Finally they brought out two long ribbons, one embroidered with gold and one with silver. These were so arranged that they crossed on his back and breast while both encircled his waist. The costume was apparently public property, intended for use on such occasions.

"Two panditas now came in. The groom squatted on the floor and the panditas squatted before him. A saucer of live coals was set between them, and incense burned in it. One of the priests took five large rings and put them on the fingers and thumb of the groom's right hand; then, holding the hand in a peculiar way he recited a long rigmarole, which was, unfortunately, lost on us. At its end the groom and his friends made some sudden exclamation.

"The other pandita now began to sing, very softly at first, then louder and louder. At this signal six young ladies, whom we may as well call bridesmaids, entered the room and seated themselves among the cushions at some distance from the groom. One of them had false finger-nails of silver, two inches long. Their faces were painted white with rich paste. Their eyebrows were artificially broadened, and brought together between the eyes. "Beaucatchers," pasted flat to their cheeks, ran around their ears. Their front hair was banged, and their back hair—but only a woman could describe that. They sat down with great deliberation, and, with one exception, kept still as statues until the ceremony was over.

THE ENTRANCE OF THE BRIDE.

"The bride entered, but people crowded around her so that we could not at first see her. She was dressed like her maids, but rather more elegantly. She took position near the groom, turned her back on him in a very pointed manner, and sat down. He and his friends now rose, formed in line, and made a slow and circuitous pilgrimage to where she was sitting. After many pauses and much marking time they reached their destination, and the groom made some advances which the bride promptly repulsed. He then sat down and gazed disconsolately at her back.

"The crowd extended their sympathy to him, and urged the bride to relent, but she refused. One of the bridesmaids at last arose and favored the audience with a long solo which we could not well understand, but she seemed to be giving the groom a very bad reputation. She finally finished and resumed her place. After more entreaties from the crowd the bride arose, turned toward the groom, and sat down again. This ended the ceremony, but when we went to supper the newly wedded man and wife were still sitting there and staring stupidly at each other."

OTHER ISLANDS OF THE ARCHIPELAGO.

The island of SAMAR, which is about 5,300 square miles in area, has as its capital Catbalogan. It is a small town, much more clean than most of these towns on the smaller islands, and lies on the north shore of a picturesque bay on the west coast. There are several shops in the town, but very little else to attract one's attention. The main business of the place is dealing in abaca, that is, buying, curing, and balling it. Plenty of fish can be obtained there, but poultry, eggs, and even fruit are scarce, and very expensive.

The island itself is much overgrown with vegetation, and is, practically, a series of jungles. To travel there means to run the risk of scorpions and centipedes, which are liable to give one much annoyance, if not proving even more serious. There are ants, too, in extraordinary quantities, consequently the enjoyment of exploration in Samar is limited. All through the hills are a number of clearings made by natives who take this method of avoiding the payment of taxes or escaping from the oppression of priests and public officials. Besides its large crop of abaca, the island also produces quantities of valuable timber. Several of its rivers are quite large, but the mountains, for the most part, are low and unimportant. The climate is favorable and fairly healthful.

PALAWAN has an area of about 4,150 square miles. Its chief city is Puerto Princesa. This island is known to the Spaniards as

Paraqua. It was formerly part of the territory of the Sultan of Borneo. The northern end was fortified by the Spaniards in the eighteenth century in order to protect themselves from the Moros. Some years afterward the Sultan of Borneo gave up the whole island to Spain, and another garrison was established, in order to hold it, at Tay-Tay. The capital of the island, which is situated on the bay, is a fairly prosperous place, without the defences. It is called a naval station because it has a place for repairing vessels, and two gunboats are usually quartered there. It is a very unusual thing for any vessels, except the regular mail steamers, to touch at this place, so when a man lands there, he is practically shut off from the rest of the world until the next steamer is due.

Palawan is the most western of all the more important islands of the Philippine group. It is about 300 miles long, and has an average breadth of about twenty miles. It is well watered by many streams, and has a high range of mountains, as a sort of backbone, in the interior. It is rich in splendid timber lands, which contain valuable hard woods, such as ebony. As to mineral wealth there is very little known. Puerto Princesa is, perhaps, better known as a penal settlement than anything else. Convicts and prisoners are sent there from other places, and they usually settle there after their term of imprisonment expires, as they have no money to pay their passage home. The natives are divided into three classes. The Moros, who are the most warlike of the inhabitants, live in the southern part; the Tagbanuas live along the northern coast, and the Battaks live in the northern mountain region. The Tagbanuas are the most peaceful of the residents. All through the island there are plenty of large-sized pythons, some of which measure twenty-three or twenty-four feet in length, and weigh about 350 pounds.

MINDORA has an area of about 4,500 square miles. It is directly south of Manila Bay. Its capital is Calapan, and the whole island is very much avoided by all white men, owing to its deadly fevers. There was a time when it was very prosperous and produced large quantities of rice, but to-day the once rich fields are overgrown with trees and shrubbery, and have become haunted by escaped criminals, who know that no possible inducement could persuade the Spanish to follow them. The island is chiefly inhabited by a tribe called Mang-

A POPULAR STREET CONVEYANCE.

As elsewhere, carriages and street cars are used in Manila, but there are hundreds of the above "native cabs," for carrying single persons short distances, and they are liberally patronized.

DRYING SUGAR.

Large pans containing the sugar are set in the sun to evaporate the moisture. No refining or clarifying machinery has been introduced into the Philippine Islands.

A NATIVE MINING CAMP IN LUZON

Gold, sulphur, iron and tin are found in the Philippines, and recent researches have caused experts to believe "the whole country is a virgin mine." Scientific mining, however, is as yet unknown. The natives have washed gold from the sands of the streams from time immemorial. Magellan had hardly landed before he began to barter with the natives for their golden ornaments.

yans, who have a very bad reputation; but, according to more recent travelers, this is undeserved. They are, for the most part, friendly natives.

NEGROS is nearby Cebu, and has an area of 2,300 square miles. Its capital is Dumaguete, a much better class of town than one usually finds. The Chinese are the merchants of the place, and the population is made up almost entirely of natives of the island. In this town are public buildings of unusual size, together with a church and convent. On the island, is an active volcano called Malaspina or Canlooan, which is over 8,000 feet high. This is, probably, the richest island of its size in the archipelago, and much of the land near the coast is cultivated. Its chief product is sugar, although there is some fine tobacco in the Escalante region. So great is the sugar crop that a number of modern sugar mills have been established upon the larger estates.

CEBU contains about 1,650 square miles. It has a capital of the same name, which has already been spoken of. MASBATE is another island of importance, with an area of 1,315 square miles. The chief town is Palanog, which is built on high ground quite near the bay. It is very small, and the only buildings of importance are the church and the schoolhouse. The natives of the island are, for the most part, quite civilized. Rice is raised in parts of the island, and live stock forms the chief industry. BOHOL, the next island in size, has an area of 925 square miles. CATANDUANES has an area of 450 square miles, and there are a dozen or more islands which vary in size from 100 to 250 square miles.

Little is known of these smaller places, and, indeed, the whole series of islands in the archipelago offer a fruitful field to the explorer. They will probably be of little use to Uncle Sam, and may be a source of great annoyance, inasmuch as the natives on many of them are still followers of piratical leaders, and given to taking the law in their own hands.

CHAPTER XIII.

The Future of the Islands

How they will Develop under the Care of the United States.—The Treaty of Peace at Paris and its Effect.—What President McKinley says about the Situation. —Extracts from his Famous Speeches on the Subject.—Views of Anti-Expansionists.—Extracts from Speeches made by Senators and others.—Freedom and Prosperity in Sight for the Long Misgoverned Islands.

SUCH are the islands of the past and present, but what of the future? The wings of peace, hovering over the two battling nations, brought a cessation of hostilities. The war was over, practically, and there lay before both Spain and America the task of formally agreeing to terms of peace and the adoption of a peace treaty. The President appointed a commission consisting of Ex-Secretary of State W. R. Day, Senator Cushman K. Davis, Senator George E. Gray, Senator William P. Frye, and Hon. Whitelaw Reid to go to Paris and meet a similar body appointed to represent Spain in the negotiations. There was a long struggle between the two before any agreement could be reached; but finally, after two months of debate, a treaty embracing seventeen articles was signed by the representatives of both countries.

TERMS OF THE TREATY OF PEACE.

Under the terms of the treaty Spain agreed to renounce all sovereignty over Cuba, and when the island was evacuated it should be occupied temporarily by the United States until a stable government could be established by the Cubans. Spain ceded to the United States Porto Rico and her other islands in the West Indies, and the Isle of Guam, in the Ladrones, and, most important of all, the whole of the Philippines, the United States agreeing to pay $20,000,000 within three months after the ratification of the treaty. Spanish ships are to be admitted to the ports of the Archipelago under the same conditions as ships from the United States during a term of ten years. All prisoners of war are to be liberated under the treaty. Both countries renounce all claims for national or private indemnity resulting from the war.

These, in a nutshell, are the main terms of the treaty. The greatest stumbling block to the agreement of the commissioners was the disposal of the Philippines. Spain gave them up with the greatest reluctance, and for a time it looked as though, on account of the islands, all of the negotiations would come to naught and that hostilities would again be resumed. And not only was this question of the possession of the Philippines warmly debated by these commissioners. Immediately people of prominence in the United States arrayed themselves on one side or the other as to the advisability of our keeping the islands. Every speech by the leaders of politics for months rang with sentiments bearing upon this important national issue, the most important that has faced the country for many years. Arguments of expansionists clashed with those of the anti-expansionists. The administration and its closest allies favored expansion, and most of the prominent Republicans of the country espoused this side of the cause. The Democrats for the most part were against expansion, led by Ex-President Grover Cleveland and William J. Bryan.

There was a warm debate over the treaty in the Senate, and just as its passage seemed to be in jeopardy news came from Manila of the savage attack of the insurgents, led by Aguinaldo, upon the American troops, and the fierce fighting that followed turned the tide of feeling. The next day the treaty of peace was ratified, and the Philippines became ours by the double right of conquest and purchase.

But the great question of the future of these beautiful and rich islands remains unsolved. The treaty of peace leaves the matter of their government to be regulated later, and the great issue of the coming presidential campaign will probably swing around this pivot. The ablest minds of our nation seem to differ on the question of territorial expansion. Their arguments are interesting. Without comment *pro* or *con* the opinions of the most distinguished men of the day on this question are given herewith. These opinions are chosen with a view to giving the ablest representatives both for and against expansion.

President McKinley gave his views on this vital question in a speech made at the Atlanta Peace Jubilee. He said:

"The flag has been planted in two hemispheres, and there it remains, the symbol of liberty and law, of peace and progress. Who will withdraw from the people over whom it floats its protecting folds? Who will haul it down?

"The peace we have won is not a selfish truce of arms, but one whose conditions presage good to humanity. The domain secured under the treaty yet to be acted upon by the Senate came to us not as the result of a crusade of conquest, but as the reward of temperate, faithful, and fearless response to the call of conscience which could not be disregarded by a liberty-loving and Christian people.

"We have so borne ourselves in the conflict and in our intercourse with the powers of the world as to escape complaint or complication, and give universal confidence of our high purpose and unselfish sacrifices for struggling peoples.

"The task is not fulfilled. Indeed, it is only just begun. The most serious work is still before us, and energy of heart and mind must be bent, and the impulses of partisanship subordinated to its faithful execution. This is the time for earnest, not faint, hearts.

"New occasions teach new duties. To this nation and every nation there come formative periods in its life and history. New conditions can be met only by new methods. Meeting these conditions hopefully and facing them bravely and wisely is to be the mightiest test of American virtue and capacity. Without abandoning past limitations, traditions and principles, but by meeting present opportunities and obligations we shall show ourselves worthy of the great trust which civilization has imposed upon us.

"At Bunker Hill liberty was at stake; at Gettysburg the Union was the issue; before Manila and Santiago our armies fought, not for gain or revenge, but for human rights. They contended for the freedom of the oppressed, for whose welfare the United States has never failed to lend a helping hand to establish and uphold, and I believe never will.

"The glories of the war cannot be dimmed, but the result will be incomplete and unworthy of us unless supplemented by civil victories harder, possibly, to win, in their way no less indispensable

"We will have our difficulties and embarrassments. They follow all victories and accompany all great responsibilities. They are inseparable from every great movement or reform. But American capacity has triumphed over all in the past. Doubts have in the end vanished.

"Thus far we have done our supreme duty. Shall we now, when the victory won in war is written in the treaty of peace, and the civilized world applauds and waits in expectation, turn timidly away from the duties imposed upon the country by its own great deeds? And when the mists fade, and we see with clearer vision, may we not go forth rejoicing in a strength which has been employed solely for humanity and always been tempered with justice and mercy, confident of our ability to meet the exigencies which await, because confident that our course is one of duty and our cause that of right."

POSTMASTER GENERAL SMITH'S VIEWS.

One of the most vigorous orations in behalf of the new policy was made by the Postmast-Gereneral, Charles Emory Smith, at Omaha, during the Exposition. He said:

"This war has opened a new career, and we joyfully turn from its thrilling drama to the grandeur of the peaceful mission which it ushers in. We turn to the contemplation of peace and its duties with the consciousness of a new position and a new power. We have stepped out on the broad stage of the world's action; we have advanced from continental dominion to world influence; we have moved out of the isolation of a great but still limited and self-circumscribed sphere into the large arena of the world's activities; and if in this departure there are the risks and possibilities which attend all human progressive enterprise there are also necessities and obligations from which we cannot shrink and opportunities and glories which beckon us onward.

"The world's acknowledged tribute is the measure of its estimate of the potency of our new position. Our use of that position will be the measure of our wisdom and rulership. Equal to every crisis in the past, we shall deal with this new emergency in the true American spirit. It makes us responsible for Cuba. It gives us Porto Rico. It plants our outposts on the farther side of the globe. Whatever we hold, whether it be more or less, will be held not for territorial aggrandizement, but solely in acceptance of responsibilities which Providence has laid upon us.

"Men lightly talk of 'imperialism.' Our imperialism is not territorial lust, but benignant trade expansion and civilizing influence, and our flag is at Manila, not in a spirit of spoliation, not in either the greed or the glory of conquest, but, let it be reverently said, under the controlling force of a providential guidance, at the ripe hour in the development and requirements of our national growth.

"For the coincidences are clear and unmistakable. This has come just at the time when we needed broader commercial scope and new outlets. It came just at the time when all the great powers are engaging in a keen, vigilant and aggressive rivalry of trade opportunity and extension. It came just at the time when the ancient and colossal empire of China, with a quarter of the world's population, is opening her doors. It came just at the time when we were turning our longing eyes across the Pacific for a share of the trade and when we needed a base of commercial enterprise in the Orient. And the thunder of our cannon at Manila, under the sudden uplifting of a veil which no vision could have penetrated, gave us in a day the prestige, the position and the opportunity which years of ordinary history and endeavor would never have brought.

"It is treated in many quarters simply as a question of territorial expansion, but that is a secondary and incidental consideration. The great and overshadowing question is one of commercial openings. The heart of the issue is not mere territory, but trade necessities and facilities. Beyond and behind and beneath this departure lies the broad problem of America's destiny in the commerce and civilization of the world.

"Others speak, and rightly speak, of what is due to those darkened people to whom our starry flag has brought the radiant sunshine of hope and life. Let me suggest what is due to ourselves and our future in the steady march of our development? Our growth has been so marvelous that we need new opportunities; and our fate is so happy that the opportunities are here for our taking.

"The imperial Louisiana acquisition, in the heart of which we now stand, and which has become the seat of twelve mighty States and fifteen millions of happy people, was dictated by the demand for the commercial outlet of the Mississippi; and under the stress of that necessity Thomas Jefferson broke away from old ideas and rose to a larger statesmanship. Our need to-day, like that of a hundred years ago, is for commercial outlets, and it is for the descendants of our fathers to rise to our occasion and duty as our fathers rose to theirs.

"Our past policy has established our industrial independence. It has enabled us to outstrip all other nations, and has endowed us with a present attainment and a potential force which almost baffle the imagination. We are immeasurably the greatest consumers among men, but our productive capacity has grown beyond our wants, and now looks to the markets of the world. We make one-half as much iron and steel, the basic fabrics of civilization, as all other countries put together. We produce one-half as much coal. We use one-half as much wool. Our motive power, our railroad operations, our general business are in the same or greater ratio. The savings out of our earnings in the last thirty years amounted to one-sixth of all that the world has saved and handed down since the dawn of the Christian era. We are the only great commercial nation which sells more than it buys. We are the only nation which is absolutely independent, untrammeled and self-supporting within itself. While we were growing up we sent abroad food and brought home equipment. But now that our American policy has realized its ultimate aim and its full fruition in our unchallenged industrial supremacy we are sending not only the products of our farms, but the products of our forges and factories.

"We place our pipes in the streets of London; we land our tubing at Singapore; we sell our paper in Japan; we send our machinery all over the world. The hour when our manufactured exports passed our manufactured imports marked the turning point of commercial mastery and opened new vistas before us. Having gained the undisputed control of our vast domestic market, we boldly enter into the world's trade competition.

"Yet, with all this achievement, we have in many fields but just begun the development of our enormous resources. We grow seven-eighths of the world's cotton, but we manufacture only a fourth of it. We consume more of some leading products of the tropics than all

BRIDGE OVER THE PASIG RIVER.

This bridge connects the old walled city on one side of the river with the new unwalled city on the other. Sea-going vessels ascend the river as far as the bridge.

A WEDDING PROCESSION.

As in Asiatic countries, weddings in the Philippines are occasions of great ceremony. This engraving shows a wedding procession in the Philippine Islands as photographed by an enterprising American. The bride and groom are inside the chairs born on the shoulders of the men.

ALL-CHINESE-SHOP QUARTER ON THE ROSARIO

The Filipinos despise the Chinese for their cowardice and duplicity. Spain imposed a special tax upon all Chinamen in the islands. Nevertheless, they have always been the leaders in commerce, the natives and Europeans not being able to compete with them. Their superior industry, shrewdness cunning, and frugality enable them to amass fortunes easily. Many of them are fabulously rich.

other nations; but we have had no proportionate share of their trade. While the amazing multiplication of our productive capacity, there is no limit to our possible development but the world's needs. In twenty-five years we shall be a nation of a hundred millions, equalling all Europe in energy of creation, and to contemplate the dazzling splendor of that beneficent destiny, if only the growth of the past twenty-five years shall be maintained, seems like the rhapsody of a dream.

"If we are to fulfill that destiny we must have commercial expansion; and it is a profoundly significant fact which shows a guiding hand that overrules the will of man that this war should have come just as this great necessity begins to be realized. This opportunity matches the need. The elevation of the United States to a new rank among the nations; the universal acceptance of its obligation to stretch forth its civilizing hand where the fate of war has carried it; the fortunate possession of an established emporium on the very theatre of the world's seeking have brought the occasion and the duty together. Is it not for enlightened American statesmanship, watchful of American interests, to use the opportunity, not in territorial avarice, but for commercial extension and civilizing influence in the Orient with the base and the bulwark that are needed for its support?

"Trade follows the flag. Around the waters of the Orient dwell more than a quarter of the human race. Among these ancient peoples there is agitation and awakening. The old walls of isolation and seclusion will be broken down, and in throwing off the thraldom of ancient prescription and primitive life, there will be the invitation and the inroad of civilizing instruments and influences. We shall enter into no struggle of imperial division; but why should we not share the opening traffic of that vast region? Why should not our mills use our own cotton, now sent abroad, and multiply our spindles in clothing China? Why should we not furnish her electric power and materials? Why should we not join in laying the rails of the new lines of communication that are to set her sluggish life in motion? Why should we not find in the requirements of a vast people, arousing from their ages of torpor, one of the openings that are needed for our surplus manufactures?

"The Pacific is rightfully within our commercial sphere. We hold one shore, and we are nearest the other. Europe must cross two oceans to the Orient, and we but one. Why should we not peacefully and providently avail ourselves of the commercial advantages within our grasp? We have, besides, learned the value and the needs of a navy. Dewey, respecting the neutrality of Hong Kong, had nowhere on the broad Pacific to rest his foot save on his own deck, and under the signal from Washington he steamed straight to Manila, defiant of mine and of fort, because the Spanish fleet was there, and because he needed and proposed to make an American harbor! And we have come to understand that under modern necessities our Olympias and Oregons and our commercial fleets bearing our flag over the world must have harbors where they can ride in safety in their own unchallenged right.

"And so, as we move forward to the new duties before us, let us try to realize the majesty of our position and the grandeur of our destiny. Picture the strength and the promise of the commanding place our mighty Republic now holds in the realms of nations. A continental domain washed by the two great oceans; midway and overarching the Orient and Occident, and impregnable because buttressed by the seas; the home of the only civilized people on earth who are economically independent and self-sustaining and boundless in their resources; along the granary and now fast becoming the workshop of the world; gaining in its new acquisitions the gates of the Caribbean, the mastery of the Isthmus and the key of Asia, embracing within its own wide territory, as no other nation does, the varied and exchangeable products of the temperate and tropic zones, and all the necessities of complete and self-centered national existence; and thus fronting the coming time of world-wide rivalry with a rounded development beyond any other nation, with the new need of commercial extension which springs from those unlimited capabilities, and with the stepping-stones and facilities brought within our possession by providential events which the imagination had not dreamed six months ago. Surely, as we contemplate this vision, we can justly feel that the mistress of the future is the noble figure of the Republic, whose torch of liberty, enlightening the world, is no less the beacon of commerce and humanity."

Hon. Whitelaw Reid, of New York, just before he was appointed one of the Peace Commissioners, said in an article in the *Century Magazine*:

"The question of the Philippines is different and difficult. They are not within what the diplomatists of the world would recognize as the legitimate sphere of American influence. Our relation to them is purely the accident of recent war. We are not in honor bound to hold them, if we can honorably dispose of them. But we know that their grievances differ only in kind, not in degree, from those of Cuba; and having once freed them from the Spanish yoke we cannot honorably require them to go back under it again. That would be to put us in an attitude of nauseating national hypocrisy, to give the lie to all our professions of humanity in our interference in Cuba, and to prove that our real motive was conquest. What humanity forbade us to tolerate in the West Indies it would not justify us in re-establishing in the Philippines.

"The chief aversion to the vast accessions of territory with which we are threatened springs from the fact that ultimately they must be admitted into the Union as States. No public duty is more urgent at this moment than to resist from the very outset the concession of such a possibility. In no circumstances likely to exist within a century, should they be admitted as States of the Union.

"With slight modifications, the territorial form of government which we have tried so successfully from the beginning of the Union, is admirably adapted to such communities. It secures local self-government, equality before the law, upright courts, ample power for order and defence, a voice in Congress for the presentation of local wants and such control by Congress as gives security against the mistakes or excesses of people new to the exercise of rights.

"The power of the government to deal with territory, foreign or domestic, precisely as it chooses, was understood from the beginning to be absolute, and at no stage in our whole history have we hesitated to exercise it. The question of permanently holding the Philippines or any other conquered territory as territory is not and cannot be made one of constitutional right; it is one solely of national duty and of national policy."

One of the most striking speeches made in the United States Senate during the debate on the treaty, was that of Senator Lodge, of Massachusetts. He said:

"In connection with these resolutions and others which have been introduced, two questions have been raised, one of Constitutional law and one of public policy. It is not my purpose to enter at length into the former discussion. The Constitutional questions are many, and the hypothetical situations which have been imagined with much ingenuity as tests of the Constitution, are almost countless. It is an inviting field, rich in casuistry and subtle distinctions, but I do not think that I could add much to the sum of human information or misinformation by attempting its elaborate cultivation.

"My own views as to our Constitutional rights and powers are simple and well defined, and have not been formed without some study, both of our Constitution and our history. I shall content myself with stating them. I believe that the United States has the undoubted power, which it has frequently exercised to acquire territory, and to hold and govern it. I am ready to admit, if necessary, that action in these directions must be taken for Constitutional purposes, but the constitutionality of the purposes must be determined by Congress itself through its majority. I believe that the power of the United States in any territory or possession outside the limits of the States themselves is absolute, with the single exception of the limitation placed on such outside possessions by the XIII Amendment. Such, at all events, has been the policy of the United States and its course of action in practice.

"Constitutions do not make a people; people make constitutions. Our Constitution is great and admirable, because the men who made it were so, and the people who ratified it and have lived under it were and are brave, intelligent and lovers of liberty. There is a higher sanction and a surer protection to life and liberty, to the right of speech and trial by jury, to justice and humanity, in the traditions and beliefs, the habits of mind, and the character of the American people than any which can be afforded by any constitution, no matter how wisely drawn. If the American people were disposed to tyranny, injustice and oppression, a constitution would offer but a temporary barrier to their ambition and the reverence for the constitution and for law and justice grows out of the fact that the American people believe in freedom and humanity, in equal justice to all men, and in equal rights before the law, and while they so believe the great doctrines of the Declaration of Independence and of the Constitution will never be in peril.

"Holding these views as to our Constitutional powers, the great question now before the American people resolves itself, in my mind, to one policy, surely.

"In our war with Spain we conquered the Philippines, or, to put it more exactly, we destroyed the power of Spain in those islands and took possession of their capital. The treaty cedes the Philippines to us. It is wisely and skilfully drawn. It commits us to no policy, to no course of action whatever in regard to the Philippines. When that treaty is ratified we have full power, and are absolutely free to do with those islands as we please; and the opposition to its ratification may be summed up in a single sentence, that the American people and the American Congress are not to be trusted with that power and with that freedom of action in regard to the inhabitants of those distant islands.

"What our precise policy shall be I do not know, because I for one am not sufficiently informed as to the conditions there to be able to say what it will be best to do; nor, I may add, do I think any one is. But I believe that we shall have the wisdom not to attempt to incorporate those islands with our body politic, or make their inhabitants part of our citizenship, or set their laborers alongside of ours and within our tariff to compete in any industry with American workmen.

"I believe that we shall have the courage not to depart from those islands fearfully, timidly and unworthily, and leave them to anarchy among themselves, to the brief and bloody domination of some self-constituted dictator and to the quick conquest of other powers, who will have no such hesitation as we would feel in crushing them into subjection by harsh and repressive methods. It is for us to decide the destiny of the Philippines, not for Europe, and we can do it alone and without assistance. I believe that we shall have the wisdom, the self-restraint and the ability to restore peace and order in those islands and give to their people an opportunity for self-government and for freedom under the protecting shield of the United States until the time shall come when they are able to stand alone, if such a thing be possible, and if they do not themselves desire to remain under our protection.

"To the American people and their Government I am ready to intrust my life, my liberty, my honor; and, what is far dearer to me than anything personal to myself, the lives and liberty of my children and my children's children. If I am ready thus to trust my children to the Government which the American people create and sustain, am I to shrink from intrusting to that same people the fate and fortunes of the inhabitants of the Philippine Islands?

"I can look at this question in only one way. A great responsibility has come to us. If we are unfit for it and unequal to it, then we should shrink it and fly from it. But I believe that we are both fit and capable, and that therefore we should meet it and take it up. There is much else involved here, vast commercial interests which I believe we have a right to guard and a duty to foster."

SENATOR PLATT'S ARGUMENTS.

During the debate on the Peace Treaty, the following was part of the notable speech made by Senator Platt, of Connecticut:

"I do not propose to discuss the policy of expansion," said Mr. Platt in the preface to his argument. "I do not propose either to discuss the features of the government we might establish in any foreign territory we might acquire. Expansion has been a law of our national growth, the mainspring of our national development. I shall maintain that the United States has shown a great capacity for government in all trying times and under many trying conditions, and that it is capable to meet any emergency likely to arise.

"I shall contend that the United States is a nation, and that as such it possesses every sovereign power not reserved by the Constitution to the States or to the people themselves; that the right to acquire territory was not reserved, and that, therefore, that right is an inherent right—a sovereign right, a right to which there is no limitation. I shall show, also, that in certain instances this inherent sovereign right is to be inferred from specific clauses of the Constitution itself."

Mr. Platt then made a constitutional argument, quoting extensively from authorities treating of the question. In maintenance of his position of the right of the United States to acquire foreign territory he quoted from the opinion of Justice Gray in the Chinese exclusion case. He declared that, in the discussion of the annexation of the Hawaiian Islands, the entire question of this Government's right to acquire foreign territory was considered thoroughly, and that the Senate had settled it satisfactorily and rightly. "We did not annex the Hawaiian Islands as a State," he said, "or with any declaration that the territory should become a State. We took it by cession. Our title to the territory is perfect and complete and constitutional."

Mr. Platt maintained that the right to Florida did not rest alone on the quitclaim from Spain, but on a deeper and broader right. He held that the United States "have the right to acquire territory in all ways that are used by other sovereign nations of the world."

"Yes; the right to acquire territory is an element of nationality; and I do not believe that there is any obligation to give to the people of acquired territory the right of self-government until such time as they are fit to exercise that right. If we believe the people of a country acquired are not fitted for the government of themselves, it is our duty to give them the most liberal government they are capable of accepting, and to educate them up, as best it may be, to the point where they will be capable of self-government. The Constitution does not confer the right of suffrage."

SENATOR CHAUNCEY M. DEPEW'S POSITION.

Senator-elect Chauncey M. Depew, when he was the guest of the Independent Club of Buffalo, speaking for expansion, said:

"In the closing hours of 1898 we are at the highest development of American prosperity and power. By a marvelous series of providences we are in the possession of vast territories, peopled by alien races in various degrees of civilization, in regard to which there have been thrust upon us the gravest responsibilities. Our success in their government depends upon the faithful application of the same oft-tried and ever-successful principles which have been worked out in such a marvelous way in our own history.

"The evolution of its administration of the affairs of the American Republic has been for one hundred years toward national supremacy. Now, in 1898, at the close of the Spanish War, the President of the United States possesses and exercises an authority beyond that of any ruler in the world, except the Czar of Russia, and without question from any source.

"We face at this time questions as vital to the future of our country as any which in the past have been met and successfully answered. The Federation of Washington, in 1798, has developed into the United States of 1898, with that inherent power which is always attached to national sovereignty—of acquiring territory by conquest or power. No constitutional lawyer will doubt this power. I do not think any body of constitutional lawyers will doubt that among the reserved powers of sovereignty which belong to us as a nation is the right to administer the affairs of territories acquired by conquest or by cession, under such form of government as Congress and the Executive may prescribe.

"To maintain order in Cuba, until the people shall be able to reach a stable government of liberty and law, is humanity. To incorporate Porto Rico in our domain, relieve its citizens from oppression, and give them good government, is humanity. To permit the bloody hand of Spain to again grasp the throat of ten millions of Filipinos, or to pass them over to the tender mercies of European governments, would be inhuman and cowardly; it would be refusing the mission which Providence has distinctly forced upon us. We must judge of the future of these possessions, not by the oppressions, which they have suffered, but by the liberty which they will enjoy. The Philippines to the United States, like Java to Holland, under the inspiring influences of American opportunity, of American schools and American hope, will be an immense market, and a large source of revenue over and above the cost of administration for the United States. Our Government, firmly planted, will not only enter the 'open door' of the Orient for the products of our fields and our factories, but when the great boot of Uncle Sam is put in the crack of the door which continental nations would close, there will be no musket jammed upon that boot to compel its withdrawal."

MILKMEN OF MANILA AT THEIR DAIRY.

In the city of Havana, Cuba, the milkmen drive their cows about the streets, and milk from the cow the quantity the customer wants. In Manila, the milkmen carry their milk in odd-shaped pitchers hung by the handle on sticks over their shoulders. In a similar manner water is carried about the streets and sold. The men carry their loads across their shoulders while the women bear their burdens on their heads

SPANIARDS EXECUTING INSURGENT CHIEFS, MANILA

Such executions took place on the beautiful Luneta driveway in the cool of the morning, and the elite of the city came out to grace the occasion. The condemned were marched with arms bound below the shoulders, before a company of soldiers, to the place of execution, and made to stand upon the sea wall facing the bay. A quick command—the sharp rifle reports, and the grim figures on the wall would fall headlong dead or writhing, to the ground.

William J. Bryan, of course, emphatically disapproved of the stand taken by the Government. He said:

"Spain, under compulsion, gives us a quitclaim to the Philippines in return for $20,000,000, but she does not agree to warrant and defend our title as against the Filipinos. To buy land is one thing, to buy people is another. Land is inanimate, and makes no resistance to a transfer of title; the people are animate, and sometimes desire a voice in their own affairs. But, even if measured by dollars and cents, the conquest of the Philippines should prove profitable or expensive, it will certainly prove embarrassing to those who still hold to the doctrine which underlies a republic. Military rule is antagonistic to our theory of government. The armaments which are used to defend it in the Philippines may be used to excuse it in the United States. Under military rule much must be left to the discretion of the Military Governor; and this can only be justified in the theory that the Military Governor knows more than the people whom he governs, is better acquainted with their needs than they are themselves, is entirely in sympathy with them, and is thoroughly honest and unselfish in his desire to do them good. Such a combination of wisdom, integrity, and love is difficult to find; and the Republican party will enter upon a hard task when it starts out to select suitable Military Governors for our remote possessions.

"We cannot afford to destroy the Declaration of Independence; we cannot afford to erase from our Constitutions, State and National, the Bill of Rights; we have not time to examine the libraries of the nation and purge them of the essays, the speeches, and the books that defend the doctrine that law is the crystallization of public opinion, rather than an emanation from physical power.

"But even if we could destroy every vestige of the laws which are the outgrowth of the immortal law penned by Jefferson; if we could obliterate every written word that has been inspired by the idea that this is 'a government of the people, by the people, and for the people', we could not tear from the heart of the human race the hope which the American Republic has planted there. The impassioned appeal, 'Give me liberty, or give me death', still echoes around the world. In the future, as in the past, the desire to be free will be stronger than the desire to enjoy a mere physical existence. The conflict between might and right will continue here and everywhere until a day is reached when the love of money will no longer sear the national conscience, and hypocrisy no longer hide the hideous features of avarice behind the mask of philanthropy."

WHAT EX-PRESIDENT CLEVELAND THINKS.

Ex-President Grover Cleveland, lent the weight of his influence against expansion. On one occasion he gave the following sarcastic interview :

"Assuming that my ideas on the subject are antiquated and unsuited to these progressive days, it is a matter of surprise to me that the refusal of certain natives of our new possessions to acquiesce in the beneficence of subjecting them to our control and management should, in the least, disturb our expansionists. This phase of the situation ought not to have been unanticipated, nor the incidents naturally growing out of it overlooked.

"The remedy is obvious and simple. The misguided inhabitants of our annexed territory who prefer something different from the plan for their control which we propose, or who oppose our designs in their behalf, should be slaughtered. The killing of natives has been a feature of expansion since expansion began, and our imperialistic enthusiasm should not be checked by the prospective necessity of destroying a few thousand or a few hundred thousand Filipinos. This should only be regarded as one stage in a transcendentally great movement a mere incident in its progress. Of course, some unprepared souls would then be lost before we had the opportunity of christianizing them, but surely those of our clergymen who have done so much to encourage expansion could manage that difficulty."

SENATOR HOAR'S ARGUMENTS.

Senator Hoar, of Massachusetts, calls it a spasm of folly. In his speech before the Senate, he said :

"The persons who favor the ratification of this treaty without conditions and without amendment differ among themselves certainly in their views, purposes and opinions, and as they are so many of them honest and well-meaning persons, we have the right to say, in their actual and real opinions. In general, the state of mind and the utterance of the lips are in accord. If you ask them what they want, you are answered with a shout: 'Three cheers for the Flag! Who will dare to haul it down? Hold on to everything you can get. The United States is strong enough to do what it likes. The Declaration of Independence and the counsel at Washington and the Constitution of the United States have grown rusty and musty. They are for little countries and not for great ones. There is, no moral law for strong nations. America has outgrown Americanism.

"In general, the friends of what is called imperialism or expansion content themselves with declaring that the flag which is taken down every night and put up again every morning over the roof of this Senate Chamber, where it is in its rightful place, must never be taken down where it once floated, whether that be its rightful place or not—a doctrine which I shall have occasion to say before I get through is not only without justification in international law; but if it were implanted there would make of every war between civilized and powerful nations a war of extermination or a war of dishonor to one party or the other.

"The power to conquer alien peoples and hold them in subjugation is nowhere expressly granted.

"The power to conquer alien peoples and hold them in subjugation is nowhere implied as necessary for the accomplishment of the purposes declared by the Constitution.

"It is clearly shown to be one that ought not to be exercised by anybody—one that the framers of the Constitution thought ought not to be exercised by anybody—

"1. Because it is immoral and wicked in itself.

"2. Because it is expressly denied in the Declaration of Independence, the great interpreter and expounder of the meaning of the Constitution, which owes its origin to the same generation and largely to the same men.

"3. It is affirmed that it is immoral and unfit to be exercised by anybody—in numerous instances by contemporary State Constitutions and the contemporary writers and authorities on public law, who expressed the opinion of the American people in that generation who adopted the Constitution as well as of the men who framed it.

"The power to hold property is implied whether that property be land or chattels. And, Mr. President, you are not now proposing to acquire or own property in the Philippines with dominion as a necessary incident, you are not to own a foot of land there. You propose now to acquire dominion and legislative power and nothing else. Where in the Constitution is the grant of power to exercise sovereignty where you have no property.

"Now, there are Senators here, yet hesitating as to what their action may be in the future, who will tell you that they loathe and hate this doctrine that we may buy nations at wholesale; that we may acquire imperial powers or imperial regions by conquest; that we may make vassal states and subject peoples without constitutional restraint, and against their will and without any restraint but our own discretion.

"The one great lesson which sums up the teachings of American history during our century of constitutional life is the dignity of labor. It is an unquestionable truth that no tropical colony was ever settled by men not born in tropical climes, for the purpose of finding work. There was scarcely ever a tropical colony successful at all. There was never a tropical colony successful except under the system of contract labor. That is to be set up, enforced and administered by the agencies of the Republic of the United States, if we are to succeed in such administration at all.

"The Senator from Connecticut seems to contemplate that we shall embark on a permanent system of national expenditure which will put this nation under an obligation, the equivalent of which will be a national debt greater than that of any other nation on the face of the earth. Our civil list, already so enormous, must be enormously increased. Instead of taking from the people by fair competition, or even by fair selection, men to take their share in self-government, we must have in the future, as they have in England, a trained class whose lives are to be spent not in self-government, but in the government of other men."

SENATOR VEST'S VIEWS.

Senator Vest's speech, in starting the opposition to the Peace Treaty, stated that our forefathers had fought for years against taxation without representation. The Declaration of Independence had been drawn up with the idea that all governments derived their just powers from the governed. It was incredible that the founders of the Government could have looked forward to the time when millions of human beings could be held without their consent, merely as chattels, to be disposed of as the sovereign powers of the mother country might choose. It seemed to him the historic argument that the just powers of the Government were derived from the consent of the governed fully covered his position, inasmuch as it had been fully maintained by the courts.

Mr. Vest thought it was the purpose of the expansionists to adopt the European system of colonization. He pointed out that Great Britain had in the mother country 120,979 square miles of territory, and in her colonies 16,667,071 square miles. The disproportion of population was about the same. He maintained that the fundamental principle of this Government was the granting of citizenship to all within the jurisdiction of the Government, except alone the Indians. The question, Mr. Vest thought, was the result of the efforts of desperate disputants who appear in the public press day by day and attack public men because they adhere to the Constitution and resist this new evangel.

"To say," declared Mr. Vest, "that citizens of a territory are excluded from the privileges guaranteed by the Bill of Rights and are merely subjects of the arbitrary will of Congress, is a monstrous proposition; but fortunately the Supreme Court had determined that question in many cases.

"I do not deny the power of the Federal Government to acquire territory, but I do deny its power to acquire territory peopled with millions without their consent and with no intention of conferring upon them citizenship. I may be answered that the point is not good; that it may be evaded by the taking in of vast tracts of lands peopled with barbarians, to be held merely for commercial advantages. When the Congress of the United States shall become so degraded as this, it is only a question of time when the end shall come."

"We are a great people," concluded Mr. Vest. "We are told that this country can do anything, Constitution or no Constitution. We are a great people, it is true, but we cannot do more than another great people did—a people that conquered the world, not with steel ships and modern cannon, but with bare swords and primitive galleys. The colonial system destroyed all hope of republicism in the old time. It is an appendage of monarchy. It can exist in no free country, because it uproots and eliminates the bases of all republican institutions—that governments derive their just powers from the consent of the governed. I know not what may be done with the glamour of foreign conquest and greed of the money-making classes of this country. For myself, I would rather quit public life this minute—nay, I would be willing to yield life itself—rather than give my consent to this fantastic and wicked attempt to revolutionize our Government and to substitute the principles of our hereditary enemy for the teachings of Washington and his associates."

HON. CARL SCHURZ'S VIEWS.

Perhaps none of the anti-expansionists received as much criticism as Hon. Carl Schurz, the noted New Yorker. In an address, he said:

"If we take these new regions, we shall be well entangled in that contest for territorial aggrandizement, which distracts other nations and drives them far beyond their original design. So it will be inevitably with us. We shall want new conquests to protect that which we already possess. The greed of speculators working upon our Government will push us from one point to another, and we shall have new conflicts on our hands, almost without knowing how we got into them. It has always been so under such circumstances, and always will be. This means more and more soldiers, ships and guns.

"We are already told that we shall need a regular army of at least 100,000, three-fourths of whom are to serve in our 'new possessions.' The question is, whether this necessity is to be only temporary or permanent. Look at the cost. Last year the support of the army proper required about $23,000,000. It is computed that, taking the increased costliness of the service in the tropics into account, the army under the new dispensation will require about $150,000,000; that is, $127,000,000 a year more.

"It is also officially admitted that the possession of the Philippines would render indispensable a much larger increase of the navy than would otherwise be necessary, costing untold millions for the building and equipment of ships, and untold millions every year for their maintenance and for the increased number of officers and men. What we shall have to spend for fortifications and the like cannot now be computed.

"But there is a burden upon us which, in like weight, no other nation has to bear. To-day, thirty-three years after the Civil War, we have a pension roll of very nearly 1,000,000 names. And still they come. We paid to pensioners over $145,000,000 last year, a sum larger than the annual cost of the whole military peace establishment of the German empire, including its pension roll. Our recent Spanish war will, according to a moderate estimate, add at least $20,000,000 to our annual pension payments. But if we send troops to the tropics and keep them there, we must look for a steady stream of pensioners from that quarter, for in the tropics soldiers are "used up" very fast, even if they have no campaigning to do.

"The cry suddenly raised that this great country has become too small for us is too ridiculous to demand an answer, in view of the fact that our present population may be tripled and still have ample elbow-room, with resources to support many more. But we are told that our industries are gasping for breath; that we are suffering from over-production; that our products must have new outlets, and that we need new colonies and dependencies the world over to give us more markets. More markets? Certainly. But do we, civilized beings, indulge in the absurd and barbarous notion that we must own the countries with which we wish to trade? Here are our official reports before us, telling us that of late years our export trade has grown enormously, not only of farm products, but of the products of our manufacturing industries; in fact, that 'our sales of manufactured goods have continued to extend with a facility and promptitude of results which have excited the serious concern of countries that, for generations, had not only controlled their home markets, but practically monopolized certain lines of trade in other lands.'

"That our victories have evolved upon us certain duties as to the people of the conquered islands, I readily admit. But are they the only duties we have to perform, or have they suddenly become paramount to all other duties? I deny it. I deny that the duties we owe to the Cubans and the Porto Ricans and the Filipinos and the Tagals of the Asiatic islands absolve us from our duties to the 75,000,000 of our own people and to their posterity. I deny that they oblige us to destroy the moral credit of our own Republic by turning this loudly heralded war of liberation and humanity into a land-grabbing game, and an act of criminal aggression. I deny that they compel us to aggravate our race troubles, to bring upon us the constant danger of war and to subject our people to the galling burden of increasing armaments. If we have rescued those unfortunate daughters of Spain, the colonies, from the tyranny of their cruel father, I deny that we are therefore in honor bound to marry any of the girls, or to take them all into our household, where they may disturb and demoralize our whole family. I deny that the liberation of those Spanish dependencies morally constrains us to do anything that would put our highest mission to solve the great problem of Democratic government in jeopardy, or that would otherwise endanger the vital interests of the Republic. Whatever our duties to them may be, our duties to our own country and people stand first; and from this standpoint we have as sane men and patriotic citizens to regard our obligation to take care of the future of those islands and their people.

" They fought for deliverance from Spanish oppression, and we helped them to obtain that deliverance. That deliverance they understand to mean independence. I repeat the question whether anybody can tell me why the declaration of Congress that the Cubans of right ought to be free and independent, should not apply to all of them? Their independence, therefore, would be the natural and rightful outcome. This is the solution of the problem first to be taken in view. It is objected that they are not capable of independent government. They may answer that this is their affair, and that they are at least entitled to a trial."

VIEW IN BANCA SHOWING DUTCH FORTIFICATIONS.
For many years the East India Islands were a bone of contention between the Dutch and the Spaniards. The Dutch owned Java, Sumatra, and other islands; but the Spaniards finally drove them entirely from every point in the Philippines.

THE NATIVE FARMER AND HIS FAITHFUL SERVANT.
The Carabao, or large Water Buffalo of the Philippine Islands is the chief domestic animal of the natives. It is generally captured wild when young. It is large and as strong as two horses.

SENOR MONTERO RIOS
President of the Spanish Peace Commission, whose painful duty required him to sign away his country's colonial possessions.

GENERAL RAMON BLANCO
Who succeeded Weyler as Captain General of Cuba in 1897. He was formerly Governor-General of the Philippine Islands.

ADMIRAL CERVERA
Commander of Spanish Fleet at Santiago.

SAGASTA
Premier of Spain during the Spanish-American War.

CHAPTER XIV

The Ladrone Islands.

The Bloodless Battle of Guam.—When the Charleston Opened Fire on the Little City of Agaña, the Governor Thought we were Saluting Him.—A Population which has Twice Disappeared.—Poverty and Laziness on all Sides.—The Value of the Island as a Military Station.

ON July 4, 1898, the United States steamship *Charleston* had a little celebration all by itself in the middle of the Pacific Ocean, during which it captured an island and hoisted the American flag in a new land. It was an incident of war which was unexpected. The inhabitants of the island did not even know that war existed between the United States and Spain. The country was so far removed from the seat of Spanish government and so out of touch with the things that were going on in the world, that when the war vessel of Uncle Sam came near to this Spanish possession and fired her shot upon the frowning forts that guarded the little city of Agaña, there was no reply, and when troops were landed to take possession of the city, and the Governor of the island was asked to surrender, he expressed his great surprise at the demand and was startled to learn that his country had become involved in a struggle with the United States.

He had heard the roar of the guns of the *Charleston*, but he thought "the noble Americans were saluting him, and he was deeply humiliated because he had no powder to return their salute." It followed that he had no powder with which to fight, so he immediately surrendered the island of Guam to the American officers, and soon the flag of Spain was lowered over the little isle where it had fluttered for so many years, and in its stead waved a new flag, a symbol unknown to the people of that place, a symbol that is to bring them peace and prosperity greater than any they have ever known, guaranteed by the Stars and Stripes of the United States.

The Governor of the island and all his soldiers were taken on board the *Charleston* as prisoners of war. Then the vessel continued her voyage to Manila, leaving a handful of men to garrison the fort of Guam. Later on, when the Treaty of Peace was signed, this little island of Guam was ceded to the United States as a coaling station. Its situation makes it valuable to the United States from a naval standpoint, for it is in a direct line across the Pacific, giving us Hawaii, Guam and the Philippines as keys to practically the whole commerce of the Pacific Ocean, which if the prophecies of the present are fulfilled will be the great highway of commerce in the years to come.

This little Island of Guam is not intrinsically a valuable possession. As a coaling station, however, it will more than repay for its keep, for this only of all the islands possessed by the United States is not self-supporting, and has not been for years.

THE DISCOVERY OF THE LADRONES.

It was a welcome sight to Magellan and his crew when, one day in March, nearly four hundred years ago they beheld the verdant and beautifully sloping hills of the Ladrone Islands. Eighteen weary months before they had sailed from the coast of Spain, and all that time, first to the southwest and then to the northwest, they had followed the setting sun. Theirs were the first vessels manned by white men that had ever plowed the trackless Pacific; and this was the first land ever seen by white men within that unknown ocean.

It was a pitiable crew on these small, weather-beaten ships, who drew, that March morning, toward the coast of the present island of Guam. Hunger and thirst had driven them to the verge of madness. They had eaten even the leather thongs from their sail fastenings, and only a small mug of water per day was the portion of drink for a man. " Land! Land!" It was a glad cry from the watch aloft. There were palm trees, cocoanuts, green grass, tropical fruits, an abundance of fresh water, and—though naked—a curious and friendly people. No wonder Magellan paused to rest himself and his sailors. But the welcome he got on this 16th day of March, 1521, was such that his stay was not a very long one. The sight of these strange ships from a foreign land aroused the curiosity of the natives to such an extent that they swarmed around in their native canoes, and some even swam out to meet the newcomers. They climbed over their ships' sides, and overran them so that they had to be expelled by force. As a farewell token these natives took one of the ships' boats, and nearly a hundred men had to be sent on shore to recover it. There was a bloody combat, in which many lives were sacrificed, but the Spaniards eventually recovered their lost possession.

IT WAS CALLED THE ISLE OF ROBBERS.

Magellan named the place Islas de las Velas Latinas, or islands of the Lateen Sails, but Legaspi called them Ladrones, which is the Spanish word for "robbers," and by that name they have been known ever after.

Since that time they have been visited by many explorers. In 1662 one of these roving vessels, the *San Damian*, while on a voyage from Mexico to Manila, anchored on the Island of Guam. It had on board a missionary, Fray Diego Luis Desan Victores, who was very much struck by the wretched poverty of the natives and their terrible condition, both physically and spiritually. When he reached Manila he tried to get prominent members of his Church interested in these natives, and so much did he plea for them to his superiors that they had to order him to drop the subject. Finally, however, he secured a good word on behalf of his project from the Archbishop, who brought the matter to the attention of King Philip the Fourth. Other pressure was also brought on that monarch so that in 1666 a royal decree was received sanctioning the establishing of a mission in the Ladrones, so Fray Diego, finally successful in the scheme that had taken possession of his whole life, set sail from Spain for the islands, intending to stop in Mexico on the way. But the owners of the vessel in which he sailed wished to change her destination to Peru, so that they might carry a full cargo. All of the pleas of the priest could do nothing, and finally when the cargo was put on it shifted to one side, so that the vessel leaned and was not able to right herself. This decided the owners to lighten her, and they dispatched the vessel to Mexico, as was desired by the priest. So Fray Diego finally arrived safely in that city, but there he encountered more trouble. The Viceroy declared that he had no orders to send an expedition to the Ladrones, and remained inflexible to all entreaty. Even his wife begged him on her bended knees to yield to the call for help from these far-away islands, and it is said that while she besought him an earthquake shook the city. The friar called it a manifestation of the disapproval of Heaven, and so superstition accomplished what entreaties could not accomplish, and the expedition started in March, 1668, in charge of a Jesuit mission.

THE NAME OF THE ISLANDS IS CHANGED.

Subsequently Queen Maria Anna, who had succeeded King Philip IV. to the throne, gave the mission a pension of $3,000 per year, to commemorate which liberality the Spaniards formally named the islands the Islas Marianas, by which name they are known in Spain up to this day, although the older name Ladrones is better known elsewhere.

As soon as the mission of Fray Diego became fairly established on the island, a small body of troops, consisting of 12 Spaniards and 19 Filipinos was sent there, with 2 pieces of artillery. For a time the natives accepted the dominion of the invaders, but as they became more and more trodden under the feet of these foreigners, they arose in rebellion. But here, again, Fray Diego was lucky, for once more Nature came to him as a powerful ally working upon the superstition of the ignorant islanders. While the rebellion was going on, a severe storm came up and swept all of the huts of the natives before it. Thereupon the priests told them that Heaven was angered at their uprising, and finally peace was declared. Fray Diego went over to Visayas shortly after, where he was killed. No sooner had he gone than the natives again revolted against the oppression of these foreign priests, who wished to force them to adopt a religion of which they knew nothing, and rites which were mysterious to them. From time to time they sacrificed the priests, either in warfare or in massacre. In 1778 a Governor of the islands was appointed. He came from Mexico with thirty soldiers, but, after two years' service, resigned, finding the field unfruitful and the honor barren; for so great is the poverty there that, during the first century of Spanish rule, the Government was never able to collect a cent of tribute from the natives, and, even at the present time, the revenue from the islands is not nearly sufficient to pay expenses.

THE EXTENT OF THE ARCHIPELAGO

There are two groups of islands in the Ladrones, divided by a broad channel. Altogether they have an area of about 417 square miles. The northern group consists of ten islands, which are uninhabited. The southern group comprises five islands, one of which is not inhabited,—Guahan or Guam, as it is known, Rota, Aguigan, Tinian, and Saypan. The chief one of these is Guam, which is the largest, the most settled, and the most southern of the islands. It contains the only city in the colony, San Ignacio de Agaña, and the fortified harbor of Umata.

The former is situated on a creek called the Port of Apra. Vessels are not able to get up to Agaña, and they come at anchor about two miles off Punta Piti, where passengers and cargo, as well as the mails, are taken over to a very little wooden landing place. Not far from there, at a distance of about 500 yards, is the office of the harbor master. The road from there to the capital is a hard one to travel, and extends for a distance of five miles. So difficult is communication between the harbor and the capital of the islands that it has been a mooted question for many years as to whether it would not be better to change the location of the chief city of the colony, but, as yet, nothing has been done.

In the capital there are some fairly good-sized buildings, including a government house, a military hospital and pharmacy, an artillery depot, infantry barracks, a prison, a tribunal and administrator's office, as well as some ruins which mark the spot where once stood what was known as the Public Buildings. There are also a College of San Juan de Letran for boys and a school for girls there.

In the city there are eight so-called stores, besides small wretched huts, where native aguardiente is sold. It is made out of fermented cocoanut milk. The stores are classed as follows: First, Manila; second, Japanese; third, Chinese; fourth, Chamarro (native); and fifth, American. There are three of the Manila stores where ready-made articles of apparel, notions in general demand, and high-priced canned goods of poor quality are sold; also poor cigars made of native tobacco. The Japanese store is one of the best, carrying the same class of goods with some additions. It has eggs and bread, the latter baked every other day, and of a poor quality. The Chinese store is very poor. The native store has a supply of native coffee of fair quality and excellent chocolate, also cotton goods. The American store is more pretentious, but inferior to the Japanese. It carries a large supply of canned goods, clothes, notions, shoes, and furniture. Flour is difficult to obtain. Butter and lard are not good, owing to the warm climate. Chickens and eggs are plentiful. The beef is poor, and no sheep are raised inland. There are plenty of pigs. Yams, sweet potatoes and corn are abundant. Bananas, cocoanuts, and breadfruit are the chief sources of food of the natives. There is little fishing. The clams are fairly good, and the oysters are very small and have a sweet taste. There are plenty of deer, goats, wild turkey, plover, ducks and other game birds.

Nine other towns exist on the island, which boast parish priests and churches built of stone and roofed with reed patching. All of these towns have tribunals, six made of bamboo and reed, one built of wood, and another of stone. In seven of these towns there are schools, four for boys, five for girls and nine for both sexes, under the direction of twenty-six teachers.

The islands themselves are of little value. The general surface of the southern group is low, while that of the northern is mountainous, although the mountains are not very high. Volcanic formations occur, and on two of the islands there are smoking craters. All of the archipelago practically is densely wooded, and the vegetation is much like that of the Philippines.

THE DISAPPEARANCE OF POPULATION.

When first visited by Europeans, the archipelago contained from 40,000 to 60,000 souls, represented by two distinct classes, the nobles and the people, between whom marriage and even contact was forbidden. But the Spanish conquest soon ended this distinction by reducing all alike to servitude. For a long time after Spanish occupation, the natives complained and finally rebelled against the oppressive measures of their rulers; but by the end of the seventeenth century they ceased their resistance, and it was found by a census that fully half of them had perished or escaped in their canoes to the Caroline Islands, and that two-thirds of their 180 villages had fallen to ruins. Then came an epidemic which swept away nearly all the natives of Guam, and the island of Tinian (one of the group) was depopulated and its inhabitants brought to Guam. Nearly all the new arrivals soon died. In the year 1760, a census showed a total of only 10,654 inhabitants left in all the islands, and the Spaniards repopulated them by bringing Tagals from the Philippines.

The population of the islands in 1899 was estimated at about 9,000. The people are generally lacking in energy, loose in morals and miserably poor. Their education has been seriously neglected. The natives of the islands are about as much domesticated as the Philippine islanders, and their features are much more regular. The introduction of Spanish language has practically driven out their own language, which is called Chamorro, and which much resembles the dialect of the Visayas. Some of the natives also speak English, as these islands used to be the resort of some English speaking whalers. The Spaniards have taught the natives the use of firearms, and all are pressed into service and trained in the arts of war.

The climate of the islands is damp but salubrious, and the heat is so tempered by trade winds that it is very much milder in temperature than the Philippines. The yearly mean temperature at Guam is about 81 F. August and September are the warmest months, but they do not differ greatly from the rest of the year.

There is a wet and a dry season, although in the latter there is considerable rain at times. From October to May the winds are usually northeasterly, while during the rest of the year they are northwesterly and southwesterly as a rule, the latter being accompanied by much rain.

The islands are full of rivers, although in Guam the clearing away of the woods has caused many of the largest streams to dwindle down to mere brooks. Cocoanut and other palms, the bread tree and other tropical trees and plants generally thrive. The large fruit bat which abounds in the Philippines is indigenous to the Ladrones, and, despite its objectionable odor, is a popular article of food. Swine and oxen are allowed to run wild, and are hunted when needed. There are only a few species of birds; even insects are rare; and the reptiles are represented by several kinds of lizards and a single species of serpent. No domestic animals were known in the islands until introduced by the Spaniards.

CHAPTER XV

The Hawaiian Islands, "The Paradise of the Pacific."

Annexed to the United States by Act of Congress, July 7, 1898.—Truly a Paradise in Climate, Fertility and Healthfulness.—Discovery by Captain Cook.—Something about the Inhabitants.—Old times in Hawaii.—A Pen Sketch of Queen Lilioukalani, the Last of the Royal Line.—The Revolution of 1893.—The Plea for Admission to the United States.—The Mission of Senator Blount.—The Work of American Missionaries.—Some Hawaiian Superstitions and Amusements.—Products and Commerce.—Sugar is to the Islands what Wheat is to our Northwest.—Honolulu, the Capital City.—A Beautiful and Delightful Resort.—On the Threshold of a Great Industrial Era.

RIGHT in the pathway which leads across the sea, to the shores of our new possessions gained by war, appears another possession, obtained through peace, the Hawaiian Islands. Five years ago the American flag which had been hoisted above the buildings of Honolulu, taking the "Paradise of the Pacific" under the protection of its folds, was lowered, and now by a joint vote of Congress, the flag has again been hoisted over the islands, and they have been formally annexed to the United States.

When the flag was raised for the second time on August 12, 1898, in obedience to the act of Congress of July 7th, some of the richest, most fertile and most valuable of all of the islands of the globe, became the property of our Government. In climate, fertility, and healthfulness, they are truly the "Paradise of the Pacific." There are eight inhabited islands in the Sandwich archipelago, including Hawaii, Maui, Kahoolawe, Lanai, Molokai, Oahu, Kaui, Niihau. Altogether they have an area of 6,700 square miles, a little less than that of the State of New Jersey, and about 500 square miles greater than the combined areas of Rhode Island and Connecticut. They extend from northwest to southeast over a distance of about 380 miles, the several islands being separated by channels varying in width from 6 to 60 miles. They lie entirely within the tropics, not far from a direct line from San Francisco and Japan, 2,089 miles from San Francisco.

CAPTAIN COOK DISCOVERS THE ISLANDS.

The islands were first discovered in January, 1778, by Captain Cook, who named them the Sandwich Islands after Lord Sandwich, but the native name Hawaii, is more generally used. There is good evidence that Juan Gaetano, in the year 1555, that is 223 years before Captain Cook's visit, landed upon their shores. Old Spanish charts and the traditions of the native bear out this theory, but they were not made known to the world until Cook visited them. The original inhabitants came from New Zealand, according to popular belief, although that island is some 4,000 miles southwest of them. The physical appearance of the people is very similar and their language is so much alike that a native Hawaiian and a native New Zealander, meeting for the first time can carry on a conversation. Their ideas of the Deity and some of their religious customs are nearly the same. That the islands have been peopled for a long time is proven by the fact that human bones are found under lava beds and coral reefs where geologists declare they have lain for at least 1,300 years.

Captain Cook's visit to the islands was a notable event, according to an old historian. The captain was worshiped as a god; the people declined to charge him for anything, but loaded up his ship freely with the best productions of the islands. "The priests approached him in a crouching attitude, offering prayers and exhibiting all the formalities of worship. After approaching him with prostrations, the priests cast their red capas over his shoulders and then receding a little they presented hogs and a variety of other offerings, with long addresses rapidly enunciated which were a repetition of their prayers and religious homage.

"When he went on shore most of the people fled for fear of him, and others bowed down before him with solemn reverence. He was conducted to the house of the gods, and into the sacred enclosure, and receive there the highest homage. Kalaniopuu, the King, arrived from Maui, on the twenty-fourth of January, and treated Captain Cook with much kindness, giving him feather coats, and fly brushes and paid him divine honors.

Describing the death of Captain Cook, this historian says that Cook had established a blockade to stop thieving in canoes. He continues: "A canoe came from an adjoining district bound within the bay. In the canoe were two chiefs of some rank, Kekuhaupio and Kalimu. The canoe was fired upon from one of the boats and Kalimu was killed. Kekuhaupio made the greatest speed till he reached the palace of the King, where Captain Cook also was, and communicated the intelligence of the death of the chief. The attendants of the King were enraged and showed signs of hostility, but were restrained by the thought that Captain Cook was a god. At that instant a warrior with a spear in his hand approached the Captain, and was heard to say, that the boats in the harbor had killed his brother and he would be revenged. Cook, from the warrior's enraged appearance and that of the multitude, was suspicious of him and fired upon him with his pistol. Then followed a scene of confusion and in the midst Captain Cook, being hit with a stone and perceiving the man who threw it, shot him dead. He also struck a certain chief with his sword. The chief instantly siezed Captain Cook with a strong hand designing merely to hold him, and not to take his life, for he supposed him to be a god, and that he could not die. Captain Cook struggled to free himself from the grasp and, as he was about to fall, uttered a groan. The people immediately exclaimed, " He groans,—he is not a god," and instantly slew him. Such was the melancholy death of Captain Cook.

"Immediately the men in the boat commenced a deliberate fire upon the crowd. They had refrained in a measure before for fear of killing their captain. Many of the natives were killed. The body of Captain Cook was carried into the interior of the island by the natives, the bones secured according to their customs, and the flesh burned in the fire.

"The heart and liver of Captain Cook were stolen and eaten by some hungry children, who mistook them in the night for the inwards of a dog. Some of his bones were sent on board his ship in compliance with the urgent demands of the officers, and some were kept by the priests as objects of worship."

The people of that period were about as wild and ignorant and superstitious as people well could be. They numbered at the time of discovery about 400,000. Forty years after, when a census was taken, there were 142,000. These diminished one-half during the next fifty years; and the native population of the islands in 1897 was only 31,019. The total population by the last census, when the islands became a part of the United States, was 109,020, made up, in addition to the natives mentioned, of 24,407 Japanese, 21,616 Chinese, 12,191 Portuguese, and 3,086 Americans. The remainder were half-castes from foreign intermarriage with the natives, together with a small representation from England, Germany, and other European countries.

A RACE BECOMING EXTINCT.

That the original Hawaiians must soon become extinct as a pure race is evident, though they have never been persecuted or maltreated. They are a handsome, strong-looking people, with a rich, dark complexion, jet black eyes, wavy hair, full voluptuous lips, and teeth of snowy whiteness; but they are constitutionally weak, easily contract and quickly succumb to disease, and the only hope of perpetuating their blood seems to lie in mixing it by intermarriage with other races.

Prior to 1795 all the islands had separate kings, but in that and the following year the Great King of Hawaii, Kamehameha, with cannon that he procured from Vancouver's ships, assaulted and subjugated all the surrounding kings, and since that time the islands have been under one government. Previous to this the natives had been at war, according to their traditions, for three hundred years. The fierceness of their hand-to-hand conflicts, as described by their historians, has probably not been surpassed by those of any other people in the world.

Kamehameha I. was succeeded by Kamehameha II., who made for himself a record as reformer. He broke through the sacred priestly law which prevented a man from eating at the same table with his female relatives, and finally succeeded in breaking up, to a great extent, but not completely, the old barbaric rites and customs. It was during his reign that the missionaries from this country first succeeded in making headway. The last Kamehameha died in 1872, leaving one child. He was the fourth of his race, and is perhaps best remembered by the reputation of his Queen, Emma, who became a great favorite with Queen Victoria when she visited England. She was a woman of lovely character, and attracted much attention to herself and her people.

On the King's death the succession lay between Prince Luralilo, a grandson of the original Kamehameha and David Kalakaua, who was the son of a chief of royal blood. Luralilo was given the throne by a popular election, but lived only two years. He died in 1874, without naming a successor, and Queen Dowager Emma announced her readiness to rule over Hawaii, but there arose, as an aspirant to the throne, this Kalakaua, who was a boatman in the harbor of Honolulu, and who, if rumor is to be believed, used to pick up extra money at night by playing the banjo in one of the waterfront dives. He was a descendant of the old Hawaiian chiefs, and had a strain of Kamehameha blood in his veins. He cast eager eyes on the throne, and, by using American influence, he was able to secure thirty-nine out of forty-five votes of the Legislature, which had been convened in extra session to decide the matter, and, consequently, was declared King of the islands, much to the disgust of the people who were in sympathy with Queen Emma.

During his reign the Government of Hawaii entered into various negotiations with the Government of the United States which resulted in a treaty of reciprocity being established in 1876. By this treaty rice and the lower grades of sugar were admitted duty free into the United States. This was of an immense advantage to Hawaii during the period in which the tax on sugar was unusually high in this country, and she was able to realize $45 or $50 per ton more than any other on her sugar. This was instrumental in drawing American capital and American people to the colony, and they began immediately to take a controlling position in the political and social affairs of the islands.

In 1887, under President Cleveland's first administration, additional provisions were made to the treaty and its time lengthened, in return for which the King ceded to the United States the exclusive right to establish and fortify a naval station on the Hawaiian Islands. Pearl Harbor was designated as the station; but in 1889 Secretary of the State, James G. Blaine, dissatisfied with the imperfect cessions of this harbor, as well as with the general status of affairs between our country and Hawaii, urged upon the Hawaiian Minister at Washington, H. A. P. Carter, an enlargement of the treaty provisions. It was proposed to make the treaty permanent, to create absolute free trade between the two countries in all articles except intoxicants, to make the cessation of a naval station permanent as well as exclusive, and to pledge to Hawaii full participation in any bounties to be given American producers of sugar. In short, Hawaii, in all its commercial and productive interests, was to enjoy all the privileges of one of the United States. In return, besides the cession of Pearl Harbor, Mr. Blaine asked a pledge of Hawaii to enter into no treaty engagement with other powers without the full consent of the United States.

Canada, however, put its finger in the pie, and so worked upon King Kalakaua that he rejected the treaty, and before another could be made, he died. Queen Liliuokalani, his sister, ascended the throne, and made immediate provision for her succesor. As she had no children of her own, there was, of course, no direct heir to the crown, but she announced that the heir to the crown would be Princess Kaiulani, one of the most beautiful, cultured, and fascinating of the children of the islands. She was the daughter of Honorable Archibald Cleghorn, an Englishman, who was the Governor of the Island of Oahu, and Princess Likelike. But, as fate would have it, this beautiful Hawaiian never ruled in Hawaii; she died early in March, 1899.

Queen Liliuokalani had not only inherited a throne, but she had inherited the discontent of a people who had been imposed upon by Kalakaua. He had shown himself a great champion of his own people, but a great foe to foreigners, and, as the latter were the most powerful and richest of the dwellers upon the islands, he laid up trouble, not only for himself, but for his successor. He was a great seeker after personal power, and used every means possible to surround himself with subservient officeholders. Through his follies, in the seven years up to 1887, the national debt grew from $389,000 to $1,936,000. Finally matters went from bad to worse, until an open revolt was precipitated by his accepting two bribes, one of $80,000, the other of $75,000, for which he gave the same exclusive privileges in the opium traffic to each of two rival bidders.

Immediately there was an uprising of such magnitude that it took the King's breath. The foreigners organized a united movement for reform, and they secured concessions which took all the real power away from the King and placed it in the hands of a cabinet, subject only to the Legislature.

In 1889 Robert W. Wilcox headed a revolution against the methods employed by the King. He was a full-blooded Hawaiian, and he protested not only against the King's extravagance, but the way in which in his later years he allowed the Government affairs to be dictated practically by the business men of other countries. His uprising was not a success. He seized the military school, the palace yard and the Government house, but the movement was suppressed within a few hours.

When the Queen took her seat she insisted on her right to appoint a Cabinet of her own. This right was granted her, and for some time she lived up to the Constitution which the previous King had signed.

Later, however, she made up her mind to take matters into her own hands and again turn the Government into a personal one. In 1892 there was a Legislative session which was protracted over a space of eight months, chiefly through her desire to get matters into her own control. Opium and lottery bills were championed by her, which were of such a nature as to arouse violent opposition. But the final crash came later. The Queen had a Constitution drawn up which would have had the effect of making her absolute monarch of the islands, and would have disfranchised a class of citizens who paid a large proportion of the taxes to the Government. She attempted to promulgate this new Constitution on January 14th. The matter had been ready for two weeks previous to that, and in expectation of it a large crowd of Hawaiians had assembled around the palace gates and in the grounds. Natives were also gathered in large groups in the Government building yard and elsewhere in the neighborhood.

The Queen retired to the blue room and summoned her ministers. She was seated at a table dressed in a magnificent costume with a sparkling coronet of diamonds. She presented the ministers upon their arrival with a draft of the new Constitution, demanding their signatures, and declaring her intention of promulgating the document immediately. Two of the ministers refused to accede to her wishes, and somewhat hesitatingly the others joined in the refusal. They urged Her Majesty not to violate the law, but she was not to be dissuaded from her revolutionary course.

Bringing her clenched hand down upon the table, the Queen said: "Gentlemen, I do not wish to hear any more advice. I intend to promulgate this Constitution, and to do it now." Then she told her Cabinet that unless they abandoned their resistance at once she would go out upon the steps of the palace and tell the excited crowd that she wished to give them a new Constitution, but the ministers were preventing her from doing it. Remembering a previous riot, and the fate of the unlucky men who fell into the hands of the insurgents, and knowing that the Queen had prepared just such a trap for them, the ministers fled before her threat could be put into execution.

From the Government building they sent word all around town asking citizens what support could be expected to resist the revolutionary movement begun by the Queen. There was but one opinion, and all joined together to support the law and the liberties of the people. When this was learned, great pressure was brought upon the Queen to retrace the steps she had already taken. While her troops stood drawn up before the palace waiting for the final word of command, the Queen hesitated. There was another conference which lasted for a long time, and finally, although she could not be persuaded to give up her plan, the Queen consented with bitter reluctance to a postponement. She was a very angry woman when later she entered the throne room where were assembled the leading men of her rule, but she announced publicly that the new Government would not yet be declared.

A PROCLAMATION.

Knowing that the Queen would eventually carry out her plans, the foreign element in the community called a mass meeting and appointed a committee of public safety, which issued a proclamation stating that: "It is firmly believed that the culminating, revolutionary attempt of last Saturday will, unless radical measures are taken, wreck our already damaged credit abroad and precipitate to final ruin our already overstrained financial condition, and guarantees of protection to life, liberty and property will steadily decrease. The political situation is rapidly growing worse. In this belief, and also in the belief that the action hereby taken is and will be for the best personal, political and property interests of every citizen of the land, we, citizens and residents of the Hawaiian Islands, organized and acting for public safety and common good, hereby proclaim as follows:

"The Hawaiian monarchical system of Government is hereby abrogated. Provisional Government for the control and management of public affairs and the protection of public peace is hereby established, to exist until terms of union with the United States of America have been negotiated and agreed upon. Such Provisional Government shall consist of an Executive Council of four members, who are hereby declared to be S. B. Dole, J. A. King, P. C. Jones, and W. O. Smith, who shall administer the Government of the islands, the first named acting as President and Chairman of such Council, administering the Department of Foreign Affairs, and the others severally administering the Departments of Interior, Finance and Attorney-General, respectively, in the order in which enumerated, according to the existing Hawaiian law, as far as may be consistent with this proclamation and also of an Advisory Council, which shall consist of fourteen members, who are hereby declared to be S. D. Damon, A. Brown, L. A. Thurston, J. F. Morgan, E. Emmelsmith, H. Waterhouse, J. A. McCandless, E. D. Tenny, F. W. McChesney, F. Wilhelm, W. R. Castle, W. G. Ashley, W. C. Wilder, and C. Bolte. Such Advisory Council shall also have general legislative authority. Such Executive and Advisory Councils shall, acting jointly, have power to remove any member of either Council, and to fill such or any other vacancy.

"All officers under the existing Government are hereby requested to continue to exercise their functions and perform the duties of their respective offices excepting the following named persons: Queen Liliuokalani, Charles B. Wilson, Marshal; Samuel Parker, Minister of Foreign Affairs; W. H. Cornwell, Minister of Finance; John F. Colburn, Minister of Interior; Arthur P. Peterson, Attorney-General, who are hereby removed from office. All Hawaiian laws and constitutional principles not inconsistent herewith shall continue in force until further order of the Executive and Advisory Councils.

 Henry E. Cooper,   J. A. McCandless,
 Andrew Brown,   Theodore F. Lansing,
 John Emmelsmith,   C. Bolte,
 Edward Suhr,   Henry Waterhouse,
 W. C. Wilder,   F. W. McChesney,
     William O. Smith."

The following day, the Provisional Government was organized, and at once issued a proclamation reciting the arrogance of the Queen, enumerating the broken promises of Her Majesty and detailing the wrongs inflicted on the residents and property.

The new Government called on volunteers, who assembled, armed, to the number of 500. The old Government surrendered without striking a blow, although it had about 400 men under arms and a battery of Gatling guns. The Provisional Government then notified the representatives of foreign Governments of the change, and asked recognition. It was at once granted by all the powers except England.

The Government assumed formal control of the palace and barracks. The Ex-Queen retired to her private residence at Washington Place, and the Government granted her an honorary guard of 16 men. The household guards were paid off to February 1st, and disbanded. A strong force of volunteers took possession, and is now in charge of the palace, the barracks, the police headquarters and other Government buildings.

At the headquarters the work of military organization was pushed rapidly forward, and volunteers continued to pour in steadily from all quarters. The Provisional Government spent a large part of the night in perfecting its organization and adjusting the wheels of Government to changed order. In the meantime the ordinary routine work of the Government was going ahead with but little break. The Hawaiian steamer *Claudine* was chartered, and left Honolulu on the morning of Wednesday, January 19th, four days after the revolt, with five commissioners aboard instructed to proceed to Washington, and negotiate a treaty of annexation. The commissioners were Lorrin A. Thurston, William C. Wilder, William R. Caset, Charles L. Carter and Joseph Marsden.

During the critical time, just as the reformers were about to sieze the throne, the United States warship *Boston* arrived unexpectedly and landed marines to protect the lives and property of Americans on the island. This turned out to be an important event in the subsequent history of the islands, for President Cleveland used it against the new Government. The deposed Queen openly charged that these troops were part of a conspiracy against her. In the proclamation issued when she was deposed, she said:

"I, Liliuokalani, by grace of God, and under the Constitution of the Hawaiian Kingdom Queen, do hereby solemnly protest any and all acts done against myself and the Constitutional Government of the Hawaiian Kingdom, by certain persons claiming to have established a Provisional Government of and for this Kingdom; that I yield to the superior force of the United States of America, whose Minister Plenipotentiary, His Excellency John L. Stevens, has caused United States troops to be landed at Honolulu, and declared that he would support the said Government.

"Now, to avoid any collision of armed forces and perhaps loss of life, I do under this protest and impelled by said force, yield my authority until such time as the Government of the United States shall, upon facts being presented to it, under the action of its representative reinstate me in the authority which I claim as constitutional sovereign of the Hawaiian Islands.

Done at Honolulu, this 17th day of January, A.D., 1893.

   (Signed)   LILIUOKALANI."

United States Minister Stevens immediately recognized the new Government in the following communication:

"To S. B. Dole, Esq., and others, composing the Provisional Government of the Hawaiian Islands: A Provisional Government having been duly constituted in place of the recent Government of Queen Liliuokalani, and the said Provisional Government being in full possession of the Government buildings, archives and treasury, and in control of the capital of the Hawaiian Islands, I hereby recognize said Provisional Government as the de facto Government of the Hawaiian Islands. JOHN L. STEVENS,
Envoy Extraordinary and Minister Plenipotentiary of the United States,"

When the matter officially reached our Government, a treaty of annexation was negotiated by President Harrison, and was sent to the Senate for confirmation, but was not passed before that body adjourned.

The election of President Cleveland put a new phase on the subject for he did not take the same view of the question as did his predecessor. It seemed to him that the protectorate established on the islands, and the control of the reform Government had been the result of conspiracy in which our own consul and the captain of the *Boston* had played a conspicuous part. Even before his inauguration he started an investigation into the matter, and one of the first things he did after he entered the White House was to withdraw the treaty which was in the hands of the Senate, and to send the Hon. James H. Blount, of Georgia, to the islands with instructions to investigate the whole affair. Such were Mr. Blount's powers that he was ever known afterward as "Paramount" Blount. He had been in Honolulu but two days, when he ordered the American flag hauled down from the Government building where it was flying and ordered the marines, which were doing duty there to return on board the *Boston*, and other ships to which they belonged. He immediately took a position which was higher in authority than either the naval officers there, or the American Minister. He started to take a testimony, but according to the unprejudiced mind it seems to have been testimony chiefly of the people allied to the deposed Queen, and was filled with perversions of facts which are well known, and was not at all convincing.

His report, however, was accepted by President Cleveland without more ado, and the latter sought to restore the Queen to her throne. Here, however, he met with an unexpected difficulty. One of the conditions which he laid before the Queen was that, when the throne should be restored to her, she should not punish the officers of the Provisional Government and the leaders of the revolution. This she bitterly refused to accede to, demanding that it was her right not only to confiscate the property of the people who sought her crown, but to behead them as well. This gave Mr. Cleveland a better idea than he had had before of the blood-thirstiness of Queen "Lil", and, even though she agreed finally to forego the pleasure of chopping off the heads of her foes, it was done in such a way that the United States, through its Minister, merely went through the formality of requesting the Provisional Government to vacate, and, when the latter declined to do so, the whole matter was dropped, and the incident was declared closed.

Owing to President Cleveland's feeling on the subject, no efforts were made during his Administration to push the annexation of the islands, and, consequently, the Provisional Government began to strengthen itself, and to look forward to becoming a permanent one. For that purpose a constitutional convention was called, which met on May 20th, and it continued in session until July 3d. On July 4, 1894, the Constitution of the new Republic of Hawaii was proclaimed, and Sanford B. Dole was elected the first President of the Republic, the same position which he occupied in the Provisional Government. And so, on the anniversary of the birthday of the greatest of all republics, there was born on this island, in the midst of the Pacific Ocean, a new republic, which was destined to become a territorial part of the United States.

But, although the islands and their throne had passed from beneath the sway of the dusky Queen "Lil" and the beautiful Kaiulani, they were not content to allow themselves to be deposed without at least a protest; so both the Queen and her niece visited this country with a view to enlisting the sympathies of President Cleveland and of the Senators and Representatives, who were to pass upon the subject of what was to become of the islands in the future.

The Princess Kaiulani was received everywhere with open arms. Her beauty, her culture, her grace and tact won for her hosts of friends wherever she appeared. Her journey was a series of social ovations. Not so with the Queen. She created but little stir, and outside of the newspaper cartoons which ridiculed her, and the frigid reception accorded her by Mr. Cleveland, she had but little attention paid her during her visit. Her reputation had preceded her, and though she stayed for a long time lobbying against the annexation of the islands to the United States, she finally left, unsuccessful and disconsolate.

On June 15, 1898, by a vote of 209 to 91, the bill providing for the annexation of Hawaii passed the House; and July 7th, the Senate passed the same resolution by a vote of 42 to 21, and President McKinley immediately signed it. The measure brought forth one of the most spirited debates ever known in the halls of the Legislature, inasmuch as it was the first step of our Government, outside of the domain which it had set down for itself, the first Congressional act of expansion. These resolutions declared that the islands were thereby annexed to the United States, and provided for five Commissioners, two at least of whom are to be residents of Hawaii, who should recommend such legislation to Congress as they thought advisable. The United States assumed the Hawaiian debt up to $4,000,000; Chinese immigration was prohibited; the treaties existing between Hawaii and the other powers were declared void; all civil, judicial, and military powers exercised by the officers of the Hawaiian Republic were to be exercised according to the directions of the President, and that officer was given power to appoint those who are to put in effect the Provisional Government of the islands. And so, on August 12, 1898, the flag of Hawaii was hauled down forever, and the new Republic began its life under the Stars and Stripes.

The American flag was raised above the Government Building with due solemnity, at which American marines and sailors from the United States vessels *Philadelphia* and *Mohican* attended. Shortly before 12 o'clock President Dole, attended by his Cabinet and Chief Justice Judd, arrived, and was joined by Minister Sewall, Admiral Miller and members of the Legislature and the Diplomatic Corps. There, on behalf of the Government of Hawaii, President Dole transferred the islands to the care of the United States, and, as the last salute to the old Government died away, and the flag that had floated for years over the islands was hauled down, the Hawaiian national anthem gave way to the "Star Spangled Banner," and the American flag was raised, while salute after salute greeted it.

Thus ended the hopes of Queen Liliuokalani, and the still greater hopes for the far future of the beautiful Princess Kaiulani for the crown which she was never to wear; but that the good of Hawaii was conserved, cannot be doubted. Neither of them attended the ceremony; the latter, with her eyes filled with tears, sat alone at her own home and passed through the bitterest moments of her life, denying herself friends and comforters.

President McKinley, under the terms of the resolution which annexed Hawaii, appointed as Commissioners to visit the islands Senator Shelby M. Cullom, of Illinois; Senator John T. Morgan, of Alabama; Representative Robert R. Hitt, of Illinois; President Sanford B. Dole, of Hawaii; and Justice W. F. Frear, of the Hawaiian Supreme Court. They visited the islands in August in order to formulate a plan for the Government. The bill which they formulated and presented to Congress provided for the government of Hawaii as a territory. Provision was made for a legislature of two houses, and the people were practically allowed to govern themselves according to the rules of the other territories of the United States. And so this possession of peace, which came to the United States in time of war, begins a new era of prosperity.

All of the American troops who have gone to Manila are enthusiastic about Hawaii. It was the first stop which they had on their long voyage halfway around the world, and when they reached it the weather was as delightful and the islands as beautiful as anyone could wish. The men stopped for a little breathing time there, and it proved a time of delight to those who visited these shores for the first time. The beauties of Honolulu, its civilization, the culture and refinement of many of the people, the richness of the coloring of flowers and foliage, and the novelty of everything that met their sight shattered all their former belief that Hawaii was an unknown, uncivilized land.

The Astor Battery boys were particularly enthusiastic about the reception they received. Everywhere they met with an ovation, as indeed did all the troops of Uncle Sam, and they were entertained by some of the residents of the place at a native dinner. This function is one that will long live in the minds of those who enjoyed it for the first time. A member of the Astor Battery tells of such a dinner which he attended, and at which Princess Kaiulani was present. He says: "The guests sat on the floor facing each other, and the good things, from a Hawaiian point of view, were placed on the floor before them. There were no courses, but in eating one helped himself, and then passed the dish on to the next neighbor, who in turn helped it circulate around the company. One of the dishes was the favorite Honolulu dish called "Poi," which was served in a bowl, and each guest helped himself with his fingers. This was all right for the first one, but when one was seated at the other end, unless he was used to the habit, or had a soldier's appetite, or had had assurances that the others had washed their hands, he was likely not to relish this dainty of the Sandwich Islands.

"I was very much surprised with the appearance of Princess Kaiulani. I had read of her in the papers, but was not prepared to find a woman of such rare intelligence and refinement as she proved to be. She is extremely fascinating, and came dressed in the fashion peculiar to the high class members of Hawaiian royalty. Around her throat she wore a necklace which might more strictly be called a boa. It was a magnificent piece of art and had been in her family for generations. It was made entirely of feathers, each feather of which had been separately plucked from beneath the wing of one bird of a rare native species, after which the bird was killed. It took years to complete this necklace, and thousands of birds were sacrificed in its making.

"The Princess spoke English fluently, also French, and, in fact, any of the languages which her guests were able to speak. She was very bright and vivacious, and gave no symptom of not being in the best of health."

This last remark was apropos of the sad news that recently came from Honolulu that the lovely Princess passed away in the early part of March, 1899, and was buried with all possible ceremonies on the 12th of the same month.

The manners and customs of the native Hawaiians are most interesting, but space forbids a description of them here. Their religion was a gross form of idolatry, with many gods. Human sacrifice was freely practiced. They deified dead chiefs and worshiped their bones. The great king, Kamehameha I., though an idolater, was a most progressive monarch, and invited Vancouver, who went there in 1794, taking swine, cattle, sheep, and horses, together with oranges and other valuable plants, to bring over teachers and missionaries to teach his people "the white man's religion."

But it was not until 1820, after the death of the great King, that the first missionaries arrived, and they came from America. The year previous, in 1819, Kamehameha II. had destroyed many of the

RAISING THE AMERICAN FLAG IN HONOLULU, AUGUST 12, 1898.
The cut in the corner shows the Royal Palace formerly occupied by the Hawaiian Kings.

CHURCH IN HONOLULU, HAWAIIAN ISLANDS.
Built of lava stone. Seating capacity about 3000.

SUGAR CANE PLANTATION, HAWAIIAN ISLANDS.
About one-fifth of the entire population is engaged in sugar culture. The average product is about three tons per acre.

temples and idols and forbidden idol worship in the islands; consequently, when the missionaries arrived, they beheld the unprecedented spectacle of a nation without a religion. The natives were rapidly converted to Christianity. It was these American missionaries who first reduced the Hawaiian language to writing, established schools and taught the natives. As a result of their work, the Hawaiians are among the most generally educated people, in the elementary sense, in the world. There is hardly a person in the islands, above the age of eight years, who cannot read and write. In spite of education, however, many of the ancient superstitions still exist, and some of the old stone temples are yet standing. What the United States will do with these heathen temples remains to be seen. The natives revere them as relics of their savage history, and as such they may be preserved.

Aside from the horrors of superstitions, the Hawaiians lead a happy life, full of amusements of various kinds on the land and water —for Hawaiian men, women and children live much of their time in the water. Infants are often taught the art of swimming before they can walk. The surf riding or swimming of the natives astonished Captain Cook more than any of their remarkable performances. The time selected was when a storm was tossing the waves high and the surf was furious. Then the men and women would dive through the surf, with narrow boards about nine inches wide and eight feet long, and, swimming a mile or more out to sea, mount on the crest of a huge billow, and sitting, kneeling or standing, with wild gesticulations ride over the waves and breakers like gods or demons of the storm. This practice is less indulged now than formerly. But the swimming of the Kanaka boys, who flock around incoming steamers, and dive after and catch coins which tourists throw into the water, like so many ducks diving after corn, shows what a degree of perfection the natatorial art has attained among the native Hawaiians. Sledging down the mountain sides, boxing and tournament riding are other popular amusements; and, with the exception of boxing, the women compete with the men in the amusements.

PRODUCTS AND COMMERCE.

Sugar is king in Hawaii as wheat is in the Northwest. In 1890 there were 19,000 laborers—nearly one-fifth of the total population—

engaged on sugar plantations. Ten tons to the acre have been raised on the richest lands. The average is over three tons per acre, but it requires from eighteen to twenty months for a crop to mature. Rice growing is also an important industry. It is raised in marsh lands, and nearly all the labor is done by Chinese, though they do not own the land. Coffee is happily well suited to the soil that is unfitted for sugar and rice, and the Hawaiian coffee is particularly fine, combining the strength of the Java with a delicate flavor of its own.

Diversified farming is coming more into vogue. Fruit raising will undoubtedly become one of the most important branches when fast steamers are provided for its transportation. Sheep and cattle raising must also prove profitable, since the animals require little feeding and need no housing.

Almost all kinds of vegetables and fruits can be raised, many of those belonging to the temperate zones thriving on the elevated mountain slopes. Fruit is abundant; the guava grows wild in all the islands, and were the manufacture of jelly made from it carried on on a large scale the product could doubtless be exported with profit. Both bananas and pineapples are prolific, and there are many fruits and vegetables, which as yet have been raised only for local trade, which would, if cultivated for export, bring in rich returns.

Of the total exports from the Hawaiian Islands in 1895, the United States received 99.04 per cent., and in the same year 79.04 per cent. of the imports to the islands were from the United States. The total value of the sugar sent to the United States in 1896, was $14,932,010; of rice, $194,903; of coffee, $45,444; and of bananas, $121,273.

THE CHIEF CITY.

Honolulu, the capital city, is to Hawaii what Havana is to Cuba, or better, what Manila is to the Philippine Islands. Here are concentrated the business, political and social forces that control the life and progress of the entire archipelago. This city of 30,000 inhabitants is situated on the south coast of Oahu, and extends up the Nuuanu Valley. It is well provided with street-car lines—which also run to a bathing resort four miles outside the city—a telephone system, electric lights, numerous stores, churches and schools, a library of over 10,000 volumes, and frequent steam communication with San

Francisco. There are papers published in the English, Hawaiian, Portuguese, Japanese, and Chinese languages, and a railroad is being built, of which thirty miles along the coast are already completed. Honolulu has also a well-equipped fire department and public waterworks. The residence portions of the city are well laid out, the houses, many of which are very handsome, being surrounded by gardens kept green throughout the year. The climate is mild and even, and the city is a delightful and a beautiful place of residence. Hawaii is peculiarly an agricultural country, and Honolulu gains its importance solely as a distributing centre or depot of supplies. Warehouses, lumber yards and commercial houses abound, but there is a singular absence of mills and factories and productive establishments. There are no metals or minerals, or, as yet, textile plants or food plants, whose manufacture is undertaken in this unique city.

The Hawaiian Islands are, without question, on the threshold of a great industrial era, fraught with most potent results to the prosperity and development of that land. Its climate is delightful and healthful, and its soil so fertile that it will easily support 5,000,000 people.

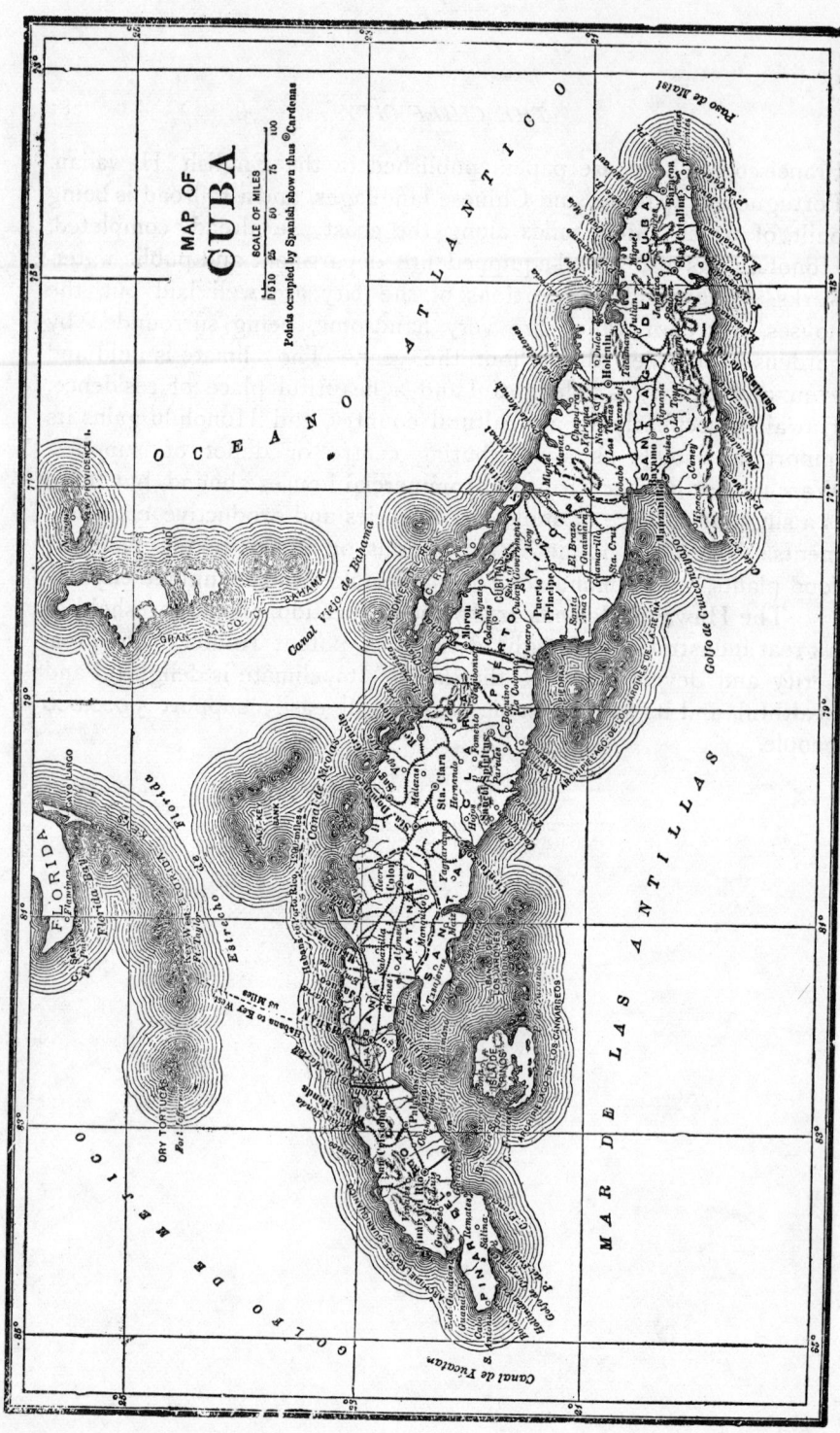

CHAPTER XVI

Cuba, "The Child of Our Adoption."

The Island whose Cry to Humanity Brought the War of Relief.—How It Received its Name.—The Founding of the Capital, Havana.—A Terrible History of Spanish Cruelty.—The Extermination of a Great People, Beginning in the Time of the Son of Columbus, before 1560 the Whole of the Population had Disappeared from the Island.—The First Cuban Revolt.—The Capture of Havana by the English.—Its Restoration to Spain.—A Long Series of Insurrections.—The Seven Years' War.—The Last and Final Uprising.—The Advent of Weyler, "the Butcher."—Atrocities before which the whole World Stood Aghast.—His Motto was "Subjugation or Death."—American Filibusters Lend a Helping Hand.—The Death of General Maceo, through Treachery, a great Blow to the Insurgents.—Weyler and the Reconcentrados.—Two Hundred Thousand Men, Women and Children Die of Disease and Starvation.—Insurgents the Masters of almost the whole Island.—The Fearful Cost of the War.—The Cuban Debt Reached Nearly $300,000,000.

ALTHOUGH Cuba is not a part or a possession of the United States, it has since the war with Spain, in 1898, come under the protection of this government, and is, therefore, entitled to a place in this volume. In the hand of Providence, this island became the doorway to America. It was here that Columbus landed, October 28, 1492. True, he touched earlier at one of the smaller islands to the north; but it was merely a halting before pushing on to Cuba. "Juana" Columbus called the island, in honor of Isabella's infant son. Afterward it was successively known as Fernandina, Santiago, and Ave Maria; but the simple natives, who were there to the number of 350,000, called it *Cooba*, and this name prevailed over the Spanish titles, as the island has finally prevailed over Spanish domination, and it has come under the protection of America with its Indian name, slightly changed to *Cuba*, remaining as the sole and only heritage we have of the simple aborigines, who have utterly perished from the face of the earth under Spanish cruelty.

In 1494 Columbus visited Cuba a second time, and once again in 1502. In 1511 Diego Columbus, the son of the great discoverer with a colony of between three and four hundred Spaniards, came, and, in 1514, he founded the towns of Santiago and Trinidad. Five years later, in 1519, the present capital Havana, or *Habana*, was founded. The French reduced the city in 1538, practically demolishing the whole town. Under the governor De Soto, it was rebuilt and fortified, the famous Morro Castle and the Punta, which are still standing, being built at that early date.

THE ORIGINAL INHABITANTS.

The natives, whom Columbus found in Cuba, were agreeable in feature, and so amiable in disposition that they welcomed the white man with open arms, and, besides contributing food, readily gave up their treasurers to please the Spaniards. Unlike the warlike cannibal tribes of the Lesser Antilles, known as the Caribs, they lived in comparative peace with one another, and had a religion which recognized the Supreme Being. Columbus held several conferences with these simple natives, who numbered, according to his estimate, from 350,000 to half a million souls, and his associations and dealings with them on his first visit were always friendly and of a mutually pleasing nature. But when he returned to Spain he left soldiers, who brutally maltreated them, until the natives rose in revolt and exterminated every white man. Even Columbus himself, in 1494, had to fight the Indians at the landing-place.

A salubrious climate, a fertile soil, and simple wants rendered it unnecessary for the native to do hard work; and although it is well proven that he did mine copper and traded in it with the mound builders of Florida, yet the native was not accustomed to arduous toil, and rebelled against it. This, perhaps, was unfortunate, for the perpetuity of his race at that time depended upon this very quality. The Spanish "friend" who came to the island was incapable of work. He neither would nor could, under his ethics of self-respect, abase himself to labor, so he proceeded to enslave the native to labor for him. The Cuban rebelled, and fled before the superior Spanish weapons from the coasts to the mountain fastnesses of the interior.

Then began that cruel and long-continued war of extermination, of which history has recorded the most shocking details. The conquest was begun under Diego Columbus, the son of the great discoverer.

The merciless Velasquez was his general, and the frightful cruelties which he inaugurated upon the simple natives have been continued for nearly four hundred years by his successors in the island, though the annihilation of the aboriginal tribes themselves was a brief and bloody work. Velasquez rode them down and trampled them—regardless of age or sex—under the iron hoofs of his war-horses slashed them with swords, devastated their villages, and bore them away into slavery. The Cuban had no weapons; the mountain fastnesses could not hide him from his relentless pursuer. African slaves, who were brought to the island in Spanish ships, were armed and forced by their masters to chase the natives, and not a forest or mountain top was a place of refuge for these doomed children of the soil. One historian declares: "There is a little doubt that before 1560 the whole of this native population had dissapeared from the island. They were so completely exterminated that it is doubtful if the blood of their race was even remotely preserved in the mixed classes who followed African and Chinese introduction."

A PERIOD OF REST.

For nearly two hundred years after the extermination of the natives, Cuba rested without a struggle in the arms of Spain The early settlers engaged almost wholly in pastoral pursuits. Tobacco was indigenous to the soil, and in 1580 the Cuban planters began its culture. Later, sugar-cane was imported from the Canaries, and found to be a fruitful and profitable crop. The beginning of the culture of sugar demanded more laborers, and the importation of additional slaves was the result. In 1717, Spain attempted to make a monopoly of the tobacco culture, and the first Cuban revolt occurred. In 1723 a second uprising took place, because of an oppressive government; but these early revolts against tyranny were insignificant as compared with those of the last half-century.

In 1762, the city of Havana was captured by the English, with an expedition commanded by Lord Albemarle, but his fighting troops were principally Americans under the immediate command of Generals Phineas Lyman and Israel Putnam of Revolutionary fame. The story of Putnam's command in this war is thrilling and sad. After first suffering shipwreck and many hardships in reaching the island they lay before Havana, where Spanish bullets and fever almost annihilated the whole command. Scarcely more than one in fifty lived to return to America. By the Treaty of Paris, 1763, Cuba was unfortunately restored to Spain, and it was afterward that her troubles with the "Mother Country," as Spain affectionately called herself to all her provinces, began. The hand of oppression for one and a quarter centuries relaxed not its grasp, and year by year grew heavier and more galling.

DISCONTENT AND INSURRECTIONS.

Some of the most prolific seeds of modern revolutions may be said to have been sown when the African slave trade assumed important proportions, in 1791. About the same time began a large importation of Chinese coolies, for which Cuba paid a bounty of $400 apiece to the importer. These coolies bound themselves to the Spaniards for eight years, for which they received $4.00 per month as wages. The new influx of labor and the coming of Las Casas as Captain-General to Cuba, in 1790, mark the beginning of Cuba's great period of prosperity. This enterprising ruler introduced numerous public improvements, established botanical gardens and schools of agriculture, with a view to developing and increasing Cuba's resources and commercial importance. Owing to his wise administration, Cuba prospered and remained undisturbed for a long while. An insurrection occurred among the slaves in 1812, which was promptly put down with characteristic cruelty, and the blacks remained "good niggers" for a third of a century. By the year 1844, the slave trade with Cuba had grown to enormous proportions. In that year alone, statistics tell us, 10,000 slaves were landed from Africa upon the island. Another wild and fanatical insurrection occurred the same year among them, in which thousands of their lives were sacrificed, but, as before, they failed. By 1850, the slaves had so multiplied and the importation had been so large that the census showed there were nearly 500,000 on the island.

Meantime, in 1830, a revolution on the part of the Creoles (descendants of Spanish and French settlers) and other free Cubans had broken out. It was put down, but the blood of the martyrs was seed in the ground. Revolutionist and enslaved insurrectionist

ENTRANCE TO THE PUBLIC GROUNDS, HAVANA, CUBA.

MAGNIFICENT INDIAN STATUE IN THE PRADO, HAVANA, CUBA.

ANTONIO MACEO.
Lieutenant-General in the Cuban Army. Killed December 4, 1896. Eight of his brothers had previously given their lives for Cuban freedom.

GENERAL CALIXTO GARCIA.
Hero of three wars for Cuba's freedom. Died of pneumonia in Washington, D. C., December, 1898.

GENERAL MAXIMO GOMEZ
The Washington of Cuba is the title applied to this hero, who, as Commander-in-Chief of the patriot army, made Cuban liberty possible.

JOSE MARTI.
President of the Cuban Revolutionary Party. Led into ambush and killed by the Spaniards, May 19, 1895.

CUBAN HEROES AND MARTYRS.

gradually drifted together. They had a common cause—to struggle for freedom against oppression. The bondsman was little or no worse off than the creoles, Chinese coolies, and free negroes—all native-born Cubans were shut out from the enjoyment of true citizenship. They must do the work and pay the tribute, but Spaniards, born in Spain, were alone allowed to hold office of profit or trust under the government; and they looked with inexpressible contempt upon the rest of the population, and, with the backing of the army, preserved their domination in spite of their inferior numbers. The Governor-General was appointed from Spain and held office from three to five years, and was expected to steel or extort himself rich in that time. It is said that not one Governor-General ever failed to do so.

THE TEN YEARS' WAR.

The first long and determined struggle of the oppressed people of Cuba for liberty began in 1868. In that year a revolution broke out in Spain, and the patriots seized the opportunity, while the mother country was occupied at home, for an heroic effort to liberate themselves. They rose first at Yara, in the district of Bayamo, and on October 10th of that year made a declaration of independence Eight days later the city of Bayamo was taken by the patriots, and early in November they defeated a force sent against them from Santiago. The majority of the South American republics hastened to recognize the Cubans as belligerents; but—though they held the entire interior of the island throughout a period of ten years, continually winning battles, and it was evident to all the world that Spain could not subdue them—there was not one great power in the world willing to extend to the patriots the recognition of belligerent rights. The cruelty of the Spaniards toward the soldiers they captured, and to all inhabitants who sympathized with the patriots' cause, was equaled only by the courage, fortitude, and exalted patriotism which animated their victims. The following instances, selected from scores that might be cited, are given in the Spaniards' own words translated, *verbatim*, into English :

Jacob Rivocoba, under date of September 4, 1896, writes :

"We captured seventeen, thirteen of whom were shot outright; on dying they shouted, 'Hurrah for free Cuba! hurrah for independence!' A mulatto said, 'Hurrah for Cespedes!' On the following day we killed a Cuban officer and another man. Among the thirteen that we shot the first day were found three sons and their father; the father witnessed the execution of his sons without even changing color, and when his turn came he said he died for the independence of his country. On coming back we brought along with us three carts filled with women and children, the families of those we had shot; and they asked us to shoot them, because they would rather die than live among Spaniards."

Pedro Fardon, another officer, who entered entirely into the spirit of the service he honored, writes on September 22, 1869:

"Not a single Cuban will remain in this island, because we shoot all those we find in the fields, on the farms, and in every hovel."

And, again, on the same day, the same officer sends the following good news to his old father:

"We do not leave a creature alive where we pass, be it man or animal. If we find cows, we kill them; if horses, ditto; if hogs, ditto; men, women, or children, ditto; as to the houses, we burn them: so every one receives his due—the men in balls, the animals in bayonet-thrusts. The island will remain a desert."

These atrocities were perpetrated not alone by the common soldier. In fact, the above reports come from men who were officers in the Spanish army, and they show that such actions were approved by the highest authority. A well-authenticated account assures us that General Count Balmaceda himself went on one occasion to the home of a patriot family, Mora by name, to arrest or kill the patriots he had heard were stopping there; but, finding the men all absent, he wreaked his vengeance and thirst for blood by butchering the two Mora sisters and burning the house over their bodies.

PEACE AND FAIR PROMISES.

At last, Spain, seeing that she could neither induce the Cubans to surrender nor draw them into a decisive battle; and finding, furthermore, that her army of 200,000 men was likely to be annihilated by death, disease, and patriot bullets, made overtures, which, by promising many privileges to the people that they had not before enjoyed, effected a peace. As a result of this war, slavery was abolished in the island; but Spain's promises for fair and equitable government were repudiated, and the civil powers became more extortionate and severe than ever. This war laid a heavy debt upon Spain, and Cuba was taxed inordinately. The people soon saw that they had been duped. The world looked upon Cuba and Spain as at peace. To the outsider the surface was placid, but underneath "the waters were troubled." Such heroic spirits as Generals Calixto Garcia, Jose Marti, Antonio Maceo, and Maximo Gomez, leaders in the ten years' struggle, still lived, though scattered far apart, and in their hearts bore a load of righteous wrath against their treacherous foe. While such men lived and such conditions existed another conflict was inevitable.

THE LAST GREAT STRUGGLE FOR FREEDOM.

It was on February 24, 1895, that the last revolution of the Cuban patriots began. Spain had heard the mutterings of the coming storm, and hoped to stay it by visiting with severe punishment every Cuban suspected of patriotic affiliations. Antonio Maceo, a mulatto, but a man of fortune and education, a veteran of the Ten Years' War, and a Cuban by birth, was banished to San Domingo. There were other exiles in Key West, New York, and elsewhere. Jose Marti was the leading spirit in forming the Cuban Junta in New York and organizing revolutionary clubs among Cubans everywhere. Antonio Maceo was selected to lead the patriot army. He went secretly to Cuba and began organizing an army, and when war was declared the flag of the new republic, bearing a red lone star in a red field, was flung to the breeze in three of the six provinces. Captain-General Campos declared martial law in the insurgents' vicinity, and troops were hastily summoned and sent from Spain. The revolutionists from the start fought by guerrilla methods of warfare, dashing upon the unsuspecting Spanish towns and forces, and escaping to the mountains before the organized Spaniards could retaliate.

Jose Marti and Jose Maceo—brother of the General—were prompt to join the active forces, and on April 13, 1895, General Maximo Gomez, a native of San Domingo, came over and was made commander of the insurgent forces. This grizzled old hero, with nearly seventy years behind him, was at once an inspiration and a host within himself. An army of 6,000 men was ready for his command, and the revolution took on new life and began in all its fury. On May 19th the insurgents met their first great disaster, when Jose Marti was led into an ambush and killed. But his blood was like a seed planted, from which thousands of patriots sprang up for the ranks. Within a few days there were 10,000 ill-armed but determined men in the field. They had no artillery, nearly half were without guns, and there was little ammunition for those who were armed.

THE PLANS OF CAMPOS THWARTED.

Captain-General Campos formed a plan to march with the Spanish troops from end to end of the island, and drive the insurgents into the sea if they refused to surrender. Information of this plan was carried to Gomez, who proved so wily that Campos could neither capture him nor force him into an engagement. Everywhere Gomez marched he gathered new patriots into his army, and captured many carloads of Spanish stores and arms. Near the city of Bayamo, Maceo attacked Campos, and the Spanish commander barely escaped with his life. He was besieged in Bayamo, and had to stay there until 10,000 soldiers were sent to escort him home. That was the last of Campos' fighting. By August, Spain had spent $21,300,000 and lost 20,000 men by death, and 39,000 additional soldiers had been brought into the island, 25,000 of them the flower of the Spanish army, and she was also forced to issue $120,000,000 bonds which she sold at a great sacrifice, to carry on the war.

The patriots met in September 13, 1895, at Camaguey and formed their government by adopting a constitution and electing a president and other state officers. This body formally conferred upon Gomez the commission of Commander-in-Chief of the army. Before the close of the month, there were 30,000 rebels in the field. Spanish warships patroled the coast, but the insurgents held the whole interior of Santiago province, and the government forces dared not venture away from the sea. The same was true of Santa Clara and Puerto Principe. Matanzas was debatable ground; but Gomez made bold raids into the very vicinity of Havana. Spain soon had an army of 200,000 and the insurgents 50,000.

As if the cup of Cuba's sorrow were not sufficiently bitter, or her long-suffering patriots had not drunk deep enough of its gall, General Campos was recalled, and General Valeriano Weyler (nicknamed "The Butcher") arrived in February, 1896. He promptly inaugurated the most bitter and inhuman policy in the annals of modern warfare. It began with a campaign of intimidation, in which his motto was "Subjugation or Death." He established a system of espionage that was perfect, and the testimony of the spy was all the evidence he required. He heeded no prayer and knew no mercy. His prisons overflowed with suspected patriots, and his sunrise executions, every morning, made room for others. It was thus that General Weyler carried on the war from his palace against the unarmed natives, his 200,000 soldiers seldom securing a shot at the insurgents, who were continually bushwhacking them with deadly effect, while yellow fever carried them off by the thousands. How many lives Weyler sacrificed in that dreadful year will never be known. How many suspects he frightened into giving him all their gold for mercy and then coldly shot for treason, no record will disclose; but the crowded, unmarked graves on the hillside outside Havana are mute but eloquent witnesses of his infamy.

Under these conditions Gomez declared that all Cubans must take sides. They must be for or against. It was no time for neutrals and there could be no neutral ground, so he boldly levied forced contributions upon planters who were unfavorable to his cause, and who extended protection to those who befriended the patriots.

THE DEATH OF GENERAL MACEO.

On the night of December 4, 1896, the insurgents suffered an irreparable loss in the death of General Maceo, who was led into an ambush and killed, it is believed, through the treachery of his staff physician. Eight brothers of Maceo had previously given their lives for Cuban freedom.

At the close of 1896, the island was desolate to an extreme perhaps unprecedented in modern times. The country was laid waste and the cities were starving. Under the pretext of protecting them, Weyler gathered the non-combatants into towns and stockades, and it is authoritatively stated that 200,000 men, women, and children of the "reconcentrados," as they were called, died of disease and starvation. The insurgents remained masters of the island except along the coasts. The only important incident of actual warfare was the capture of Victoria de las Tunas, in Santiago province, by General Garcia at the head of 3,000 men, after three days' fighting. In this battle the Spanish commander lost his life and forty per cent. of his troops were killed or wounded ; the rest surrendered to Garcia, and the rebels secured by their victory 1,000 rifles, 1,000,000 rounds of ammunition, and two Krupp guns.

In the spring of 1898, the United States intervened. The story of our war with Spain for Cuba's freedom is elsewhere related,

Spain has paid dearly for her supremacy in Cuba during the last third of the nineteenth century. Notwithstanding the fact that the revenue from Cuba for several years prior to the Ten Years' War of 1868–78 amounted to $26,000,000 annually—about $18 for every man, woman, and child in the island—$20,000,000 of it was absorbed in Spain's official circles at Havana, and "the other $6,000,000 that the Spanish government received," says one historian, " was hardly enough to pay transportation rates on the help that the mother country had to send to her army of occupation." Consequently, despite this enormous tax, a heavy debt accumulated on account of the island, even before the Ten Years' War began.

FEARFUL COST OF THE WAR.

At the close of the Ten Years' War (1878) Spain had laid upon the island a public debt of $200,000,000, and required her to raise $39,000,000 of revenue annually, an average at that time of nearly $30 per inhabitant. But Spain's own debt had also increased to nearly $2,000,000,000, and during this Ten Years' War she had sent 200,000 soldiers and her favorite commanders to the island, only about 50,000 of whom ever returned. According to our Consular Report of July, 1898, when the last revolution began, 1895, the Cuban debt had reached $295,707,264. The interest on this alone imposed a burden of $9.79 per annum upon each inhabitant. During the war, Spain had 200,000 troops in the island, and the three and one-half years' conflict cost her the loss of nearly 100,000 lives, mostly from sickness, and, as yet, unknown millions of dollars.

CHAPTER XVII

Possibilities of the Island

Its Possibilities, its Hopes.—The Extent of the Island, its Soil and its vast Products.
—Rich in Sugar, in Timber and in Minerals, it is a Place Promising Wealth,
Rivaling that of the Klondike.—Its Commerce and its Climate.—Havana, the
Capital City, and other Ports.

WHAT the future of Cuba may be under new conditions of government remains to be seen. Certainly, in all the world's history few sadder or more devastated lands have gathered their remnants of population upon the ashes of their ruins and turned a hopeful face to the future. So far as the people themselves are concerned, a more hunted, starved, wasted, and wretched mass of humanity never lay upon the bosom of their desolated land.

But the soil, the mineral and the timber, not even Spanish tyranny could destroy; and in these lie the hope, we may say the sure guarantee, of Cuba's future. In wealth of resources and fertility of soil, Cuba is superior to all other tropical countries, and these fully justify its right to the title, "Pearl of the Antilles," first given it by Columbus.

Under a wise and secure government its possibilities are almost limitless. Owing to its location at the entrance of the Gulf of Mexico, which it divides into the Yucatan and Florida channels, on the south and north, the island has been termed the "Key to the Gulf of Mexico," and on its coat of arms is emblazoned a key, as if to imply its ability to open or close this great sea to the commerce of the world.

Cuba extends from east to west 760 miles, is 21 miles wide in its narrowest part and 111 miles in the widest, with an average width of 60 miles. It has numerous harbors, which afford excellent anchorage. The area of the island proper is 41,655 square miles (a little larger than the State of Ohio), and including the Isle of Pines and other small points around its entire length, numbering in all some 1,200, there are 47,278 square miles altogether in Cuba and belonging to it. The island is intersected by broken ranges of mountains, which gradually increase in height from west to east, where they reach an elevation of nearly 8,000 feet. The central and western portions of the island are the most fertile, while the principal mineral deposits are in the mountains of the eastern end. In Matanzas and other central provinces, the well-drained, gently sloping plains, diversified by low, forest-clad hills, are especially adapted to sugar culture, and the country under normal conditions presents the appearance of vast fields of cane. The western portion of the island is also mountainous, but the elevations are not great, and in the valleys and along the fertile slopes of this district is produced the greater part of the tobacco for which the island is famous.

FERTILITY OF SOIL AND ITS PRODUCTS.

The soil of the whole island is well-nigh inexhaustible. Except in tobacco culture, fertilizers are never used. In the sugar districts are found old cane-fields that have produced annual crops for a hundred years without perceptible impoverishment of the soil. Besides sugar and tobacco, the island yields Indian corn, rice, manioc (the plant from which tapioca is prepared), oranges, bananas, pineapples, mangoes, guava and all other tropical fruits, with many of those belonging to the temperate zone. Raw sugar, molasses and tobacco are the chief products, and, with fruits, nuts and unmanufactured woods, form the bulk of exports, though coffee culture is rapidly coming to the front, and its fine quality indicates that it must in time become one of the most important products of the island.

As a sugar country, Cuba takes first rank in the world. Mr. Gallon, the English Consul, in his report to his government in 1897 upon this Cuban crop, declared: "Of the other cane-sugar countries of the world, Java is the only one which comes within 50 per cent, of the amount of sugar produced annually in Cuba in normal times, and Java and the Hawaiian Islands are the only ones which are so generally advanced in the process of manufacture." Our own Consul, Hyatt, in his report of February, 1897, expresses the belief that Cuba is equal to supplying the entire demands of the whole western hemisphere with sugar—a market for 4,000,000 tons or more, and requiring a crop four times as large as the island has ever yet produced. Those who regard this statement as extravagant should remember that Cuba, although founded and settled more than fifty years before the United States, has nearly 14,000,000 acres of uncleared primeval forest-land, and is capable of easily supporting a population more than ten times that of the present. In fact, the Island of Java, not so rich as Cuba, and of very nearly the same area, with less tillable land, has over 22,000,000 inhabitants as against Cuba's—perhaps at this time—not more than 1,200,000 souls.

MINERAL AND TIMBER RESOURCES.

The mineral resources of Cuba are second in importance to its agricultural products. Gold and silver are not believed to exist in paying quantities; but its most valuable mineral, copper, seems to be almost inexhaustible. The iron and manganese mines, in the vicinity of Santiago, are of great importance, the ores being rated among the finest in the world. Deposits of asphalt and mineral oils are also found.

The third resource of Cuba in importance is its forest product. Its millions of acres of unbroken woodlands are rich in valuable hard woods, suitable for the finest cabinet-work and shipbuilding, and also furnish many excellent dye woods. Mahogany, cedar, rosewood and ebony abound. The palm, of which there are thirty-odd species found in the island, is one of the most characteristic and valuable of Cuban trees.

CITIES AND COMMERCE.

The commerce of Cuba has been great in the past, but Spanish laws made it expensive and oppressive to the Cubans. Its location and resources, with wise government, assure to the island an enormous trade in the future. There are already four cities of marked importance to the commercial world: Havana with a population of 250,000, Santiago with 71,000, Matanzas with 29,000, and Cienfuegos with 30,000, are all seaport cities with excellent harbors, and all do a large exporting business. Add to these Cardenas with 25,000, Trinidad with 18,000, Manzanillo with 10,000, and Guantanamo and Baracoa, each with 7,000 inhabitants, we have an array of ten cities such as few strictly farming countries of like size possess Aside from cigar and cigarette making, there is little manufacturing in Cuba; but fruit canneries, sugar refineries, and various manufacturing industries for the consumption of native products will rapidly follow in the steps of good government. Hence, in the field of manufacturing, this island offers excellent inducements to capital.

SEASONS AND CLIMATE.

Like all tropical countries, Cuba has but two seasons—the wet and the dry. The former extends from May to October, June, July and August being the most rainy months. The dry season lasts from November to May. This fact must go far toward making the island more and more popular as a winter health resort. The interior of the island is mountainous, and always pleasantly cool at night, while on the highlands the heat in the day is less oppressive than in New York and Pennsylvania during the hottest summer weather; consequently, when once yellow fever, which now ravages the coasts of the island on account of its defective sanitation, is extirpated, as it doubtless will be under the new order of things, Cuba will become the seat of many winter homes for wealthy residents of the United States. Even in the summer, the temperature seldom rises above 80°, while the average for the year is 77°. At no place, except in the extreme mountainous altitude, is it ever cold enough for frost.

THE EVACUATION OF HAVANA.

The complete transfer of authority in the island of Cuba from Spain to the United States took place on Sunday, January 1, 1899. At noon on that day Captain-General Castellanos and staff met the representatives of the United States in the hall of his palace, and with due formality and marked Spanish courtesy, in the name of the King and Queen Regent of Spain, delivered possession of Cuba to General Wade, head of the American Evacuation Committee, and he in turn transferred the same to General Brooke, who had been appointed by President McKinley as Military Governor of the Division of Cuba. No unpleasant incident marred the occasion. General Castellanos spoke with evident, yet becoming emotion on so important an occasion. Three Cuban generals were present, who, at General

Castellanos' request, were presented to him, and the Spaniard said, with marked grace and evident sincerity "I am sorry, gentlemen, that we are enemies, being of the same blood;" to which one of the Cuban patriots courteously responded, with commendable charity, "We fought only for Cuba, and now that she is free, we are no longer enemies."

THE STARS AND STRIPES HOISTED.

The formal transfer had scarcely taken place within the palace hall, when the flag of Spain was lowered from Morro Castle, Cabanas Fortress, and all the public buildings, and the Stars and Stripes instantly arose in its place on the flagpoles of these old and historic buildings. As its graceful folds floated gently out upon the breeze, the crowds from the streets cheered, the band played the most appropriate of all airs, while voices in many places in the throng, catching up the tune, sang the inspiring words of the "Star-Spangled Banner."

HAVANA, THE BEAUTIFUL CAPITAL.

When one mentions Cuba, the first thought that enters the minds is of Havana, the beautiful capital of this beautiful Isle. For many years it has been the Mecca of social pilgrims who journey south during the winter to escape the cold. It is supposed to have been founded by Diego Velasquez, the conqueror of Cuba in 1508, who, being so delighted with the harbor and its general position, called it La Have del Nuevo Mondo, which means the key to the new world. In 1528, it was burned to the ground, but it was soon built anew, and protected by a chain of fortifications, which made it a great stronghold. In 1802, it was again largely destroyed by fire and instead of wood, it was rebuilt in stone and masonry.

GRIM MORRO CASTLE

The first thing that impresses the traveler as he enters Havana by the sea, is Morro Castle, which stands at the mouth of the harbor, cold, gloomy, but powerful, and one naturally shudders a little at its sight, because around it cluster tales of the most horrible brutality and savagery ever known in this continent. Here all the prisoners were kept to be led out later to pay the penalty of patriotism, for

crimes real or imaginary against the Spanish Government. Here
in its dungeons, prisoners were starved and tortured to madness,
and here too men, women and children whose only crimes were that
they had relatives in the ranks of the insurgents, were huddled together like rats in a cage, and made to suffer atrocities which have
shocked the whole civilized world.

The harbor of Havana is a beautiful one, and from a military
point of view, is practically impregnable. The city proper is quite as
beautiful. The commercial quarter consists of a labyrinth of narrow
lanes, traversed by one or two streets, which are wider and more
striking, the principal of which is the Calle Oreilly, which runs from
the Governor's palace out to the very walls of the City. Few of the
houses which line the little streets are more than one story in height,
but a Spanish one-story is almost equal to three stories of an average
house. The lower half of every house is painted either a dark blue,
deep red, or vivid yellow, while the upper part is always a dazzling
white. The columns of the buildings, which are plentiful, are usually
treated in the same way, one-half being one color, and the other half
another. The lower windows are protected for the most part by
heavy iron bars, which would make the place look like a prison,
especially as in passing one sees the fair face of some senorita looking from between them, were it not for their bright colors. Some of
the finer houses of the city are very handsome indeed, but there is
little variety in their architecture; they are all built in the style
which reminds one of Rome, with an inner courtyard surrounded by
handsome marble or stucco columns.

THE BEAUTY OF THE COURTYARDS.

In this inner courtyard is usually to be found a garden, with a
fountain in the centre, or perhaps some statues, and here the women
of the house entertain in the evening or enjoy themselves quietly
beneath the blazing glare of the lights, and as one passes up the
street outside, he cannot resist the temptation to glance in through
the doorway and see this brilliant scene, which adds so much to the
beauty of the city at night.

The Cerro is the handsomest residence street in Havana. It
runs up the hill at the back of the town, and has on either side

large old villas, which are surrounded by magnificient gardens. Upon this street is the former summer villa of the Bishops of Havana, in the midst of a forest of cocoa palms. It is now used as a private residence. One hears a great deal of the old time volante, which was to Cuba what the gondola is to Venice. It is not as common in Havana nowadays as it used to be, but occasionally one sees this remarkable vehicle with its wheels so thin that one wonders why they do not break, its long shafts and the driver perched upon the animal which draws it. Sometimes the characteristic volantes are magnificently decorated with silver and costly cloths. In these later days the usual vehicles of America are much more common in the city proper than this famous old Cuban equipage, although it is still to be generally seen in other parts of the island.

As one walks along he notices that the lamp-posts are painted various colors to tell the district—red for the central district, blue for the second, and green for the outside district. This enables even a stranger to compute the carriage hire of public conveyances. The laws are very strict in the matter of charges, and one is able to keep from being imposed upon by the hack drivers, owing to the fact that he can tell exactly how far he is going.

THE SPLENDID CHURCHES OF HAVANA.

There are one or two very fine churches in this city, the largest of which is the Mercede. Here the fashionable people wend their way on Sundays and holidays, the young men lining up in rows outside the church door after services as they do in this country. The most magnificent edifice, however, is the great Cathedral of Havana, which was erected in 1724. It has one big dome and two little towers on either side of the centre much like the other churches of Spanish-American architecture, and both inside and outside it is beautiful and effective.

The columns of the church are of mahogany so highly polished that they look like deep-red marble. They are strikingly relieved by great gilt bronze capitals. The choir place is the most striking of its kind probably on this continent; and in it is the tomb of Columbus, from which the body of the great discoverer was recently taken and sent to Spain. The stalls are of mahogany, magnificently carved, and highly polished. The ceiling, too, is very artistic, and is made almost entirely of mosaic work in rare woods.

Another prominent building of Havana is the Jesuit College for boys, which has connected with it one of the best observatories outside of the United States. It also has a museum and a library, in which are relics and manuscripts illustrating Cuban affairs from the sixteenth century down to the present day. Throughout the city there are a number of large charitable institutions, which are, for the most part, very clean and well carried on.

One of the things that the traveler first notices in Havana is the great number of beggars. They appear everywhere, and from them there is little escape, as their boldness is something amazing.

SHOPS AND THEATRES.

The shops in Havana are numerous, but most of them are built on the principle of the bazaars in the far East, without windows and with all the wares exposed to the passer-by.

As for amusements, the chief opera house of the city, the Tacon, is considered a very fine place, and the attractions there are nearly always of the best. It seats about 5,000 persons, and the boxes are arranged in tiers, which are separated by gilded lattices. The topmost gallery is given over to colored people entirely. The first two rows of boxes are usually filled up with the aristocracy of the city and the wealthy merchants, and on a gala night the display of jewelry and costumes may be said to quite rival that of the large cities of the United States. In the lower part of the house are a pit and orchestra stalls. The stage is large and well managed according to the most approved American ideas. The orchestra is largely made up of colored people, some of them full-blooded negroes, but the music they give is such that the most captious critic could not find fault with it.

Salvini, Duse, and Bernhardt have appeared here, and the audiences which greeted them would compare favorably with the audiences which cheer them in any other country.

A GLIMPSE AT CUBAN SOCIETY.

In an article recently published in the *Fortnightly Review*, Richard Davey gives the following very interesting account of Cuban society:

"Of society, in our sense of the word, there is little or none in Havana, and one may count upon the fingers of one hand the houses where balls and parties are given. Conversation soon flags in a country where education is so backward, especially among the women, whose intellectual pabulum consists generally of the very worst French novels and their prayer-books—a singular combination. The education of the males is a little better. The wealthier families send their sons either to the Jesuits at Havana, to Europe, or the United States. So far so good; but when they come home for their holidays, or their education is finished, the home influence is disastrous. Waited on hand and foot by the negroes, and pampered by their parents, they soon fall victims to the relaxing climate and to every sort of vicious influence. Lack of energy is the result of this lamentable system, which fosters most unhealthy love of ease and sensual indulgence.

"The usual way of spending the evening in a Cuban house is to place a long, double row of rocking-chairs opposite each other, and sit there chattering, everybody meanwhile smoking the inevitable cigarette. In some houses music of a high order may be heard, and some of the ladies sing charmingly—otherwise the place is socially dull.

"The Cuban lady is a very fascinating creature. She is elegant, walks gracefully, has pretty features, beautiful eyes, admirable teeth, and splendid hair, but spoils herself by her insane fashion of coating face, neck, shoulders and arms with rice powder to such a thickness as to give her a most ghastly appearance, not unlike that of a Pierrette. Coquettish as a young girl, she is generally both devoted and blameless as a wife and mother. On the other hand she is capable, on provocation, of displaying fiendishly vindictive and cruel traits, a fact only too well known by many a poor ex-slave.

"Religion occupies a great deal of the time of the Cubans of both sexes, but I am afraid it is considered rather a pastime than a moral factor. Among the men of the better class, who have been educated in Paris, it is never allowed to interfere with their passions, pleasures, or caprices. In the days of slavery they considered their duty to their dependents ended with the wholesale administration of baptism, which was obligatory by law, but it never entered their head to teach them any duties beyond those of implicit obedience to their own will, even the rudiments of the catechism being absolutely neglected. That there are many admirable men among the Cubans cannot be gainsaid, but unfortunately the mass of them is corrupt, as must ever be the case with a people whose slaves have for generations been only too eager to pander to their worst vices.

"Much more sincere than the Spaniards, they have always been distinguished for their hospitality and for the grace and dignity of their manners. If they offer you a thing they wish you to accept it, and do not say so for the mere form. They welcome you heartily, and regret your departure.

BRUTAL TREATMENT OF SLAVES.

"In former times their treatment of their slaves was notoriously cruel, and I shall never forget the contrast between the splendid hospitality which I myself enjoyed on a Cuban plantation, and the horrid sights which I witnessed in its coffee-fields, where the negroes were whipped by the overseers for the most trivial offences. An appalling incident occurred, too, during my stay, which can never be effaced from my mind, and which I discovered by the merest chance, for I was to have been kept in total ignorance of its occurrence. A strikingly handsome young mulatto had escaped into the woods and had been recaptured. For nearly a week he was tortured every day regularly for two hours, and in the presence of all the other hands, and, needless to say, in that of his master. I chanced one afternoon to go for a walk, accompanied by one of the children of the family, a lad of twelve years, who thoughtlessly asked me to come and see what they were 'doing to Pedro.' They were flaying him alive with pincers, burning him with hot wires, and rubbing his wounds with saltpetre! The poor wretch, who was shrieking desperately and writhing in agony, was tied hand and foot to the stump of a tree. The strangest part of it all was that the negroes for whose intimidation this diabolical torture, which eventually ended in slow death, had been devised, did not seem to be particularly impressed by its horror, for they were laughing and shouting like so many fiends. Needless to say, I left that hacienda somewhat hurriedly.

"The house slaves, however, were treated with extreme indulgence, petted and spoiled to their heart's content, and a more idle, vicious, happy-go-lucky lot I never came across in all my life. The house on this plantation was a very fair specimen of its class. It was enormous, built of stone with spacious verandas, and, although but one-story high, the rooms were so prodigiously lofty that the external appearance was quite majestic. Its wide, inner courtyard, numerous saloons, billiard-room and corridors were luxuriously furnished in excellent taste, and were cool and delightful. The garden was a veritable paradise. I wish I had the space to describe the many pleasant days I passed there, marred alone by the dreadful incident above alluded to."

A CITY FILLED WITH ODORS.

Notwithstanding the fact that Havana is a pleasant city, taken as a whole, yet there are many things which cause it to be a place to be avoided at certain seasons of the year. The odor which comes up from the harbor is such that one can scarcely enjoy life while it exists. So offensive was it that as soon as the United States came into possession of the city under the terms of the protocol, Colonel George E. Waring, of New York, was sent to Cuba by the Government to look into the matter of cleaning up Havana and making it as sanitary as possible. The trip proved a fatal one for Colonel Waring. While in Havana he contracted yellow fever, and came home to die from this terrible scourge. However, the work he did in Havana was of such a nature that the Government was able immediately after taking possession of the city to start in its task of cleaning the Cuban capital.

Vigorous action was also begun to improve the moral sanitation of Havana. Vans now go around the city after midnight and pick up the vagrant and homeless persons who fill the porticos everywhere. Those who are able to labor are turned over to the public work of the city, such as sweeping the streets and cleaning up the gutters. For this they are paid ninety cents a day. Those who are not able to work, and these form by far the larger class, are provided for either at the San Isidro Asylum or the hospitals. It is hoped to clear the streets entirely of these people.

The children, too, are being looked after, and provided with home in the San Jose Asylum. This formerly had a manual training school in connection with it, which will be revived, and the children taught to do some trade.

RECONCENTRADOS DIE BY THOUSANDS.

Another attractive part of Cuba is Matanzas, near which, during the recent uprising, the Cuban insurgents had their headquarters. Here under the edict of General Weyler, 11,000 Reconcentrados gathered together, and here, too, 9,000 of them died of starvation and want. The whole of the province is about as large as the State of Delaware.

The city, although smaller than Havana, is better built, and the streets are very much more regular. It is perhaps the most delightful place to live in on the island, and is in the midst of a wonderfully fertile district. Near it is the valley of the Yumurri, the "happy valley," which is so pleasant in temperature, even in the hottest days in summer, that it is the most charming of places to spend either summer or winter.

But perhaps the best known city of the island, after Havana, a city which has been brought into the greatest prominence by the war, is Santiago de Cuba. Here the American forces gathered both by land and sea, and after an attack more brilliant perhaps than any other of which we have known, captured this stronghold against fearful odds. And when they marched into it, they found this little town, nestling at the base of the hills, in an awful state of filth and decay. Fever, more terrible even than Spanish bullets, began to wage war in the ranks of our army, and after the city had completely yielded itself into our hands the first great work of those appointed to take care of it was to cleanse it and remove as far as possible the danger of plague. This work was placed in charge of Doctor Leonard Wood, the famous Colonel and commander of the Rough Riders, who after winning the most notable laurels as a fighter, added to them laurels equally notable, through his remarkable work in ridding the city of filth and disease.

THE CLEANING OF SANTIAGO.

Perhaps the best idea of what was accomplished may be gained from the report of Robert P. Porter, Special Commissioner for the

United States to Cuba and Porto Rico. "The disagreeable smells of the typical Cuban city," his report says, "are less pronounced in Santiago, while whitewash, limewash, fresh paint and all sorts of disinfectants have deodorized the surrounding atmosphere and made the old town quite habitable. The streets are no longer used as sewers, and the unhappy individual who violates the law and escapes the lash of the Sanitary Commissioner's whip is compelled to work on the streets for thirty days. This official, Major Barbour, with 126 men dressed in spotless white, and 32 good United States mule teams and carts, having dug out from the streets of Santiago the filth of ages, is now able to keep them absolutely clean. Every day, by the aid of petroleum, the garbage of the city is burned.

"The work of sanitation is not confined to the streets, but extends to the dwelling houses, shops and buildings of all kinds. To accomplish this, however, the doors of houses had to be smashed in, and people making sewers of the thoroughfares were publicly horsewhipped in the streets. Eminently respectable citizens were forcibly brought before the commanding general and sentenced to aid in cleaning the streets they were in the habit of defiling.

"The campaign has ended in a complete surrender to the sanitary authorities, and the inhabitants of Santiago, regardless of class, have had their first object lesson in the new order of things inaugurated by the war. Several important streets have been repaved; all the public buildings have been thoroughly cleaned, the work even extending to the Opera House."

Continuing in his report, Mr. Porter says,—in speaking of the general condition of the island:

"The rural districts of Santiago have been so depleted that it would be impossible to collect taxes over and above those needed for the bare necessities of schools for the poor, and possibly small sums to improve sanitary conditions.

"The dawn of prosperity, however, should be the signal for inaugurating systematic work on the country roads. The British Government spends annually for the roads in Jamaica about $500,000, where there are now 2000 miles already constructed. The money expended on roads, whether from the general funds of the island or from the local budgets, would come back a hundred fold, it is stated, and make Santiago one of the richest sugar, coffee and fruit growing districts in the West Indies. Bananas can be grown at a profit, and, as it takes only fourteen months to grow, unlike coffee and oranges, the poorer classes could undertake its cultivation to their great advantage. The internal, industrial, professional, licensing and other miscellaneous taxes have so far been remitted in this part of Cuba, but the authorities are now preparing to enforce them."

Now that the customs tariff has been disposed of, Mr. Porter recommends that an immediate scheme be prepared for levying and collecting internal revenue for the entire island. The question of separating these taxes from purely municipal taxes should also be considered. The large total of delinquencies during the last three years, which amounted to about $6,000,000, was, of course, due to the war. In normal times we have here $4,000,000 or $5,000,000 of revenue that must not be overlooked, revenue which, if properly and economically employed, would aid in the industrial rehabilitation of Cuba.

WHERE SUGAR AND TOBACCO GROW.

The other divisions of the island are Pinar del Rio, Santa Clara and Puerto Principe. Each has a capital of the same name, which is more or less a copy of Havana. One of the most notable ports of the island is Baracoa, which formerly was a place much visited by American traders dealing in bananas, cocoanuts and chocolate. In one year this port did a business amounting to 2,000,000 bunches of bananas and 4,000,000 cocoanuts, together with large quantities of other fruit. But since the war, importations from Baracoa practically amounted to nothing. The great tobacco district of the island is in the Santa Clara and Santiago de Cuba Provinces, the former giving what is thought to be the finest tobacco in Cuba. The export from this Province reached about 250,000 bales and 175,000,000 cigars, but like all the other industries of the island, it was laid waste during the war of the insurgents, and almost all of the tobacco plantations were destroyed.

The great sugar belt comprises the Provinces of Havana, Santa Clara and Matanzas, while Santiago de Cuba also has a share of the big plantations. Some idea may be had of the enormous production of sugar in Cuba, when it is known that the yield of 1894 was 1,040,-000 tons. As soon as the regions which usually were productive of large harvests of sugar came into the hands of the insurgents, they either burned the mills and the houses on the plantations, or kept the planters from working, with the result that in one year after the beginning of the war the production of sugar fell from over a million to 225,000 tons, and, as the war proceeded, this was greatly reduced until it amounted to practically nothing.

But such is the remarkable fertility of this island, and such are its wonderful resources that the future seems promising, although there is little left of the land but ruins since the march of the devasting insurgent troops. Under the conditions which are promised to the beautiful isle, when a staple government has been assured by the United States, and when the people will be free to carry on their work without fear of molestation, there seems to be no limit to the financial success of this country, which has so long been held down and kept from progressing by the iron hand and the bloody rule of Spain.

CHAPTER XVIII

The Explosion of the "Maine," and War

Awful Catastrophe to the Big Battleship in the Harbor of Havana.—Firm Belief that the Vessel was Blown up by Spaniards.—A Naval Board of Inquiry.—A Wave of Feeling Sweeps the Whole Nation.—McKinley Places the Matter Before Congress.—War is Entered upon for the Sake of Humanity.—The First Call for Troops.—All the States of the Union Respond Immediately with their Quota of Men.—The Mobilization of the American Army.

DIPLOMATIC relations between the United States and Spain became somewhat strained in the latter part of 1897, through the dissatisfaction of Spanish political leaders, with the sympathy manifested by the American public toward the struggle of the Cubans for independence. A number of prominent Americans had made tours of Cuba, and others had seen for themselves the situation in Havana and its immediate vicinity, and the facts thus ascertained were laid before the Congress of the United States in the form of reports or petitions, so vigorously presented and so eloquently supported, that many debates occurred in the National Legislature over resolutions that had been introduced for the recognition of the Cubans as belligerents, and more than one effort was also made to secure American recognition of the insurgents.

THE "MAINE" SENT TO HAVANA.

The newspapers of both countries were full of pointed and semi-sarcastic editorials on the opposing national attitudes, and the air was full of the possibilities of war, though the hope ran high in the hearts of thoughtful people that such a serious consequence might be avoided. In the last week in January, however, the battleship *Maine*, which had been lying at Key West with the rest of the South Atlantic Squadron, was ordered to proceed to Havana at once. The vessel left Key West on January 25, 1898. The order for her departure had not been heralded in advance, and there was no time for speculation as to the why and wherefore of her journey until she was already at the Cuban port.

The Secretary of the Navy and other important officials at Washington declared that the visit of the warship to Havana meant only the friendly relations with Spain were now formally resumed in that particular, since for some time previously there had been no American war vessels in that port. Nevertheless, the feeling was strong that the *Maine* would not have been sent there unless Consul-General Fitzhugh Lee had believed there was special need for a protector of Americans and American interests.

Officials of the McKinley Administration were quoted as having said that a mistake was made by the Cleveland Administration in deciding, at the very beginning of the Cuban insurrection, not to send any warships to Havana or to permit any of the naval vessels to stop at that port as they had occasionally been in the habit of doing. It was always maintained in these utterances that the decision to keep our war vessels away from Havana was uncalled for, and was a wholly unnecessary concession to the sensibilities of the Spanish public. If that decision had not been reached by the Cleveland Administration our warships could have visited Havana in 1896 and 1897 just as they had done previously, and then there would have been no thought that the sending of the *Maine* to Havana in 1898 was an indication of trouble with Spain.

It was ascertained that Consul-General Lee had reported to the State Department that he feared serious disturbances might take place in Havana at any moment, and that, while he would not himself take the responsibility of asking for a warship, he wished the Administration to understand that the conditions of affairs in Havana was such as might lead to disturbances almost any day, which would involve the lives of American citizens.

THE VIEWS OF SENOR DE LOME.

The Spanish Minister, De Lome, called at the White House on the day that the battleship went to Havana, was shown the orders that had been issued for the departure of the *Maine*, and publicly expressed himself to the effect that, so far as his advice was concerned, the Spanish Government would not regard the sending of the

THE ROUGH RIDERS DRIVING BACK THE SPANIARDS, PREVIOUS TO THE ATTACK ON SANTIAGO.

MAJOR-GENERAL NELSON APPLETON MILES.

MAJOR-GENERAL FITZHUGH LEE.

MAJOR-GENERAL WESLEY MERRITT.

MAJOR-GENERAL WM. R. SHAFTER.

LEADING COMMANDERS OF OUR ARMY IN THE SPANISH-AMERICAN WAR

Maine to Havana as a hostile act, or a threat against the friendly relations that were in existence between the two countries. Still, there was a decidedly uneasy feeling throughout the country, not because a war with Spain was feared, but because the people seemed not to have been taken into the confidence of those who had the power to prevent war or to bring it about.

Naval and army officers were particularly interested in the matter, and promptly expressed themselves as confident that the time was near at hand when the chance for active service in front of an enemy, which is the height of every officer's ambition, would not be much longer delayed. The fact that there was a large fleet assembled at Key West, within a few hours' run from the port to which the *Maine* had been sent, and the further fact that unusual activity was being manifested in the navy yards and arsenals throughout the country, gave color to much of the war talk, and turned all eyes in the direction of the *Maine*, though no one seemed to expect the fate that was about to befall her.

The situation was rendered very much more serious by the publication in American newspapers, on February 9, 1898, of a remarkable letter said to have been written by the Spanish Minister in Washington. It was addressed to a Spanish editor who was stopping at a hotel in Havana, and contained, among other comments on the American attitude toward the Cubans, a characterization of President McKinley as "weak, and catering to the rabble; and, besides, a low politician, who desires to leave a door open to me and to stand well with the jingoes of his party."

DE LOME RESIGNS.

This letter was made public through the Cuban Junta, who secured it at Havana. The Junta claimed that the receiver of the letter was so astonished at its contents that he could not help telling some of his friends about it, and that in this way it had come into the hands of their agents. The authenticity of the letter was not doubted for a moment; but the officials at Washington promptly afforded Minister De Lome an opportunity to deny it if he cared to. Nothing came from De Lome, however, and the State Department then sent a request to him for immediate information as to the genuineness of the letter. De Lome called at the State Department. He admitted that the letter was genuine, but explained that the translation was inaccurate, and he volunteered the further information that he had cabled his resignation to Madrid.

The resignation of the Spanish Minister was accepted, and he withdrew to Canada. The Spanish Government made a feeble attempt to disclaim responsibility for this gratuitous insult to the President of the United States, but this incident filled the cup of the Nation's patience almost to overflowing, and there was, therefore, less surprise manifested than would have been the case a week or so earlier, when, on the morning of February 16th, the whole world was electrified by the news of the blowing up of the *Maine*, as she lay moored in the harbor of Havana, and the loss of several hundred lives.

The news of the catastrophe was officially communicated to Washington in a message to the Secretary of the Navy, from Captain Sigsbee, of the *Maine*, which was received just after midnight, and read as follows:

"*Maine* blown up in Havana harbor and destroyed. Many wounded and doubtless more killed and drowned. Wounded and others on board Spanish man-of-war and Ward Line steamer. Send lighthouse tenders from Key West for crew and a few pieces of equipment still above water. No one has other clothes than those upon him. Public opinion should be suspended until further report. All officers believed to be saved. Jenkins and Merritt not yet accounted for. Many Spanish officers, including represensative of General Blanco, now with me and express sympathy.   SIGSBEE."

The first reports received from the scene of the disaster placed the loss at something over a hundred, but at that time it was still dark and it was impossible to obtain more accurate information. This, however, was bad enough as it was, but when it became known that the great majority of the crew of the big battleship had been killed or drowned, the anxiety for further details was deep and universal.

On the day following the explosion, it was ascertained that the total victims of the disaster were 264 men and 2 officers killed, and many men wounded. The officers killed were Lieutenant Friend W.

Jenkins and Assistant Engineer Darwin R. Merritt. Captain Charles D. Sigsbee, the Commander, and Lieutenant-Commander Richard Wainwright, were both on board at the time, and, with all the other officers, escaped. The Navy Department was besieged with inquiries from the friends of the members of the crew, and the whole Nation was aroused to fever heat by the disaster.

None of the Government officials would say that they thought the *Maine* had been purposely blown up, but thousands of citizens so expressed themselves, and there was a general feeling throughout the country, while waiting for further particulars, that if the explosion was shown to be due to bomb, torpedo or mine, it would mean nothing less than war with Spain.

The officers of the *Maine*, promptly recognizing the possible significance of the catastrophe, were somewhat reticent as to the details of the occurrence. Various descriptions of the disaster were given, but it was some time afterward that a perfectly connected story was available.

Lieutenant-Commander Wainwright, at a quarter to 10 o'clock on the night of February 15th, was half undressed and was smoking in his cabin. Suddenly an explosion occurred, which put out the electric lights. Wainwright struck a match and made his way to the adjoining cabin of Captain Sigsbee. The Captain had been thrown from his bunk, but was uninjured. Wainwright's belief was that the explosion was due to a short-circuited dynamo. Captain Sigsbee and he hastened on deck and ordered a man to flood 2,500 pounds of gun cotton which was on board. The order was carried out, but the man never returned, for by the time he could go to the place where the flood cocks were and get back again to the quarter-deck, a second explosion had taken place, and he was undoubtedly added to the victims.

THE DISASTER DESCRIBED BY AN EYEWITNESS.

One officer described the disaster as follows:

"Three of us were sitting in the mess-room, when a heavy explosion occurred. We rushed on the upper deck and found that the vessel was on fire and sinking. All efforts were then directed toward lowering the boats and saving lives, but the *Maine* settled quickly on the bottom of the harbor, only her upper works remaining above the water. Boats from the Spanish warship *Alfonso XII*, and boats from the Ward Line steamer, *City of Washington*, came alongside and rendered assistance."

All the officers agreed that the explosion occurred somewhere in the forward part of the midship section of the battleship. Many of the crew who were below at the time of the first explosion were unable to escape, and those who succeeded in reaching the upper decks saved their lives with great difficulty.

The *Maine*, at the time of the explosion, was at anchor, about 500 yards from the arsenal, and about 200 yards from the floating dock. The explosion put out the lights near the wharf, and blew down telephone and telegraph wires in that vicinity. The smokestacks of the battleship fell at 11.30. The first of the American sailors to reach the wharf were swimming. Three of those who thus escaped fell senseless just as they reached a place of safety. The total number of those saved, out of a crew of 350 was less than a hundred.

OTHER VESSELS LEND ASSISTANCE

Eyewitnesses of the scene of the explosion, within a few minutes after its occurrence painted striking word pictures of the struggles of wounded men in the water, and of the excitement that prevailed in and about the harbor. Boats from the Spanish warship and merchant vessels, searching for the wounded, more frequently encountered the bodies of the dead, and each hour seemed to add to these ghastly accumulations, until the wharves on shore became open-air morgues, and the victims of the disaster lay in long rows side by side, waiting for identification.

The wounded were taken to Key West as rapidly as possible, but many of the dead were temporarily buried in Havana, and in these burials the sympathy of the citizens of Havana was certainly made manifest, though the feeling of suspicion that the disaster was due to treachery had a strong hold in the minds of the surviving sailors as well as in the minds of their friends at home.

The interment of twenty-two martyrs of the *Maine* took place on the afternoon of February 17, 1898. The flags on the public buildings of Havana were at half-mast and many of the houses were draped in mourning. All classes were represented in the throngs that filled the streets along which the funeral procession passed to the cemetery. The procession included the Municipal Guards on horseback, the City Fire Brigade, representatives of various official bureaus, officers of the Spanish army and navy, and committees representing the Chamber of Commerce and other trade organizations.

BURYING THE DEAD.

The bodies rested in coffins in the City Hall, and were profusely covered with flowers. A great crown from the City Council bore the inscription: "The People of Havana to the Victims of the *Maine*." There was also a handsome crown of silk ribbons in the Spanish national colors with the inscription: "The Navy Department at Havana to the Victims of the *Maine*." The Mayor of Havana headed the funeral procession; General Solana represented Captain-General Blanco. The population that lined the route of the procession gave every indication of the profoundest sympathy.

Others of the victims of the *Maine* were subsequently buried at Key West. The bodies of many were claimed by friends and taken to their homes for burial. Many bodies were never recovered, and some were found by the divers who subsequently worked upon the wreck of the *Maine*, wedged in between the decks, where they had met their death by drowning. A few of those who had been picked up in a wounded condition died in the hospitals, but the great majority of the injured were only slightly hurt and rapidly recovered.

A BOARD OF INQUIRY APPOINTED.

Captain Sigsbee, of the *Maine*, had asked, immediately upon the occurrence of the disaster, for a Board of Inquiry to determine the cause of the explosion. This was in line with the usual custom of commanders of vessels which have met with any mishap, so that the record of the commander may be established, but in this instance there came also a demand from the entire American nation, and, while the Board that was appointed was officially named in response to Sigbee's request, it was equally in answer to the popular demand, and its proceedings and findings were eagerly watched and waited for.

The Spanish authorities in Havana, taking the cue from those higher in authority at Madrid, continuously deplored the "unfortunate accident" which had befallen the *Maine*, and straightway instituted an investigation of their own, the manner of conducting which, and the subsequent findings that were promulgated, all going to show that the Spanish Government had no intention of listening for a moment to any theory concerning the affair except that it was purely an accidental occurrence.

Divers were sent down into the wreck of the battleship by the Spaniards secretly, when no other divers were there, and on the reports made by these Spanish submarine investigators a document was formulated, which was widely circulated through Spanish official channels, to the effect that the *Maine* had been blown up by an interior explosion. The wreck of the *Maine* was so complete, its compartments were so utterly shattered, and its constructive iron so twisted and broken, that the Spaniards found it comparatively easy to mystify themselves, if indeed they failed to delude the rest of the world.

Meanwhile, the divers engaged by the Government of the United States conducted an investigation which was scientifically superintended, and the results of which were accurately recorded. Diagrams were made for presentation to the Board of Inquiry, and nothing was left undone that could in any way be expected to throw light upon the cause of the disaster. The Government of the United States was fully determined that the truth should be made known.

BLOWN UP BY AN OUTSIDE EXPLOSION.

When the exact condition of the wreck had been determined, and when the circumstances came to be considered in the new light afforded by the official investigation, naval engineers throughout the world, and scientific men of international prominence, promptly gave it as their opinion that the *Maine* had been blown up from the outside. It then became known that the *Maine* had been moored at a certain buoy in the harbor of Havana, to which she had been conducted by a Spanish official, and it was also ascertained that this buoy was in the immediate vicinity, if not exactly over, mines that had been placed in the harbor bottom.

One theory was that the American warship had been thus placed with the direct purpose of accomplishing her destruction. Others accepted that portion of this theory which included the destruction of the vessel, but were charitable enough to say that perhaps Spain's managers of the affair did not intend to explode the mines except in the event of war being declared between the two countries.

This left it an open question for the public mind as to whether the *Maine* had been blown up by a secret order on the part of the Government, or whether some over-enthusiastic individual enemy of the United States had exploded a mine beneath her bottom without waiting for orders. There was considerable talk about torpedoes, and about electric connections with the shore batteries, but there had been ample time for every outward evidence of treachery to be removed before the official American investigation began, and it only remained for the Board of Inquiry to establish the nature of the explosion and leave the world to judge as to its cause.

On February 18th, three days after the explosion, Congress appropriated $200,000 for the employment of divers, for the raising of the vessel if it was found practicable, and for the preliminary expenses of the Court of Inquiry. On February 20th the divers began their work; on the 25th the Court of Inquiry began its investigations at Havana, and on the 22d Consul-General Lee informally advised Americans not necessarily detained in Cuba to leave for home at once.

CAPTAIN SIGSBEE'S STORY.

The sessions of the Court of Inquiry were held behind closed doors. The first witness was Captain Sigsbee. The record of the testimony was strictly guarded until the conclusion of the investigation, but when once an officer had been a witness before the Court, he seemed to be at liberty to speak more freely of experiences on that dreadful night.

Captain Sigsbee himself, after being a witness, told to correspondents in Havana the following story of his vessel's destruction. He said: "I find it impossible to describe the sound or shock, but the impression remains of something awe-inspiring, terrifying, noise-rendering, vibrating, all-pervading. There was nothing in the former experience of anyone on board to measure the explosion by.

"After the first great shock, I cannot myself recall how many sharper detonations I heard, but it was not more than two or three. I knew my ship was gone. In such a structure as the *Maine*, the effects of such an explosion are not for a moment in doubt. I made my way through the long passage, in the dark, groping from side to side, to the hatchway and thence to the poop deck, being among the earliest to reach that spot."

"So soon as I recognized the officers, I ordered high explosives to be flooded, and I then directed that the boats available be lowered to rescue the wounded or drowning. Discipline, in a perfect measure, prevailed. There was no more confusion than a call to general quarters would produce, if as much. I soon saw, by the light of the flames, that all my officers and crew left alive and on board, surrounded me."

"I cannot form any idea of the time, but it seemed five minutes from the time I reached the poop until I left, the last man it was possible to reach having been saved. It must have been three quarters of an hour or more, however, from the amount of work done. I remember the officers and men worked together, lowering the boats, and that the gig took some time to lower."

PLACED ABOVE THE FATAL MINE.

Captain Sigsbee testified before the Court of Inquiry that an investigation was sometimes made of the bottoms of harbors in which men-of-war are moored, but that in connection with the mooring of the *Maine* in the harbor of Havana, presumably the port of a friendly power, he had taken the berth officially assigned without question as to its safety; but that he had taken the usual precautions against attack. The quarter-watch being ordered to have ammunition for the smaller guns ready to hand, so that, in the improbable event of an attack on the ship, it would have been found ready. This ammunition exploded when the heat reached it, and is supposed to account for the detonation that occurred after the two first and greater explosions.

From the testimony of other officers, it was learned that the usual rounds of the ship had been made at eight bells on that fatal evening, and everything had been reported all right. There was nothing in prospect but another night of untroubled dreams. One

SPANIARDS REPELLING THE ATTACK OF CUBAN INSURGENTS.

Nearly all of the fighting between Spaniards and Cubans in the "Ten Years War," 1868-'78, and the last war, 1895-'98, was conducted on guerrilla methods. The Cubans were never strong enough to risk an open battle with Spain's armies of drilled soldiers. The

This magnificent second class battleship was blown up in Havana Harbor, February 15, 1898, and 266 American sailors lost their lives through the explosion. The vessel was left a complete wreck. It was popularly believed that the ship was destroyed through Spanish treachery; and this sentiment did much to of the seamen testified that, looking over the side in the dark, at about half past nine, he fancied he saw a black shining object silently approaching the vessel, but it was supposed that the man's mind had probably been set on edge by the gossip of his mates, and that he was perhaps over-keen to scent danger. He testified that he was about to give warning to the officer of the deck, when the explosion occurred. The whole forward part of the ship seemed to be lifted from the water. Then followed the second explosion with outflaming.

The crash had been so terrific as to deprive some who heard it of their reason, to stun others, to astound many, but for 250 gallant seamen it was, if they heard it at all, the last sound that was to ring in their ears in this world. The portholes of nearby ships were smashed in, also the windows of houses facing the harbor. The lights on the water front were extinguished. Great masses of the vessel's iron substance were torn from her, and sent flying through the air. Some witnesses testified to having heard an awful chorus of groans from those not yet dead but dying between the vessel's decks.

As the hearings of the Court of Inquiry drew near their close, more and more secrecy was maintained in regard to the evidence. This led to the belief that developments were being made that threatened the peace of the nations. Consul-General Lee's advice to Americans in Cuba, that they had better get off of the island as soon as possible, particularly annoyed the Spaniards, and an urgent effort was made at Madrid to get United States Minister Woodford to suggest General Lee's recall. This effort, however, signally failed, and the temper of the American people in the emergency was magnificently manifested, on March 8th, when Congress voted unanimously for a defense fund of fifty millions of dollars, which President McKinley was authorized to expend as he might deem best in the interest of peace or war, as the case might be

SPAIN PREPARES FOR TROUBLE.

Nor was Spain lying upon her oars in the matter of preparation. She was making strenuous efforts to purchase warships, and to provide for a big war loan. Another thing that she undertook at this time was to create an impressive moral effect by dispatching a fleet of vessels westward, as if to let the Americans see that she was ready for anything that might happen. It turned out, however, that the destination of this fleet was the Cape Verde Islands, and the length of time it remained at those islands, subsequently gave it the name of the Cape Verde Fleet, and this was the fleet that really did venture further west several months later, and never went back.

The *Maine* Court of Inquiry finished its work on March 19th, and a summary of its findings was forwarded to the President and the Navy Department on the following day. Then followed more than a week of delay, during which time every detail of the report was carefully considered by the Cabinet, and after this consideration had been taken, the report in full, with all the evidence taken, was, on March 28th, submitted to Congress. Meanwhile, all vessels of the American Navy were donning their smoke-colored warpaint, and everybody's mind was being made up to the fact that war was inevitable.

The tension of feeling throughout the nation was so great at this time that the report of the Board of Inquiry was not altogether satisfactory. It positively declared that the explosion by which the *Maine* was wrecked was external, but it was impossible for the Board to make any statement as to the responsibility. This omission was the part that failed to give universal satisfaction; but subsequent events developed the fact that the Administration felt that there were grounds for war, if war must come, even grander and more praiseworthy than any that could be based upon the idea of revenge for a national insult, or of reprisal for loss of life.

THE REPORT OF THE BOARD OF INQUIRY.

In any event the report of the Board of Inquiry was submitted without attempt to fix the responsibility, though the public was left free to draw its own conclusions from the findings. These findings were substantially as follows :

1. That the battleship *Maine* was conducted to buoy No. 4 in the harbor of Havana by the regular Government pilot, and that the United States Consul-General at Havana had notified the authorities, on the previous evening, of the intended arrival of the *Maine*.

2. The state of discipline on board the *Maine* was excellent, and all orders and regulations in regard to the care and safety of the

vessel were strictly carried out. The fire alarms were in working order, and there had never been a case of spontaneous combustion of coal on board. On the night of the destruction of the *Maine*, everything had been reported secure for the night at 8 P.M. by reliable persons, through the proper authorities, to the commanding officer; and, at the time of the explosion, the vessel was quiet, and, therefore, least liable to accidents caused by movements from those on board.

3. The destruction of the *Maine* occurred at 9.40 P.M. on February 15, 1898, in the harbor of Havana, Cuba, she being at that time moored to the same buoy to which she had been taken upon her arrival. There were two explosions. By the first, the forward part of the ship was lifted to a marked degree. The second explosion was, in the opinion of the Court, caused by the partial explosion of two or more of the forward magazines.

4. That portion of the portside of the protected deck, which extends from about frame 30 to about frame 41, was blown up aft and over to port. The main deck, from about frame 30 to about frame 41, was blown up aft and slightly over to starboard, folding the forward part of the middle superstructure over and on top of the afterpart.

5. In the opinion of the Court, these effects and others developed in evidence could have been produced only by the explosion of a mine situated under the bottom of the ship at about frame 18, and somewhat on the portside.

6. The Court finds that the loss of the *Maine* was not, in any respect, due to fault or negligence on the part of any of the officers or members of the crew.

7. In the opinion of the Court, the *Maine* was destroyed by the explosion of a submarine mine, which caused the partial explosion of two or more of her forward magazines.

8. The Court has been unable to obtain evidence, fixing the responsibility for the destruction of the *Maine* upon any person or persons.

The report was signed by Captain W. T. Sampson, U. S. N., President, and Lieutenant-Commander A. Marix, U. S. N., Judge-Advocate, and the proceedings and findings of the Court were approved by Rear-Admiral Sicard, Commander-in-Chief of the United States Naval force on the North Atlantic Station.

No further evidence has been officially recorded as to the cause of the explosion; but many stories were subsequently circulated in apparent confirmation of popular opinion that Spain should have been held responsible. One of these stories was to the effect that dynamite had been purchased in England by private agents of General Weyler, and that it was to the desire of his friends to resent his recall from Cuba that the disaster to the *Maine* was due.

CONGRESS STIRRED TO ACTION.

The United States Government authorities, however, studiously avoided laying the blame for the explosion at the door of Spain, but there was no cessation of the preparations for war. Members of the Senate and of the House of Representatives emphatically declared that the time had come for America to intervene in Cuban affairs, and, within two or three days after the report of the Board of Inquiry was made public, resolutions to that effect were introduced in both houses of the National Legislature.

Senator Foraker, of Ohio, on March 30th, presented resolutions recognizing the independence of Cuba, and favoring armed intervention. He declared that autonomy had absolutely failed, and that just as this failure was realized the country was confronted by the De Lome incident. Scarcely had this begun to attract less interest when the explosion of the *Maine* threw the country into a hurricane of excitement, but that the proper action for Congress to take was upon the general Cuban question.

Senator Frye, of Maine, also introduced a resolution, based on the declaration that the war in Cuba had been conducted by the Spanish Government in violation of the rules of civilized warfare; that the President be authorized "to take such effective steps as, in his discretion, may be necessary to secure a speedy termination of the hostilities between the Government of Spain and the people of Cuba, the withdrawal of the military and naval forces of Spain from said island, and the complete independence of said people."

Senator Rawlins, of Utah, offered a resolution for the recognition of Cuba's independence, and for a declaration of war against

Spain. Senator Allen, of Nebraska, introduced a resolution recognizing the independence of Cuba, and that the United States should immediately intervene and put an end to the war that was being waged by the Spaniards against the citizens of that island. Similar resolutions were introduced in the House of Representatives, all being referred to the Committees on Foreign Affairs, with instructions for an early report.

ALL POWERS STRIVE FOR PEACE.

Spain began to have inquiries made through devious diplomatic channels as to what would satisfy the United States in regard to Spanish conduct of Cuban affairs. Several propositions passed backward and forward, unofficially, and there was every evidence of an effort on the part of Spain to gain more time. Meanwhile, there was a great rush at all the navy yards. The squadron at Key West, of which the *Maine* had been a part, was rapidly put into fighting trim.

The Spanish vessels *Viscaya* and *Almirante Oquendo*, which had been in Havana harbor since a few days after the destruction of the *Maine*, withdrew to Porto Rico, and thence to the Canaries, being subsequently attached to the Cape Verde fleet under command of Admiral Cervera.

Representatives of the great powers called upon the Secretary of State at Washington in the interest of peace, but, recognizing at once the trend of events, reported their opinions to their home Governments, and the importunities of the powers were then directed toward influencing Spain to see the folly of allowing war to be declared.

The excuse put forward by Spain for not agreeing to the suggestions of the United States was that the Spanish dynasty would be imperiled by the rising of the people in revolution if too great concessions were made in Cuba. The powers, however, agreed to take care of the dynasty and to keep down rebellion if Spain would give up; but Sagasta refused to negotiate for the preservation of peace, Minister Woodford prepared to leave Madrid, and it became plainly apparent early in April that the United States Consul-General could be of no more service in Havana.

On the evening of April 9th, General Lee and his staff left Havana on board the lighthouse tender *Fern*. The wharf was crowded, but no discourtesy was shown. General Lee had called at the palace of the Governor-General to say good-bye to General Blanco, but the Governor-General was very busy and could not receive General Lee. The American flag upon the Consulate Building was taken down by consular employees during the afternoon, and American interests were left in the hands of the British Consul. A great many Americans accompanied General Lee from the Cuban capital, but Havana seemed to be absolutely indifferent to the evacuation.

AN ARMISTICE TO INSURGENTS.

On the same day that General Lee quitted Havana, the Spanish Cabinet decided to grant an armistice to the insurgents in Cuba. The Ambassadors of foreign powers had induced the Spaniards to make this concession in the hope of averting the war. The conditions of the armistice were to be the withdrawal of the American squadrons from Cuba and the Philippines. The armistice was to last for five days. The temper of the American Congress, however, was not favorable to any deviation from the programme that had been laid down. Prominent leaders of both political parties insisted that Congressional action should be taken regardless of the armistice, and it was also necessary for the Cubans to be communicated with in regard to the proposed cessation of fighting.

Meanwhile, however, the authorities in Madrid appeared to imagine that armistice meant peace, for they still believed there would be some way found for them to meet America's demands and still retain sovereignty in Cuba; but, on April 11th, President McKinley sent to Congress his famous message asking for power to intervene in Cuba. The message referred to the fearful starving and desolation which had followed General Weyler's policy of devastation and concentration; it denounced the policy of reconcentration as uncivilized; and it opposed the recognition of the belligerency of the insurgents, or the recognition, at this time, of the independence of the present insurgent Government.

The President declared forcible intervention to stop the war to be justifiable in the cause of humanity and for the protection of our citizens, and to prevent further loss to our commerce and trade. He spoke of the inexpressible horror over the destruction of the *Maine;*

and referred to the report of the Naval Court of Inquiry as commanding the unqualified confidence of the Government, adding that the only hope of relief and repose from a condition, which could no longer be endured, was the enforced pacification of Cuba.

"In the name of humanity, in the name of civilization, in behalf of endangered American interests, which give us the right and the duty to speak and to act," said the President, "the war in Cuba must stop. In view of these facts and of these considerations, I ask the Congress to authorize and to empower the President to take measures to secure a full and final termination of hostilities between the Government of Spain and the people of Cuba, and to secure in the island the establishment of a stable government, capable of maintaining order and of observing its international obligations, ensuring peace and tranquility, and the security of its citizens as well as our own, and to use the military and naval forces of the United States as may be necessary for these purposes."

THE RESULT OF THE MESSAGE.

The President's message was referred to the Committees on Foreign Affairs of both Houses of Congress, and was taken under consideration in connection with the various resolutions for intervention and recognition which had recently been introduced, and, on April 18th, a joint resolution was agreed upon. The Senate had declared for recognition, but the House had directly sustained the President in his views upon this question, and the result was a non-recognition measure, the full text of which was as follows:

WHEREAS, The abhorrent conditions which have existed for more than three years in the Island of Cuba, so near to our own borders, have shocked the moral sense of the people of the United States, have been a disgrace to Christian civilization, culminating, as they have, in the destruction of a United States battleship, with two hundred and sixty-six of its officers and crew, while on a friendly visit in the harbor of Havana, and cannot longer be endured, as has been set forth by the President of the United States in his Message to Congress of April 11, 1898, upon which the action of Congress was invited; therefore,

Resolved, By the Senate and House of Representatives of the United States of America in Congress assembled—

First.—That the people of the Island of Cuba are, and of right ought to be, free and independent.

Second.—That it is the duty of the United States to demand, and the Government of the States does hereby demand, that the Government of Spain at once relinquish its authority and government in the Island of Cuba, and withdraw its land and naval forces from Cuba and Cuban waters.

Third.—That the President of the United States be, and he hereby is, directed and empowered to use the entire land and naval forces of the United States, and to call into the actual service of the United States the militia of the several States, to such extent as may be necessary to carry these resolutions into effect.

Fourth.—That the United States hereby disclaims any disposition or intention to exercise sovereignty, jurisdiction or control over said Island except for the pacification thereof; and asserts its determination when that is accomplished to leave the government and control of the Island to its people.

The adoption of this resolution was looked upon at home and abroad as a practical declaration of war, and the preparations which had been rapidly pushed forward since the destruction of the *Maine*, now began to be rushed at high speed. The President signed the joint resolution of Congress on April 20th, and the Government's ultimatum was forwarded to Spain on the same day. Spain was given three days in which to make a satisfactory reply, but Minister Polo y Barnabe, who had succeeded DeLome temporarily, withdrew to Canada. On April 21st, Minister Woodford was handed his passports at Madrid, before the American ultimatum was presented, and he promptly left the Spanish capital. On the following day, April 22d, orders were given the American fleet at Key West and the Flying Squadron to seek the fleet of Spain, which was supposed to be on its way across the ocean, and on the same day President McKinley issued a call for troops, summoning 125,000 men for service in Cuba.

This call was in the form of a proclamation, as follows:

THE PEACE COMMISSIONERS.

Appointed September 9, 1898. Met Spanish Commissioners at Paris, October 1st. Treaty of Peace signed by the Commissioners at Paris, December 10th, and ratified by the United States Senate at Washington, February 6th, 1899

THE FLEET OF ADMIRAL CERVERA AT CAPE VERDE, DESTROYED BY THE AMERICAN FLEET AT SANTIAGO, JULY 3, 1898.

By the President of the United States:

WHEREAS, By a joint resolution of Congress, approved on the 20th day of April, 1898, entitled, " Joint Resolution for the Recognition of the Independence of the People of Cuba, Demanding that the Government of Spain Relinquish its Authority and Government in the Island of Cuba, to Withdraw Its Land and Naval Forces from Cuba and Cuban Waters, and directing the President of the United States to use the land and naval forces of the United States to carry these resolutions into effect " ; and,

WHEREAS, By an Act of Congress, entitled " An Act to provide for temporarily increasing the military establishment of the United States in time of war and for other purposes," approved April 22, 1898, the President is authorized in order to raise a volunteer army to issue his proclamation calling for volunteers to serve in the army of the United States.

NOW, THEREFORE, I, William McKinley, President of the United States, by virtue of the power vested in me by the Constitution and the laws, and deeming sufficient occasion to exist, have thought fit to call for, and hereby do call for, volunteers to the aggregate number of 125,000 in order to carry into effect the purpose of the said resolution, the same to be apportioned, as far as practicable, among the several States and Territories and the District of Columbia, according to the population, and to serve for two years, unless sooner discharged. The details of this object will be immediately communicated to the proper authorities through the War Department.

IN WITNESS WHEREOF, I have hereunto set my hand and caused the seal of the United States to be affixed.

Done at the City of Washington, this 23d day of April, A.D., 1898, and of the Independence of the United States the 122d.

[SEAL]   WILLIAM MCKINLEY.

By the President.

JOHN SHERMAN, Secretary of State.

Among the lasting glories of the United States of America, will ever be prominent the manner in which all the States of the Union responded to this call for national defenders. The quota of each

State was fixed according to the population of those of the militia age. On this basis the State of New York was to furnish 12,512 volunteers; Pennsylvania, 10,762; Illinois, 8,048; Ohio, 7,248; Missouri, 5,411; and all other States in the same proportion, down to 351 men from Delaware; 237 from Nevada; 231 from Wyoming; 181 from Arizona, and 142 from Oklahoma.

These volunteers were speedily mobilized at central points in their respective States, and everything possible was done to perfect their equipment. The members of the State Guards went into camp under their own officers, and all, officers and men, were submitted to a rigorous physical examination. The response to the call had been so generous, that the War Department determined to take only those who were best fitted for the arduous service which was to be expected of them in Cuba. The result was that the ranks of the State Guards, though they had been only slightly impaired by failure to volunteer, were considerably thinned by the weeding done by the regular army surgeons. So eager were men in all parts of the country to have a chance to fight against Spain, that all sorts of subterfuges were resorted to in the hope of deceiving the examiners in regard to actual physical conditions, but the weeding out was successfully accomplished, the vacancies in the State regiments were filled by men selected through the same process, and the result was as fine a body of men as ever enlisted for any service in any part of the world.

THE FIRST STATE TO REPORT.

The first State to complete her quota was Pennsylvania, notwithstanding the fact that hers was second only to New York in point of numbers. The Keystone soldiers were mobilized at Mt. Gretna, the site of the annual State encampments, forty miles from Harrisburg. The President's call had been issued on April 21st; on April 28th, the entire National Guard of Pennsylvania was in camp, and within thirty days its ten thousand men had been selected, uniformed and equipped, and many of them were on their way to camps of preparation nearer to Cuba, while one of its regiments, the Tenth, was already on its way to Manila.

And what Pennsylvania had accomplished was approximated in the other states throughout the Union. Camps of preparations were established at Falls Church, Va., near the historical battlefield of Bull Run, and in the National Military Park at Chickamauga, Ga., which had been the scene of memorable battles during the War of the Rebellion. Other temporary camps of further preparation were established at different points, but the great majority of the troops were eventually mobilized at these two most important rendezvous, and from them the different regiments were forwarded to Tampa, Charleston, Newport News, and other ports from which embarkation was subsequently made for service in Cuba. The bulk of the troops that went to Manila was selected from the Western States, the Tenth Pennsylvania being the only volunteer regiment to serve in that campaign from east of the Mississippi.

The regiments of the regular army were perfected in numbers and equipment, and these were the nucleus of the army corps, which were organized for the earliest service. The First Corps, however, under Major-General Brooke, which was organized at Camp Thomas, Chickamauga, was made up entirely of volunteers, but the Second Corps, which did such gallant service before Santiago, under General Shafter, was made up largely of regulars, but with a grand leaven of volunteers who fully shared the honors of that eventful campaign. Many officers who had been prominent in the Civil War were given commissions as general officers in the volunteer service. Among them were General Joseph Wheeler, who had been the great cavalry leader of the Rebellion, General Fitzhugh Lee, of Va., General Gordon, of Georgia, and others. Soldiers of all states were equally eager. There was no longer any North or South, East or West. It was one flag and one country, and "On to Cuba" was the cry.

WAR IS DECLARED.

These unmistakable preparations constituted a declaration of war in themselves, but, for the sake of avoiding complications that might arise in connection with blockades, etc., President McKinley, recommended and Congress passed, on April 24th, a bill, as follows:

"*First.*—That war be, and the same hereby is, declared to exist, and that war has existed since the 21st day of April, A.D., 1898, including said day, between the United States of America and the Kingdom of Spain.

"*Second.*—That the President of the United States be, and he hereby is, directed and empowered to use the entire land and naval forces of the United States, and to call into actual service of the United States, the militia of the several States to such an extent as may be necessary to carry this bill into effect."

Then followed the active operations that were conducted by the Navy upon the Atlantic coast and far away among the islands of the Pacific. The victory of Admiral Dewey over the Spanish fleet in the harbor of Manila, on May 1st, seemed to set the pace for the rest of the war. The news of this glorious achievement stirred the hearts of every American to such an extent that all efforts against the national enemy seemed to have been accelerated thereby. The plans of the War Department began more rapidly to mature, and the naval vessels in the vicinity of Havana could scarce restrain their impulse to make a decisive onslaught, but the Administration had the situation well in hand, and the advance of the army and navy was near at hand.

CHAPTER XIX

The Campaign in Cuba

A Close Blockade Established at Havana.—The First Shot of the War.—The Buena Ventura Captured as the Initial Prize of the Conflict.—The First Death of the War.—Ensign WorthBagley, of the Torpedo Boat Winslow, Killed.—Admiral Cervera's Fleet Leaves Spain for the Cape Verde Islands.—A Period of Search and Apprehension.—The Spanish Vessels Reach Santiago.—Commodore Schley Bottles up the Fleet in Santiago Harbor.—"I've got them, and they Will Never Get out Alive."—Sampson takes Charge of the Blockade.—Lieutenant Hobson's Daring Deed of Heroism.—The Brilliant Young Naval Officer Sinks the Merrimac at the Mouth of the Harbor to Prevent the Enemy from Coming Out.—Afloat on a Raft Amid the Shells of Spanish Forts and Cruisers.—Taken Prisoner and Landed in Morro Castle.—The American Vessels Shell the Castle, although the Captured Men were Exposed to the Deadly Fire.—The Magnificent Naval Battle of July 3d.—The Capture of Admiral Cervera and the total Annihilation of the Spanish Fleet.

THE blockade of Havana by the vessels of the American navy included in the North Atlantic Squadron, under Admiral Sampson, began in the latter part of April, 1898. One by one the vessels had gathered at Key West from different points on the Atlantic coast, and on the 22d of the month, soon after 5 o'clock in the morning, the entire squadron of sea-fighters, except the monitors *Terror* and *Puritan*, and the smaller cruisers, sailed from Key West headed for the Florida Straits.

This movement was made in pursuance of a proclamation issued by President McKinley, and was really the first concerted movement of the war. The call of the President for 125,000 volunteers was not made until the following day, but it had been promptly determined that not a moment should be lost in blockading the principal seaport of Spain's chief possession in the West Indies, so that the effect of the declaration of war might be immediately felt.

It was known throughout the fleet, and on shore as well, that the long-expected advance on Havana was near at hand. Key West was in a fever of anticipation. Advices from Washington on the 21st indicated the probability of a movement during the night or on the following morning, but naval men kept their knowledge to themselves as long as they could. Early in the evening, however, signals were hoisted recalling to the ships all men who were on shore, and this was accepted as a foregone conclusion that the movement was certainly near at hand.

Still later at night this idea was further confirmed by the arrival of a special boat from the flagship with orders for every officer to go on board. Midnight found Key West empty of gold braid and blue jackets. The theatre of action was transferred to the harbor, where a glittering panorama was enacted until daybreak, and then it was apparent to everybody that the vessels would soon be beyond the offing.

For many days past the flagship *New York* had majestically swung at anchor about seven miles out, flanked by her big sisters, the *Iowa* and the *Indiana*. To the eyes of Key West their great smokestacks were barely visible, while the hulls lay like shadows in the distant water. The inner harbor, however, offered a striking picture, crowded as it was with monitors, cruisers, gunboats, and torpedo boats, flitting noiselessly in and out of the maze of greater vessels lying at anchor.

THE MESSAGES OF THE LIGHTS.

When twilight fell, on the evening of April 22d, this scene was unchanged, but in the darkness that followed, signal lights glimmered their messages across the skies almost without cessation, and in the early dawn, while it was still dark enough for the same sort of signalling, on the morning of the 23d, a great line of fire appeared on the sky above where lay the flagship. A moment later and the signal staff of the *Cincinnati*, in the inner harbor, flashed into colored lights, answering the call. Then the *Puritan* and the *Helena* joined in the incandescent conversation, and soon the skies were kaleidoscopic, as ship after ship answered and new lights ticked messages fraught with the gravest import, and creative of the Nation's history.

Those on shore knew not the words that had been transmitted; they saw the ships of the inner harbor move out toward the larger ones when the daydawn had advanced a little further, and everyone knew that the flagship was drawing the rest of the fleet toward her.

It was just 5.42 A.M. when the *New York*, without unnecessary display, moved slowly toward the outer waters of the Gulf. The *Iowa* and the *Indiana* followed on either side, but separated from her by a good stretch of water. As the line advanced toward the horizon, the ships spread out until there was perhaps a distance of three miles between the tips of the crescent. Those following the three leaders were the cruisers *Cincinnati*, *Detroit* and *Nashville*; the gunboats *Wilmington*, *Castine*, *Machias* and *Newport*; the monitor *Amphitrite*, the torpedo boat *Foote*, the *Mayflower* and the cable repair-boat *Mangrove*. The *Marblehead* was taking on water and followed within a day or two.

Although it was a fact that the departure of the squadron was in pursuance of orders merely to establish a blockade, there were many rumors in Key West, and throughout the entire country, when the departure was made known, that an attack was to be made upon Havana without delay. It became apparent subsequently, however that it was nothing but blockade duty that was expected of the squadron at this time. The vessels patrolled the northern coast for many miles east and west of Havana, and carried out the instructions of the President concerning the stoppage and overhauling of all vessels bound to and from Havana. The care exercised in carrying out these instructions was made manifest by the paucity of complications growing out of the seizures that were made, and the energy of the blockaders was emphasized in the many interesting incidents that occurred.

THE FIRST SHOT OF THE WAR.

On the very first day out from Key West a prize was captured. The *Nashville* saw a steamer flying the Spanish flag and overhauled her. She first fired a blank shot, which the Spaniard ignored. This was followed by a six-pound shot fired across the bows of the fugitive—the first shot of the war. The Spaniard then came to a stop and surrendered. She proved to be the *Buena Ventura*, of 1,000 tons, having on board a cargo of lumber. The *Nashville* towed her prisoner into Key West, thus having secured the first prize.

The first fight of the war, however, was the bombardment and reduction of the outer fortifications at Matanzas on the afternoon of April 27th, by Admiral Sampson's flagship *New York*, with the monitor *Puritan* and the cruiser *Cincinnati*. Matanzas is about fifty miles east of Havana. Before the destruction of the *Maine*, its only protection consisted of two old-fashioned forts near the entrance to the harbor, with old-fashioned guns that were not at all formidable ; but the Spaniards, anticipating trouble, had hundreds of men employed on the works for several weeks previous to this attack, and it was rapidly becoming almost as formidable as Havana itself.

The extent of the fortifications was not known to Admiral Sampson, but it was known that whatever was being done, was being rushed. Hence the determination of the Admiral, to vary the monotony of blockade duty by a little target practice. The flagship started out alone to do the work. The *Puritan* and *Cincinnati* were already in front of Matanzas doing blockade duty. The *New York* signalled what she was going to do as she started for the point furthest from Matanzas, where the fortifications of Point Rubalcava were being pushed ahead, and the *Puritan* and *Cincinnati* fell in behind.

The *New York* ran provokingly close to the fortifications and in a few minutes there was a puff of smoke from Rubalcava, followed by the roar of a heavy gun and the whistle of a shell. At the same time there was another puff of smoke to the east and the roar of another gun. These two shots were the invitation that the men of Admiral Sampson's ship had been looking for, and in less time than it takes to tell it, the big 8-inch gun on the starboard side forward on the *New York*, sent a shell directly into the fortification at Rubalcava. At the same time, the *Puritan* steamed up behind the *New York*, and the *Cincinnati* sailed directly toward the mouth of the harbor.

AMERICAN GUNNERS PROVE THEIR SKILL.

Before the Spaniards in the fortifications had recovered from the suprise the first shell gave them, the *New York* had planted three more almost in the same spot, and the *Puritan* and *Cincinnati* had unlimbered their guns and were paying the same sort of compliment to the other fortifications. Every shot they fired struck the fortifications and tore them asunder. Great clouds of dust arose, and lumps of masonry went flying.

The marksmanship of the Americans was excellent. The Spaniards fired wide of their mark. When the firing began the *New*

PRESIDENT McKINLEY AND THE WAR CABINET.

PRESIDENT McKINLEY.
JOHN W. GRIGGS, Attorney-General.
JOHN D. LONG, Sec'y of the Navy.
WM. R. DAY, Sec'y of State.
RUSSELL A. ALGER, Sec'y of War.
CHAS. EMORY SMITH, Postmaster-General.
LYMAN J. GAGE, Sec'y of the Treasury.
JAS. WILSON, Sec'y of Agriculture.
C. N. BLISS, Sec'y of the Interior.

AMERICANS STORMING SAN JUAN HILL.
The most dramatic scene, the most destructive battle of the Spanish War.

York was about 6,000 yards from the shore, but she gradually reduced the distance to less than 3,000 yards, and she increased the rapidity of her fire to three shots a minute, and every shot had a telling effect.

The *Puritan* did not fire quite so rapidly, but her shots were not more than a minute apart, and she did not miss anything she shot at. The *Cincinnati* fired broadsides with equal effectiveness, and after about fifteen minutes of this rapid work, the firing from the fortifications had practically ceased, and the flagship signalled to back away.

At that moment Rubalcava fired her last shot. The *Puritan* was a long distance from her, but her gunners saw the smoke puff out and aimed for that spot with one of the big 12-inch guns. The aim was magnificent. The huge 1,000-pound shell of the *Puritan* struck exactly where the smoke had been, hit the cannon from which it had come, smashed it, and drove on into the earthworks, carrying destruction before it exploded. When it exploded it seemed to those who were watching the shot, as if about all that was visible of the island of Cuba went up into the air.

This was the last shot of the first fight of the war. The three vessels then sailed out several miles off shore. There was no sign of life about the fortifications of Matanzas after they left. Not one of the Spanish shots had taken effect on the vessels, so, of course, no one was injured. The casualties among the Spaniards have never been known. It will be remembered that Blanco sent his famous message to Madrid, which said: "Killed one mule," as the report of loss in this engagement, but there is reason to believe that the mule had plenty of Spanish company in the happy hunting grounds.

THE FIRST LIVES LOST FOR THE FLAG.

The first lives to be offered up in connection with the war, that had been inaugurated, were those of Ensign Worth Bagley and four men of the torpedo boat *Winslow*, which bore the brunt of a terrific fire from batteries in the harbor of Cardenas, on May the 11th. The harbor of Cardenas had been a refuge for Spanish gunboats, and the gunboat *Wilmington*, with the gunboat *Hudson* and the *Winslow*, had been ordered to rout them out. It was in the carrying out of these orders that death came to these initial heroes.

Only one Spanish gunboat could be seen from the entrance to the harbor. The *Wilmington* was too deep of draft to enter, so the *Winslow* was sent in to capture her by threatening to blow her up with a torpedo, and the *Hudson* stood by to lend a hand. When the *Winslow* had advanced to within a thousand yards of the shore, a masked battery opened fire on her. The plucky torpedo boat replied sturdily with her small guns and continued to advance, but as she swung around to move out of range, a 10-inch shell struck her, wrecking her steam steering gear, and rendering her helpless.

Still the little vessel replied vigorously with her three guns until one of them was disabled by a fragment of a shell, but the others continued to operate while some of the crew attempted to connect the hand steering apparatus. In the meantime another 10-inch shell struck the *Winslow* on the port side, wrecked her forward boiler, filling the compartment with dense clouds of steam, and driving the men who were at work there to seek the deck for air.

The Spaniards quickly recognized the helpless plight of the torpedo boat and began to cheer. Shore batteries and the guns of two or three Spanish boats, which had not been visible from outside the harbor, all concentrated their fire upon the little American vessel. The entire engagement lasted for nearly an hour, and while it lasted it was terrific. The *Hudson* steamed forward to the aid of the *Winslow*, and attempted to tow her out of harm's way. The Spaniards seemed to pay no attention to the *Hudson*, so intent were they upon destroying the *Winslow*. Ensign Bagley and several of his men stood on the deck of the latter, doing the best they could to answer the fire of the enemy. When the *Hudson* approached within hailing distance, Bagley called out: " Pass us a line quickly; it's getting too hot here for comfort." The *Hudson's* crew threw the line and it was made fast, but it was too late to save the lives that seemed to have been doomed.

Just as the hawser drew taut, a 10-inch shell exploded in the midst of the group of men on the deck of the *Winslow*. Every man in the party was thrown backward, all dead or mortally wounded. The plucky ensign, who had been in an exposed condition during the entire conflict, was instantly killed. So also were John Denfee, a fireman, and John Varvarves, an oiler. Two others, George B. Meek, fireman, and E. B. Tunnell, cook, were so grievously injured that they died a short time afterward. For a moment after the explosion the *Hudson* wavered, and then she started with her heavy tow for the mouth of the harbor. The hawser parted, however, before she had gone far, and she turned, in the midst of a perfect hail of missiles, to aid her disabled consort. This time the cable held, and the *Winslow* passed out safely.

The shore batteries did not fire another shot after the *Winslow* was towed away by the *Hudson*. On account of the smoke and the masking of the battery, it was impossible to know what the Spanish loss in killed and wounded was ; but it has always been thought that the *Winslow* did much more damage by her answering fire than the Spaniards were willing to concede, particularly because of the moral effect of casualties at that early stage of the war. The bodies of Bagley and his men were taken to Key West by the *Hudson*, and their death was deeply mourned throughout the nation.

Another incident of this eventful week was a ruse resorted to by the wily Spaniards to send a couple of Sampson's ships to the bottom. They baited the trap as one would bait a rat-trap. A small schooner was sent out from Havana harbor, shortly before daylight, to draw some of the Americans into the ambuscade. The ruse worked like a charm. The *Vicksburg* and the *Morill*, who had been added to the blockading fleet, in the heat of the chase, and in their contempt for Spanish gunnery, closed in upon their quarry almost under the guns of Morro Castle, but the poor marksmanship of the Spanish gunners gave them warning of their danger, and allowed them to escape without damage.

THE FIRST AMERICAN FLAG IN CUBA.

On May 11th, while the *Wilmington*, *Winslow*, and the *Hudson* were engaged with the enemy at Cardenas, where Ensign Bagley and his men were killed, the steel gunboat *Machias* undertook to silence the Spanish fire at Diora Bay, the barracks located a short distance from the main batteries of Cardenas. The fight was spirited, and in less than half an hour the Spaniards retreated from their wrecked fortifications. Scarcely waiting for the firing to cease, Ensign Willard, accompanied by three men, went ashore in a launch, hauled down the Spanish flag, which the enemy had left behind in their haste to get away, and raised in its stead the Stars and Stripes. This was the first American flag erected over the enemy's works in Cuba.

On May 12th, while Admiral Sampson and several of his warships were reducing the fortifications at San Juan de Porto Rico, the *Manning*, *Dolphin*, and *Gussie* reached Mariel, on the Cuban coast, and the latter succeeded in landing a quantity of Winchester rifles, ammunition, and supplies for the Cuban insurgents. On the 14th, four boat crews, from the *Marblehead* and *Nashville*, cut the cables at Cienfuegos, losing one man killed and several officers and men wounded.

Commander McCalla, of the *Marblehead*, had signalled to the *Nashville* that morning that he proposed cutting the cable, and he ordered that volunteers be called for. So hearty was the response to this call that the officers of the vessels had to make selections from the entire crews. Four boats were fitted out. There were about forty men in the party. In each boat beside the crew were several marines, and each of the launches had a one-pound gun in its bow. All four boats made their way in, directly toward the shore, until they were not more than thirty yards from the beach. The men in the cutters were to work at the cables, so the launches stood between them and the shore, and the men in the latter promptly began firing at the Spanish soldiers who had gathered on the beach, while the *Marblehead* and the *Nashville* shelled the woods on either side.

The men in the boats cut a long piece out of the first cable, and then began to grapple for the other. Meantime the Spaniards were firing low in an evident desire to sink the cutters. Several men were kept at the oars to hold the cutters in position, and the first man wounded was one of these. No one else in the boat knew it, however, until he fainted in his seat from the loss of blood. Others took the cue from this, and there was not a groan or complaint from the two boats as the bullets, coming thicker and faster, began to bite flesh every now and then. The men simply possessed themselves in patience, and went on with their work. They did not even have the satisfaction of returning the Spanish fire, but the marines in the bow of the boats shot hard enough for all, and the men at the oars again and again grunted approval when they saw Spaniards on the beach fall victims to the shots that were fired.

BOTH CABLES ARE CUT.

This sort of thing kept up for about two hours before both cables had been successfully severed, the Spaniards all the while keeping up a fire on the daring cable-cutters, and the marines defending the workmen. When it became too hot for comfort, a few cans of shrapnel were exploded over the heads of the Spaniards. This was too much for the Dons, and they ran to cover behind a lighthouse, and to this place they dragged a number of their machine guns and again opened fire. By this time, however, the work that the Americans had started out to do was fairly well accomplished. The cutters and launches withdrew from the shore, and were soon at the side of the *Marblehead* and the *Nashville*. The warships trained guns upon the lighthouse, where the Spaniards had taken refuge, and speedily knocked it into fragments. The only man killed instantly in this engagement was Patrick Regan, a marine. A sailor, who had been shot at the oars, died of his wounds on the same day. Five other sailors were wounded, Commander Maynard, of the *Nashville*, was grazed in the shoulder, and Lieutenant Winslow was wounded in the hand.

AN EFFECTIVE BLOCKADE KEPT UP.

The blockade was kept up at all ports on the northern coast of Cuba, and, though some of the Spanish skippers succeeded in eluding the watchfulness of the Americans, many prizes were captured, and the blockade was satisfactorily successful. Its effectiveness was soon made very evident in Havana, where provisions grew to be very scarce. It was impossible to prevail upon merchants to embark in such a dangerous enterprise, as running the blockade, and shipowners were equally loath to risk the almost certain capture and condemnation of their vessels. The exigencies of the war, however, demanded from time to time, the withdrawal of a part of the blockading force, and thus it was made possible to introduce into Havana occassional small consignments of supplies.

Among the earlier captures made by the blockading squadron, was that of the steamer *Lafayette*, of the French transatlantic line, which was taken by the gunboat *Annapolis* just off the harbor of Havana, but the *Lafayette* was subsequently released on a technicality. The gunboat *Vicksburg* captured the schooner *Oriente*, and the dispatch boat *Uncas* captured the *Antonio Suaves*. The cruiser *Montgomery* brought into port the Spanish brigantine *Franzquito*, bound for Havana, also the brigantine *Lorenzo;* the *Newport* captured the *Padre de Dios*, the *Morrill* overhauled the sloop *Espana*, and the auxiliary cruiser *Yale* secured a rich prize in the steamship *Rita*. The flagship *New York* also made several notable captures including the *Carlos F. Rosas*. In a secret chamber of the *Argonauta*, were found rifles and ammunition to the value of $6,000. A United States prize court was established at Key West, and the Spanish vessels that remained unclaimed were condemned and ordered sold.

A feature of the naval operations off the coast of Cuba, at this time was the arrival at Key West, May 26th, of the battleship *Oregon*, having made the voyage from San Francisco since March 19th, a distance of more than 13,000 miles, which it covered in 65 days of actual travel.

HUNTING FOR THE SPANISH FLEET.

The monotony of the blockade was broken nearly every day by news of the supposed movements of the fleet of Admiral Cervera, which was known to have left Spain for the Cape Verde Islands, and which was supposed to be on its way to the West Indies. Marvelous stories had been told of the prowess of these Spanish men-of-war, and the appetite of the entire American Navy had been whetted to a keen point. The desire to try conclusions with the enemy on the sea was uppermost in the minds of every sailor, and there was sincere disappointment when each succeeding rumor of the discovery of the fleet proved to be without foundation, and there was equal satisfaction when the enemy was at last definitely located.

Admiral Sampson had reduced the fortifications at San Juan de Porto Rico and had seen nothing of the enemy's fleet in that direction. He then returned to Havana. Commodore Schley had been placed in command of the Flying Squadron. Orders had been sent him to establish a blockade at Cienfuegos with the least possible delay. His instructions were, that if the Spanish vessels showed themselves in that vicinity, and, finding him on the lookout, should try to come around the island, whether east or west, he was to send word by the swiftest vessel he had, so that Sampson might be ready for them at Havana.

The first definite information as to the whereabouts of Cervera's fleet came through the United States Minister to Venezuela, who cabled when he learned from a confidential source that the Spaniards were seen on May 17th, headed in the direction of Cuba. They did not appear off Cienfuegos, as expected, and Sampson sent instructions to Schley on May 21st, that word had come to Washington that the Spanish squadron, consisting of four ships and three torpedo destroyers, were probably at Santiago de Cuba.

"If you are satisfied that they are not near Cienfuegos," were Schley's instructions, "proceed with all dispatch, but cautiously, to Santiago de Cuba, and, if the enemy is there, blockade him in port."

STARTED TO CRUISE EASTWARD.

Meanwhile, Sampson assembled a powerful squadron off Havana and started to cruise eastward, with a view to prevent the possible approach of Cervera's fleet from that direction, but not so far as to make it impossible to fall back to Havana in case of Cervera's fleet coming around the western end of the island. It was not believed by the Navy Department that Cervera, if he was in Santiago, would remain there, unless the port was closely blockaded,

Schley did not reach Santiago on May 24th, as expected, because, as he telegraphed to Sampson, he "was not satisfied that the Spanish squadron was not at Cienfuegos." "The large amount of smoke seen in the harbor," were the words of Schley's message, "would indicate the presence of a number of vessels, and under such circumstances it would seem to be extremely unwise to chase up a probability at Santiago, reported via Havana, no doubt as a ruse. I shall therefore remain off this port, with this squadron, availing myself of every opportunity for coaling and keeping it ready for any emergency."

Admiral Schley also embodied in his message to Sampson, the following paragraph :

"I am further satisfied that the destination of the Spanish squadron is either Cienfuegos or Havana. This point, being in communication with Havana, would be better for their purposes, if it was left exposed, and I think we ought to be very careful how we receive information from Havana, which is, no doubt, sent out for the purpose of misleading us."

On May 23d, Schley further reported that a steamer leaving Santiago on the 18th, had brought word of seeing the lights of seven vessels several miles to the southward of Santiago, and, notwithstanding this report, Schley added that, "on Saturday, May 21st, when about 40 miles southwest of Cienfuegos, I heard, from the bridge, firing of guns towards Cienfuegos, which I interpreted as a welcome to the Spanish fleet, and I am convinced that the fleet is here. Latest Bulletin from Jamaica, received this morning, asserts that the fleet has left Santiago. I think I have them here in Cienfuegos almost a certainty." In reply to this message from Schley, Sampson sent him the following:

"ST. NICHOLAS CHANNEL, May 27, 1898.

Sir:—Every report, particularly confidential reports, state Spanish squadron has been in Santiago de Cuba from the 19th to the 25th inst., inclusive, the 25th being the date of the last report received. You will please proceed with all possible dispatch to Santiago to blockade that port. If, on arrival there, you receive positive information of the Spanish ships having left, you will follow them in pursuit.   Very respectfully,   W. T. SAMPSON."

SCHLEY PROCEEDS TO SANTIAGO.

Schley's response to this message was that he should proceed to Santiago at once, though he was embarrassed by the short coal supply of the *Texas*, and her inability to coal in the open sea; furthermore, that he would not be able to remain off Santiago, on account of the general short coal supply of the squadron. Upon learning this, Admiral Sampson at once decided to go to Key West, coal, and if authorized by the Department, proceed to Santiago. Colliers were sent with all haste to Schley, and he was instructed to blockade the Spanish squadron at all hazards. Admiral Sampson cabled to the Navy Department as follows:

"Notwithstanding the apparent uncertainty of Schley's movements, I believe Spanish squadron is still in the port of Santiago." The same dispatch said that Sampson's orders to Schley had included the sinking of a collier across the entrance to Santiago, and this was the origin of the incident in which naval constructor Hobson afterward played so prominent a part. Meanwhile, however, there was great unrest at Washington as to what Schley was doing and what he was going to be able to do at Santiago.

The dispatches that passed between Sampson and the Department regarding Schley's movements included one sent by Sampson on the afternoon of May 29th, as follows: "The importance of absolutely preventing the escape of the Spanish squadron is so paramount, that promptness and most efficient use of every means is demanded." To this the Secretary of the Navy replied with the statement: "Schley telegraphs from Santiago that he goes to Key West with his squadron for coal, though he has 4,000 tons of coal with him in a broken-down collier." Following this statement from the Secretary was the following query: "How soon after arrival of Schley at Key West could you reach Santiago with the *New York*, *Oregon* and the *Indiana*, and lighters, and how long could you blockade there, sending your vessels singly to coal from our lighters at Gonaives, Hayti? Consider if you could seize Guantanamo and occupy as a coaling station. Schley has not ascertained whether Spanish squadron is at Santiago."

The Admiral's response to the above was: "Answering telegram regarding time of reaching Santiago: three days. Can blockade indefinitely. Think can occupy Guantanamo. Would like to start at once with *New York* and *Oregon*, arriving in two days. Do not quite understand the necessity of awaiting the arrival of Schley, but would propose meeting and turning back the principal part of the force under his command if he has left. Try to hold him by telegraph. Failure of Schley to continue blockade must be remedied at once if possible. There can be no doubt of presence of Spanish squadron at Santiago."

SAMPSON TAKES COMMAND AT SANTIAGO.

Meanwhile Schley sent word that he had been able to repair his broken-down collier; that he would endeavor to coal the *Texas* and the

Marblehead in the open sea and to retain his position off Santiago as long as the coal lasted. To this information Sampson sent Schley a message of congratulation, warning him, however, to maintain a close blockade, especially at night, but Secretary Long ordered Sampson to proceed at once to Santiago and take command.

In pursuance of these direct orders, therefore, the *New York*, with Admiral Sampson on board, left Key West for Santiago, just before midnight of May 29th. The next morning the *Oregon*, *Mayflower*, and the *Porter* joined the flagship, and they all raced eastward as fast as they could go. Up to that time no word had been received from Schley as to whether he knew where the Spanish squadron really was, but on the way along the northern coast of Cuba the *St. Paul* and the *Yale* were encountered bound for Key West for coal. Captain Sigsbee, of the *St. Paul*, had with him a copy of a dispatch he had sent from Mole St. Nicholas, to Secretary Long, from Schley, announcing the "bottling up" of the Spanish squadron, in the following terms: "Enemy in port. Recognized *Christobal Colon*, *Infanta Maria Teresa*, and two torpedo boats moored inside Morro, behind point. Doubtless others are here."

SUSPENSE APPEARED AT AN END.

The suspense of the past few days appeared to be at an end after learning of this dispatch, but it was not until the early morning of June 1st, when Admiral Sampson reached a point off the port of Santiago and found Schley and his ships still there, that all anxiety was removed and the fate of the Spanish squadron was sealed beyond peradventure. Sampson assumed command, by virtue of his orders from Washington, and at once began the arrangements for sinking the Merrimac and in other ways making it impossible for Cervera to escape.

It will perhaps never be quite understood why the Spanish squadron did not get out of Santiago harbor before the Americans had established their blockade. Some of the Spanish captains, who were afterward captured, said it was owing to lack of coal, but others intimated that Cervera had preferred to be blockaded in the tortuous harbor of Santiago rather than in Cienfuegos, and that it had not occurred to them that Santiago would become so untenable by reason of land and sea bombardment. The fact that they had not escaped, however, was enough for the Americans to know at that time, and the next step was to "put a cork in the neck of the bottle."

THE SINKING OF THE MERRIMAC.

The original plan for sinking a vessel at the mouth of the harbor of Santiago, had embodied the selection of the collier *Stirling* for that purpose, and it was that name that had been given to Commodore Schley, when Admiral Sampson sent his instructions regarding the proposition. It was the *Merrimac*, however, that the Admiral had in mind, and the name *Stirling* had been used through a mistake of the stenographer. Schley had found no opportunity to carry out this order, and Sampson at once went to work to perfect his plan. He had no idea that a sunken vessel would prove a lasting impediment to Cervera's escape, because he was of the opinion that the Spanish would be able to blow her up sufficiently to gain a path of egress. His main object was to keep Cervera in Santiago until the troops were landed.

On the passage from Key West to Santiago, Hobson, as assistant naval constructor, had been called into the Admiral's cabin for consultation as to the proposed blowing up of the ship. He took up the subject with so much intelligence and enthusiasm that Sampson put him in charge of the work of preparing the *Merrimac*. When the call was made for volunteers, on the night of June 1st, Hobson begged the Admiral to let him retain charge of the ship on her adventurous trip. Other men begged for the same privilege, and every man in the fleet volunteered for service on board of the *Merrimac*, but the Admiral did not wish to risk any more lives than would be absolutely necessary, and Hobson was so perfectly acquainted with all the details, that Sampson finally put him in charge and refused to allow any other officer to go on the expedition. The Admiral seems to have been almost the only man on board the *New York* who expected to see Hobson and his crew come out of the adventure alive. He said, before the start was made, "It is a dangerous undertaking, and a brave act on the part of those who are going, but it is not so easy to shoot a few men on a big ship in a dark night, and, you know, the Spaniards are very poor shots."

The *Merrimac* was a steel cargo steamer of about 5,500 tons burden. She was built at Newcastle-on-Tyne, for a Norwegian company, but was burned at Newport News, in 1896. The hull was sold to a New York firm. It was overhauled and refitted, and the reconstructed vessel was sold to the Government for a collier in April, 1898. In fitting her up for the purpose of sinking her, a line was run along the portside of the ship, parallel to the water line. Along this line were suspended, in 8-inch copper cases, ten charges of ordinary brown prismatic powder, each charge weighing about 80 pounds; over this an ordinary igniting charge of brown powder was placed, and the whole was covered with pitch for protection against water, with a primer and a wire for exploding the charges. The first plan contemplated the simultaneous explosion of all the charges. It was found, however, that the battery on hand was not sufficient to explode with certainty more than six of the charges, so only six were connected. The ship's anchors were lashed over the rail, ready for instant dropping. The cargo ports, two on each side, were opened to aid in the submerging of the vessel.

PREPARATIONS.

Below, in the engine room, the nuts holding the bonnets of the main injection valve, and the sea-suction valve of the big fire pump, were slackened off ready for instant removal, and wooden props were wedged in on top of the bonnets, so that after the nuts had been taken off, one blow with a sledge would knock out the prop, allow the bonnet to fly off and admit the sea. All these preparations were made with the greatest haste, as it was decided to send the ship in before daybreak on the morning of the 2d. One of the ships liferafts was to be towed from a line amidships on the starboard side.

Hobson, of course, was to be in charge; Deignan was stationed at the wheel; Boatswain Murphy was to cut the lashings of the starboard bower anchor; and Montague was to similarly cut the lashings of the quarter anchor; Charette was to explode the charges on signal. At the first signal, Phillips was to knock out the props, Kelly was to cut the small sea pipes and then run on deck to haul in the liferaft. At the second signal, Phillips was to stop the engine, then run on deck and jump over the starboard side. The strong floodtide was relied on to head the ship properly and to assist in sinking her. It was the intention of Hobson to remain on the bridge until he felt the ship settle. He expected that a mine would be exploded under the ship by the enemy, thus materially aiding his own plan.

THE FAREWELL OF HOBSON AND HIS MEN.

Finally all preparations were completed. By this time it was broad daylight, but the *Merrimac's* crew had said "good-bye" to the rest of the fleet and she was already headed in toward her fate. Suddenly came an order to return, from the flagship. Some slight changes in the original plan were made. Hobson decided also that it would be safer to explode each powder charge separately. It was also decided to follow the *Merrimac* in with a steam launch. These details having been arranged, Hobson at 7 P.M., June 2d, went below on the flagship, to get a little rest, and the men who were going with him also took what rest they could get. At 1.30 A.M., Hobson and his men were all on board the *Merrimac*, Cadet Powell was prepared to follow with a steam launch, and the expedition finally got under way.

The moon was partly obscured by clouds and those on the other vessels of the fleet could not see the movements of the *Merrimac* after she neared the entrance to the harbor. At 3.15 A.M., June 3d, a shot was fired, which evidently came from one of the guns of the Socapo battery on the hill to the westward of the harbor mouth. The shot was seen to splash seaward from the *Merrimac* having passed over her. Firing became very general soon after that, being especially fierce and rapid from inside the harbor on the west. For fifteen minutes a perfect fusillade was kept up, and the whole fleet knew that the *Merrimac* was having a hot time of it. Then the fire slackened, and by 3.30 A.M., had almost ceased. A close watch was kept on the mouth of the harbor in order to pick up the steam launch, which was confidently expected to return with definite news, if not with Hobson and the men who had accompanied him.

Cadet Powell brought the launch alongside the *Texas* and reported that "no one had come out of the entrance of the harbor." His words sounded like the death-knell of all who had gone in on the *Merrimac*. It seemed impossible that any of them could have lived through the awful fire that had been directed at the vessel. The launch had followed behind the ship at a distance of about 400 yards. The collier was in plain view of Cadet Powell until she rounded the bend of the channel, and until the helm had been put to port to swing her into position across the channel. Powell heard or saw and counted seven explosions, which were undoubtedly those of the powder charges under the collier. He remained in the entrance as long as he deemed it safe to do so. No wreckage or bodies floated out, but everything had evidently been swept inside by the strong floodtide, and those who made up the launch party were convinced that Hobson and his men were dead.

THE MERRIMAC'S MEN PRISONERS.

Much to the surprise of every one, therefore, a tug, flying a flag of truce, came out of the mouth of the harbor in the afternoon and made for the American fleet. The *Vixen*, flying a tablecloth at the fore, went to meet the tug. A Spanish officer went aboard the *Vixen* from the tug, and was taken aboard the flagship. He announced to Admiral Sampson that the collier's crew were prisoners of war. Two had been slightly wounded, but the others were all well. The Spanish officer also said that the prisoners were confined in Morro Castle. He said further that Admiral Cervera considered the attempt to run in and sink the *Merrimac* across the channel an act of such bravery and desperate daring that he thought it only proper that the American Admiral should be notified of the safety of those who went on such a perilous expedition.

So far as blocking the channel was concerned the attempt was not distinctly successful. The firing from the shore batteries did so much damage to he collier that the original plan could not be closely followed. Hobson maintained his place on the bridge, and the crew was distributed as planned, but the crushing of shells through the side of the vessel caused her to begin to sink before the details that had been agreed upon could be carried out. When the vessel began to settle, Hobson exploded some of his powder charges and ordered the men in the engine room to come on deck.

A perfect shower of shot came from the forts on shore, and it seemed as if the men would surely all be killed. Hobson ordered the men to lie on the deck. The water came up until only their heads were above water, but they remained there until it was apparent that the vessel was going down as she lay, and that they had better try to save their lives. They all managed to get on board the raft and cast loose from the sinking ship. They saw her settle until only the upper half of her masts were above the water, and while they were watching these, and wondering whether they had accomplished their object or not, a Spanish craft, on board of which was Admiral Cervera himself, came alongside and took them off. The Spanish Admiral took Hobson by the hand and complimented him and his men upon their bravery, promising them to send the message to Admiral Sampson, which gave the fleet its knowledge of the safety of the crew.

LOCKED UP IN MORRO CASTLE.

The prisoners were taken on shore at once and promptly conducted up the hill to Morro Castle. There they were confined for several days They were kept in separate cells and were not allowed to communicate with each other. It was reported to the fleet that the quarters of the prisoners were in an exposed portion of the Castle, so that they would be directly in the line of fire if any bombardment was attempted. Hobson afterwards said however, that this was not the fact, though from his place of confinement on the further side of the Castle he could hear the sound of the striking of the missiles that were fired in the bombardment that did follow, and could see the shells that soared over the castle and fell into the fields beyond. The British Consul, however, protested against the prisoners being kept at Morro, and they were thereupon removed to the hospital nearer the City of Santiago, where they were kept imprisoned until an exchange was agreed upon.

The Spaniards succeeded in blowing the *Merrimac* partially to pieces, so that she really formed no obstruction in the way of ingress or egress to the harbor. When this had been done, the officers of the American fleet were convinced that Cervera intended to make a dash for the freedom of the seas. Everybody, therefore, was upon a constant lookout. There was no time of the day or night that the eyes of the Americans were not fixed upon "the neck of that bottle;" but a whole month passed by after the daring exploit of Hobson and his men before the happening of the expected. Meanwhile a bombardment of the city of Santiago had been undertaken by throwing shells over the hills by which the harbor was enclosed, and the Morro and other batteries were persistently hammered at whenever the fleet seemed in need of target practice.

THE DAWN OF JULY 3D.

Sunday, July 3d, the fifth Sunday spent by the American vessels before Santiago, and the ninth recurrence of that sacred day since the victory of Dewey at Manila, broke with no particularly different situation from that which had marked preceeding Sundays. The monotony, the heat of the tropical sun, the wonder why something was not being done beside waiting, all these were there, and no one outside the harbor had reason to believe that anything unusual was about to occur.

The American fleet swung lazily at a distance of from four to five miles from the harbor entrance. The line which was at all times supposed to be in a half circle, inclosing the harbor entrance as a central point, was more than ordinarily broken up this awfully hot morning. The big battleships had drifted to the east considerably, and the *Massachusetts*, the *New York*, the *New Orleans* and the *Newark*, were not in sight. The *New York* had taken Admiral Sampson down to Altares, eight miles east from the blockade, to make a visit to the camp of the American army, while the other missing vessels were at Guantanamo forty miles to the east.

The vessels on the blockade were the *Iowa*, *Indiana*, and *Oregon*, battleships; the flagship of Commodore Schley, the *Brooklyn*, and the small yachts *Gloucester* and *Vixen*. The *Iowa* was swinging a mile further out than the rest of the squadron, trying to arrange matters in her forward 12-inch turret, which was a little out of repair, while the *Indiana* was doing the same with her forward 13-inch turret. The absolutely available ships in the squadron, therefore, were only the *Oregon*, *Texas*, and *Brooklyn*, although the *Iowa* and the *Indiana* were not long in coming forward and getting a share in the fight.

It is a custom on naval vessels that there shall be a general muster, at least once every three months, and that the articles of war shall then be read. First call for this purpose had been sounded on board the *Brooklyn* at 9.15 A.M., and the men were assembling on the decks. The lookout in the masthead had some time before reported smoke in the harbor, but, as the same thing had been noticed several times, no special attention was paid to it. Presently the lookout fairly yelled, "There is a big ship coming out of the harbor, sir." Navigator Hodgson, who was on the forward bridge at the time, looked toward the harbor's mouth, and then, grasping the megaphone: "After bridge there, tell the Commodore, the enemy's fleet is coming out."

Commodore Schley was sitting under the awning on the quarter-deck. Going to the bridge, he said: "Raise the signal to the fleet", and, turning to Captain Cook, who stood by his side, he added, "Clear ship for action." Then the Commodore, who was to have charge of this important engagement in the temporary absence of the Commander of the fleet, went forward, and took his place on a little platform of wood running on the outside of the conning tower, which had been built expressly for his point of lookout in the event of the *Brooklyn's* getting into a battle. He was dressed in blue trousers, a black alpaca jacket, and the regulation cap without the commodore's broad band of gold braid.

THE DASH FOR LIBERTY.

The *Brooklyn* and the *Vixen* were the only vessels to the west of the entrance, the others having all drifted well to the east. Schley, therefore, had the first good view of the oncoming vessel, which proved to be the *Infanta Maria Teresa*. The *Oregon* was the first to fire. She opened with her 13-inch shells, and the *Texas* followed suit. Even the *Indiana* and the *Iowa*, coming up as rapidly as possible from their greater distance, began to fire, though the range was so long that their first shots were not particularly effective.

Still the *Brooklyn* waited, but down below the coal was being forced into the furnace, every boiler was being worked, and every gun made ready to fire. Schley wanted to know which way the vessels of the enemy were all going; whether they would follow in a line to the westward, or whether they would scatter. Lieutenant Sears, who had been sharing the Commodore's watchfulness, remarked, "They all seem to be coming west, sir." Schley nodded, and gave the order, "Full speed, ahead; open fire, and don't waste a shot." In an instant the *Brooklyn's* terrific 8- and 5-inch batteries on her port side opened, and the cruiser headed for a point in front of the first escaping ship, firing at and receiving the fire from two of them.

The *Maria Teresa* came on directly toward the *Brooklyn* with the evident intention of ramming her. "Hard aport your helm!" shouted Schley, and his vessel began to turn. She turned so quickly that in a minute her big steel ram was pointing at the oncoming enemy; and the *Maria Teresa* had to work inshore to avoid the same fate which she had planned to inflict upon the Commodore's flagship. But the shells of the *Texas* and *Oregon*, with a terrible shower of shot from the *Brooklyn*, had done their work. The smoke began to appear pouring from the decks of the enemy's advance guard, and everybody knew that the *Maria Teresa* was on fire.

THE "GLOUCESTER'S" PLUCKY FIGHT.

In the meantime, the converted yacht *Gloucester* could be seen pluckily engaged with two torpedo boat destroyers that had followed the last ship out, and "Dick" Wainwright won undying fame by sinking them. At 10 o'clock the entire Spanish squadron was outside the harbor, and going rapidly westward. The *Iowa* and the *Indiana* could not quite keep the pace, but they did excellent execution while they had the range. The *Oregon*, however, came across to the assistance of the *Brooklyn*, which was now engaging the *Christobal Colon* and the *Viscaya*. At 10.10 the Spanish ships seemed all to be concentrating their shots on the *Brooklyn*. She was in a perfect rain of shells, though most of them went over her.

Standing in this hail of shells, Schley asked Yeoman Ellis, who was near at hand with a stadimeter: "What is the distance to the *Viscaya*?" The man took the observation. "Twenty-two hundred yards, sir," he said. There was a whistle, followed by a splash, and his head was literally torn from his shoulders by an 8-inch shell.

The *Maria Teresa* ran her nose on the beach, and in an instant was a mass of flames. The fire of the *Brooklyn*, the *Oregon*, and the *Indiana* was then concentrated on the *Almirante Oquendo*, and in ten minutes she, too, was sent ashore a burning wreck just a short distance from Santiago. The *Iowa*, in the meantime, had sunk one torpedo boat destroyer, and the other one had been driven ashore by the *Gloucester's* terrific rapid fire. The *Iowa* and *Texas* also poured hot shot into the *Oquendo* at a distance of 1,100 yards. Many 12- and 8-inch shells were seen to explode inside of her, and smoke came out through her hatches.

Next the *Viscaya* slowly drew abeam of the *Iowa*, and for the space of fifteen minutes it was give and take between these two ships. The *Viscaya* fired rapidly but wildly, not one shot taking effect on the *Iowa*, while the shells from the latter tore great rents in the sides of the Spaniard. The *Viscaya* finally drew ahead of the *Iowa*, but then she came under the murderous fire of the *Oregon* and *Texas*. A moment later and she was raked fore and aft, clean along her gundeck, by an 8-inch shell from the *Brooklyn*. Another moment and a shell exploded in her superstructure with terrific force, killing eighty people; then she headed for the beach at Acerraderos, and was out of the running.

A LIVELY CHASE.

The *Christobal Colon* seemed to be the greyhound of the Spanish fleet. Only the *Brooklyn* and *Oregon* were able to keep near her. At 11 o'clock the other vessels were from six to eight miles behind. Firing was suspended and all interest centred in the chase. The men came up on deck and began to cheer. They cheered for Schley and for Captain Clark, of the *Oregon*, and the *Oregon's* men returned the cheer. Up to the masthead of the *Oregon* went a pennant. "Remember the Maine," read the signal officer. "Tell them we have," said Schley, and there was a roar, as the answer went up, that might have been heard almost in Santiago.

The *Colon*, at a distance of five miles, hugged the shore, but Schley ordered the *Oregon* to follow her, and then, with the *Brooklyn*, he made a straight course for Cape Cruz, around which the *Colon* would have to steer on a long detour if she hoped to get away. The three vessels pumped along at great speed. In an hour the pursuers had made a considerable gain on their victim. Captain Clark, of the *Oregon*, signalled: "A strange ship, looking like an Italian, in the distance." He alluded to the fact that the *Colon* was bought from Italy. Schley, sitting on the edge of the forward 8-inch turret, swinging his legs and happy, said: "Tell the *Oregon* she can try one of those 13-inch railroad trains on her."

There was a terrible roar as the big shell went by the *Brooklyn*, a moment of suspense and watching, and then a hearty cheer as the missile struck the water close astern of the *Colon*, four miles away. Another was tried. That reached the mark, and there were more cheers. Then the *Brooklyn* opened her forward and starboard 8-inch guns, and one shell was seen to go through the *Colon* at the top of her armor belt. At 1.15 P.M. the *Colon* turned toward the shore and gave up the fight. As she hauled down her flag the sailors on the *Brooklyn* and the *Oregon* began a cheer that lasted for fully five minutes.

THE SPANISH ADMIRAL'S SURRENDER.

A boat was lowered from the *Brooklyn*, and Captain Cook went aboard to receive the surrender. The Spanish Rear Admiral, with tears in his eyes, said: "I surrender unconditionally to Commodore Schley. We were badly hurt and could not get away." While Captain Cook was returning to the *Brooklyn*, the *New York*, with Admiral Sampson on board, came along, ran in between the *Brooklyn* and the prize, and ordered Captain Cook to send the prisoners on board the *New York*. Commodore Schley, seeing this, megaphoned over: "I request the honor of receiving the surrender of the officers of the *Christobal Colon*." No answer was vouchsafed him from the *New York*. Commodore Schley then raised the pennant: "A glorious victory has been won; details later." The answer from the *New York* was: "Report your casualties."

Meanwhile the *Iowa* headed for the wreck of the *Viscaya*, which was burning furiously fore and aft. When the big battleship had approached as near as the depth of the water would permit, Captain Evans lowered all his boats and sent them to the assistance of the unfortunate men who were being drowned by dozens or roasted on the decks. It was soon discovered that insurgent Cubans on the shore were shooting at men who were struggling in the water after having surrendered to the Americans. Evans immediately put a stop to this, but he could not put a stop to the mutilation of many bodies by the sharks inside the reef. All the Spaniards were practically without clothes. Some of them had their legs torn off by fragments of shells. Others, who had been in the water, were mutilated in every conceivable way.

Admiral Cervera surrendered to Commander Wainwright, of the *Gloucester*, who had been a deck officer on board the ill-fated *Maine*, and who thus by the irony of fate had an opportutnity to "Remember the Maine," indeed. The crews of the *Maria Teresa* and of the *Almirante Oquendo* were taken on board the auxiliary cruiser *Harvard*, which vessel had nearly 1,000 prisoners on board by midnight.

The annals of naval history record no more complete destruction of an enemy's fleet than this. Nor had there ever been a more notable act of implicit obedience to a superior power under such awfully adverse circumstances as those which confronted the Spanish Admiral in this connection. It was subsequently learned that Cervera received direct orders from Madrid to make the sortie, and that he had no thought of escaping, except by a mere chance. This heroic feature of the enemy's position was prominent in the minds of his conquerors, and the Admiral and his men were treated with every consideration, so much so that Cervera, during his detention in the United States as a prisoner of war, never ceased to speak of it.

PRAYER ON BOARD THE "TEXAS."

The scenes and incidents of this great naval conflict would fill the pages of many books, but some there are which were particularly striking. Notable among these was the assembling of his crew upon the quarter-deck, by Captain Philip, of the *Texas*, immediately after the consummation of the victory, and his public acknowledgement, then and there, of his belief in Almighty God, by the offering of a prayer of thanksgiving for the success that had attended the efforts of the American ships.

"Fighting Bob" Evans, the Commander of the *Iowa*, when some one referred in his presence to Captain Philip's action in this regard, and asked him why he had not followed the example, said: "I found my ship surrounded by boats carrying dying and wounded prisoners. To leave these men to suffer for want of food and clothing while I called my men aft to offer prayer was not my idea either of Christianity or religion. I preferred to clothe the naked, feed the hungry, and succor the sick, and I am strongly of the opinion that Almighty God has not put a black mark against me on account of it, for every drop of blood in my body on that afternoon of July 3d was singing thanks and praise to Him for the victory we had won."

The official announcement of the destruction of the Spanish fleet was cabled to Washington as follows:

"SIBONEY, July 4th, 3 A.M.

"*To the Secretary of the Navy:*

The fleet under my command offers the Nation as a 4th of July present the destruction of the whole of Cervera's fleet. Not one escaped. Their attempt to escape was made at 9.30 A.M. yesterday, and at 2 P.M. the last, the *Christobal Colon*, ran ashore 60 miles west of Santiago, and let down her colors.

"The *Infanta Maria Teresa*, *Oquendo* and *Viscaya* were forced ashore, burned and blown up within 20 miles of Santiago. The *Furor* and *Pluton* were destroyed within four miles of the port.

"Enemy's loss probably several hundred from gun fire, explosions and drowning. About 1,300 prisoners, including Admiral Cervera. Our loss, one killed and two wounded. The man killed was George H. Ellis, chief yeoman of the *Brooklyn*.

SAMPSON."

The Spanish prisoners were transferred at once to Portsmouth, N. H., and from there Admiral Cervera was taken to Annapolis, Md., where he remained until his release. The *Maria Teresa* was subsequently raised under the supervision of Naval Constructor Hobson, but was lost on her way to Hampton Roads. The other Spanish vessels were left upon the beach where they had been driven by the fierce onslaught of the American gunners. Most of the victorious American vessels returned to American ports soon after their notable achievement; others remained at Santiago to aid the army in the final capture of that city. This great victory, however, is conceded to have practically ended the war, for there was no longer any hope that the beleaguered city could withstand the operations that were being made against it.

CHAPTER XX

The Invasion of Cuba by the Army

General Shafter Starts from Tampa with Transports.—The Shutting up of the Spanish Fleet Changes the Campaign from Havana to Santiago.—The Landing of Troops at Baiquiri.—The Brilliant Charge of the "Rough Riders" under Colonel Wood and "Teddy" Roosevelt.—Marvelous Bravery at El Caney and San Juan Hill. The Small American Force though Handicapped on all Sides Wins Victory from the Better Armed and Better Protected Spaniards by Sheer Bravery, and the Mad Rush of their Battle.—Terrible and Costly Hours of Waiting.—Shafter Ill in the Rear, Generals Wheeler, Lawton, Chaffee, Colonels Wood and "Teddy" Roosevelt Lead the Men to a Marvelous Victory.

THE troops that had been mobilizing at the different camps were more than longing for a chance to join in an attack upon Havana, and when the orders for a forward movement were given, many who were not in the secrets of the campaign thought they were bound for the Cuban capital. Word had come to the President, however, and to the Departments in Washington, that the situation in the harbor at Santiago demanded immediate operations on shore. The fleet was maintaining a perfect blockade, but could not coax the rat from its hole. To get behind the enemy, therefore, and to grind him, if possible, between the upper and the lower millstones was an absolute necessity. The original plan, which had Havana for the objective point, was therefore changed, and the eyes of the leaders of the military expeditions to Cuba were turned towards Santiago.

It was on June 13, 1898, that troops began to leave Tampa and Key West to play their part in the operations against Santiago. Seven days later all the transports bearing them arrived off the harbor. The start from Florida had been much delayed. There was ground for the criticism that everything had not been well planned, but the plans, such as they were, were pushed forward as rapidly as possible under the circumstances, and the fleet, when it finally loomed in the offing opposite the neck of the bottle in which Cervera's fleet was held in bondage, presented quite a formidable spectacle.

The transports rolled about in that vicinity for the next thirty-six or forty hours, but on the second day, the 23d, General Shafter landed his army of 16,000 soldiers at Baiquiri, a few miles east of the Castle of Morro. This landing was accomplished with a loss of only two men, and these met their fate by drowning. Before the coming of the troops the Spanish had evacuated the village of Baiquiri, which is just a little back from the landing. They set fire to the town, destroyed the powder magazines, and utterly demolished a railroad roundhouse in which were several locomotives.

LANDING THE TROOPS FOR BATTLE.

Admiral Sampson had escorted the transports with men-of-war, and when the soldier-bearing vessels approached the landing places the warships shelled the vicinity and opened fire also upon the forts to the east and west for a distance of several miles so that the attention of the enemy was perfectly distracted, and the soldiers landed unmolested.

To have made this landing on the imperfect wharves and from the beach boats which were best available would have been terribly disastrous if the enemy had been actively opposed, but under the circumstances it was only the crowded condition of the transports, and the awkward arrangements that were made, that caused it to be at all disagreeable to these men who had long been eager to gain a foothold upon Cuban soil.

Colonel Huntington's marines, who had already landed at Guantanamo and had established Camp McCalla at the sacrifice of several lives, had expected that the army of Shafter would land where they did. The facilities at that point, however, were far from being good. The marines themselves had found it hard to reach the shore, and it would have been practically impossible for the regulars and artillery to have disembarked at that point. Shafter had thought of making the landing at Acerraderos. The Government map shows a road running from this point to the city of Santiago, but the engineers found that this so-called road was simply a mule path over which it would be killing work to attempt to transport artillery.

CITY OF HAVANA AND HARBOR, SHOWING WRECK OF THE BATTLESHIP "MAINE."

Cuba has four cities of marked importance to the commercial world: Havana with a population of 250,000, Santiago with 71,000, Matanzas with 29,000 and Cienfuegos with 30,000 are all seaport cities with excellent harbors and do a large exporting business.

GENERAL JOSEPH WHEELER.

RICHMOND PEARSON HOBSON.

THEODORE ROOSEVELT.

MAJOR-GENERAL ELWELL S. OTIS.

POPULAR HEROES OF THE SPANISH-AMERICAN WAR.

For this and other reasons Baiquiri was selected as the place for disembarkation. Back of the town, already referred to as having been burned by the Spaniards upon the approach of the transports, there is a high plateau extending along the coast almost to Santiago. Behind this plateau a coral road runs for some distance, occupying a good strategic position for part of the way. Moreover, there is a famous iron pier at Baiquiri, built by American capital for the sake of facilitating the loading of ore brought down from the Cuban mines which were being worked by a Chicago corporation. This pier was particularly well built for the purpose for which it was designed, but as its height above the water was about 15 feet it was really not satisfactorily available for the landing of troops. Its shore approaches, however, were advantageous in this connection, and it is probable, therefore, that Baiquiri presented as good advantages for the disembarkation as could have been found at any other place along the coast.

The fleet of transports consisted of about 40 vessels. The convoy was made up of 16 warships of different rates. The expedition comprised 14,564 enlisted men, and 773 officers. The great majority of the the troops were regulars. The only volunteer organizations were the Seventy-first New York, Second Massachusetts, and two dismounted squadrons of four troops each from the First Volunteer Cavalry, with Colonel Leonard Wood in command and Theodore Roosevelt as Lieutenant-Colonel. There were also two dismounted squadrons of four troops each from the First, Third, Sixth, Ninth and Tenth regular cavalry, making a total of 2,875 enlisted men of dismounted cavalry and 159 officers.

Of artillery, there were light batteries E and K of the First Artillery, A and F of the Second, and G and H of the Fourth; a total of 18 officers and 445 enlisted men from this branch of the service. There were also 200 enlisted men and 9 officers of engineers, and one detachment from the Signal Corps, comprising 45 enlisted men and two officers.

The regiments of regular infantry were the First, Second, Third, Sixth, Seventh, Eighth, Ninth, Tenth, Twelfth, Thirteenth, Sixteenth, Seventeenth, Twentieth, Twenty-first, Twenty-second, Twenty-fourth, and Twenty-fifth, making, with the volunteers, a total of 561 officers and 10,709 enlisted men.

When the army began to disembark there was a great deal of undue haste on the part of different commands to be the first to get on shore. Life on board the troopships had not been pleasant. They had all been fearfully crowded. Everybody suffered greatly. The thermometer had been close to a hundred down in the holds of the vessels where the troops were packed in like sardines at night. On one transport alone, the *Cherokee*, five regulars, inured though they were to all kinds of hardships, fainted away, while one or more cases of prostration had been reported from nearly every other transport.

THE SCENE AT THE LANDING.

A thousand men could have prevented ten times that number from landing at Baiquiri, but the Spaniards apparently had their hands full at other points. Still, a few warships could have made the position very hot for any one who undertook to prevent the landing. The woods and the hillsides for miles around Baiquiri were shelled by the vessels of Sampson's fleet, and the Spaniards practically kept out of the way. From their point of observation, the fleet of transports with the convoy of battleships, must have presented a decidedly formidable appearance, and when the soldiers began to swarm in the rigging and over the sides, cheering wildly, the bands playing national airs, interspersed with popular songs, the men joining in the choruses, the warships banging away at the beach, smoke enough hanging over the water to suggest war indeed, the scene so impressed the Spaniards who saw it, that they apparently stood not upon the order of their going but went at once.

Throughout the day smoke rose up from the buildings which the retreating Spaniards had fired in the town, and made a sort of a screen between the transports and the lower foothills. The higher ground, however, was plainly in sight from the vessels, and detachments of Spanish horse and foot, scurrying along upward and away from this scene of impressively active operations, could be seen to halt and look back as if taking in the full import of the picture.

Outside, stretching to the offing, were the transports, ranging from the huge coastwise steamer built on the models of Atlantic liners to side-wheelers and nondescript vessels half-way, apparently, between the ark and a tugboat. All were moving constantly to overcome the drift of the current. Among them, and spread out on either side toward the shore, were the convoys, whose keen-eyed lookouts constantly scanned the beach and the hills beyond, and which occasionally sent a shot whizzing through the air.

Small boats were everywhere. They came and went singly, in pairs, and in long strings. They were rowed, towed and allowed to drift. They clung to the ships, lined the landing wharf, and filled all space between. The soldiers, scrambling over the sides of the vessels as best they might, packed themselves away in these boats, and it was in connection with this haste and recklessness that the only fatalities occurred. Each man carried his gun and field accoutrements, and his blankets were slung in a roll over his shoulder.

It usually happened that men from several different commands would find themselves in the same small boat, but when they landed at a low wharf inside the iron pier, straggling up to a level bit of sand beyond it, or if they had stepped overboard in shallow water and waded ashore, they managed to fall into their own companies without much delay, and, marching off, were almost immediately out of sight in the tangle of tropical underbrush. Of the thousands that landed not more than two or three hundred were in sight at any one time during the three days in which the disembarkation was going on.

Some of the men were packed in the small boats for four hours between the time they came over the side of the transport and the time when it was their turn at the wharves. This is the reason why so many became restless, and why hundreds of the impatient soldiers left the small boats and waded, sometimes up to their waists, though even this did not cool their desire to be on terra firma.

Those transports which had stock on board drew up along the dock of the coal company. One of the side-wheelers got jammed against the wharf in such a position that in self-defence it had to discharge its cargo of 100 mules into thirty feet of water, and these poor beasts, apparently as eager as the soldiers to get ashore, swam gamely to the beach, fully forty yards away.

During the first day of the disembarkation the volunteers all got ashore and a great part of the regulars. This day extended far into the night, and the next day began where its predecessor had finished.

The searchlights from the men-of-war turned night into day, and quite as good progress was made at midnight as at noon. The Engineer and Signal Corps were among the first to land. The artillery, including the siege guns, were among the last. The cavalry had things pretty much their own way, for Roosevelt had set their pace at Tampa by practically pre-empting a vessel to which some other command had been assigned, and here at Baiquiri, Colonel Wood having left the details of the disembarkation to him, it turned out the Rough Riders were on shore among the first, and the other cavalry were not far behind. There was a great deal of pulling and hauling, and it looked for a time as if it would take a week to get everybody landed. General Shafter and Admiral Sampson came ashore in the same boat, and were loudly cheered by those who had preceded them.

General Joe Wheeler, in command of the cavalry division, promptly pushed forward to Siboney. General Young and Colonels Wood and Roosevelt were with him. These knew that the first work to be done in the way of facing the enemy would probably fall upon them. Shafter established temporary headquarters at Playa del Este, and the great bulk of the infantry bore off toward Jaragua, the artillery being instructed to come on as rapidly as possible. The Rough Riders, making a forced march, found themselves, the first night after their landing, in a position which gave them a surety of being in the very van of those who were to have this early opportunity to show the stuff they were made of.

THE ENEMY PREPARES FOR BATTLE.

On the afternoon of June 23, 1898, while the artillery and infantry were still moving toward Jaragua, word came to General Wheeler, through a Cuban officer, that the enemy had gathered in considerable numbers at Guasimas, and that they were blocking the way to Santiago in that direction. There is no town at Guasimas, not even so much as a village. It is merely the junction of two trails that meet at the point of a V, one coming from Siboney and the other from Baiquiri, and both proceeding as one toward Santiago. That same afternoon General Wheeler took with him a handful of Cubans and reconnoitered this trail. That night he sat around a camp fire with General Young, Colonel Wood, and Lieutenant-Colonel Roosevelt, and, after discussing the situation thoroughly, it was decided to attack the enemy on the following morning.

Little sleeping was done that night. The news soon flew through the cavalry quarters that there was to be "business" the next day. Moreover, stores and ammunition were still being landed on the coast only three or four miles away, and the searchlights on the vessels in the harbor were throwing their great arms of light athwart the sky in every direction, so that the whole place was almost as light as day. In this night light, and in the midst of this wakefulness, the men did their best to dry their uniforms, and considerable time was spent in cooking coffee and bacon.

At 5 o'clock in the morning, the men having had not more than two or three hours sleep at the best, the forward movement began. General Young started first toward Guasimas with the First and Tenth (dismounted) Cavalry, taking the eastern trail. The Rough Riders climbed the steep hill above Siboney and struck in on the western trail. There was about half a mile between the Rough Riders and General Young's command. Within less than half an hour after the men left Siboney, Colonel Wood took the very precautions which the earliest reports said had been neglected. He sent Captain Capron forward with his troop as an advance guard. There were Cuban scouts in front of these and flankers on the right and left.

At about 6 o'clock Colonel Wood ordered a halt. Several of the officers were mounted. They had been moving slowly to give the men a chance to keep up. Every few moments a pause had been made for the purpose of resting, so when this halt order came the men thought it one of the ordinary stops that had been allowed them during the hard march. But those who were in sight of the leaders had noticed a Cuban scout dropping back and whispering softly in the ear of Colonel Wood. A dozen men were sent back with the scout, but there was otherwise no evidence of the seriousness of the situation. The country was covered with high grass and chaparral. Thousands of Spaniards might have been hidden without betraying their whereabouts, and in it, as a matter of fact, thousands were concealed and ready to do much damage.

It was fully ten minutes before Colonel Wood gave the signal for the entire command to advance. Colonel Roosevelt took a third of the regiment into the forest on the right. Firing was begun by the hidden foe, so our men quickened their pace, and were preparing for a rush toward a point from which firing could be distinctly heard, when one of the men who had been sent with the Cuban scouts a few moments before met them. He had been wounded. His face was covered with blood. He was sobbing like a child.

"I am not hurt," he said, in an apologetic tone, "but I am a fool. I set off one of my own cartridges while I was loading. My face and eyes are full of powder and I can't fight." Then he sat down on the grass, and the others went on, leaving him alone there sobbing and swearing alternately.

THE FOE IN AMBUSH.

In the meantime the enemy was pouring a telling fire into the men. General Young, with the regulars, was off at the left, Colonel Wood occupied the centre, and Roosevelt was on the right. These three gradually drew together at the apex of the V, pushing forward through the high hot grass and undergrowth right into the face of the firing that came from the dense thickets, and with never an opportunity at this stage of the proceedings to get a fair shot at those who were firing upon them from ambush.

Every little while a comparatively open space would be encountered. Then it was like breaking through the walls of a maze. In other places the troopers could not see those who were nearest them. If they heard a twig break, or the heavy breathing of a man, they knew they were not alone, but there was no sign of human beings except in the intervals when they came out into the open.

The fire of the enemy was awfully accurate. Nine men of the Rough Riders were killed in the short space of three minutes. The wounded were dragged into the shade when opportunity offered, but many of those who had fallen were left to lie, where they fell, until the first-aid men or the surgeons could find them.

The enemy was firing very low. The Rough Riders had to advance oftentimes on their hands and knees. It was mighty hot work, and it didn't take long for everybody to strip to the waist. If a fellow kept his cartridge belt and canteen, he had all he wanted to carry, so the trail along which they passed was strewn with bits of uniforms and articles of equipment, and looked more as if a retreating army had passed that way than that an army of advance had fought its way to victory. Blanket rolls, haversacks, carbines, canteens, hats and even shoes were cast aside, and here and there an empty cartridge belt was found in evidence of some one having used the last of his precious ammunition.

THE TERRIBLE ROLL OF DEATH.

It has been estimated that there were about 3,000 Spaniards engaged in this fight, The Americans were less than 1,000. The Americans had 16 killed and 52 wounded, 42 of the casualties occurring to the Rough Riders and 26 among the Regulars. The Spanish killed were about 100, notwithstanding their advantage of ambush. Thirty-seven Spaniards were found dead on the ground. The wounded had been carried off, and it was ascertained after the battle that many of the killed had also been carried away and buried.

Prominent among those who were killed along the bloody trail of Guasimas was Captain Capron. He was the fifth generation of soldiers that his family had produced, and his father was at the head of a battery of artillery only a few miles away. The younger Capron was only 28 years of age. He was shot in the shoulder. The wound was known to be fatal from the first. One or two of his friends saw him as the surgeon was trying to do what he could for the man.

The death of Sergeant Hamilton Fish was another sad event of this day's experiences. Fish, defiant in life, had met death standing. Half a dozen of the troopers had called to him to crouch and creep along with the rest of them, but he was at the head of his men and stalked across the occasional open spaces without a thought of himself until finally he fell like a log across the trail.

Some of the escapes from death were miraculous. Champney Marshal, of Washington, had one bullet pass through his sleeve. Another passed through his shirt, where it was pulled close to the spine. The holes where the ball entered and went out again were clearly cut. Another man's skin was slightly burned by three bullets in three distinct lines, as though it had been touched for an instant by the lighted end of a cigar. Roosevelt himself was so close to one bullet, when it struck a tree, that it filled his eyes and ears with splinters, and his color sergeant, Wright, following close at his heels, was clipped three times in the head and neck, and four bullets passed through the folds of the flag he carried.

THE MAN WHO WOULDN'T GIVE UP.

A cowboy named Heffner was shot through the body. He asked to be propped up against a tree with his canteen and cartridge belt beside him. As those who placed him in this position turned away they saw him firing over their heads in the direction of the enemy. Subsequently this man was taken to a hospital apparently half-dead, but when he heard an ambulance coming to take wounded men to the hospital ship, he rolled off of his blanket under the edge of the tent, and the ambulance went off without him. Next day he dragged himself to the firing line. He was sent back by Colonel Roosevelt, but when it came to the battle of El Caney this man appeared among the rest of the Rough Riders and insisted on handling a gun.

"I thought I told you to go to the hospital and stay there," said Colonel Roosevelt.

"I believe you did, Colonel; but there was nothing going on back there, and I thought I had better be with the rest of the boys."

This man recovered from his wound sufficiently to come home with his regiment to Montauk Point, and subsequently helped to make some of the noise that the Rough Riders made during Colonel Roosevelt's successful campaign for the governorship of New York.

Another of the men who fell in the first volley was Captain McClintock. A private who had been sick for some days, seeing McClintock lying on the field, crawled up between the latter and the firing line and said:

"Never mind, Captain; I am between you and the enemy. They can't hurt you now."

Edward Culver, a Cherokee Indian, was alongside of Hamilton Fish when the latter was shot. As Fish fell to the ground, he called out, "I am wounded." Culver called back, "And I am killed."

Culver was shot through the left lung, the ball coming out the muscle of his back. He believed he was dying, but he said if he was

LANDING AT TAMPA.

HAVANA HARBOR.

CAMP SCENE AT CHICKAMAUGA.

THE SURRENDER OF SANTIAGO, JULY 17, 1898

After a little ceremony the two commanding generals faced each other, and General Toral, speaking in Spanish, said: "Through fate I am forced to surrender to General Shafter the American Army the city and strongholds of the city of Santiago." General Shafter in reply said: "I receive the city in the name of the Government of the United States."

to die he would do the Spaniards as much damage as possible before leaving. He braced himself up against a bush and sent forty-five bullets at the enemy before being taken away.

THE HEROIC WORK OF "BOB" CHURCH.

"Bob" Church, of Princeton football fame, was junior surgeon of the Roosevelt regiment. He carried as many as half a dozen wounded men on his back half a mile from the firing line to a temporary dressing station, and those who knew of the work he did on that day say that these and many others owe their lives to his indefatigability and nerve.

There was no difference in the bravery of the two predominating elements in the Rough Riders' organization, but there was a difference in their style of fighting. The cowboys of the western frontier slipped cautiously from cover and dodged deftly behind the next protecting thicket, but the eastern athletes made wild rushes and were reckless in exposing themselves. On every hand, however, evidence was constantly accumulating that there was never a body of men possessing such varied elements, and yet it was easily welded into an effective fighting-machine so easily that a foreigner would not have known that all these men were not as much brothers in blood, character, occupation, mutual faith and long companionship as any soldier organization that ever took the field.

The dominant element was the big-game hunter and the cowboy. Every field officer and captain had at one time or another owned a ranch. The majority came from Arizona, New Mexico, Oklohoma, and the Indian Territory, though nearly every State in the Union was represented. There were graduates of Harvard, Yale, Columbia, Princeton, Cornell, University of Pennsylvania, of Virginia, of Colorado, Iowa, and other western and southern colleges. There were members of the Knickerbocker Club of New York, the Somerset Club of Boston, and of famous horse organizations of Philadelphia, New York, and New Jersey. There were revenue officers from Georgia and Tennessee, policemen from New York City, half a dozen deputy marshals from Colorado, several Texan rangers, three or four Cherokees and Chickasaws, Choctaws and Creeks, and one Pawnee Indian. There were Catholics, Protestants, and Jews in this organization; there was one strapping Australian, and one of the Queen's Mounted Police from the British-American possessions, though 90 per cent. of all were native born Americans.

This is the sort of material that forced the Spaniards along the Guasimas trail back from the position they had occupied and gradually drove them out of reach. The result was that the way was cleared through this defile to the immediate vicinity of Santiago. Furthermore, the fact that the Spaniards who had occupied this commanding position were not re-enforced, demonstrated the further fact that the enemy knew how useless it would be to stop the onrush of the Americans, and established in the minds of the American commanders the idea that their strongest opposition would be met much nearer the beleaguered city.

The position of the Spanish in the vicinity of Guasimas was naturally so strong that, if it had been held in force, the United States troops must have had several days of hard fighting before they could have driven the enemy from the mountainous ridges commanding the road. But after the onslaught of the dismounted cavalry squadrons, the Spaniards made no attempt to utilize the natural advantages afforded by the lay of the land, and fell back immediately on the line of defences at San Juan and El Caney, almost within firing distance of Santiago.

ROOSEVELT TAKES COMMAND OF THE ROUGH RIDERS.

Soon after noon, on the day of the Guasimas fight, the advance guard of the cavalry was pushed forward to the plateau at Sevilla. Here the country was fairly open with stretches of grass land at intervals. The distance from Siboney, which had become the base of supplies, was not more than five miles, and General Wheeler, in command of the cavalry division, and General Lawton, commanding the Second Infantry division, decided to make this point their headquarters for the present. On the following day Colonel Wood was placed in command of a brigade, and Roosevelt's Rough Riders from that time on were Roosevelt's in fact as well as in name.

With the cavalry at Sevilla, General Shafter maintained his headquarters at Playa del Este. One reason for this was that the cable station was located at this point. The Commanding General also felt that he wanted to be near the coast until the very last of the troops and munitions of war had been disembarked. When the Spaniards had been driven out of Guasimas, and it became evident that their firmest stand would be made near Santiago, Shafter transferred his headquarters to La Redonda, about six miles from Siboney, and only a little way from Sevilla. Generals Kent, Lawson, and Chaffee were also in that immediate neighborhood, so that Sevilla, as a matter of fact, may be said to have been the location of the entire army immediately after the exploit of the Rough Riders and other cavalry along the Guasimas trail

The encampment was continued at this point for three or four days, and it became a common remark of field and company officers that any enemy with a small degree of enterprise could have attacked the invaders and done them great damage, if, indeed, the entire force could not have been routed and driven back in confusion. The camps were in a jumbled condition, supplies were irregular, and the men soon became pretty well disgusted with what seemed to them to be an interminable delay.

Meanwhile news was constantly being brought to General Shafter that the Spaniards were improving their position, particularly in the vicinity of El Caney and along the San Juan hills. They had evidently been indifferent to the easy prey that the invading army might have been, merely because they had already seen something of the valor of the American troops, and had chosen the battleground on which they preferred that the bulk of the fighting should take place.

The natural conformation of the country could hardly have been more favorable to a defensive campaign. The Wilderness in Virginia presented far less difficulties to the invading Northerners than did the San Juan valley to Shafter's army. The greater part was covered with young undergrowth, interlaced with thorny vines, and the roads were little more than blind trails.

SHAFTER IS TAKEN ILL.

General Shafter was taken ill while the army was at Sevilla, and his condition was made worse by the extreme heat. He kept in touch with what was going on, however, but for several days the duty of personal observation had to be delegated to others. He and all his officers saw, within forty-eight hours after the fight at Guasimas, that an early advance must be made upon El Caney. The subsequent capture of this point and the really brilliant engagement at San Juan constitute one event, and it has always been so regarded by all the general officers who took part in the fighting.

The reinforcements that General Pando was known to be offering to the beleaguered garrison at Santiago would have found their easiest approach through El Caney, and it was decided, therefore, to put this possibility out of the way as soon as circumstances would permit. The Spaniards had apparently expected that the army would reach Santiago by detour along the coast, but Shafter evidently had his own reasons for sending his men directly across the country.

Progression and protection of the American position was rendered imperative by the problem of feeding the men who had penetrated into the enemy's country. The roads were impassable. The dry weather had given place to tropical rains. Every pathway had become a sunken road. There seemed to be only one of two things for the invaders to do—they must either hold the ground they had gained and advance therefrom or some of the troops must move westward along the coast, where the Spaniards had made special preparations to receive them, and try to capture some little port, thus shortening up the line of supplies between the fleet and the troops. The forward movement was decided upon. Moreover, the officers all felt that July 4th was approaching, and everybody wanted to celebrate that day by some great event.

A COUNCIL OF WAR.

On June 29th a council of war was held. Every man who took part in it had learned a great deal regarding the use of rapid-fire guns and smokeless powder. Older officers, who had served in the Civil War, saw that the rapid-fire guns of to-day, where smokeless powder is used, give to each man the value of five men during the Rebellion. More than that, with the accuracy of aim now possible, a good marksman can kill ten men with such a gun where he could only kill one thirty years ago. The new arms, with their low range and rapid fire, had wholly altered the manœuvres that must immediately precede and occur during the battles of the future. The play, therefore, was to be for a flank attack, and that was the plan decided upon at this conference in front of Santiago.

Generals Young and Chaffee favored clearing the right flank first, and not exposing both of our flanks to the scientifically posted Spanish infantry. It was decided, therefore, to take El Caney by assault early on the morning of July 1st, and let the other two divisions conform to the movement that was to be made by Lawton, who was to deliver the swinging, jugular-vein blow. General Lawton wanted to go out that very night and get into position to deliver his blow, but every commander was as zealous as he was, and the result was that this disposition was not made. The plan was further developed during the final day of June, and on the following night bivouac was made at 10 o'clock, and the men slept on their arms.

Before daylight General Chaffee had worked his men forward so that he might approach El Caney from the east of north. He got his men well entrenched, personally supervising every detail. It was subsequently discovered that the Spaniards also well understood the trick of digging good trenches. Their rifle-pits consisted of a deep, narrow hole in which a marksman could crouch, making the earth itself his guardian angel, and when, at the first sight of dawn, Chaffee ordered the advance, and line after line of rifle-pits was encountered, there was an occasional hesitation, not inspired by fear, but by indecision.

The fighting was stubborn from the very outset. Resistance was determined, and the patience of the two divisions on the left, already under fire from the San Juan forts, was sorely tried. Their commander sent over to know if the movement of Chaffee could not be hurried or abandoned, so that they could go into action against the enemy in front of them, but Chaffee was too far committed to consider the proposition of withdrawing. The effect of this message, however, was to redouble the energy of the men before El Caney, and many acts of individual courage were performed that day.

Captain Capron, father of the young man who had been killed with the Rough Riders along the Guasimas trail, concentrated the fire of his battery upon the blockhouses by getting two of them in line. So accurate was the aim of his battery that he knocked whole corners out of these stone structures. His guns were so placed tha after the shells went through one blockhouse they would land and explode in the next one, rending it apart like a box of pasteboard.

While this sort of thing was going on, Adjutant-General Gilmore had ridden over from the San Juan way with the information that the fight had its heart in front of the forts at that point, and that reinforcements must be hurried there to insure success. General Lawton turned to the officer who brought this news and said : " There is important business to be done here, and I can't quit." A hurried consultation was held, however, and it was decided that the village must be taken. It was done in thirty minutes by a splendid assault led by Captain Haskell, of the Twelfth Infantry. Those who saw this gallant officer lead the charge up that hill will never forget it. He rushed along at the head of his men with his long, white beard flying in the air and surrounding his face like a patch of fog. His men followed him without question, and one blockhouse was carried almost before the Spaniards knew that the enemy was upon them.

A TERRIBLE FIGHT IN A BLOCKHOUSE.

This blockhouse stood at the top of a hill, facing the pathway, leading up to it and into the town. Intrenchments were all around it, and no one knew how many soldiers of Spain were in and behind these fortifications. There were about fifty inside the blockhouse, shooting through the holes. A company of the Ninth Infantry reached this point first, and twenty of them climbed up to the roof and dropped inside. A terrific fight took place in these close quarters. The first Americans who entered were awfully slaughtered by the Spaniards. Some of them were badly mutilated. Fifteen others of the Ninth regulars also mounted the walls of the blockhouse and jumped down into this pit of death. The sight of their outraged comrades galled them. It took only a moment for vengeance to be wrought. One man was shot in the wrist, but he killed the Spaniard who shot him and brought away the pistol that the Don had used. One American is known to have killed four Spaniards in this hand-to-hand encounter. One of the regulars had a piece of his nose shot off. Turning on the Spaniard who had maimed him he ran him through with his bayonet, pinned him to the wall and held him there until he died.

Meanwhile others of the Americans were doing desperate work in the immediate vicinity of the blockhouses. The rush that had been made seemed to take away the breath of the Spaniards, and the shower of leaden hail which was fired upon them created awful havoc. When our men got into the Spanish ditches they found some of them three to five feet deep with dead Spaniards, but no wounded were found, these evidently having been taken along with the retreating force. The Spaniards, however, made a desperate resistance at many points. Their firing was much more accurate than many have been led to suppose, Their artillery was well placed and did a great deal of damage, but it was the intrepidity of the Americans that staggered them. The fact that their advantage with smokeless powder did not deter the onslaught, seemed to be more than they could understand.

WHAT FOREIGN REPRESENTATIVES SAID OF THE FIGHT.

The assault and capture of El Caney took the breath of the foreign attaches who were watching the manœuvres. One said : " It is very gallant, but very foolish." "It is slaughter ; absolute slaughter," said another, " they never can take it, you know." The little Japanese attache merely shrugged his shoulders and said nothing. But they all watched the assault with eagerness, and when it was crowned with victory they could hardly believe their own eyes.

The Rough Riders' dynamite gun, handled by Alsop Borrowe, did good execution against the fortifications at El Caney. This was the first opportunity afforded for work with this weapon, and everyone was well pleased with what it accomplished. It was located in a position that was guarded by several troops of the Rough Riders, who were particularly anxious to have more active work to do than they seemed likely to get in this connection. Later in the day, however, Colonel Roosevelt made good use of his opportunities, but it was in the second day's fighting that the regiment again distinguished itself.

The lack of more artillery was very disheartening. Had it not been for the marvelous prowess of the infantry, the Spaniards would not have been driven out of El Caney. The slightest faltering on the part of the Americans would have resulted in their having been hurled back further than their starting point. It was their continuous forward movement that won the day.

The first wounded man to reach headquarters was a private of the Second Massachusetts, who had two fingers shot away. His battalion had been within 200 yards of the enemy when the Spaniards opened fire. He spoke particularly of the disadvantage he and his comrades had had in not being able to see where the shots came from. They felt like rats in a trap at first, but they soon learned the Spanish tactics of fighting under cover. This wounded man complained bitterly that his regiment had not been allowed to light fires for twenty-four hours, and had started into battle with only ten pieces of hardtack and a piece of bacon an inch wide.

THE WORK OF THE SHARPSHOOTERS.

During the progress of the fight, the Eighth Infantry was under a heavy fire, in the neighborhood of a big mango tree. Some of the men were under the tree, and the fruit fell on them in showers, knocked down by the bullets. The greatest annoyance experienced by all the troops was from the sharpshooters who were posted with their smokeless powder pieces in the surrounding trees. It was impossible to get at these fellows until their companions had been driven from the rifle-pits. Then one of these roosting birds would occasionally drop down to join in the flight, and the chances were very much against his getting away alive.

It had been thought before this fight began that El Caney could be captured in very short order. The first blockhouse fell into the hands of the Americans within half an hour after its fierce assault was undertaken, but the day was well spent before all the trenches were cleaned out, and the enemy was entirely driven back. It had been a day of bravery, and a day of slaughter on both sides, though the exact loss could not be reckoned until the following day's work was complete. The United States troops had stuck their finger nails into the crest of the bluff and stayed there. They were victorious as far as they had gone, but there was much more to be accomplished. Westward from El Caney, on the top of the ridge, were the forts of San Juan. These constituted the outer stronghold of Santiago, and these must be captured at once.

Officers and men all knew that this was the work cut out for them on the 2d of July. There was very little sleep that night, but a great deal of work was done in perfecting the intrenchments and getting ready for the morrow. The morning broke clear and beautiful. The men could be seen on the crest of the hill, in the holes they had dug in the ground during the night, and the entire army was eager to go to their support. The enemy was evidently quite as wide awake and anxiously awaiting the attack.

San Juan hill is a long and steep irregular ridge. It is of unequal height, and the highest point was crowned by an old building which had been converted into a fort with trenches in front of it, and the ordinary broken-stone construction of the Spanish blockhouse. In front of the blockhouse the hill was at least a hundred feet higher than the plateau before it. The ascent was at an angle of fully forty-five degrees. The face of the hill was stony and thorny, and on the margin of the plateau was a wilderness of trees and thick brush through which the American soldiers had to fight their way, and when they had penetrated this thicket they were out in the open fully exposed to the fire of the fort and those who were in the intrenchments at the top of the hill.

WHY ROOSEVELT KEPT AHEAD.

The original order had been not to advance beyond the San Juan River, which flowed sluggishly through the thicket, but the fire in this brushwood was too effective to engender patience, and as each regiment came to the stream, which really was not much of an impediment to progress, they rushed over it and up on the hill without waiting for further orders. It was at this point where Colonel Roosevelt dismounted and led his Rough Riders up the slope. Afterward, when complimented on the good time he had made at the head of his command, he smiled and said: "I had to move quick to keep out of their way." The men of several commands got separated in this advance, and it was this fact, particularly in the case of the Seventy-first New York, which led to contradictory reports as to obedience of orders and manifestations of indifference. Those who neared the top of the hill first saw that they could do nothing, unsupported, against the enemy, and, as they looked around in their anxiety, each on-coming command was warmly welcomed, and thus each moment it grew warmer for the Spaniards.

On this hillside also the barbed wire fence played no unimportant part. Several companies of the Sixth Infantry ran plump against one of these obstructions halfway up the hill. Captain Burns saw a big Cuban fighting with a machete a little way off and called to him in Spanish to cut the wires. He did so, and the men rushed through and onward. The hill was so steep at that point that the men had to drag themselves up by catching at roots and bushes, stopping every other second to kill a Spaniard or two, and some of them stopping to be killed.

Several of the cavalry regiments became seriously mixed up owing to the utter impossibility of moving straightforward at anything like regular intervals. Captain Morton commanded a battalion of the Third Cavalry. When he finally approached the open space across which the dash was made for the right of the San Juan position, he found himself surrounded by men of two or three different regiments, mostly, however, of his own. He did not hesitate. There was no time for hesitation. Mauser bullets and shrapnel were singing thick and fast through the air, and men were falling on every side. Morton simply put all the men near him into line, led them forward and quickly took the most advanced position on the right, driving the Spaniards back upon a battery of theirs down under the walls of San Juan barracks.

SKILL OF SPANISH ENGINEERS.

The artificial strengthening of the Spanish line of defense showed the very highest order of engineering skill. The utmost advantage was taken of the conformation of the ground. Each fortified point or angle commanded some other one. In many places, on gaining certain intrenchments, the American troops found themselves under a crossfire from other portions of the original line. The result was that the Americans seemed sometimes to be almost surrounded, and it was like fighting their way out of a hollow square when any advance was made.

It was under these conditions that all the regiments, engaged in that day's fighting, did so nobly. The rush of the Ninth and Tenth cavalrymen was noted by the commanders of many other regiments, and those colored regulars became heroes from that hour. The regulars naturally gained the most of the glory, for they were in a large majority, but the commanding officers have accorded a full meed of praise to all concerned.

General Kent, commanding the first division of the Fifth Army Corps, gave special credit to Brigadier-General H. S. Hawkins, who, placing himself between the two regiments leading his brigade, the Sixth and Sixteenth Infantry, urged and led them by voice and bugle calls to the attack so successfully accomplished.

The total number of killed on July 1st in the First Division was 89, the wounded nearly 500. On July 2d, 9 were killed and 94 wounded. The total for the three days' fighting, from the morning of the attack upon El Caney until the truce on the afternoon of July 3d, was 12 officers and 87 men killed, 36 officers and 561 men wounded, and 62 unaccounted for. General Lawton lost 410 men, the cavalry lost 285 men, and the grand total, as given by General Shafter in his official report, was 1,593 men, killed, wounded and missing.

PERSONAL IMPRESSIONS OF OFFICERS.

The large proportion of officers killed in these engagements has been attributed by many to the fact that this was a junior officers' campaign. General Wheeler was unable to be in the field on July 1st and 2d. Generals Kent, Lawton and Chaffee were active, of course, but General Shafter was practically confined at headquarters, and the bulk of the work fell upon the juniors. These were mowed down with the men under their command, and have taken, with them, their place among the heroes who swept away the obstructions to the approaches to Santiago and made the subsequent surrender of the city a certainty.

The personal impressions of some of the officers who were engaged against the Spaniards on these earliest days of July tell the story at first hand. Lieutenant Joseph A. Carr, of the Rough Riders, speaking of the fight at San Juan Hill, has said: "We were not supported by artillery, and it was a test of what American nerve and determination could do. Most of my men were shot down from ambush. I was left in command of what remained. After we had driven the Spanish back and taken possession of San Juan hill, I was sent to occupy another eminence about 500 yards away. The

Spanish fire never ceased. We had no earthworks and no artillery. I saw no flinching. No man seemed to think of retiring, but every nerve was strained to its utmost, and our boys made a display of courage and coolness that I cannot help feeling is somehow a part of American blood."

Captain Hunter said: "It occurred to me, as we were going up San Juan Hill, that just twenty-five years before, to the very day and hour, Grimes' battery had opened the battle at Gettysburg. This coincidence was no unpleasant thought. I knew we had a hot day's work ahead, but I also knew that we were bound to win. As the battle proceeded our loss was heavy indeed, but when we saw the terrible execution our own men were doing we began to feel more than satisfied. When the artillery firing began the very first shell fired by the enemy killed one man and seriously wounded two others under my very eyes, but they paid for this a hundred times over before the day was done."

The large number of killed and wounded in the engagements which took place before Santiago was very galling to the commanders, and even more so perhaps to the authorities at Washington. General Shafter has been criticized in this connection for allowing the fighting to proceed without the aid of the siege guns, and without the artillery to support the infantry, but it is claimed, on the other hand, that there was a certain amount of work to do, and that it had to be done at once, and that the loss of so many men, deplorable as it was, could not have been prevented under the circumstances.

The sacrifice of these lives, however, occurred in the midst of onslaughts that powerfully impressed the Spaniards as to the mettle of Uncle Sam's soldiers. There was no longer any thought in the minds of the enemy that they had to deal with novices in war, or that they would have no difficulty in driving the invaders into the sea. Quite the contrary. The news was carried into Santiago that the American army could, and probably would, sweep everything before it, and it was this sort of tidings, emphasized by the accumulating assurances of the next few days, that paved the way for the subsequent surrender.

CHAPTER XXI

The Surrender of Santiago

Truce Proclaimed and Prolonged from Day to Day.—Consultation for Surrender of Santiago—General Miles, Commander-in-Chief of the Army, Joins Shafter and Takes part in the Negotiations.—General Toral Surrenders.—Terms of Evacuation.—Raising the Stars and Stripes above the City.—Hobson and His Fellow-Heroes Exchanged.—A Rousing Reception by Land and Sea.

"IF you do not surrender the city I will bombard it." That, in effect, was the ultimatum which General Shafter sent the Spanish commander in Santiago on the 3d of July. General Linares had been wounded. General Toral was in command. He refused to surrender. With this refusal came to General Shafter an appeal from foreign residents in the town for an opportunity to get out of the city before the bombardment began. The representatives of foreign nations came out to have a consultation with General Shafter, and the result was that notice was given that the bombardment would not take place until noon of July 5th.

General Toral was urged to aid the rapid departure of foreigners and non-combatants, and notices were posted in the streets of the city advising all women, children and non-combatants, that, between 5 and 9 o'clock in the morning of July 5th, they might pass out of any gate of the city. Everybody must go on foot. There could be no carriages. Stretchers would be provided for the ill and infirm. A great company of pilgrims took advantage of this opportunity, and there was a continuous line of refugees pouring out of the threatened city between the hours that had been named, and nearly 400 persons were carried out on litters.

All this took place, of course, under a flag of truce, and while the flag was still flying a communication was received from General Toral requesting that the truce be still further extended. He wanted to communicate again with the Spanish Government at Madrid concerning the surrender of the city, but all the telegraph operators, being Englishmen, had gone out with the refugees. General Shafter extended the truce until 4 o'clock on Sunday, July 10th, and the operators returned to work the wires for the Spanish commander. During all this time the refugees continued to throng the roads to Siboney and El Caney until there were nearly 20,000 of them congregated at these two points. Meanwhile the Spanish soldiers were helping themselves to everything that had been left behind by the families who had departed, and no effort seems to have been made on the part of the Spanish commanders to stop the looting.

GENERAL MILES ARRIVES ON THE SCENE.

General Miles arrived upon the scene on the day set for the expiration of the truce. The first of the two expeditions containing reinforcements landed on July 8th, the second on the 9th, and another on the 10th, so that Shafter's army had been strengthened by 6,000 men. General Toral knew of the arrival of General Miles, and with this knowledge came the impression, strongly urged on the part of the American emissaries, that further resistance on the part of the Spanish commander could only result in a useless loss of life.

The answer of the Spanish commander was that his home government had not yet given him permission to surrender the city, and that, if the Americans could not wait any longer, he and his men would die fighting. A joint bombardment by the army and navy therefore was promptly begun.

The response of the Spanish guns to the firing of the Americans on sea and shore was feeble. When the Americans fired with small arms the answer was more vigorous, but Shafter's lines were well protected with sandbags, and not much damage was done. The vessels of the fleet kept up a rain of shot and shell on the water forts and the approaches to the city, and the artillery was used much more than smaller arms in the trenches.

This bombardment continued until the afternoon of the second day. Then another flag of truce was hoisted over the city, and the general impression was that Toral was about to surrender, but he only asked for more time. Generals Miles and Shafter held a consultation. Another truce was consented to, and, at last, on July 14th, General Toral agreed to surrender the city on condition that the

THE CONDITIONS OF THE SURRENDER

Spanish army be returned to Spain at the expense of the United States. On July 16th, the agreement of surrender, the points of which had been communicated by cable to Washington and Madrid, and had been approved, was signed in duplicate by the commissioners of both sides.

THE CONDITIONS OF THE SURRENDER.

The conditions of the surrender involved the following points: (1) The 20,000 refugees at El Caney and Siboney to be sent back to Santiago, (2) An American infantry patrol to be posted on the roads surrounding the city and in the country between it and the American cavalry. (3) Our hospital corps to give attention, as far as possible, to the sick and wounded Spanish soldiers in Santiago. (4) All the Spanish troops in the province, except ten thousand men at Holguin, under command of General Luque, to come into the city and surrender. (5) The guns and defenses of the city to be turned over to the Americans in good condition. (6) The Americans to have full use of the Juragua Railroad, which belongs to the Spanish Government. (7) The Spaniards to surrender their arms. (8) All the Spaniards to be conveyed to Spain on board of American transports with the least possible delay, and be permitted to take portable church property with them.

The American army took formal possession of the city of Santiago on the morning of July 17th. General Shafter had notified General Toral of his wish in this regard, and no obstacle was interposed. At 8.30 o'clock on the morning of that day, therefore, General Shafter, accompanied by General Miles, General Wheeler and General Lawton approached Santiago on foot, walking down the road from headquarters in a leisurely manner. Under a great mango tree, just outside the walls of the city, they were met by General Toral in full uniform, accompanied by nearly 200 officers. The commanding generals faced each other, and General Toral, speaking in Spanish, said:

"It is by fate that I am forced to surrender to the American army the city of Santiago."

General Shafter replied:

"I receive the city in the name of the Government of the United States."

This was all of the simple ceremony which transferred the ancient capital of Cuba to our forces. The officers of the Spanish General wheeled about and presented arms as General Shafter, with the American officers and troops that had been chosen for the occasion, passed on into the city and to the Governor's palace.

That picturesque building is in the centre of the city fronting the Plaza, at the other end of which stands the Cathedral. The watching soldiers in the American trenches could see their commanders as they proceeded in the direction of the Plaza, and all along the lines they gave voice to cheer after cheer.

In front of the palace about 3,000 persons had gathered to see what was going to take place. The Civil Governor, the Mayor of the city, the Chief of Police, and perhaps two score of the minor officials of the municipality were waiting with the rest. There were also present some of the English and French residents of the city. Irrepressible cheers by American sympathizers were objected to by some of the Spaniards, and one or two fist-fights occurred. But the trouble was quelled almost as soon as it began.

After the Americans had arrived at the palace, the Archbishop of Santiago, the most powerful ecclesiastic in Cuba, accompanied by ten priests, came forward, gravely saluted General Shafter, and entered into conversation with him, the Archbishop speaking excellent English.

Preceding the formal ceremony of handing over the city to the Americans, luncheon was served at the palace. The only Cuban present at any of the ceremonies was General Joaquin Castillo and one of his aides, who were the personal guests of General Shafter.

RAISING THE FLAG OVER SANTIAGO.

Just before noon, Lieutenant Miley, General Shafter's chief of staff, disappeared from the crowd at luncheon, and shortly afterward every one went out on the plaza in front of the palace, where American cavalry and infantry were drawn up. General Shafter and the other Americans, followed by the Spanish military officers and officials, took up a position in front of the soldiers. Lieutenant Miley appeared on the top of the palace, accompanied by two other officers.

Every eye was riveted upon them as they stood silhouetted against the sky. Every voice was hushed expectantly, and then, as the great bell of the tower of the Cathedral gave the first stroke of 12, Lieutenant Miley ran the Stars and Stripes up to the top of the staff which had before known only the emblem of Spain. Its folds spread to the southwest breeze, and as it fluttered there, all hats were removed, and Americans and Spanish officials alike stood bare before the flag of the victor.

As the last stroke of the hour tolled out, the military band played the "Star Spangled Banner," following it up with "Three Cheers for the Red, White and Blue." Again and again the soldiers cheered, and so did more than half of the people. The crowd was composed largely of men and women of a half-starved appearance, most of whom seemed to be grateful that the Americans were in possession of the city, evidently anticipating that their days of hunger and misery were over. One enthusiastic Cuban started the cry, "Viva los Americanos!" and hundreds of his compatriots joined in the acclaim.

As the American flag floated over the city, one of the batteries of artillery at the right centre of the American line fired a national salute. As the guns thundered, our 20,000 men, from the Third Regiment on the left of the line, to the Eighth Regiment far off on the El Cobre road on the west, yelled, cheered, shouted, threw their hats in the air, and jumped up and down. The soldiers stood on the crests of the trenches, which they had won at the cost of so many lives, and, though they could not be seen from the city, their cheers were easily caught by the ear, and it was thus made plainly evident how completely Santiago and the Spanish army had been hemmed in.

After cheering the flag on the palace, the soldiers in the city cheered for General Shafter and for the army as a whole. General Shafter and his officers then left for the American camp, and soldiers were assigned to patrol duty in the city.

The navy also had its share in the ceremonies of surrender. Admiral Sampson had received requests from every small vessel in the fleet for permission to enter the harbor, but the danger from submarine mines was not yet well defined, and nothing but launches were allowed to enter. Three of these felt their way into the harbor, passing the wreck of the *Reina Mercedes* and the *Merrimac*, with only her topmasts above the water, and so on up the bay, at the head of which the surrendered city lay. They arrived in time to take part in the final cheering. They found the army already in possession of everything.

The only war vessel in the harbor was the small gunboat *Alvarez*, which mounts a modern 4-inch gun forward and a machine gun aft. The Spaniards requested that the American flag be not raised on her until all her crew had left her. This request was granted. The Spaniards took the boat up to the dock and all disembarked. Lieutenant Marble then ran up a new American flag on the vessel, and a ship of war was added to our navy. The Lieutenant also took possession of all the other vessels in the harbor. One of them was a big steamer that had been used as a transport; the others were two tugs, four lighters, twelve schooners, and a number of small boats. The American flag was raised on all of them.

Lieutenant Marble boarded the gunboat which had been captured and returned on her to the fleet. He had with him two Spanish officers who knew all about the mines in the harbor. On the way down the bay he told them of the destruction of the Spanish fleet at Manila. They said that the Spanish official reports declared that Admiral Montijo had won a glorious victory at Manila, and that, if the soldiers in Santiago had known of the Spanish defeat in the Philippines, they would not have been so willing to fight the Americans.

Before the gunboat reached the sea, the men on the vessels of Sampson's fleet saw American infantrymen and cavalry at Morro Castle and on the side batteries. They knew then that the surrender was complete, and the sailors added their full quota of cheering to the shouts that had been sent up by the soldiers. Some of the vessels moved up close under the castle, and then they saw for the first time the awful havoc their guns had wrought.

The Morro was literally a pile of ruins—at least on the side next the sea. The rock on which it had been built had crumbled to dust wherever shot and shell had struck; there was a dozen holes in the lighthouse, and the building around the semaphore had been completely destroyed. All but two of six guns that had been mounted on a battery to the east of the castle were wrecked. This battery was protected by barrels of sand, and it was evident that the reason the Spaniards had shot too high in answering the American fire was that some of the sand barrels in front of the guns were so high that it was necessary to greatly elevate the guns in order to shoot over them. Several of the guns were dismounted the earth was badly torn up, and the sand bags were ripped open in many places.

Inside the harbor entrance some tremendous holes were seen that had evidently been made by the coughdrops administered by the *Vesuvius* on Dr. Dynamite's prescription. The first close inspection of the wrecks at the entrance of the harbor revealed the fact that the *Reina Mercedes* did not block the channel. Further examination showed two twelve-inch holes in her side, plainly establishing the fact that she was sunk by one of our ships, and not by the Spaniards themselves. The Spanish officers volunteered to help remove or explode the mines in the harbor. Four had been exploded against the *Merrimac*, but there were yet half a dozen that were dangerous. There were also several contact mines at the right of the *Merrimac*, going in. Those on the left of the *Merrimac* the Spanish officers said, had been removed to let Admiral Cervera's fleet out. Half a dozen launches from the warships went about with the Spanish officers, and eventually the mines were made harmless

An incident of the surrender was the raising of a Cuban flag on the western end of the fortifications known as water batteries. This was discovered on board the *New York*, and orders were sent to haul it down. It was an American victory on land and sea, and Old Glory was the only flag to float.

Meanwhile the soldiers left on duty in Santiago had restored comparative order. Immediately upon hoisting of the Stars and Stripes over the Governor's palace the refugees began to crowd back into the city, and the Spanish soldiers began to leave. They did not pretend to go in any sort of marching order, and as they reached the rifle-pits they stacked arms and went into camp. They spent the time in good-natured chaffing with the men they had been seeking to destroy, and ate greedily of the hard-tack that was given them. General Linares and General Toral were not in the city when our flag was hoisted. They remained in houses outside of the town, and they remained there until a transport was ready for them to go on board.

The formal surrender of Santiago and its possession by the army of the United States was announced to the Government at Washington by General Shafter, as follows:

"I have the honor to announce that the American flag has been this instant, 12 noon, hoisted over the house of the civil government in the city of Santiago. An immense concourse of people was present, a squadron of cavalry and a regiment of infantry presenting arms, and a band playing national airs. A light battery fired a salute of twenty-one guns. Perfect order is being maintained by the municipal government. The distress is very great, but there is little sickness in town and scarcely any yellow fever.

"Battalions of Spanish troops have been depositing arms since daylight in the armory over which I have a guard. About 7,000 rifles, 60,000 cartridges, and many fine modern guns were given up.

"This important victory with its substantial fruits of conquest was won at a loss of 1,593 men killed, wounded and missing. Lawton, who had the severe fighting around El Caney, lost 410 men; Kent lost 859 men in the still more severe assault on San Juan and the other conflicts of the centre; the cavalry lost 285 men, many of whom fell at El Caney. The feint of Aguadores cost 37 men. One man of the signal corps was killed and one wounded. Trying as it is to bear the casualties of the fight, there can be no doubt that in a military sense success was not dearly won."

In forwarding to the War Department at Washington a copy of the agreement between the American and Spanish commissioners for the surrender of Santiago, General Shafter stated that the men, surrendered by Toral, numbered between 22,000 and 23,000, about 6,000 more than the Americans themselves. The following is his report of the situation as he found it after the surrender:

"The city of Santiago is simply a network of fortifications at every street corner. I had no proper conception of its strength until I went into it, although I knew those old stone towns were naturally very strong. Everything is going admirably, so far as the transfer is concerned, and the Spanish troops are behaving well. They seem perfectly delighted with the idea of returning to Spain.

"I send you a copy of a telegram of General Linares to his Government, which one of the Consuls gave me. It shows the straits in which the Spaniards were and the feeling that animated them. He stated the case exactly. I did have him so surrounded that it was impossible for him to get away, and I could wait, and he could not.

"To-morrow morning I shall send out to receive something over 2,000 men about thirty miles in the interior, and in two or three days we shall send to Guantanamo to receive the 7,000 who have surrendered there. There are also about 800 men each at Baracoa and Sagua de Tanamo, on the north coast, to whom I will send an officer with a Spanish guide to take their arms and military supplies.

"We have secured a great deal more than I had any idea of getting in the way of munitions of war. In everything except food the Spaniards were well supplied. My only fear is that we shall have some sickness, and it is for that reason that I have wired so earnestly about getting the prisoners away so that we can go up into the mountains with our soldiers, fifteen or twenty miles, at the end of the railroad, at San Luis, which is said to be very healthy. It is at any rate about 1,500 feet above the sea, and has communication by rail with Santiago.

"Of those here who served throughout the Civil War, all declare they never had anything that could compare with it for hardship. With only one set of clothes, officers have been, until now, rained on nearly every day, carrying three days rations, like the men, on their persons, and suffering every privation in addition to all the horrors of disease in an unknown land, and very limited accomodations in case of sickness or injury. The spirit shown by the whole army has been simply grand."

The following schedule of ordnance surrendered at Santiago was officially reported to the department at Washington:

Rifles.—Spanish Mausers, 16,902; Argent, 872; Remington, 6,118.

Carbines.—Mausers, 833; Argent, 84; Remington. 330; Revolvers, 75.

Ammunition for small arms.—Mauser rifles, 1,500,000 cartridges; Argent rifles, 1,471,200 cartridges; Remington rifles, 1,660,000 cartridges.

The worthless small arm ammunition amounts to 973,000 cartridges.

Forty-four smooth-bore siege guns and 5 mortars were also captured, besides 30 bronze, 10 cast-iron and 8 steel guns, all rifled.

Projectiles captured.—Solid shot spherical 3,551; shells spherical, 678 ; shells cylindrical, 1,879 ; shrapnel, 437.

GENERAL LINARES' PITIFUL STORY.

The cablegram of General Linares to the Government at Madrid, referred to by General Shafter as having disclosed the true state of affairs at Santiago, before the surrender was written by the Spanish Commander while confined to his house by reason of wounds received in battle. It was sent to Madrid by way of Havana, and is therefore presumed to have had the endorsement of General Blanco. It certainly set forth the situation in a deplorable light, and those who afterward entered the city agreed with General Shafter that it presented actual facts. The dispatch in full is as follows :

To the Minister of War :—

" Although prostrated in bed by excessive weakness and sharp pains, I am preoccupied to such an extent by the terrible condition of these long-suffering troops that I consider it my duty to address your Excellency the Minister of War in order to expose the true condition of affairs.

" The enemy's position is very strong, and his outposts are very close to the limits of this city. The natural formation of the surrounding country gives our besiegers great advantages. Our lines extend fourteen kilometers.

" Our troops are attenuated and the proportion of sick is considerable, but they are not allowed to go to a hospital, owing to the necessity of keeping them in the trenches. Our horses have no grain or forage. Under a veritable deluge we remained for twenty hours at a stretch in the trenches and breastworks, soaked to the marrow, with no earthly shelter or protection possible for the unfortunate soldiers, who eat nothing but rice, and cannot even change or dry their clothes.

" The great losses among our officers—either dead, wounded, sick or disappeared—deprive our men of the neccessary direction and command at critical moments.

"Under such conditions it would be impossible to attempt to break through the enemy's ranks, as one-third of our men are too feeble to walk, and would have to be left behind, while the rest would be decimated and routed by the superior forces of the enemy. The result of such an attempt would be a wholesale slaughter and disaster. The attempt would utterly fail in the object desired by your Excellency, which is the salvation of these eleven thinned and impoverished battalions.

"In order to attempt a sortie under the protection of the Holguin division, it is in the first place necessary for those forces to break through the enemy's ranks and reinforce ours before we could move. On the other hand, the Holguin forces would have ahead of them eight days of forced marches, and would have to bring a great quantity of commissary supplies and rations, which it would be impossible for them to do. Altogether the gravity of the situation is appalling. The surrender of the town is inevitable; a prolonged resistance would simply mean a protraction of our death agony. The sacrifice would be sterile and fruitless.

"The enemy appreciates our position perfectly, and, with our lines circumvented and walled in as securely as they are, he is able to drain and wipe out our forces without exposing his own, as he did yesterday, cannonading us with vertical fire, while we could not see or make out his batteries. Moreover, his navy has our range down to so fine a point that his ships can bombard the town by sections with mathematical precision.

"Santiago de Cuba is not Gerona, which was defended inch by inch to the last drop of blood by women and children, by the old and by the feeble, all moved by the sacred spirit of independence, and animated and encouraged by the hope and promise of relief, which they did actually receive.

"Here solitude alone reigns. The total population, native as well as Spanish, has left the city. Not only have private individuals abandoned it, but public officials and Government employes as well. The clergy alone remain within our wall, and they, too, are preparing to flee to-morrow, with their prelate at their head.

"Our troops are not starting to-day, fresh and vigorous, full of energy and enthusiasm, on a campaign; they are men who have struggled three long years against climatic perils, fatigue, hardships, disease, and hunger, and who to-day when called to face these trying and critical conditions, are wasted away in body and soul, with no earthly means or possibility of relief.

"They are fighting without spirit or nerves. They have no sacred fire, no ideal to defend, for the very property they are called upon to defend and protect has been abandoned before their eyes by its veritable owners, many of whom are allied to the American forces, strengthening those ranks against ourselves.

"The honors of arms and of war have limits, and I appeal to the judgment of the Government and of the whole nation as to whether these troops have not given repeated illustrations of courage, valor, and devotion, and whether they are to be further sacrificed for a lost cause.

"If, for reasons of which I am ignorant, their sacrifice is demanded, or if some person is required who will assume the responsibility for the inglorious end predicted in my former despatches, I offer myself loyally on the altar of my country, to assume command and responsibility in either case, and I will, if necessary, be alone answerable for the surrender of this place, as my modest reputation is of small value compared with the national welfare.

LINARES."

THE SURRENDER MUST HAVE COME.

The entry into Santiago, and the discovery of the exact situation, as so pathetically described in General Linares' dispatch, was a source of great gratification to the army. Every one was convinced that, if General Toral had not voluntarily relinquished the defense of the city, he would have lost it by force of arms within forty-eight hours of fighting, and that too, without a great loss to the Americans. The position of the besiegers had been constantly improved. The investment of the city had daily been growing more and more complete. Not only had the lines been stretched further and further around, but they had been advanced and set in better places. The artillery had been put in most effective stations, so that, if firing had begun again, awful damage would have been inflicted. Many of the Spanish lines had been enfiladed, so that they could have been swept clear in a short time.

The enemy appears to have known all this, for the certainty of a vast destruction and the unavoidable necessity of an early capitulation undoubtedly led Toral to yield when he did.

The plight among the Americans who were sick was pitiable indeed, but there were enough well men to have taken Santiago with less ado than many may have thought possible. Sick and well alike, profited immediately from the surrender. A day's ration for some of the soldiers consisted of five or six pieces of hard-tack, two potatoes and an onion, but the pack trains began to come in regularly just before the surrender, and with them came not only food of better variety and quality, but many appliances for the sick and wounded. Quantities of rations were distributed among the refugees every day, at least until they began to pour back into the city, and everybody was glad indeed when the tension was relaxed and the matter of supplies could be systematized.

ON THE VERGE OF STARVATION.

A Cuban woman from El Caney staggered into the camp of the Ninth Cavalry on the morning of the surrender. She was pale and pinched, and the ragged silk dress that half covered her attenuated body spoke no more of past luxury and refinement than did her features, her despair, and her utter exhaustion. She did not ask for food. She wanted work. She washed clothes from the hospital tent for half a day in return for food, and sat down to the welcome army fare with hands bleeding from the unaccustomed labor. At dusk she turned wearily back toward El Caney, six miles away, richer, at least, by one meal. There had been many visits paid to the camps by Cuban soldiers, but none of them were as willing to work for what they got as this poor woman.

On the afternoon of the surrender of Santiago, the relief ship *State of Texas* came up the harbor loaded with food enough to give something to eat to every one within the city. She was moored at the principal wharf, opened her ports, and began to issue food to the people who thronged to her side. Questions to the applicants were unnecessary. Their emaciated faces and eager eyes told that they were desperately hungry. The plight of the children was particularly pitiful. The skin was drawn tight over their pinched faces, and the eyes of many of them had an unnatural lustre. They stretched forth their skinny hands timidly, and the beseeching look in their eyes went straight to the heart of every American. The Spanish soldiers did not openly beg for food, but when questioned they said earnestly that they were hungry, and when food was given to them they devoured it ravenously.

The supplying of food to the destitute was soon reduced to a system, and the policing of the city of Santiago was rapily placed upon a satisfactory basis. There was no offensive display of military force by the American soldiers, and the occupation of the city was practically accomplished without disturbance. There was no scarcity of liquor in the town, but it was not sold openly. There was no clashing between the forces that had been so bitterly opposed to each other, and thus within thirty days after the landing of Shafter's army on Cuban soil, the entire province, as well as the city of Santiago, was in the peaceful possession of our arms.

THE EXCHANGE OF LIEUTENANT HOBSON.

Among the incidents preceding the raising of the Stars and Stripes at Santiago was the exchange of Lieutenant Hobson and the seamen who had composed the crew of the *Merrimac* when she was sunk in the harbor. Hobson and his men were held as prisoners of war by the Spaniards until the 6th of July; the fleet of Cervera had been sunk, the battles of Guasimas, El Caney, and San Juan Hill had been fought, and these brave sailors were shut away from the active operations. Several efforts had been made to secure their exchange, but for some time these efforts were unavailing. Admiral Cervera had taken such a deep interest in Hobson's exploit that it was tacitly understood that he had become personally responsible for the hero of the *Merrimac*, and there was no doubt, after the first few days, that an exchange would eventually be made.

It was thought at first that the Spanish Government would excuse their delay in consenting to an exchange on the ground that Hobson had had full opportunity during his detention to observe the character of the defences, and to gather other military information that might be disastrous to the Spanish, if disclosed to the American naval and military commanders. Captain-General Blanco, in Havana, authorized a statement to this effect; but the point was made on the part of the United States that this reason would, of course, disappear upon the capture of Santiago, and when Cervera's fleet had been destroyed, and the surrender of the city was only a matter of time, it was easier for an exchange to be brought about.

On the morning of the 6th of July the Spanish authorities consented to make the exchange, and a truce was established for that purpose. The place selected for the exchange was under a tree between the Spanish and American lines, two-thirds of a mile beyond the entrenchments occupied by the Rough Riders, near General Wheeler's headquarters. The American prisoners left the Reina Mercedes Hospital, on the outskirts of Santiago, where they had been confined after their first week or so in the Morro, just before 3 o'clock in the afternoon, in charge of Major Irles, a Spanish staff officer, who spoke English perfectly. The prisoners were conducted to the meeting place on foot, but were not blindfolded. The Spanish prisoners to be exchanged were Lieutenants Volez and Aurelius, both of the Twenty-ninth Regiment Infantry, who had been captured at El Caney on the preceding Friday, and Lieutenant Adolfo Aries, of the First Provisional Regiment of Barcelona, one of the most aristocratic organizations of the Spanish army. There were also fourteen non-commissioned officers and privates. Lieutenant Aries and a number of the men had been wounded in the fight at El Caney, but none of them seriously. The Spanish prisoners were brought through the American lines mounted and blindfolded, in charge of Colonel John Jacob Astor and Lieutenant Miley, accompanied by Interpreter Maestro.

The meeting between Colonel Astor and Major Irles was extremely courteous and extremely formal. No attempt was made by either of them to discuss anything but the matter in hand. To Major Irles was given a choice of one of the three Spanish lieutenants in exchange for Hobson; and he was also informed that he could have all of the fourteen men in exchange for the American sailors. Lieutenant Aries was selected, and the other two Spanish officers were conducted back to Juragua.

The exchange took place at 4 o'clock. Just as the two parties were separating, Major Irles turned and said, courteously enough, but in a tone which gave his hearers the impression that he desired hostilities to be renewed at once:

"Our understanding is, gentlemen, that this truce comes to an end at 5 o'clock."

Colonel Astor looked at his watch, bowed to the Spanish officer, without making any reply, and then slowly started back to the American lines, with Hobson and his companions.

WILD WELCOME FROM AMERICAN TROOPS.

The meeting of the two parties and the exchange of prisoners had taken place in full view of both the American and Spanish soldiers who were entrenched near the meeting place, and the keenest interest was manifested in the episode. As Hobson and the men of the *Merrimac* approached the first line of entrenchments, which happened to be occupied by the Rough Riders, low murmurs ran from one end of the line of cowboys and athletes to the other, and by the time the party reached them every man was on his feet cheering wildly and rushing over every obstacle that chanced to be in the way, in the effort to reach Hobson and his party and grasp them by the hand.

The released prisoners were soon surrounded. They were compelled to stop and receive the greetings, congratulations and heartfelt handshakings of men they had never seen before. Sunburned cavalrymen who had spent their lives on the plains, and who did not know the difference between a ship's maintop, bilge or keel, threw their arms around the sailor boys and literally dragged them over the entrenchments, all the time sending out yells that, under other circumstances, might well have struck terror to hearts even as gallant as the heroes of the *Merrimac*.

In the entrenchments next to the Rough Riders were the Seventy-first New York Volunteers, and Hobson and his men now had to run the gauntlet of their greeting. Almost immediately afterward the Ninth and Tenth Cavalry, both colored regiments, joined in the general enthusiasm, and cheer after cheer arose as Hobson and his companions forced their way through the lines of white and colored soldiers.

Hobson, as far as possible, grasped each hand extended toward him, and neither he nor his men made any protest against the uncomfortable crowding and jostling which they had to undergo. If the young officer, whose home is in Alabama, had any race prejudice he certainly forgot all about it as he passed through the lines of soldiers.

These prisoners, so recently set free, saw only the uniforms of the United States army, and the Southerner who had distinguished himself so gallantly cared not for the color of the wearers of the uniform. He grasped the hands of the colored cavalrymen and expressed his thanks for their patriotic welcome with as much heartiness as he displayed toward men of his own color. He and all of his men were completely overcome by the reception accorded them, and tears rolled down their cheeks as the soldiers crowded around.

When the crew of the *Merrimac* approached Grimes' Battery, a great cry went up for the firing of a salute in their honor. Hobson protested against this, and called out to the artillerymen, who had caught the infection, not to fire their guns. Some of the more enthusiastic soldiers, however, appealed to Colonel Astor, and he, entering into the spirit of the occasion, told the men they need not obey Hobson's orders, as he was "only a lieutenant anyway." The officers of the battery, however, prevented the men from firing the guns for fear the Spaniards might mistake it for the re-opening of the attack, and if the latter had responded the American soldiers were in no position, in their state of disorder and enthusiasm, to repel an assault.

HOBSON MEETS GENERAL SHAFTER.

Hobson first paid his respects to General Wheeler, who was nearest at hand, after which he started for General Shafter's headquarters, still accompanied by his men. Word of the coming of the party ran along ahead of them, and regiment after regiment lined up to greet and hail the heroes. On the way to Shafter's position they met Captain Chadwick, of the *New York*, and Lieutenant Staunton, assistant chief of staff, who had been conferring with General Shafter, and who were then on their way to visit the firing lines. Warm greetings were exchanged by the naval officers, and Hobson pressed forward. After a short visit to General Shafter, Hobson rode to Siboney, off which place the *New York* was lying. Here he and his men were greeted with another tremendous ovation.

The single street of the little village was blocked with soldiers, Cuban camp followers and sailors from the transports. Cheer after cheer went up for Hobson and his sailors. They kept up a continuous smiling, bowing, all the while insisting that they had merely done what every American soldier or sailor would do if the opportunity offered.

Hobson's reception on board the *New York* was equally enthusiastic as it was throughout all the fleet. He had very little to say about himself, but one thing he did say was that from his place of confinement in the hospital, after being taken from Morro Castle, he saw the battle of the preceding Friday, and, as he looked on that gallant charge of the Rough Riders and the colored troops of the Tenth Cavalry up the San Juan Ridge, he had said to himself that none but American soldiers could have won such a victory.

Lieutenant Hobson impressed all who met him with his evidently sincere desire not to have the incident of the sinking of the *Merrimac* made more of than a simple performance of a sailor's duty. He talked in a straightforward manner about the incident, and did not seem to think that he and his men had been in any great danger while confined in Morro.

"In Morro," said Lieutenant Hobson, "we were confined in cells in the inner side of the fortress, and were there the first day the fleet bombarded the castle. I could only hear the whistling of the shells and the noise they made when they struck, but I judged from the conversation of the guards that the shells did considerable damage. After this bombardment Mr. Ramsden, the British Consul, protested, and we were removed to the hospital. There I was separated from the other men in our crew and could see them only by special permission. Montague and Kelly fell ill from malaria two weeks after we were captured, and I was permitted to visit them twice. Mr. Ramsden was very kind to us, and demanded that the sick men be removed to better quarters in the hospital. This was done. As for myself there is little to say. The Spanish were not disposed to do much for any of the prisoners at first, but, after our army had taken some of their men as prisoners, our treatment was better. Food was scarce in the city, and I was told that we fared better than the Spanish officers."

The announcement of the exchange of Lieutenant Hobson and his men was officially made to Washington by General Shafter as follows:

PLAYA DEL ESTE, July 6, 1898.
HEADQUARTERS FIFTH ARMY CORPS.

Secretary of War, Washington:—

Lieutenant Hobson and all of his men have just been received safely in exchange for one Spanish officer and other prisoners taken by United States   All in good health, except two seamen convalescing from remittent fever.   SHAFTER,
Major-General, Commanding.

THE FIRST TROOPS IN CUBA.

The engagements which resulted in the capture of Santiago were the last battles that took place on Cuban soil. It was only two months, however, before this that the first landing of troops had been made. A portion of the First Regiment, U. S. Infantry, did the fighting in the original instance, and the vessel on which they proceeded from Key West to Cuba, was the *Gussie*.

The commander of the expedition was Colonel J. H. Dorst, U. S. V., and the troops accompanying him were as follows:

Company E, First Infantry, 60 men and Captain J. J. O'Connell and Second Lieutenant W. M. Crofton; Company G, First Infantry, 60 men and Captain M. P. Phister, First Lieutenant F. E. Lacey and Second Lieutenant D. E. Nolan. The object of the expedition was to effect a junction with the Cuban troops that were supposed to be in the western part of the island, and to provide for the landing of stores and ammunition for the insurgents.

One bright May morning, the *Gussie* left Key West and essayed to make a landing on the north coast of Cuba, a little to the east of Mariel. The Cubans on board, who were to be put on shore at the first opportunity, to act as scouts and guides for the expedition, made an inspection of the lay of the land from on shipboard, and decided that they would prefer to land elsewhere. The whole country-side seemed to know of the coming of the expedition. Whenever the *Gussie* got anywhere near the shore, a Spanish soldier would take a shot at her, but without effect, and as the vessel proceeded on down the coast, squads of Spanish cavalry could be seen keeping her in sight, evidently determined to prevent the carrying out of her plans. Off Cabanas a drizzling rain began to fall which soon turned into a regular drenching tropical downpour. After that, nothing more was seen of the Spanish cavalry, and the commander of the *Gussie* decided to land his scouts at Arbolitos Point.

FIERCE FIRING IN THE JUNGLE.

Three Cuban scouts went off first in a light skiff, to show the way over the reef, but their boat was capsized, and they had to swim and wade to shore. Two boats carrying about 40 men of Company E, commanded by Captain O Connell and Lieutenant Crofton, next started. O'Connell's boat was upset on the reef and Lieutenant Crofton's command therefore, was the first to land upon Cuban soil. Captain O'Connell presently reached the beach about 300 yards to the right.

Both parties went ahead in skirmish lines and dissappeared from the sight of those on board the *Gussie* in a network of shrubbery. Two minutes later the silence was broken by heavy volleys of musketry followed by the sharp cracking of skirmish firing. It was hard to tell exactly what had happened, but evidently the skirmishers had stumbled upon Spaniards in the jungle.

The advancing Americans had clambered over a line of Spanish rifle-pits, unoccupied, but when Captain O'Connell and his party finally came out upon a grass-grown road, they encountered about 50 Spanish guerillas, some mounted and some on foot, all evidently pushing on with the greatest haste to reach the rifle-pits.

The guerillas were the first to fire. One bullet found lodgement in the arm of a newspaperman, but all the rest went wild of their mark. Our men, facing about and firing at ease, brought down four of the Spaniards. The exhibition of marksmanship thoroughly demoralized the guerillas, who made off into the jungle, firing wildly as they retreated. Private Metzler, of Company E, brought down the commanding officer of the band, who proved to be a Lieutenant of that crack corps, the Civil Guard.

Lieutenant Crofton and his command now came up from the left and both commands gave chase to the fugitives. The gunboats tore the jungle and the chapparal at the right of the skirmishers with shot and shell, and the infantry fired half a dozen volleys in the same general direction. Now and again a shot came back in reply, but the Spaniards were more fleet of foot than accurate of aim, and nothing more was seen of them.

The first action of the war fought on Cuban soil between Spanish and American troops resulted decidedly in favor of the United States. The enemy had lost at least four dead, whose bodies were seen, and doubtless more were killed or wounded by the heavy firing from the vessels. Lieutenant Crofton brought back with him to the *Gussie*, as prisoner of war, a charcoal burner who had given the first landing party misinformation, and who was thought to have been a decoy in the pay of the Spaniards.

Another incident of this expedition took place after the Cubans had been landed who were to make the connection with the camp of their compatriots. The *Gussie*, still proceeding along the coast, caught sight of a white flag, extended to the breeze from a tall palm tree. It would be waved for a minute or two and then vanish, but only to reappear, some moments later, a few hundred yards to the westward.

FIRED UPON FROM AMBUSH.

The commander of the *Gussie*, and many others on board, looked upon this as a signal from Cuban friends who were kindly guiding the expedition toward a safe place for further landing, but suddenly, when the *Gussie* had been lured to within 300 yards of the beach, the Spaniards opened fire from two field batteries concealed in the jungle of shrubbery and vines. In this instance, as usual, the Spaniards displayed very poor marksmanship, and no damage was done.

Their presence and their readiness, however, convinced those in charge of the expedition that the stores and ammunitions on board the *Gussie* could not be landed with any assurance of their escaping the Spaniards. The land had been approached at three points where meetings with the insurgents had been pre-arranged, and in each case the Cubans had not been able to keep their engagement. In view of the Spanish force along the coast it would have been poor policy for them to have appeared, so the *Gussie* flew to the breeze the homeward bound pennant and sailed back to Key West.

CHAPTER XXII

The Campaign in Porto Rico

General Miles' Plans for the Invasion of the Island.—Preliminary Operations by Sampson's Fleet.—Bombardment of San Juan de Porto Rico.—Miles in Charge of the Army Expedition.—Troops Meet with but Little Resistance.—Spanish Officers and the People Cheer the American Flag.—Capture of Towns, and Movements of the Army.—The First Steps Toward Peace, in Washington.—The French Ambassador Consults our President and Secretary of State on Behalf of Spain.—As the Guns of Pennsylvania Troops were being Placed in Position for a Battle, Word Came from Washington, Announcing that Fighting Must Cease.—The Last Scenes and Shots of the War.

WHEN Santiago surrendered, the attention of the army and navy was turned toward Porto Rico. The power of the United States had already been manifested there, through the naval arm of its service, by the bombardment of San Juan, the capital of the island, about two months earlier.

When the fleet of Cervera was known to be at sea somewhere between Spain and the West Indies, it had been thought advisable to make sure that San Juan should not be a fit stopping place for the coming Spanish men-of-war; and, moreover, it had been deemed wise to obtain a moral effect that could not be overlooked by letting the world in general, and Spain in particular, see something more of what Uncle Sam's gunners could do.

At midnight of May 3d the fighting squadron of Admiral Sampson left Key West eastward bound. The Admiral really hoped to meet the Spanish fleet at Porto Rico, and, by destroying it, to strike such a blow to Spain as would force her to sue for peace. In any event the other objects enumerated were to be accomplished, so there was nothing of the nature of an experimental excursion about the expedition.

Sampson had with him the *New York* as his flagship, and the battleships *Iowa* and *Indiana*, the monitors *Amphitrite* and *Terror*, the cruisers *Montgomery* and *Detroit*, and the torpedo boat *Porter*.

The cruise was slow from the start. On the 11th the fleet crossed Mona Passage. At 5 o'clock that afternoon the Admiral moved his flag to the *Iowa*, issued orders for the disposition of the vessels of the fleet, and waited for the morning.

In the dim light of early dawn, the Morro (for every Spanish port seems to have a castle of this name) loomed up like a gray mountain of stone as the *Iowa* steamed slowly across the channel under its guns. The sentinel on the watchtower could be heard giving the alarm to the city and garrison. General quarters had been sounded on board the vessels at half-past four, and, though it was not yet sunrise, the order was given to hoist colors as the vessels were in motion, and, just as the *Detroit* passed the point of Morro, "Old Glory" was flaunted in the face of the enemy.

THE FIGHT BEGINS.

Almost on the minute of 5 o'clock the *Iowa* fired the first shot of the engagement. Quick as a flash the Dons answered, and the fight was on. With the *Iowa* in the lead, the big battleships steamed slowly by and delivered their broadsides. It was a sort of a reveille that the Spaniards were not used to being awakened by; but they were not slow in getting into action, and their responses to the guns of the Americans were a long way from feeble.

The line of the big battleships was just fifty-five minutes in passing, and, during that time, the *Detroit* stood still and allowed herself to be used as a target for the guns from the entire range of forts. It was this that caused Captain Bob Evans to remark to Admiral Sampson on the bridge of the *Iowa:* "The *Detroit* is the gamecock of the squadron." As the *Iowa* passed, however, the *Detroit* got under way and slowly moved out, and presently her guns were doing their full share in the bombardment.

From the topmast of the *Iowa* streamed in brilliant colored flags, "Remember the Maine." Behind her came the huge *Indiana*, of such enormous bulk that she rode almost steady even upon that heaving sea. Then followed the *New York*, almost as formidable as a battleship, the low-lying monitors *Amphitrite* and *Terror*, with the *Montgomery* and *Porter* marking the limits of the course over which this line of seafighters was passing.

First the starboard broadsides were brought to bear. One of the great 13-inch guns of the *Iowa* belched forth flame, and a shell sailed high toward Morro. It fell short, but the response was a roar from all the batteries and forts along the shore. It was a tremendous burst of sound and smoke and flame—a shower of shells that wasted themselves in the sea. So wild was the volley that even if the *Iowa* had been within range, none of the shots would have hit her.

Presently, however, all the vessels drew in nearer to the shore. Each ship was now firing, and each shore gun was answering. The Spanish aim was wild, but the American gunners fired with the calmness and precision of experienced target practice. The fleet and the shore were soon enveloped in smoke. Only outlines could be made out; but it was apparent that, while the Spanish shells issued from the smoke of the shore to fall into the sea, the American shells rushed from the fleet's envelope of smoke to bury themselves in the smoke on shore, and, now and then, as the wind drifted the thick gray curtain aside, it could be seen that the American ships were uninjured, and that on shore the line of fortifications, that had at first been unbroken, was torn and ruined in many places.

NO GREAT DAMAGE DONE.

When the *Iowa* came up to the "stakeboat," she turned and led the column back again across the line of fire, and the above scene was thus repeated again and again. The Spanish shells did not all go wild, though none of them did any great damage. One shell struck a boat on the *Iowa*, passed through it and entered the superstructure, scattering splinters in every direction. Three men were injured, Admiral Sampson and Captain Evans were on the lower bridge, and narrowly escaped the flying fragments.

In all, the *Iowa* was hit nine times. She was struck once by a 14-centimeter shell at a distance of about 5,000 yards. The shell came over the stern of the ship, broke off an 8-inch iron stanchion, demolished a wooden boat in which it exploded and set fire to the canvas covering and the splinters that had been made. The shell itself burst into many pieces. One fragment went downward and struck near the port 8-inch waist gun where 12 men were stationed. One man was killed and several others injured.

After two hours of this sort of work the day had become furiously hot, so hot that men were fainting below the decks and at the guns. The gunners were streaming with perspiration. A gunner's mate on the *Amphitrite* was overcome, and died in a few hours. But the battle went on. The fire from the ships was unabated. Many of the Spanish guns were silenced, but when the shore batteries could be seen it was evident that the Spanish gunners were becoming demoralized. They seemed to be drunk with fury. They loaded and fired like madmen, without aiming, without any appearance of discipline or direction, and seemed to be in such a crazed condition that they performed such absurd acts as waving their swords, shaking their fists and discharging pistols at the warships that were peppering them from far out in the harbor.

The man on the watchtower of the Morro, who had given the alarm to the city, stood at his post through the whole fight, and it was said on board the vessels that his bravery was so much admired that no one made any special effort to dislodge him from the eyrie to which his duty had assigned him. He marched up and down on the parapet through all the three hours rain of shot and shell, and was still there when the fleet, satisfied that the defences of the harbor had been badly crippled, and knowing that the city had been set on fire by the bombardment, ceased firing and drew away.

Next day, at St. Thomas, it was ascertained that San Juan had been practically destroyed. Nothing had been seen of Cervera's fleet and Admiral Sampson had thought best, after inflicting the punishment of this eventful day, to leave the enemy to their own devices for the present. No further operations were carried on against any portion of Porto Rico until two months later when General Miles and General Brooke invaded the island at another point.

THE EXPEDITION TO CONQUER THE ISLAND.

The operations against Porto Rico, following the destruction of Cervera's fleet and the surrender of Santiago, were largely prompted by the desire of the United States not to enter empty-handed into a peace parley. It was plainly evident to the authorities at Washington that the end of the war was near at hand, and the possession of Porto Rico was an important desideratum. To bring about this possession three expeditions were sent. The first, under General Miles, sailed from Guantanamo Bay, Cuba, July 21st; the second, which was part of General Brooke's command, sailed from Charleston also on July 21st, with General Ernst as brigade commander, and the third, under General Brooke himself, embarked at Newport News, on July 26th.

All these expeditions, aggregating about 11,000 men, were convoyed by warships and were successfully landed. The first, under General Miles, reached Guanica at daylight on July 25th. A Spanish force attempted to resist the landing, but a few well-directed shells from the *Massachusetts, Gloucester* and *Columbia* soon put the enemy to flight. The *Gloucester* (formerly J. Pierpont Morgan's yacht *Corsair*), commanded by Lieutenant Commander Wainwright, was then headed into the port with orders to send a party on shore.

The harbor of Guanica is a veritable haven of rest, with high mountains for a background, a bay of considerable extent, a plateau of cultivated meadow land stretching from the beach to the mountains, a score or so of prettily painted houses on the line of the shore, a sugar mill on the right, a blockhouse distant a couple of miles on the left, and, directly in front of the place, a smaller blockhouse, before which floated the Spanish flag.

The *Gloucester* made direct for this flagstaff. When she came to a stop, thirty men, under Lieutenant Huse, were sent ashore in the launch. The Spaniards began to fire upon them. The Americans replied with their rifles and machine guns, and several shots were also fired from the vessels in the harbor. This served to scatter the Spaniards from the vicinity of the flagstaff, around which the American sailors soon rallied, pulled down the red and yellow flag of Spain, and hoisted the Stars and Stripes.

This action on the part of the Americans seemed to greatly enrage the Spaniards. They set their gunners at work right merrily in all the little batteries along the shore, and their soldiers fired from around the corners of the houses in the town, but the American vessels continued to fire into their midst, and the landing party quickly threw up an entrenchment across the street, mounted a Colt rapid-fire gun on its centre, tangled some barbed wire in front of this improvised entrenchment, signalled for reinforcements, and then opened fire with the Colt. The result was that five of the enemy were killed, while not one American was even wounded, and no further resistance was made on the part of the Spaniards.

General Miles then went on shore and personally superintended the landing. Boatload after boatload of men, and long strings of boats, towed by the steam launches of the *Massachusetts*, made for the shore. The troops formed into companies and promptly occupied points of vantage in the neighborhood. A strong detachment of troops was sent to Yauco, a small place about five miles inland, which forms the western terminus of the railroad leading to Ponce, 15 miles distant, due east. The troops accompanying General Miles from Guantanamo were batteries C and F of the Third Artillery, and B and F of the Fourth Artillery, Loniras' Battery of the Fifth Artillery, the Sixth Illinois Volunteers, the Sixth Massachusetts, 275 recruits of the Fifth Corps, 60 men of the Signal Corps and Seventh Hospital Corps—3,415 men all told.

It had been expected by the War Department at Washington that the first landing in Porto Rico would have been made at Fajardo, but General Miles cabled by way of St. Thomas that the circumstances were such that he had deemed it advisable to take the harbor of Guanica first. There was considerable friction in connection with this change in the programme, which some of the Washington authorities claimed had been made unwisely by General Miles, but the General of the army, being upon the spot, evidently considered himself the best judge of the situation.

THE SURRENDER OF PONCE.

General Miles arrived at Port Ponce, having marched with his division from Guanica on the morning of July 28th. General Ernst's brigade and General Wilson's division of the First Army Corps, which had left Charleston on the 21st, arrived the same morning. They found the port already under American control. It had been surrendered to Commander C. H. Davis, of the gunboat *Dixie*, on the 27th. There was no resistance, and the Americans were welcomed with enthusiasm. General Ernst's brigade immediately started for the town of Ponce, three miles inland, which also promptly capitulated, and where a still warmer welcome was given to the invaders.

THE MARKET PLACE, PONCE, PORTO RICO.

THE CUSTOM HOUSE, PONCE, PORTO RICO, AFTER THE RAISING OF THE AMERICAN FLAG BY GENERAL MILES.

HULA DANCING GIRLS, HAWAII.

NATIVE BELLES, PORTO RICO.

Ferdinand Toro, the British Consul, acting in behalf of the Spaniards, placed the city in the possession of General Miles, with whom was General James H. Wilson, commanding the First Division of the First Army Corps. The scene was more like one on a gala day than one involving the surrender of a city. A majority of the residents remained in the city to welcome the Americans. The ceremony was unique. General Miles and General Wilson, by a pre-arranged plan, had been driven from the American headquarters at Port Ponce to Casa del Rey, in the city proper, where Consul Toro and the Mayor awaited them. The bombero, or city fire brigade, was drawn up opposite the casa, and as General Miles and General Wilson left their carriages the fire brigade band played a Sousa march. Guards in front of the building forced a way for the American generals, and through the cheering crowd they marched into the building.

Consul Toro said to General Miles that the citizens of Ponce were anxious to know if the same municipal officers and system as had been in vogue would be continued temporarily. He was assured that municipal affairs would not be disturbed for the time being, but it was explained that all would be responsible to General Wilson, as Military Governor, who would keep the city under a form of martial law which would be oppressive to none.

General Miles and General Wilson then stepped out on the balcony to view the square. The crowd cheered wildly, and the two American generals hastily withdrew. They received an ovation as they made their way back to headquarters, and all that afternoon the Porto Ricans continued to arrive in carriages, on bicycles and on foot to cheer the generals and the troops. General Miles' principle of purchasing or renting everything used by the army had a most excellent and immediate effect, and this was enhanced by the prompt employment of several hundred natives as stevedores.

A PROCLAMATION.

General Miles added still further to the good understanding between the Americans and the Porto Ricans by issuing the following proclamation:

"In the prosecution of the war against the Kingdom of Spain by the people of the United States, in the cause of liberty, justice and humanity, its military forces have come to occupy the island of Porto Rico. They come bearing the banners of freedom, inspired by a noble purpose, to seek the enemies of our Government and of yours, and to destroy or capture all in armed resistance.

"They bring you the fostering arms of a free people, whose greatest power is justice and humanity to all living within their fold. Hence they release you from your former political relations, and, it is hoped, insure your cheerful acceptance of the Government of the United States.

"The chief object of the American military forces will be to overthrow the armed authority of Spain and give the people of your beautiful island the largest measure of liberty consistent with this military occupation. They have not come to make war on the people of the country, who for centuries have been oppressed, but, on the contrary, they bring protection not only to yourselves, but to your property, promote your prosperity, and bestow the immunities and blessings of our enlightenment and liberal institutions and government.

"It is not their purpose to interfere with existing laws and customs, which are wholesome and beneficial to the people, so long as they conform to the rules of the military administration, order and justice. This is not a war of devastation and desolation, but one to give all within the control of the military and naval forces the advantages and blessings of enlightened civilization."

One of the first acts of General Wilson, as Military Governor of Porto Rico, was to release the political prisoners. One of these was charged with having cut the telegraph wire between Ponce and San Juan the night before the Americans arrived and would have been killed on the following day. The first thing these political ex-prisoners thought of, when once they breathed free air again, was to see their friends and relatives; the next was vengeance. They promptly corralled the Spaniards who had put them into prison, and dragged them before General Wilson, expecting no doubt that they would immediately be put to death, but General Wilson released the Spaniards and told the Porto Ricans that the redress they expected was not his to give.

There came also to General Wilson, a large delegation of Porto Rican priests who wanted to know what provision the United States

Government intended to make for the churches. The Military Governor informed them that, under the Constitution of the United States, no appropriations could be made to religious organizations, and that the churches would have to support themselves. The editors of several newspapers also came to General Wilson to ask, if they must suspend publication, but the General told them to "go ahead and print the news."

While these matters were running so smoothly at Ponce, however, General Garreton's brigade, which had remained in the vicinity of Guanica, had a spirited engagement on skirmish lines, July 26th. The Americans were making an advance upon Yauco when they were met by the enemy and a lively fifteen minutes' fight ensued. Four men of the Sixth Massachusetts were wounded, but none seriously, while three of the Spaniards were killed and thirteen were wounded. Yauco was reached on the 28th, and was then added to the towns that were fast coming into American possession.

ENTHUSIASM AT YAUCO.

At Yauco the enthusiasm of the Porto Ricans was even more marked than at Ponce. When the Spaniards had been driven away the citizens greeted the soldiers with as much enthusiasm as if they had been men of their own blood returning from victory over a common enemy. The Mayor of the town promptly issued the following proclamation:

"Citizens!—On to-day the citizens of Porto Rico assist in one of her most beautiful fetes—the sun of America shines upon our mountains and valleys this day of July, 1898. It is a day of glorious remembrance for each son of this beloved isle, because for the first time there waves over us a flag of the stars, planted in the name of the Government of the United States of America, by the Major-General of the American army, Senor Miles.

" Porto Ricans, we are by the miraculous intervention of the God of the just, given back to the bosom of our mother, America, in whose waters Nature placed us as people of America. To her we are given back in the name of her Government by General Miles, and we must send her our most expressive salutation of generous affection through our conduct towards the valiant troops represented by distinguished officers and commanded by the illustrious General Miles. Citizens, long live the Government of the United States of America. Hail to their valiant troops! Hail, Porto Rico, always American. "ALCALDE FRANCISCO MEGIA."

"Yauco, Porto Rico, United States of America."

This proclamation was acted upon by the people without hesitation. All day the bands played in the public square, the balconies were filled with people, and dancing with the soldiers was the popular amusement of the Porto Rican belles. At night the town was illuminated, and half a dozen receptions were given. The only disturbing elements were reports that came in from time to time that the Spaniards had been re-inforced and were coming back, but the American soldiers speedily dispelled these fears and the revelry went on till long after midnight.

Guanica had been the first town captured, Ponce was next surrendered, and Yauco was third. The fourth town to be taken possession of was Juan Diaz. This was captured by the Sixteenth Pennsylvania Volunteers, under command of Colonel Willis J. Hulings, subsequently promoted to a Brigadier-Generalship in recognition of his services here and at Coamo. This was the first Pennsylvania regiment to get a baptism of fire. The Tenth had not yet gotten into any engagements in Manila, and the Fourth, which was part of the Second Brigade of General Wilson's division, did not get an opportunity at this early date.

On August 1st, Arroyo was added to the captured towns. It came into the possession of the United States without a struggle. When the sun rose over the picturesque village that morning, it was, nominally at least, in possession of the Spanish, but the gunboat *Gloucester* arrived at 9 A.M., sent a landing party on shore, and before noon the Stars and Stripes were flying over the Custom House. The only two declared Spaniards in the place—the Captain of the port and a priest—were brought out to the *Gloucester* as prisoners, but were released on parole. A city judge and His Honor the Mayor were subsequently discovered and similarly treated.

A careful investigation of the neighborhood disclosed the fact that, if there had been any Spanish soldiers there, they had made good their escape before the appearance of the gunboat, but the

Gloucester, not wishing to seem to have made such an easy capture, dropped a couple of shells into the woods above the town, where half a dozen horsemen were seen toward evening, and if these were a squad of Spanish cavalry, they speedily joined the main body of their command somewhere far away, for no resistance of any sort was offered.

Six or eight miles to the westward of Arroyo was the more important town of Guayama. This fell into the hands of General Brooke the day after he landed with General Haines' brigade, where the *Gloucester* had made sure of a clear footing, at Arroyo. In this brigade were the Fourth Ohio, the Third Illinois, and the Fourth Pennsylvania. There was a garrison of 250 at Guayama, and General Brooke determined to send an adequate force there rather than take any chances that the strength of the garrison had not been underestimated. A message was sent demanding the surrender of the place, and word came back that the Mayor of Guayama was considering the advisability of complying with the demand. It was not consideration that General Brooke was looking for, however, but surrender. Therefore, leaving the Fourth Pennsylvania at Arroyo, General Haines was ordered to take the Fourth Ohio and Third Illinois to Guayama. These regiments appeared in front of the town on August 5th, had some slight skirmishing with the enemy, and obtained possession without strong resistance. Three privates of the Fourth Ohio were wounded in the skirmishing, none of them seriously.

FIGHTING FOR THE PENNSYLVANIANS.

The town of Coamo was captured on August 9th, after half an hour of fighting, by Generals Wilson and Ernst. General Wilson devised the method of attack, supervised the performance in person, and was one of the first to enter the town after its surrender. The troops under him, comprising General Ernst's brigade, were the Second and Third Wisconsin and the Sixteenth Pennsylvania. They left camp at 6 o'clock in the morning, taking with them two batteries of artillery with which they began a cannonading of the town with a view to disclosing the strength of the opposing force. The Sixteenth Pennsylvania, however, had the good fortune to do all the real fighting. They were guided in their advance upon Coamo by Colonel

Biddle and Captain Gardiner of General Wilson's staff, and reached the town ahead of the Wisconsin Volunteers.

Suddenly, emerging from behind a hill back of the town, they saw a line of Spanish rifles aimed at them. Then came the crash of a volley, the ping and whistle of bullets and a scramble for cover. The Americans had no shelter, while the Spaniards had a perfect breastwork in a bank of earth, which had been thrown up by the roadbuilders to protect the gutter of the road from being washed away, but the American fire was very effective. There was among the Spaniards about a dozen mounted men and officers, and in a few minutes all of them had been shot down. Six of the horses were found dead and all wounded. The Second Battalion of the Sixteenth Pennsylvania now emerged upon the road beyond the Spaniards, and, as soon as the entrapped Dons saw themselves surrounded, the whole line fluttered with white signals of surrender. Major Windsor accepted the surrender, and had them drop their arms and accoutrements in piles in the middle of the road. The prisoners included one major, one captain, three lieutenants, and 162 enlisted men, nearly all of whom belonged to the Twenty-fifth Battalion of the Spanish Infantry.

The Spanish wounded were cared for at the same time with those of the Americans who were hit. Dead and wounded were both taken to one of the official road houses near at hand. There were five dead Spaniards on the road, and one more died soon after the surrender. The Americans had a number of men slightly wounded, most of them, however, being merely clipped by the shower of Mauser bullets. Five had to go to the hospital, all privates of the Sixteenth Pennsylvania, except Corporal Barnes, of Company E, whose abdomen was cut by a Mauser bullet as if by a knife.

The Spanish dead were treated with the highest respect. Surgeon Major John McG. Woodbury, of General Wilson's staff, took charge of their burial, and gave full permission to the Spanish chaplain and the local priests to conduct the services in any manner they chose. The bodies of the officers were sent to Ponce for burial, the others were interred in the cemetery at Coamo with all the ceremonies of the Catholic Church.

The noise of the firing between the Spaniards and the Sixteenth Pennsylvania was plainly heard in the town, and, when General Wilson and the rest of the troops appeared on the outskirts, the alcalde was there to offer the place in surrender. Generals Wilson and Ernst slept that night at the residence of the alcalde, and the troops passed on through the town and made camp in the direction of Aybonito.

NOT A VERY CORDIAL RECEPTION.

The reception of the Americans in Coamo was not as cordial as it had been in Ponce or at Yauco. Many of the people were in the streets and some shouted welcomes, but there was a much greater reserve than in places previously occupied. This was due, in a great measure, to the misbehavior of some of the American soldiers who first entered the town. Some of them went into the stores and eating houses, seized what they wanted, and went off without paying for it. The result was that the stores soon closed, and it was not possible for any one to buy a thing to eat The action of the soldiers in this regard was strongly condemned by General Wilson, but the offenders could not be identified.

Meanwhile General Schwan, with a force of 1,300 men, including regulars of the Eleventh Infantry, two batteries of regular artillery and one troop of regular cavalry, had started from Guanica, where General Miles had made his landing and was undertaking a somewhat independent expedition in the direction of Mayaguez. This expedition possessed one or two peculiarities. A Brigadier-General commanded what was barely more than a single regiment. It included all three arms of the service, and it was accompanied by a wagon train. Moreover, it kept moving, and was constantly confronted with a force which was its numerical equal, if not its superior.

It occupied Savana Grande and San German practically without opposition, but about six miles beyond San German, midway between that place and Mayaguez, the enemy was met in considerable force. A hamlet at this point, bearing the name of Hormigueros, boasted an army barracks, the headquarters of a Spanish battalion, which is practically the equivalent of an American regiment in its numerical strength. Here an engagement took place. There was a bit of sharp infantry firing, with a slight casualty list for both sides. It was not much of a fight, but it put the American flag in the place of the red and yellow over a Spanish military edifice. The Spaniards might have stopped the Americans twenty times within the next few miles. They might have decimated the invading ranks by guerilla firing, but they seemed to have been terror-stricken by the appearance of an army which fired as it moved forward and moved forward always.

For General Schwan did not stop for a grand celebration at Hormigueros. He left a small detatchment as garrison and went on his way. This detatchment might easily have been swallowed up by a return of the Spaniards from their flight across the hills, but they seemed to have been too much interested in getting somewhere else.

Mayaguez was occupied practically without resistance, and the army pushed on toward Aguadilla and Lares. Anasco was occupied and Aguarda virtually so. The Spanish troops fell back on Lares, with the Americans in hot pursuit. They were overtaken on the banks of a river near Las Marias where an engagement took place in which the Spanish are known to have lost five killed and fourteen wounded, though later reports were to the effect that the losses from the American firing and from death by drowning in crossing the river were many times that number. Another twenty-four hours would undoubtedly have found General Schwan in possession of Lares and Aguadilla, and in control of all the western part of the island, but the truce had been declared before these points were reached. The American losses throughout this whole campaign amounted to two men killed and one officer and seventeen men wounded.

TRUCE IS DECLARED.

The truce had been brought about, it will be remembered, as the result of the advances made by the French Ambassador in Washington, on the part of the Government of Spain, on July 26th, asking President McKinley upon what terms he would consent to peace. This was two days before Ponce surrendered to General Miles, but the result of the negotiations was still problematical. Two days later, on July 30th, President McKinley's statement as to the conditions on which he would agree to end the war was given to the French Ambassador.

SUNRISE EXECUTIONS
Outside the prison walls, Havana. Weyler's way of getting rid of prisoners.

A MARKET GIRL, PORTO RICO.

A VOLANTE, THE TYPICAL CUBAN CONVEYANCE.

SAN JUAN, PORTO RICO.

This city, the capital of Porto Rico, was founded by Ponce de Leon in 1511. It is built on a long narrow island connected with the mainland by a bridge. The population in 1899 was estimated at 31,000, and the city is very much overcrowded, the poor being packed like rats in the tenements. San Juan is a

The proposition submitted by the Ambassador, acting for the Spanish Government was general in its terms. It was confined to the one essential point of an earnest plea that negotiations be opened for the purpose of terminating the war and arriving at terms of peace. The communication of the Spanish Government did not suggest any specific terms of peace, nor was there any reference made to Cuba, the Philippines, Porto Rico, or other Spanish possessions.

The evident purpose of the Madrid authorities was to first learn whether the United States would treat on the subject of peace, and after that to take up such terms as the two parties might suggest. Neither was there any suggestion from the Spanish Government that an armistice be established, pending the peace negotiations. It was generally expected, however, that if formal peace negotiations were entered upon a cessation of hostilities would occur.

Owing to the importance of the communication, the French Ambassador adopted the usual diplomatic procedure of reading the communication of the Spanish Government from the original, a translation being submitted at the same time. In the conversation which followed the reading of the proposition, neither the President nor the Ambassador entered upon the question of the terms of peace. The instructions of the Ambassador confined him to the one essential point of opening peace negotiations, and it was evident that the President desired to consider the proposition before giving any definite reply. It was finally determined that the President should consult his Cabinet concerning the proposition and that M. Cambon would be invited to the White House for further conference and for a final answer from the Government of the United States.

On July 30th the answer of the American Government to Spain was handed to the French Ambassador. It included the following propositions: The absolute surrender of Porto Rico to the United States; relinquishment of Spanish sovereignty in Cuba; the cession of several small islands adjacent to Cuba and Porto Rico to the United States; the cession of one of the Ladrone Islands to the United States as a coaling station, and the leaving of the disposition of the Philippine subject to future negotiations.

The Government of the United States did not put forward any claim for pecuniary indemnity, but required the relinquishment of all claim of sovereignty over or title to the island of Cuba, as well as the immediate evacuation by Spain of the Island. The United States announced its intention to occupy and hold the city, bay and harbor of Manila, pending the conclusion of a treaty of peace, which would determine the control, disposition and government of the Philippines.

It was also provided, that, if these terms were accepted in their entirety by Spain, commissioners would be named by the United States to meet commissioners on the part of Spain for the purpose of concluding a Treaty of Peace on the basis indicated.

THE PROTOCOL SIGNED.

On August 9, 1898, the Spanish Cabinet approved the terms for preliminary negotiations, and this acceptance of the conditions was communicated to President McKinley. On August 12th, protocols agreeing as to the preliminaries for a Treaty of Peace were signed by Secretary of State Day and the French Ambassador, United States naval and military commanders were ordered to cease hostilities, and the negotiation of a permanent peace was begun. The full text of the protocols was as follows:

"1. That Spain will relinquish all claim of sovereignty over and title to Cuba.

"2 That Porto Rico and other Spanish islands in the West Indies and an island in the Ladrones, to be selected by the United States, shall be ceded to the latter.

"3. That the United States will occupy and hold the city, bay and harbor of Manila, pending the conclusion of a Treaty of Peace which shall determine the control, disposition and government of the Philippines.

"4. That Cuba, Porto Rico and other Spanish islands in the West Indies shall be immediately evacuated, and that commissioners, to be appointed within ten days, shall, within thirty days from the signing of the protocol, meet at Havana and San Juan, respectively, to arrange and execute the details of the evacuation.

"5. That the United States and Spain will each appoint not more than five commissioners to negotiate and conclude a Treaty of of Peace. The commissioners are to meet at Paris not later than October 1st.

"6. On the signing of the protocol, hostilities will be suspended and notice to that effect will be given as soon as possible by each Government to the commanders of its military and naval forces."

The proclamation declaring the existence of an armistice was as follows:

"By the President of the United States of America:

A PROCLAMATION.

"WHEREAS, By a protocol concluded and signed August 12, 1898, by William R. Day, Secretary of State of the United States, and His Excellency Jules Cambon, Ambassador Extraordinary and Plenipotentiary of the Republic of France at Washington, respectively representing for this purpose the Government of the United States and the Government of Spain, the United States and Spain have formally agreed upon the terms on which negotiations for the establishment of peace between the two countries shall be undertaken; and,

"WHEREAS, It is in said protocol agreed that upon its conclusion and signature hostilities between the two countries shall be suspended, and that notice to that effect shall be given as soon as possible by each Government to the commanders of its military and naval forces;

"Now, THEREFORE, I, William McKinley, President of the United States, do, in accordance with the stipulations of the protocol, declare and proclaim on the part of the United States a suspension of hostilities, and do hereby command that orders be immediately given through the proper channels to the commanders of the military and naval forces of the United States to abstain from all acts inconsistent with this proclamation.

"IN WITNESS WHEREOF, I have hereunto set my hand and caused the seal of the United States to be affixed.

"Done at the city of Washington, this 12th day of August, in the year of our Lord one thousand eight hundred and ninety-eight, and of the independence of the United States the one hundred and twenty-third.

[SEAL] "WILLIAM MCKINLEY.
"By the President.
"WILLIAM R. DAY, Secretary of State."

This armistice proclamation was followed at once by orders from the War and Navy Departments to the several commanders in the field and of the fleets, directing that all operations be suspended. Identical cablegrams were sent to General Miles in Porto Rico, General Shafter in Cuba, General Merritt in the Philippines, and to Admirals Sampson and Dewey; but it was in Porto Rico that the principal operations were going on at that time, and it was there that the effect was most interesting.

General Miles was at Ponce when the news of the signing of the protocol was cabled from Washington. Generals Brooke and Wilson, with their brigades, were further afield. General Wilson had received instructions from General Miles to demand the surrender of Aybonito whenever he felt that the position warranted such a demand. With the view, therefore, of making a demonstration in force, and also for the sake of developing the enemy's position, General Wilson had, on the morning of August 13th, ordered Major Lancaster to take a battery of the Third Artillery, advance from the outskirts of Coamo, where they had been in camp, and shell the Spanish position at that place and Aybonito Pass.

IN A SHOWER OF LEADEN BULLETS.

These positions were very strong, consisting of a series of rifle-pits along the crests of the mountains overlooking the military road for miles. The enemy also had several fieldpieces, modern guns of small calibre, mounted behind earthworks. As the horses of the battery galloped up the road, the enemy's infantry, from the pits on the mountains, showered bullets all about them. Four of the guns were unlimbered off the road, behind a natural fortification in the shape of a ridge, while the fifth gun was taken further above and unlimbered at a turn within plain sight of the Spanish position, though the horses and caissons were sheltered by a high bank on the roadside.

Within two minutes all five guns were thundering at the hill on which the enemy's artillery was located. Instantly came the reply. Shells screamed over the heads of the Americans for the thirty minutes that the duel continued. Our fire was so well directed that, after half a dozen shots, only one of the Spanish guns replied. Twenty minutes later this also was silenced, and the Spaniards could be seen fleeing from the trenches and making for the rifle-pits on the left. The rifle-pits were promptly shelled and a sharp fire was returned for a few minutes, but silence presently prevailed along the entire Spanish line. General Wilson then ordered the artillery to cease firing. This was about 3 P.M. Another section of the battery was then ordered up the road, and when it reached the point whence the former firing had taken place, the enemy began a fusillade, and all three of the American batteries were at once turned loose upon them until silence ultimately reigned supreme.

General Wilson then sent Colonel Bliss, his chief of staff, into Aybonito under a flag of truce to demand the surrender of the city. Colonel Bliss delivered the demand and reported to General Wilson that the commandant had said: "If you want to save the further shedding of blood, stay where you are."

General Wilson promptly ordered the artillery to unlimber again, and the gunners were making preparations to fire when the message was received from General Miles, notifying General Wilson of the signing of the protocol and the ending of hostilities. The artillery-men were so put out by being stopped from again attacking the Spaniards that many of them wept.

Meantime General Brooke had been operating in the vicinity of Guayama, and his experience at the final moment of the war was equally interesting. He had instructed General Haines to advance with the Fourth Ohio and the Third Illinois from Arroyo with a view to ascertaining the truth of a report to the effect that the enemy's troops had gathered in considerable force, at a point about five miles distant up the military road to San Juan. The Fourth Pennsylvania, under Colonel David Brainerd Case, was left at Arroyo as a temporary garrison, this being the only other regiment in General Haines brigade. After proceeding about half the distance to the reported point of interest the Third Illinois was left as a reserve, and the Fourth Ohio proceeded along the main road, General Brooke and his aides being in advance of the column.

The day was beautiful. A slight breeze cooled the air and tempered the heat of the sun. A peculiar haze covered the hills with a bluish veil. There was nothing to break the stillness for a while, but presently a sharply singing "pstwing" was heard over the heads of the soldiers, a sound which nearly every one took for the whizzing of a Mauser bullet. One of the General's aides, however, called attention to a telegraph wire that had sagged by the roadside, and he insisted that it had been cut, but the discussion was immediately ended by the arrival of a great many messages, not over the wire, but through the air, and the soldiers then knew that the enemy were watching and intending to oppose their progress.

The range of the enemy's fire was evidently a long one, as many of the bullets lay spent at the very feet of the invaders, and the report of the Mausers was not heard until long after the song of the bullet. No smoke or flash could be seen in any direction. It was some time before the enemy's exact position could be ascertained. This sort of thing kept up for about an hour. Finally the Spaniards retreated toward the hills and took up positions behind rocks, from which they did some pretty brisk firing. The dynamite guns were finally brought up, five shells were thrown into the midst of the enemy, and this silenced them effectively.

This engagement occurred on August 18th. Two days later another advance was made along the San Juan road to a point where the Spaniards could be seen, distinctly with a glass, throwing up entrenchments on the opposite hills; also small bodies of them moving about upon the side of the mountain some three or four thousand yards distant. The Fourth Ohio, under Colonel Coit, was at the head of the column. The road along which they were proceeding was cut from the face of the hill. The last company was about to pass through two open ledges in which the road was laid, when a terrific volley fire was opened from the Spanish entrenchments. Colonel Coit and two members of General Brooke's staff, who had ridden up, took shelter behind a small house by the roadside, and the rest of the command lay flat upon their faces. A gutter or trench by the side of the road was the only cover. Into that rolled the men, and finally, by its cover, managed to crawl around the bend to a place protected from the enemy's fire.

The firing line was soon formed, however, the wounded were brought back, and a few well-directed volleys told the enemy that they were not to have it all their own way. In a few minutes the dynamite guns were once more brought up. These caused the

Spanish to retreat. Several of the men of the Fourth Ohio were slightly wounded in this engagement, but none were killed, and there was never any means of ascertaining the effect of the American fire upon the Spanish lines at this point.

THE FINAL OPERATION.

The final operation was on the morning of the 13th of August, when General Brooke, who had come up to General Haines' position again, with three batteries of artillery and two troops of cavalry, ordered a concentrated movement upon the enemy's position. The orders for this movement had been issued on the night of the 12th. They were that the troops should be in readiness at 6 A.M. for the advance in the direction of San Juan. There was little sleep that night. The route had been reconnoitered, and the reports that had been made upon it indicated that serious work was to be expected.

The military road along which the advance was to be made was a winding affair with deep cuts. Often there was a sheer wall of two hundred feet rising on one side, while across the road would be a descent of perhaps three times that distance. The road led directly over the mountains, and on every advantageous spot along that road of ten miles, the Spaniards had planted batteries that could not be seen from the road and were unapproachable in any other way.

Some of these entrenchments overlooked precipices three hundred feet deep. To get at them, except by way of the road, meant to scale walls of perpendicular rock. In some places tons of rocks and boulders were held in place on lofty ledges by great vines and prickly scrub growth.

From these entrenchments of the Spaniards it was possible to note every movement of the American troops. The enemy could accurately determine the strength of the invading force, but an estimate of the force of the enemy was all guesswork. It was only known that the Spaniards, many or few, were magnificently entrenched, and that it was going to be a hard job to rout them.

When the troops were led out of Guayama, on that morning of August 13th, with General Brooke and his staff at the head, the streets and balconies were crowded with natives. General Haines, with some of the infantry, was sent to flank the enemy's position on the left, while the cavalry were to perform a similar movement on the right. General Brooke continued to lead the advance in person. Part of the time he was on foot, while his staff and horses halted along the roadside. He carefully scanned the hills with his field-glass, and others who did the same could plainly see the Spaniards in their fortifications at points where they had perfect command of the road. To have taken those hills would have been as memorable a victory as that of the division of General Lawton at El Caney, or the dash up the slopes of San Juan, and General Brooke's force was eager for the chance to take them.

The troops were soon ordered forward, and, clambering up the steep slope, were formed into a firing line. The batteries followed. Battery B, of Pittsburg, Pa., having the right of the line, was the first to begin unlimbering. The guns were soon in place; their targets were marked and the range calculated. The cavalry then disappeared around the hills. General Haines was only a little distance away with the rest of the infantry. The Spanish position could be plainly noted. Eagerness and expectation were universal. There was an almost impressive silence. Even the final orders were issued in a subdued voice, and everybody believed that the next thing to occur would be the belching of artillery and a hail of leaden missiles.

THE MESSAGE THAT ENDED THE WAR.

Such was the situation when a mounted officer, closely followed by his orderly on a mule, appeared around a bend of the road, lashing his tired steed through the battery. It was Lieutenant McLaughlin, of the Signal Corps. He rode up to General Brooke, neglecting, in his haste, to dismount, and said: "An important message, sir." General Brooke took the message from the hand of the messenger, read it, passed it to one of his staff, then quietly turned about and gave the order that the troops return to Guayama.

The contents of the message were soon known to everybody. They were as follows:

"PORT PONCE, August 13, 1898.

"*Major-General Brooke:*—

" By direction of the President, operations against the enemy are suspended. Negotiations are near completion. The protocol has been signed by representatives of the two countries. All commanders will be governed accordingly.

"BY COMMAND OF MAJOR-GENERAL MILES,
"GILMORE, Chief of Staff."

Not a comment was heard. The soldiers were utterly stupefied. The retreat was made sullenly, but on the march the disappointed soldiers, officers and all, used not a little strong language in condemnation of their luck.

"Three minutes more," said General Brooke, "and we should have fired." Just then an enthusiast in the ranks, determined to give some vent to his feelings, discharged his rifle, and this was the last shot of the war. General Brooke looked around for a moment, as if wishing he knew who had committed this breach of discipline, but he merely smiled, as if perfectly understanding the situation, and led the troops back to the coast. Thus was the military feature of the expedition to Porto Rico brought to an end, and all that remains to be told is in connection with the Civil Departments.

CHAPTER XXIII

Porto Rico—Past, Present and Future

The Island and Its Population.—Its Future as a Winter Resort.—Timber in Abundance and Variety.—Minerals and Mining.—Some Facts about Its Commerce, which Amounts to over $36,000,000.—The Chief Cities and Towns of Porto Rico.—Snap-shots of San Juan, the Capital, and of Ponce, the Next Largest City.

IT was in November of the year 1493, on his second voyage to the New World, that Columbus landed on a strange island, in quest of water for his ships. He found it in abundance, and called the place *Aquadilla*—the watering place. As he had done at Cuba the year before, the great discoverer held pleasant conferences with the natives, and with due ceremony took possession of the island for his benefactors and sovereigns—Ferdinand and Isabella of Spain. From that day until it was ceded to the United States in 1898, as a result of the Spanish-American War, Porto Rico remained one of the most attractive and valuable of Spain's West Indian possessions.

The simple and friendly natives gladly welcomed their Spanish invaders, who, with the same promptness which was manifested in Cuba, proceeded to enslave and exterminate them. In 1510, Ponce de Leon founded the first settlement on the site of the present village of Puerto Viejo. The next year the noted ivader founded San Juan, the present capital of the island. One of the most interesting sights of this old city to-day is the Casa Blanca, built at that period as the palatial residence of Ponce de Leon. It was there, perhaps, after he had finished his conquest of the island, that this famous old Spaniard listened to the wonderful story of the natives, who served him as slaves, concerning the mysterious country over the sea which had hidden in its forests a fountain wherein an old man might plunge and be restored to all the vigor of youth. It was there and thus, perhaps, while sitting at leisure in his palace, that de Leon planned the voyage in search of that "fountain of youth" which resulted in the discovery and exploration of Florida.

As to the number of natives in Porto Rico when the Spaniards came old chroniclers differ. Some say there were 500,000, others 300,000. It is all surmise. Probably the latter figure is an overestimate, for Cuba, more than ten times as large, was not thought to contain more than half a million of inhabitants at most. A detailed account of their manners and customs was written by one of the early Spaniards, and part of it is translated by the British Consul, Mr. Bidwell, in his Consular Report of 1880. Some of the statements in this old book are most peculiar and interesting. Within the last forty years archæologists have discovered many stone axes, spear-heads and knives, stone and clay images, and pieces of earthenware made by the aboriginal Porto Ricans, and these are preserved in the Smithsonian Institute at Washington, in Berlin, and elsewhere. It is curious that none of these remains had been found prior to 1856. On the banks of the Rio Grande there still stands, also, a a rude stone monument, with strange designs carved upon its surface.

From the earliest times, the island, with its rich produce and commerce, was the prey of robbers. The fierce cannibal Caribs from the south made expeditions to it before the white men came; and for many decades after the Spanish conquest it suffered attacks from pirates by sea and brigands upon land, who found easy hiding within its deep forests.

ATTACKS AND INVASIONS BY FOREIGN FORCES.

In 1595, San Juan was sacked by the English under Drake, and again, three years later, by the Duke of Cumberland. In 1615, Baldwin Heinrich, a Dutchman, lost his life in an attack upon the governor's castle, and several of his ships were destroyed by a hurricane. The English failed to capture it, fifty-three years later; and Abercrombie tried it again in 1797, but had to give up the undertaking after a three days' siege. It was one hundred and one years after Abercrombie's siege, before another hostile fleet appeared before and bombarded San Juan. This was done by Admiral Sampson, May 12, 1898, with the United States squadron of modern iron-clad battleships and cruisers. In this engagement Morro Castle, which, though impregnable a hundred years before, was unable to withstand modern guns, and was in a large part reduced to ruins.

General Nelson A. Miles landed his United States troops on the island in July, 1898, and on the 12th of August, before he completed his conquest, hostilities were closed by the protocol of peace, and amid the rejoicing of the natives "Beautiful Porto Rico" became a province of the United States. The one and only attempt the Porto Ricans ever made to throw off the Spanish yoke was in 1820; but conditions for hiding from the soldiers were not so good as the Cubans enjoyed in their large island, and Spanish supremacy was completely re-established by 1823.

THE ISLAND AND ITS POPULATION.

Porto Rico is at once the most healthful and most densely populated island of the West Indies. It is almost rectangular in form—100 miles long and 36 broad. Its total area is about 3,600 square miles—a little larger than the combined areas of Rhode Island and Delaware. Its population, unlike that of Cuba, has greatly increased within the last fifty years. In 1830, it numbered 319,000; in 1887, 813,937—about 220 people to the square mile, a density which few States of the Union can equal. About half of its population are negroes or mulattoes, who were introduced by the Spaniards as slaves in the 16th and 17th centuries.

Among the people of European origin the most numerous are the Spaniards, with many Germans, Swedes, Danes, Russians, Frenchmen, Chuetos (descendants from the Moorish Jews), and natives of the Canary Islands. There are also a number of Chinese, while the Gibaros, or small land-holders and day-laborers of the country districts, are a curious old Spanish cross with the aboriginal Indian blood. In this class the aborigines are more fortunate than the original Cubans in having even a trace of their blood preserved.

This island is said to be capable of easily supporting three times its present population, the soil is so universally fertile and its resources are so well diversified. Though droughts occur in certain parts of the island, it is all extremely well watered, by more than one thousand streams, enumerated on the maps, and the dry sections have a system of irrigation which may be operated very effectually and with little expense. Of the 1,300 streams, forty-seven are considerable rivers.

Forests still cover all the elevated parts of the hill country of the interior, the inhabitants living mostly along the coast. The main need to set the interior teeming with a thrifty and healthy population is a system of good roads. The interior, with the exception of a few extensive savannas, is one vast expanse of rounded hills, covered with such rich soil that they may be cultivated to their summits. At present these forests are accessible only by mule tracks. "The timber of the island," says our official report, "comprises more than five hundred varieties of trees, and in the more elevated regions the vegetation of the temperate zones is not unknown. On the hills is found a luxuriant and diversified vegetation, tree-ferns and mountain palms being abundant. At a lower level grow many varieties of trees noted for their useful woods, such as the mahogany, cedar, walnut and laurel. The mammee, guaiacum and copal, besides other trees and shrubs valuable for their gum, flourish in all parts of the island. The coffee tree and sugar cane, both of which grow well at an altitude of a thousand feet or more, were introduced into the island—the former from Martinique in 1722, the latter from the Canaries, through Santo Domingo. Tobacco grows easily in the lowlands, while maize, pineapples, bananas, etc., are all prolific. The banana and plantain bear fruit within ten months after planting, and, like the cocoa palm, live through an ordinary lifetime."

MINERALS AND MINING.

"The mineral resources of the island," says our consul in his report, "have been very little developed, the only mineral industry of any importance being the salt works situated at Guanica, Salinas and Cabo Rojo. Sulphides of copper and magnetic oxides of iron are found in large quantities, and formerly gold to a considerable extent was found in many of the streams. At present the natives still wash out nuggets by the crude process in use in the time of Ponce de Leon. Marble, carbonates, lignite and amber are also present in varying quantities, and hot springs and mineral waters occur, the best known ones being at Coamo, near Santa Isabel."

The commerce of Porto Rico amounted, in 1896, to $36,624,120, exceeding the records of all previous years; the increase, no doubt, being largely due to the unsettled condition of Cuba. The value of the exports for the same year was, for the first time for more than a decade, slightly in excess of that of the imports; the former being valued at $18,341,430, the latter at $18,282,690. The chief exports from the island are agricultural products. The principal articles are sugar, coffee, molasses and tobacco; while rice, wheat, flour and manufactured articles are among the chief imports. The value of the sugar and molasses exported to the United States during the ten years from 1888 to 1897 made up 95 per cent. of the total value of the exports to that country. Fruits, nuts and spices are also exported to a small extent. Of the non-agricultural exports, the most important are perfumery and cosmetics; chemicals, drugs and dyes; unmanufactured wood and salt.

The leading article of import from the United States is wheat flour. Corn and meal, bread, biscuit, meats, dairy products, wood and its manufactures, iron, steel, etc., are also imported.

GENERAL HENRY REORGANIZES THE GOVERNMENT.

When the American forces took possession of the island a change was immediately felt, pointing toward a new era of success in every branch of trade. General Guy V. Henry, "Fighting Guy," as he is called, was appointed and established Military Governor of Porto Rico. He immediately set out to reorganize the affairs of the Government. How he succeeded is told by Major George W. Fishback, Chief Paymaster of the Department of Porto Rico, as follows:

"The management of the island and its affairs commands the admiration of both natives and Americans. Major-General Guy V. Henry, who is Military Governor has proved himself to be most acceptable to both. He is a forceful man and full of the kindliest sympathies for the native people. He has surrounded himself with a cabinet made up of the most intelligent men of the island, and through them, as representatives of the different branches of the Government, he rules the island firmly and justly. He summoned the leaders of the Roman Catholic Church and conveyed to them the fact that he proposed to have perfect freedom of religious worship in Porto Rico; that he would not tolerate any interference with the affairs of the Roman Catholic Church, nor would he allow that Church to interfere with free religious worship on the part of the Protestant denominations. He furthermore served notice upon the Archbishop that he would expel from the island any priest, or body of priests, who openly or in underhanded ways made any effort to influence the native people in questions of religious worship.

"I asked the Minister of Justice the other day in what esteem General Henry was held among the best people in Government circles, and he replied that he was very well liked, but was open to criticism of making his Cabinet officers do more work than they were accustomed to. The idea of working hours a day, with only a short interruption for a midday breakfast, was something that Porto Rican business men are not accustomed to.

UNDER PERFECT CONTROL.

"The whole island is under the most perfect control, under General Henry's military supervision. Disturbers of the peace have felt the weight of his iron hand and now appreciate the fact that an offender will be dealt with quickly and severely if he commits an offence against either public health or morals. The post office service is being extended to all parts of the island, and letters mailed in San Juan one evening are delivered in Ponce the following night. General Frederick D. Grant is in command of the district of San Juan, and, as a result of many inspection trips throughout his part of the island, has the military body in excellent condition. There is no sickness to speak of in any of the camps."

General Henry, immediately upon taking charge of affairs, issued a formal letter to the Presidents and Secretarys of the Council there, announcing what his program would be for the Government of the island. In this statement he says, that as far as possible he wishes to give independence of action to the Alcaldes and Consuls in the various towns, and, after the selection of these officers, to hold them responsible for the condition of affairs. He orders them to see that the town is kept in proper police law and order, to introduce sanitary regulations, to obtain in the absence of a sewer system, the odorless system of carts, used in the United States, to see that there are no overcrowded houses, and that cleanliness is kept up, taxing those people who refuse to observe the orders for health. He commends the introduction of a water supply and frequent flushings of the streets.

The choice of City officials he leaves entirely to the people themselves under certain restrictions. The men chosen are not to be removed except for cause, such as inefficiency, failure to do their duty, or crookedness.

In this letter he takes up the system of education as follows :

" The system of school education should be looked into, and it is my desire to ascertain how many teachers they can pay who can teach the American or English language, beginning with the younger children. It is believed that people who can speak English only can accomplish the purpose by object lessons. It is thought that American women for teaching can be obtained at $50 per month in gold, and they are well worth it. The young children are anxious to learn and now is the time for them to do so. If Alcaldes will report to me how many teachers they can so employ they will be brought from the United States and sent to these towns.

" It is also my desire to introduce, as soon as possible, policemen, so as to teach the native policemen what their duties are, and also to encourage them to exercise some authority, which at present they seem not desirous of doing."

He further says that men should not be put in jail except upon definite charges and upon proper evidence, and gives certain restrictions as to the punishment of criminals. The matter of customs and the value of money he leaves to the Congress. He restricts articles in newspapers of an incendiary character reflecting upon the Government or its officials, and he goes on to say : " Upon my assuming command, the cabinet selected by General Brooke handed in their resignations so as to leave me free to act. I consider it for the best interests of the island to retain those gentlemen in office until I have some reason for relieving them, for I believe they are capable men and have the good of the island at heart, and in their actions are governed simply by the interest of the island rather than by personal motives. It is the intention that the soldiers so far as possible shall preserve law and order, but as in the United States the soldiers are not needed, so the idea now is to educate the people to take care of themselves."

Such was the opinion of General Henry when he took charge, and the result was better than anyone hoped. As this is being written, Aguadilla, on the west coast, is the only city under a Military Mayor; all of the others have a native in charge. Captain T. W. Mansfield took charge of that town, not because of disruption among the people, but because of a deadlock and corruption in the town council. He was in charge for one month up to March 1st, and then a new set of councilmen was elected, but these city fathers, instead of voting for some native to act as Mayor, begged that Captain Mansfield continue in charge. He was very popular with everybody.

DISHONESTY OF OFFICIALS.

When he took the office he discovered a system of corruption in the government of the place which demanded an immediate reform. No sooner was he seated than a clerk brought in a number of documents for him to sign. "What are these?" asked the Captain. "Receipts for February," said the clerk. "Has the money been paid?" "Not yet, sir."

This opened the Captain's eyes, and he soon found out how officials had made money without much work. This was the plan: The previous Mayors signed Treasury receipts sufficient to pay all day-laborers employed by the city for a month in advance. As they were dated a month ahead they could not be cashed by the workmen until that time had expired. So when a laborer needed a loaf of bread, he was forced to sell this order for money at a big discount, and the city officials personally bought them in. They would give $30 for a $40 slip, and when it became due, they would cash it and pocket the difference, $10, and there would be no record on the books of any crookedness, although the poor laborer had been cheated out of $10. It did not take long to correct that trouble, and it served as a warning that Porto Rican officials were not the most honest creatures in the world.

A MONUMENT TO A SPANISH SOLDIER.

At Yauco, Captain C. A. Vernon has made himself exceedingly popular with the natives and has organized a street-cleaning department, strengthened the police force, and made the merchants interested in a village improvement association. Right outside of the village is a little monument which bears the following inscription: "In memory of a Spanish soldier killed in action with United States troops, July 27, 1898. Presented by officers of Yauco Post, First Battalion, Nineteenth Infantry."

In the capital of the island American officers are to be found in the Department of Justice, of Finance, the Engineering Department, and the Educational and Health Boards. They are simply assigned to duty there in order to introduce American methods.

When the United States took charge of the Treasury at San Juan, the capital of Porto Rico, investigation showed that the insular Treasury held 76 cents in copper, $3.80 in Venezuelan gold and about $900 in American bankbills. This was a great surprise, as there should have been at least several hundred thousand dollars deposited to the credit of a general guarantee fund. Investigation showed that at least $200,000 was missing from that fund, and it is probable that the full amount which should be there is nearly 500,000 pesos, between $300,000 and $400,000. There can be no doubt that the money was taken to Spain. It is generally known that the late Captain-General Macias delivered to the Government at Madrid 91,000 pesos, and that the Brigadier de Marina Vallarino delivered to his Government 46,000 pesos which rightfully belonged to Porto Rico and which were drawn from this guarantee fund.

The Spanish Bank of Porto Rico was found to be in arrears to the Government, and it was forced to pay to the Treasury 20,000 pesos collected on account of taxes and revenues, and will be forced to meet further obligations.

LIFE IN THE SMALLER TOWNS.

A glimpse of the life in one of the smaller towns of this island is not uninteresting. Take, for instance, Adjuntas, which is one of the places about which little is known, consequently it may be taken as a representative small town. It is an exceedingly pretty little place with a square plaza in the centre filled with beautiful roses, palms and flowering bushes. It has several nice stores which sell shoes and clothes and liquor. The stores generally carry very few dry goods, as the people depend chiefly on the venders who go round the streets with their baskets on their heads selling anything from a baby's rubber ring to a very pretty dress.

All the saloons, or casinos, as the Porto Ricans call them, have gambling rooms attached, for Porto Rico is a great gambling place.

Little fruit stands may be found on every corner, and the price of oranges and bananas is absurdly cheap. The people are dark in color, for even the Porto Ricans of the better class have a tinge of Negro blood in their veins, while the lowest classes show strong traces of Indian blood.

The people are for the most part lazy and dirty They never bathe, and they always wear the same clothes. Their chief food is plantains, a kind of banana, which they boil, and oranges and bread. Meat is very expensive, and therefore little used. During the coffee season the workers picking coffee receive about 30 cents a day. At the end of the season, instead of looking for more work, they gamble away the little they have saved, and when it is gone they steal. The people bury their dead in a rude box shaped like a coffin, and sometimes, if they have not enough money for this, they rent a coffin for the occasion. Some of the coffins are not even painted. Four men carry the box on their shoulders for many miles, and relief pallbearers take the places of the others when they get tired. The body is taken to a church and then to the cemetery where, if the coffin is not rented, it is buried. If the coffin is rented, however, the body is taken out and buried right in the ground.

AT A COCKFIGHT.

Porto Rico is a great place for cockfights. The season is from November until April, and Sunday is the chief day for the sport. Every village, however small, or however how far up in the mountains, has a pit dug in the earth and covered with a wooden roof to keep out the sun in the dry season and the rain in the wet. The spectators sit around on rough board seats, and yell at the top of their lungs. They become so excited, and howl so vigorously, that they sometimes scare the birds so that they turn and flee. In betting the men never deposit their money. All wagers are paid at the end of the afternoon fights. A man has to call out his bet at the top of his voice, and his ears or eyes must then catch the answer. There is no pit at San Juan, because that city is so overcrowded. But across the harbor in Catano there is a place where all the sportsmen congregate. Ten coppers is the fare and a native sailboat takes the gamblers over. Admission is 20 cents. In Ponce there is a place owned by a wealthy Spaniard. Behind the rickety board-fence he keeps more than a hundred game-birds worth from $3.00 to $200 each. Half a dozen negroes take care of his gamestock, clipping their feathers, polishing their spurs, and feeding them.

The island offers great inducements for profitable investment. It needs, however, good judgment, carefulness, and plenty of capital to get anything like big returns. Agriculture is the great source of wealth, and consequently the prosperity of the island depends on the success of the crops. It also must be taken into consideration that Cuba and Porto Rico produce about the same kind of crops, and, unless Porto Rico is given extraordinary tax advantages over Cuba, the latter will have the advantage of being so much nearer and better situated in respect to the American market, and also is capable of much larger and consequently much cheaper production.

LAND IS VERY EXPENSIVE.

Land is expensive in Porto Rico, because the island is so very thickly populated, and, of course, since the occupation by the Americans, the price has gone up remarkably. The land is divided into four classes: First-class land is the sugar land, the second class the coffee land of the interior, the third class comprises black sandy loam adjoining sugar lands, which is chiefly used for truck farms, and the fourth class comprises the sandy beach land, where cocoanuts are planted. Land is sold by the *cuerda*, which is equal to sixty-nine yards square in our measurement. The sugar lands are found in the belt of low flat land, running around the island between the foothills of the mountains and the sea. First-class property has been known to bring $400 a cuerda, but the price of to-day is about $150. This represents land that has already been drained and ditched and is ready for planting. The coffee plantations, if already planted, are considered to be worth about $150 a cuerda, although land suitable for raising coffee, if not planted, may be bought for about 10 or 25 pesos. For instance, a farm of 500 cuerdas is advertised for sale at 9,000 pesos, made up of forty cuerdas already set out with young coffee trees, one hundred more suitable for immediate planting, and the balance in woodland and pasture, part of which would grow fruits and vegetables. The black loam of the third class varies very much in value. Some farms of it are quite expensive, and others may be bought for 10 or 20 pesos, depending largely on the location in respect to the seaports. The sandy soil for cocoanut planting also ranges from 5 to 25 pesos.

THE BEST FIELDS FOR INVESTMENT.

Orange raising, together with the raising of pineapples and bananas, offers the best field, probably, for profitable investment. It is a field that may be developed to a large degree, and, if the results show sufficient production to warrant a line of fruit steamers, this industry might have good returns. Sugar depends largely upon the laws which will regulate its exportation. The Cuban crop will be its greatest rival. The tobacco of the island is of excellent quality, although it has been very badly harvested and cured of late. Here is an example of what may be realized from a good tobacco farm: A farm of 100 cuerdas produced in one year $12,000 in gold, and cost the owner $3,000 for cultivation and general expenses.

In regard to the prospects for the future, Frank A. Vanderlip, Assistant Secretary of the Treasury, who was sent there to look into currency and custom problems, says: "The people are delighted to be Americans, and there is every prospect of prosperity for our new possession. Whatever mineral wealth there is, is wholly undeveloped, and the agricultural possibilities are, apparently, boundless. Only a portion of the land is under cultivation. There are no water works, sewers, electric lights, or electric railways. There is a good field for electric roads throughout the island. With the exception of the military road, there is no railroad of any kind in Porto Rico. The franchise seekers and promoters in general, who rushed to the island almost before the American troops were landed, have begun to give place to a more solid and promising class. Undoubtedly capital will begin to seek investment there soon. There is no field for a man without capital on account of the high prices for land."

In regard to the mineral resources of the island, Robert T. Hill, of the United States Geological Survey, reports that the conditions are theoretically favorable for valuable iron deposits, and, in one or two instances these undoubtedly exist, notably north of Juncos. At this place there is a large deposit of magnetic iron ore of great purity, containing 66 per cent. of iron and less than .023 of phosphorous. A French engineer has calculated that there are at least 35,000 tons of this ore in sight. At present it is many miles from a seaport, and its development will necessitate the construction of a railway. In Mr. Hill's opinion this deposit is the most valuable metallic resource of the island at present in sight, and American capital will develop it. It has been estimated that the deposit contains 10,000,000 tons of metallic iron.

MINERAL RESOURCES OF THE ISLAND.

The best-known iron mines, which are already in operation, are situated in the Sierra Maestra, a few miles east of Santiago, and are owned by American companies. There are also rich deposits of manganese in the same range of mountains. The mines in the neighborhood of Ponupo yielded 200 tons a day before they were closed by the insurgents.

There is also plenty of asphaltum of great richness beneath the waters of Cardenas Bay and in several other places. Near Villa Clara is an unusually rich deposit, which has supplied the material for illuminating gas for the city for forty years. The copper mines of Cobre, about twelve leagues north of Santiago, used to be the greatest copper mines in the world, back in 1867, and it is generally believed that large quantities of the ore still exist in that locality, although the mines themselves have been filled up with water, and it is a question whether they can be profitably reopened.

Near Juana Diaz is a belt of beautiful marble of great hardness. It is variegated in color, consisting of a reddish matrix, mottled with small white spots. At present it is only used for structural purposes, such as piers for bridges. Green sand marl occurs in great abundance on the road from Lares to San Sebastian, immediately adjoining the most productive coffee region. Lime marls abound everywhere around the coast, and gypsum marls occur near Juana Diaz adjacent to the Rio Portugues and near Ponce. These are especially important in as much as these natural fertilizers will play a large part in the agricultural development of the island.

Gold is found along the bed of streams but only in small quantities, and Mr. Hill does not think that any quartz veins will be found.

Salt deposits exist and there are some thermal springs which are said to be of great value in curing skin diseases and rheumatic troubles.

OUR TRADE WITH PORTO RICO.

A word or two about our trade with Porto Rico may not be amiss. Frank H. Hitchcock of the Department of Agriculture, has recently made an investigation, into the exports and imports of Porto Rico. His report shows that during the year ending June 30, 1897, the commercial transactions between this country and Porto Rico amounted to $4,169,912, and, with exception of 1895, when the value of trade fell to $3,340,056, this was the smallest recorded for any year since the Civil War. The high water mark in our trade with Porto Rico was reached way back in 1872, in which the imports and exports had a combined value of $13,870,925.

Products of agriculture play the most important part in our commerce with Porto Rico, comprising in value more than 80 per cent. of the merchandise imported and exported. Among these products sugar is by far the most important. Measured in value it comprised nearly 75 per cent. of all the merchandise we received from the island during the ten years up to 1897, and if the value of the molasses be also included the combined item would form more than 95 per cent. of the total imports. After these, coffee is the most important, while fruits, nuts and spices make up the rest of the imports.

The annual receipts of sugar during 1893 and 1897 averaged 79,941,404 pounds, valued at $1,980,460. That of molasses 2,445,897 gallons valued at $558,042. The annual average imports for the past five years in coffee amounted to only 164,769 pounds, worth $32,671.

In regard to exports the United States has chiefly sent to Porto Rico breadstuffs and meat products, their combined value representing nearly 95 per cent. of the whole volume of agricultural exports. Wheat flour is the chief breadstuff exported during the five years, 1893 to 1897. The average number of barrels shipped per annum was 148,487, valued at $570,619.

During the same period our exports of wood and its manufactures reached an annual value of $292,336. Our exports of iron and steel manufactures during the year 1897 were larger than ever before, and amounted to $180,486.

There are plenty of harbors along the coast of Porto Rico, but those on the north side are mostly unprotected from the trade winds, and those on the west side are filled with sand. The whole of the north coast is lined with navigable lagoons, some of which are nearly ten miles in length. Of the twenty-one rivers, most are quite small, but several of them can be navigated for five or six miles. A number of the bays and creeks are deep enough for vessels of considerable size, but the north coast is subject to tremendous ground seas which drift against the cliffs with great violence.

CHIEF TOWNS OF PORTO RICO.

The exporting towns are Mayaguez, San German and Aguadilla, on the west, and Guanica, Guayanilla, and Puerto Ponce on the south. The eastern part of the island is less important commercially.

The capital of the island is San Juan. It is situated on a long narrow island, separated from the mainland at one end by a shallow arm of the sea. There is a bridge connecting this end with the mainland, while the other extremity ends in a great high bluff, which is crowned by Morro Castle, the chief fort of the town. Back of this bluff is a magnificent bay with a good depth of water. It is one of the best harbors in the West Indies. The town itself, built over 250 years ago, is a fine specimen of the old walled town, having a portcullis, moat, gates and battlements, which must have cost millions of dollars. The city is laid off in regular squares, with six parallel streets running the length of the island and seven at right angles with these. The city is devoid of running water and depends entirely upon rain water which is caught upon the tops of the buildings and kept in cisterns. There is no sewage system, and the risks of contaminating the water supply are very great, while in dry season the supplies are frequently exhausted.

The town is very much overcrowded. It is surprising to see the great number of poor who are packed like rats in a garret in the tenements in the upper part of the place, and it is almost impossible to rent for residential purposes second stories that are not directly over people who live in squalor, foul air and confusion. As may be imagined, dwelling houses are expensive, and our soldiers found great trouble in securing quarters.

It can be seen readily that in the absence of a good water supply and a sewage system, and with people packed together in such a manner, epidemics of disease are frequent. The Spaniards once started an expensive system of aqueducts costing $400,000, and issued municipal bonds for that purpose, but the work was never completed. The piping was almost finished, however, and steps are now being taken to push the work on a stone supply reservoir to be erected in the northern and highest part of the city which would ultimately be used in connection with the unfinished aqueduct. It will take at least a year to complete this reservoir, and even then it will hold less than 3,000,000 gallons, which would only last the city five days.

The streets of the city are wider than those in the older part of Havana and admit two carriages abreast. The pavements are good, but made of material which is easily broken. Besides the portion of the town within the walls, there are small portions just outside called the Marina and Porta de Tierra, each of which have about 3,000 inhabitants. There are also two suburbs, San Turce approached by the only road leading out of the city, and the other Catano, which may be reached by ferry right across the bay. The entire population of city and suburbs is about 30,000, one half of which consists of negroes and mixed races.

THE CITY OF PONCE.

The city of Ponce, with a population of 37,500, and in commercial importance next to the largest city of Porto Rico, is situated on the south coast of the island about two miles from the sea, and about seventy miles from the capital. It is one of the healthiest cities of Porto Rico and is regularly built, the central part of it being made of brick and the outside part of wood. Here the military commander of the island used to live. It has an appellate criminal court, besides other courts, and contains two hospitals, a military station, two churches, one of which is the only Protestant church in the West Indies, a good fire department, a bank, a theatre, three hotels, and a gas works.

The chief occupations of the people are the cultivation of sugar, cocoa, tobacco and oranges and the breeding of cattle. The port which is connected to the city by a splendid road is called the Playa. Here all the import and export trade is transacted, and here is the customhouse and all the consular offices. The port is a good one, and will hold vessels of 25 feet draft. The water supply, which is conveyed to the city by an aqueduct, is ample and good.

The third largest city of Porto Rico is Mayaguez. It is situated in the western part, 102 miles from San Juan, on Mona Channel. There are three manufactures of chocolate there, and the city exports sugar, coffee, oranges, pineapples and cocoanuts. The coffee is of the best quality and competes with Java and other first-rate brands. The population is about 20,000, the majority of whom are white. The city is connected with street cars with the town of Aguadilla near by, and a railroad is being built to Lares in the interior.

Aguadilla has about 5,000 inhabitants. Its chief industries are the cultivation of sugar, coffee, tobacco, and cocoanuts. The climate is very hot, but healthy. The city is a port for a district which has about 30,000 inhabitants.

The town of Arecibo is situated on the northern coast of Porto Rico, facing the Atlantic. It is much the same in construction as other Porto Rican towns, with a plaza in the centre and streets running at right angles from it. The harbor is not a good one, being exposed to the full force of the ocean, and having dangerous reefs close into shore. The Rio Grande de Arecibo empties into the harbor, and is a small, shallow stream upon which goods are conveyed on flat-bottom boats from the city out to the bar, and there transferred to lighters which carry them over to the vessels. It is, however, the port of about 30,000 inhabitants, and is, consequently, an important place, although the town itself has but 7,000 people in it.

Fajardo, on the east coast, has a population of 9,000. It is a good port, with a lighthouse at the entrance, and a customhouse. The town itself is a mile and a quarter from the bay. Most of the people of the district manufacture muscovado sugar, which is the chief article of export. The climate is healthy.

Naguabo, on the east side, having 2,000 inhabitants, Playa de Naguabo, with 1,500, and Humaco, the capital of the district, with

4,000, Arroyo in the district of Guayama (southeast portion), with 1,200 inhabitants, are the other well-known cities of the island.

The general healthfulness of the whole island gives rise to the belief that it will become a splendid winter resort in the future under the Stars and Stripes. It already has fame in that connection, and now, with its new affiliations, the personal safety and comfort of visitors will be such that it will probably be the land of refuge when snow and sleet chase the rich from their homes in the great cities of the North.

CHAPTER XXVI

The Closing Events of the Philippine War

A Proclamation by the Commissioners from the United States, Giving Assurance of our Good Will but Stating that American Supremacy Will be Maintained for Good Government.—Dagupan Bombarded.—General Montenegro One of the Great Insurgent Leaders Killed.—Lawton's Flying Column Sweeps Down Upon the Province of Laguna.—Santa Cruz Captured.—Lumban and Pagsangan Also Fall Before the American Troops.—Lawton's Expedition Recalled.—MacArthur's Men Gloriously Storm Calumpit's Trenches.—The Fighting Continues.

SHORTLY after the fall of Malolos, the United States Philippine Commissioners issued a proclamation on behalf of our Government to show the good will of the President and the people of the United States towards the inhabitants of the Philippines. This proclamation was one of the most important documents issued in connection with war in those islands, and is given herewith in full, inasmuch as it shows the attitude which President McKinley has taken and proposes to carry out in regard to the Filipinos.

The proclamation follows:

"The commission desires to assure the people of the Philippine Islands of the cordial good will and fraternal feeling which is entertained for them by the President of the United States and by the American people.

"The aim and object of the American Government, apart from the fulfillment of the solemn obligations it has assumed toward the family of nations by its acceptance of sovereignty over the Philippine Islands, is the well-being, prosperity and happiness of the Philippine people and their elevation and advancement to a position among the most civilized peoples of the world.

"The President believes that this felicity and perfection of the Philippine people is to be brought about by the assurance of peace and order, by the guarantee of civil and religious liberty, by the establishment of justice, by the cultivation of letters, science and the liberal and practical arts, by the enlargement of intercourse with foreign nations, by expansion of industrial pursuits, by trade and commerce, by multiplication and improvement of the means of internal communication, by development, with the aid of modern mechanical inventions, of the great natural resources of the archipelago, and, in a word, by the uninterrupted devotion of the people to the pursuit of useful objects and the realization of those noble ideas which constitute the higher civilization of mankind.

" Unfortunately, these pure aims and purposes of the American Government and people have been misinterpreted to some of the inhabitants of certain islands, and as a consequence, the friendly American forces have, without provocation or cause, been openly attacked. And why these hostilities? What do the best Filipinos desire? Can it be more than the United States is ready to give? They are patriots and wants liberty.

" In the meantime the attention of the people of the Philippines is invited to certain regulative principles by whicn the United States will be guided in its relations with them.

" These are deemed to be the points of cardinal importance :

" 1. The supremacy of the United States must and will be enforced throughout every part of the archipelago, and those who resist it can accomplish no end other than their own ruin.

" 2. To the Philippine people will be granted the most ample liberty and self-government reconcilable with the maintenance of a wise, just, stable, effective and economical administration of public affairs and compatible with the sovereign and international rights and the obligations of the United States.

" 3. The civil rights of the Philippine people will be guaranteed and protected to the fullest extent ; religious freedom will be assured, and all persons shall be equal and have equal standing in the eyes of the law.

" 4. Honor, justice and friendship forbid the use of the Philippine people or the islands they inhabit as an object or means of exploitation. The purpose of the American Government is the welfare and advancement of the Philippine people.

"5. There shall be guaranteed to the Philippine people an honest and effective civil service in which, to the fullest extent to which it is practical, natives shall be employed.

"6. The collection and application of all taxes and other revenues will be placed upon a sound, economical basis and the public funds, raised justly and collected honestly, will be applied only to defray the regular and proper expenses incurred by and for the establishment and maintenance of the Philippine Government and such general improvements as the public interests may demand. Local funds collected will be used for local purposes and not to be devoted to other ends.

"With such prudent and honest fiscal administration it is believed that the needs of the Government will, in a short time, become compatible with a considerable reduction in taxation.

"7. A pure, speedy and effective administration of justice will be established whereby may be eradicated the evils arising from delay, corruption and exploitation.

"8. The construction of roads, railroads and similar means of communication and transportation, and of other public works, manifestly to the advantage of the Philippine people, will be promoted.

"9. Domestic and foreign trade and commerce, agriculture and other industrial pursuits tending toward the general development of the country, in the interests of the inhabitants, shall be objects of constant solicitude and fostering care.

"10. Effective provision will be made for the establishment of elementary schools in which the children of the people may be educated, and appropriate facilities will be provided for a higher education.

"11. Reforms in all departments of the Government, all branches of the public service and all corporations closely touching the common life of the people will be undertaken without delay and effected conformably with right and justice in a way to satisfy the well-founded demands and the highest sentiments and aspirations of the people.

"Such is the spirit in which the United States comes to the people of the islands, and the President has instructed the commission to make this publicly known.

"In obeying his behest, the commissioners desire to join the President in expressing their good will toward the Philippine people and to extend to the leading representative men an invitation to meet them for the purpose of personal acquaintance and the exchange of views and opinions.

JACOB GOULD SCHURMAN, GEORGE DEWEY,
U. S. Commissioner. U. S. Navy.
ELWELL S. OTIS, CHARLES DENBY,
Major-General, U. S. A. U. S. Commissioner.
DEAN C. WORCESTER,
U. S. Commissioner.

Colonel Charles Denby, one of the members of the Commission, said concerning it, "This is the most important proclamation since the Declaration of Independence. Spanish, Tagalo and English versions of it have been printed and it is proposed to circulate them at all the seaports and they will be sent to the lake towns by gunboats." The effect of this publication was to bring thousands of Filipinos into our lines under the flag of surrender.

In the meantime General MacArthur's army rested at Malolos, the men sleeping in the trenches and occasionally exchanging shots with stray detachments of insurgents, who kept up just enough fire to make life unbearable to the soldiers. After the battle which resulted in the capture of the Filipino capital, a priest and two members of the so-called Filipino Congress, who hid themselves in the woods during the fighting, returned and surrendered to the American troops and stated that 2,000 of the Filipino soldiers were anxious to give up fighting and would do so, except for their officers to keep them under arms. The natives were still further depressed by the loss of one of their best leaders, General Montenegro, who was killed in the battle of Malolos. Next to Aguinaldo and General Luna, he was the greatest of the Filipino officers.

On April 3, 1899, General Otis cabled to the Adjutant-General at Washington as follows:—"Present indications denote insurgent

THE CLOSING EVENTS OF THE PHILIPPINE WAR 465

government in perilous condition. Its army defeated, discouraged and shattered. Insurgents returning to their homes in cities and villages between here and points north of Malolos which reconnoitering parties have reached, and desire protection of Americans. Views from Visayan Islands more encouraging every day."

On April 4th, General MacArthur's brigade moved out of Malolos to the northward in the hope of finding the main body of the Filipino army and effectually destroying it. They were not able however to locate the remnants of Aguinaldo's forces, although they went for twelve miles seeking some trace of them.

About the same time the United States Cruiser *Charleston*, while cruising along the west coast of Luzon Island sent a boat inshore near Dagupan to make soundings. The rebels opened fire, wounding one of the officers, whereupon the cruiser bombarded the town and the insurgents fled.

Malolos soon resumed its natural aspect. Business went on as usual and there was nothing extraordinary except the nightly attacks of the insurgents and the hard work of the soldiers who were active in cleaning up the city and turning it from a place of pestilence to a healthful spot.

Reports reached Manila about this time, that there had been trouble on the island of Negros. On March 27, 1899, a number of bandits headed by a man named Papaissio attempted a rebellion and killed several officials. A proclamation was issued calling upon the natives to rise up against the American troops. Two expeditions were sent to the scene of the disturbance and on April 2d, the headquarters of the bandits at Labzid was captured and the town itself destroyed. Thirty-five prisoners were brought back, and the rebellion was practically quelled at the start. In Samar things were reported to be quiet and the Filipinos were said to be anxious to accept American rule.

LAWTON LEADS AN EXPEDITION.

After the taking of the capital it was decided to send an expedition across the Laguna de Bay and capture Santa Cruz. General Lawton was in command and under him were three gunboats and 1,500 picked men. The expedition consisted of eight companies of the Fourteenth United States Infantry, three companies of the Fourth Cavalry, four of the North Dakota Volunteers, four of the Idaho Volunteers, two mountain guns and two hundred sharpshooters of the Fourteenth Infantry.

General Lawton captured Santa Cruz after a splendid battle. The attack was made simultaneously by land and water and the taking of the city was the result of a spirited charge. Santa Cruz is the military key of Laguna de Bay, the large sheet of water in the centre of the island of Luzon, connected with the Bay of Manila by the Pasig River. The capture of this city cut off the only telegraphic communication between the insurgent forces to the north of Manila and those south of Manila, and consequently these two bodies are forced to act independently of one another in the future.

On Saturday night April 8th, the troops started, but progress in boats was slow so that they did not reach the other side of the lake until noon of the following day. Consequently the attack was postponed until the dawn of April 10th. Then the line advanced in extended order, the gunboats moving slowly along the shore, shelling the wooded places in front of the American lines, driving the Filipinos inland. The Gatling guns were placed upon the decks of the boats and used to clear some entrenchments which were near enough for the fire to be effective. The battalion of the First Idaho had a short sharp fight against a force of Filipinos on the high ground on the right of our advancing line. They made a sudden charge upon the enemy which turned and fled leaving many of their dead on the field. In order that the prisoners taken, might be safely guarded by a few men, their hands and feet were tied. General Lawton happened to see them in that condition, and with his own hands cut the bands from the prisoners and forbade such action in the future.

THE NATIVES MAKE A BOLD STAND.

A mile south of the town on the shore of the lake the Filipinos made a strong stand against the advancing forces. They did not retreat even when the gunboat *Caste* advanced and began to shell their lines, but pluckily answered back with their muskets. A troop of Cavalry however, which was advancing on the city, wheeled round and put these insurgents to flight. They rushed forward at double

THE CLOSING EVENTS OF THE PHILIPPINE WAR 467

time, stopping now and then to fire an effective volley. The gunboat *Laguna de Bay* bombarded the entrenchments close to the town and also the stone buildings occupied by fighting men, particularly the prison which was used as a fort. The shells crushed in the roof of this building in the bombardment. The main line of the Americans in the meantime swept the Filipinos before them, driving them in full retreat through the town to the swamp beyond. The advance was conducted in perfect system, and the exhibition of tactics was enough to gladden the heart of a military expert.

General Lawton with the Fourteenth Infantry under his personal direction made a magnificent charge across a bridge over a creek on the southern side of the town. The men tore down a stone barricade with their hands and drove the enemy backward at the point of the bayonet. After the capture of the city General Lawton established his headquarters at the palace of the Governor of the Alcalda Mayor, province of Laguna of which Santa Cruz is the capital.

GENERAL LAWTON'S NARROW ESCAPE.

During the advance on the city, when the troops were half way to the town from the landing place a single Filipino remained behind when his comrades fled, and bravely met death in an attempt to kill General Lawton. He secreted himself in a house which he knew the Americans would pass. When General Lawton and his staff reached this place the insurgent, who was only six feet away, fired point blank at the group of officers. Fortunately in his excitement his aim was bad, and the bullet flew wide of its mark. After firing, the native jumped from a window and fired from the yard, but again failed to hit anybody. Before he could get out of the yard, he was surrounded and shot three times. Even then he would not surrender, until he was finally struck with a gun and completely disabled.

Two members of the Fourteenth Infantry who ventured a hundred yards beyond the American lines had a lively experience. No sooner had they gotten out of sight of our lines than they were surrounded by insurgent troops who took them prisoners. They were disarmed, but one of them managed to conceal his bayonet in the leg of his trousers, and while their captors were taking them to the insurgent line, this man whose name was Myers, suddenly drew the bayonet and stabbed the Filipino who was guarding him. At the same time the other prisoner grabbed his guard's rifle and struck out with it in every direction, the natives were so surprised that for a time they did not know what to do, and both of the Americans ran for their lives in the direction of their camp. Myers reached the American lines safely, but the other man did not arrive, and it was thought he had been lost. Searching parties were sent out to look for him, and he was finally found hidden in a tree where he had climbed to escape the Filipinos who had pursued him, and where he stayed for many weary hours.

GENERAL OTIS' REPORT.

In reference to this attack of Lawton, General Otis reported as follows :

"Enemy left ninety-three uniformed dead on the field and a number seriously wounded. Lawton captured city without destruction of property, his loss ten wounded, slightly except two. One since died. Lieutenant Elling only officer wounded, slightly in hand. Enemy retired eastward, Lawton in pursuit this morning."

In that pursuit General Lawton captured two more towns, Lumban and Pagsangan. He also captured two gunboats and four launches in the Santa Cruz river, which had been taken from their owners by the insurgents. From Lumban he advanced eight miles north and occupied Pacte the military centre of the district. The troops forded two rivers and marched through tangles of underbrush driving a small number of the enemy before them. In taking Pacte the North Dakotas were in the centre and the sharpshooters flanking, when the column suddenly encountered a cross fire of the rebels. Sharpshooters were moved out quickly and a squad of five of the North Dakota men was surprised by a volley at fifteen yards from a concealed trench. Two were killed and two wounded, one mortally. The Dakota sharpshooters rushed the steep incline and took the trenches.

As the Flying Column, as Lawton's expedition was called, moved northward, the enemy retreated everywhere before it. Late after a victorious march General Lawton was ordered to return to Manila with his expedition. All of the territory taken by him was evacuated. It was considered unwise to deplete our troops on the island

THE CLOSING EVENTS OF THE PHILIPPINE WAR 469

by leaving sufficient garrison in the various places captured to hold them. The main objects of the expedition, which had been to capture the insurgents boats and distribute copies of the proclamation issued by our commissioners had been accomplished and the strength of the American troops had been emphasized throughout the lake region, consequently it was considered that the expedition had been very successful.

AN ATTACK ON GENERAL WHEATON.

In the meantime General Wheaton had been having a lively time near Malolos. The rebels cut the telegraph line at several places between Manila and Malolos, and signal fires were lighted and rockets sent up among the foothills to the right of the railroad. All this signified that something was going to happen, and so it proved, for later the enemy attacked the outposts of the Minnesota regiment between Bigaa and Bocave, five miles south of Malolos, killing two men and wounding fourteen. Simultaneously the outposts of the Oregon regiment at Marilalo, the next station on the way to Manila, were attacked with the result that three Americans were killed and two wounded, while the enemy lost ten men killed and six wounded. Troops were concentrated along the railroad as thickly as possible and the rebels were driven back to the foothills.

WOULD NOT WAIT TO BE KILLED.

Later General Wheaton with the Tenth Pennsylvania and the Second Oregon regiments and two guns advanced to drive the rebels still further. He met with slight resistance near Santa Maria and had one man wounded. The enemy bolted when shelled by the artillery and burned and abandoned the town of Santa Maria, where a thousand rebels had been reported to have collected. During the rest of the day the enemy was in full retreat, burning the villages behind them. Occasionally a few of them dropped to the rear and fired at the advancing American troops, thinking apparently that this would check the advance and cover the retreat of the Filipinos. Finding this ineffectual, these rebels gave it up and fled with the others. As General Wheaton telegraphed to Major-General Otis, "They would not wait to be killed."

One of the sad fortunes of war was described in a cablegram from Admiral Dewey, which caused much comment in this country. The cablegram tells the whole story concisely—all else is conjecture. It said :

"The *Yorktown* visited Baler, Luzon, east coast of Luzon, P. I., April 12th for the purpose of rescuing and bringing away the Spanish forces, consisting of eighty soldiers, three officers and two priests, which were surrounded by 400 insurgents. Some of the insurgents armed with Mauser rifles as reported by natives. Lieutenant J. C. Gilmore, while making an examination of the mouth of the river in an armed boat, was ambushed, fired upon and captured. Fate unknown, as insurgents refused to communicate afterward. The following are missing :

Lieutenant J. C. Gilmore, Chief Quartermaster W. Walton, Coxswain J. Ellsworth, Gunner's Mate H. J. Hygard, Sailmaker's Mate Vendgit, Seamen W. H. Rynders and C. W. Woodbury, Apprentices D. W. A. Venville, J. Peterson, Ordinary Seamen F. Brisolese and O. B. McDonald, Landsmen L. T. Edwards, F. Andersen, J. Dillon and C. A. Morrissey."

Here again was noble sacrifice "for humanity." The little band of Spanish troops less than a hundred all told, had been keeping a large number of Filipinos at bay at Baler for months. Their condition had become critical, and just at the time when there seemed no hope, the gallant Admiral made this brave attempt to aid those who had a few months before been his sworn enemies.

The fate of the reconnoitering party is still doubtful. It was thought that they had been mutilated and tortured after the Filipino fashion of treating prisoners, but word was received some days after that the unfortunate men were being held as prisoners of war in the hope that some day they might be useful to the rebels.

A LIVELY SKIRMISH.

A lively skirmish took place on April 21st. Three companies of the South Dakota marched from Bocave, and united with three companies of the Minnesota regiment just north of that place. There they encountered about 500 insurgents and a brisk interchange of shots resulted. The insurgents finally fell back in good order, after suffering great losses. The Americans lost one man wounded, and returned to Bocave after ammunition was exhausted. The army tugs along the river took up the fighting and drove the insurgents inland.

A force of 200 insurgents attacked the outposts of the Washington regiment on the same day near Tagig, south of Pasig. They were routed after two hours hard fighting, leaving twelve killed and several wounded on the field. Three of our men were wounded in this fight.

General Lawton was put in charge of a new flying column and started to outflank the enemy before joining MacArthur north of Malolos.

A DESPERATE FIGHT.

While he was on the way, one of the most depressing of all our battles with the Filipinos occurred near Quenqua, about four miles northeast of Malolos. In the engagement two gallant officers, Colonel John M. Stotzenberg, of the First Nebraska, and Lieutenant Sisson of the same regiment were killed, and our total loss was six killed and forty-four wounded.

The insurgents had a horseshoe trench, about a mile long, encircling a rice field on the edge of a wood. Major Bell, with forty cavalrymen, while making a reconnoissance, encountered a strong outpost and at the first fire one of his men was killed and five wounded. The Americans retired, carrying their wounded back with great difficulty, closely followed by the enemy. Reinforcements were sent for, and two battalions finally arrived, under Colonel Stotzenberg. He decided that a charge was the best means of dislodging the enemy, and he led the advance in person. When about 200 yards from the enemy's breastworks, a bullet struck him, and he died instantly. Lieutenant Sisson suffered the same fate. The bullet which pierced his heart, pierced also the picture of the woman which he wore around his neck, suspended by a ribbon.

The arrival of the artillery materially aided the American forces, and the Filipinos fell back to another series of trenches, a mile away.

The eyes of the leaders now centered upon Calumpit, to which the insurgent Government had retired when Malolos was taken.

With its fall, they hoped would come the fall of the whole fabric of the so called Filipino Government, and in this it would seem they were correct.

THE TAKING OF CALUMPIT.

The taking of Calumpit was characterized by one of the most brilliant deeds of daring the war has seen—a deed which made Colonel Fred Funston,—"Fighting Fred," as they call him—the most talked of man of the day.

The troops had advanced step by step to the edge of the Bagbag River, beyond which the enemy was intrenched with great skill and was able to hold a large force at bay. The bridge over the river had been cleverly stripped by the Filipinos, and had been so fixed that the girders would part if a train were forced over thus throwing the whole into the river. Fortunately the girders fell before their time. The advance was made along the railroad. The Kansas regiment was on the right side of the road and the Utah light artillery and the First Montana on the left. In the centre was an armored train mounted with six-pounders and rapid fire guns, pushed ahead by Chinamen. The train was moved right up to the mouth of the bridge and a vigorous response was made to the fire of the enemy.

FUNSTON'S MAD FEAT.

Then Colonel Funston did one of the dare-devil feats which have made him famous. "Volunteers to cross the bridge," he cried, "and I'll go myself."

There were too many volunteers eager for the adventure, so the doughty Colonel had to pick his men. He chose Lieutenant Bell, a private of Company E, one from Company K, trumpeter Barsfield and Corporal Ferguson of Company I. This gallant half-dozen set out for their perilous feat in the storm of shot which rained around them. Slowly they crawled accross the iron work of the bridge, with Filipino bullets popping from the heights above them. When they reached the broken span, they dropped into the swift water and swam ashore. Colonel Funston was the first to reach the bank, and as the brave six Americans rose, dripping from the water, and charged upon the trenches with wild western yells, the armed Filipinos fled before them.

THE CLOSING EVENTS OF THE PHILIPPINE WAR 473

The severest fighting however was encountered by the other brigade of MacArthur's division, that commanded by General Hale, and consisting of the Nebraska, South Dakota and Iowa regiments. Six were killed and twelve wounded in this engagement, and many rebels were left dead on the field, and 350 prisoners were taken. The fiercest engagement took place at Pulillan, north of Quenqua. Here the Filipinos were strongly entrenched, and continued to receive reinforcements from Calumpit. When night closed General Hale, and General Wheaton had joined forces, and as Calumpit was too strongly fortified to be taken offhand the troops waited until morning before making the attack.

This was the last ditch of the Filipinos. They brought artillery into use for the first time since the war began, but did not handle it with much effect. The attack was pushed effectively and Calumpit fell, the enemy retiring to Apalit. They finally were forced out of that town, which they burned as they left it.

THE MOST BRILLIANT ACHIEVEMENT OF THE WAR.

In this, the last great battle of the Philippines, Colonel Funston again proved himself a man absolutely without fear. He performed what General MacArthur said was the most brilliant and daring achievement of the war, and won a victory unparalleled in the history of American arms.

The victorious march of the American troops had again been checked by a river—the Rio Grande. It was too deep to ford and the bridge across it had been stripped, as usual, by the enemy. Something had to be done and Colonel Funston volunteered to do it. He asked to be allowed to cross the river and Wheaton gave him permission. The first attempt to cross was to be made at night some miles below the bridge. The barking of dogs revealed activity in the American lines however, and the Filipinos were ready with showers of bullets to check the attempt.

Kansas and Montana volunteers had occupied the whole town except the splendid entrenchments which controlled the bridge over the river. The entire strength of the enemy had been concentrated in these trenches and they must be taken. Only the river (100 yards wide) separated the two forces. Funston first thought of taking fifteen men over the bridge at night, but Corporal Ferguson of Company I, Kansas, reconnoitered and reported that plan impracticable. He went within ten feet of the insurgent sentry on the bridge and was not discovered.

The next day Funston determined to brazenly defy the bullets of the Filipinos and cross the river before the very eyes of the enemy; with 120 Kansas men he went to a point several hundred yards from the bridge, where two privates, White and Trembly, swam with a rope to the opposite shore. They landed and attached the rope to a portion of the insurgent trench, being under the protection of the vigorous fire of our troops. Several insurgents were on the shore where the men landed, but fled when the two fearless fellows began yelling. The rope was attached to three rafts loaded with fifty men, and these were drawn to the shore in safety, although exposed to an awful fire from the enemy.

This little band advanced upon the trenches and literally scared the Filipinos out of their stronghold. The bridge was thus left without protection and our troops immediately crossed it and swept the enemy before them. General Luna, who commanded the retreating forces in person, tried to check the demoralization of his army but was powerless. They could understand some things, but such fearlessness and such fighting was too much for them, and they fled.

FUNSTON MADE BRIGADIER-GENERAL.

In recognition of his bravery in this and other battles, Funston was appointed a Brigadier-General of Volunteers on May 2d. The appointment was strongly recommended by General Otis and Major-General MacArthur, both of whom cabled to Washington the most unstinted praise of the fearless Kansan.

General Funston has been a fighter all his life. His career has been one of unusual excitement, and has served to bring out strongly those qualities which go so far toward making a popular hero. His first appearance before the public was made at a political meeting in Kansas when he was little more than a boy. The meeting was in opposition to his father who was running for Congress, and in the midst of it young Funston sprang upon the platform unannounced and spoke so eloquently to the crowd that he won many of them to his side and aided materially in securing his father's nomination.

After being educated in the common schools and graduated from the Kansas State University, he set to work as a reporter on the Fort Smith *Tribune*, a paper with strong Democratic tendencies. While the editor was absent, young Funston turned the sheet into a Republican organ and wrote some burning editorials in favor of that party. Naturally it cost him his position, and after more or less indefinite wandering he joined the troops in fighting Indians. Shortly after winning his commission in some hot fights he led the memorable expedition to Death Valley and then went on a scientific exploration to Alaska to collect flora and fauna for the Government. From there he went to Cuba and joined the army of Garcia. Here, as elsewhere, his absolute fearlessness made him conspicuous and he was soon appointed chief of artillery. His services with the Cuban army continued until the war between the United States and Spain broke out, when he took command of the Kansas regiment and began the series of triumphs which has made him one of the most admired men in the Army.

OVERTURES FOR PEACE.

At the time, it appeared as though the end of the war had come. It was no secret that the Filipino army was discouraged and dissatisfied at their condition, and this move toward peace was looked upon as a first step in the direction of surrender.

Colonel Arguelesses and Lieutenant Bernal were escorted to General Otis' headquarters with the greatest formality and there they were received by the victorious commander with courtesy and respect. They stated, in behalf of their chief, that they were desirous of ending the war as soon as possible, but that could not be done until Aguinaldo should have time to summon the Filipino Congress and place the terms before that body for action. Therefore, they requested General Otis to order his forces to cease hostilities for two weeks until that necessary step could be taken. General Otis heard the envoys to the end and then replied: "Tell your General that there must be no reservations. He must lay down his arms at once. I cannot recognize the Filipino Government or its Congress. If you wish peace, surrender. You will be allowed perfect amnesty. There will be no punishments for acts already committed. America forgives you.

"The proclamation issued by my Government is sincere, and you shall share with our own people the fullest liberty. But now you must make a complete and unreserved surrender. You are compelled to admit that you are defeated.

"America did not begin the war. It was of your making. There is a big army on the way from the United States and there is nothing for you to do but surrender. This is absolute."

This constant refusal to recognize the Filipino Congress has nettled Aguinaldo not a little, and it is an interesting commentary on his scheme that only sixty of the 300 members of the Congress have taken the necessary oath of allegiance required by their constitution.

The overtures toward peace were fruitless, and the two commissioners returned to the insurgent army, expressing the hope of being able to reach some definite decision within the next few days.

CONTINUED FIGHTING.

But the Americans continued their preparations for more fighting. Positions were strengthened and one or two small skirmishes took place. Major Bell, with a squad of scouts, occupied the town of Macabebe, about four miles southwest of Calumpit and the invading army was welcomed by the townsmen with cheers and the ringing of bells.

A Spanish prisoner who had escaped into the American lines stated that 200 Filipinos had been killed in General Hale's advance on Quingan. This was the largest number of insurgents killed in any battle for several months previous.

During the first week of May, Major-General MacArthur succeeded in capturing San Tomas after encountering strong resistance. Brigadier-General Hale attacked the enemy on the right and Brigadier-General Wheaton on the left. In a daring charge made by the latter's command, the gallant Funston added one more brilliant feat of daring to his already long record, but this time he came out with a badly wounded hand. Colonel Summers took Moasim, on the right, with a part of his Oregon and Minnesota regiments.

When Major-General MacArthur's division advanced on San Fernando, they found the town deserted by the rebels who had left only a small detatchment to cover their retreat. The success of the American arms was so marked that Aguinaldo sent an emissary to General Otis requesting passes for his commissioners to enter our lines. He was told that an unarmed emissary would never be stopped.

PRESIDENT MCKINLEY'S PROPOSED FORM OF GOVERNMENT.

Early in the morning of May 17th, General Lawton's advance guard under Colonel Summers moved on San Isidro, the insurgent capital and captured it after some fighting. The American forces were now in such strong position that they seemed to hold the key to the situation and seven commissioners from Aguinaldo met General Otis and discussed further plans for a settlement. They declared that they were not empowered to bind the Filipino Congress to any agreement and could only submit to that body the results of the conference. The United States Commissioners submitted a proposed form of government which had been approved by President McKinley. It was as follows:

"While the final decision as to the form of government is in the hands of Congress, the President, under his military powers, pending the action of Congress, stands ready to offer the following form of government:

"A Governor-General to be appointed by the President; a Cabinet to be appointed by the Governor-General; all the Judges to be appointed by the President; the Heads of Departments and Judges to be either Americans or Filipinos or both; and also a General Advisory Council, its members to be chosen by the people by a form of suffrage to be hereafter carefully determined upon.

"The President earnestly desires that bloodshed cease, and that the people of the Philippines, at an early date, enjoy the largest measure of self-government compatible with peace and order."

While the discussion was still going on, a sharp skirmish took place near San Fernando, in which fifty Filipinos were killed and many wounded. The American losses were two men killed and twelve wounded. Another small engagement took place at Santa Rita, in which the Filipinos were repulsed.

On May 8th, the President issued orders stating that in each of the new possessions—Cuba, the Philippines and Porto Rico—there would be created "the offices of Auditor of the islands; one Assistant Auditor for auditing the accounts of the Department of Customs; and one Assistant Auditor for auditing the accounts of the Post Offices, who shall be appointed by the Secretary of War, and whose duties shall be to audit all accounts of the islands.

"There is hereby created and shall be maintained the office of Treasurer of the Islands which shall be filled by the appointment thereto of an officer of the regular army of the United States."

The constant procrastination of the Filipinos in the settlement of the terms of surrender soon exhausted the patience of the authorities at Washington. The stand taken by General Otis was known to be approved and his need of more troops was recognized. During May, reinforcements were sent to Manila and arrangements made for the shipment of 2,000 more troops to leave San Francisco whenever necessary. The proposition of General MacArthur to arm the Macabebes and have them join the American forces in fighting their old enemies, the Tagalos, was also looked upon favorably as following an experiment England had so successfully made in her colonies.

Immense pressure was brought to bear upon President McKinley to issue a call for additional volunteers but as General Otis had not yet asked for such a step it became understood that nothing in that direction would be done until a request for large reinforcements was made.

ADMIRAL DEWEY TO RETURN HOME.

Meantime, Admiral Dewey, at his own urgent request, was relieved and was succeeded by Rear-Admiral John C. Watson, who was in charge of the Mare Island Navy Yard at San Francisco. As soon as it was announced that Dewey would return home, the whole country rose as one man to prepare a fitting reception to the man who, above all others, had won the hearts of the American people. Elaborate banquets were planned in all the large cities he would be likely to visit on his return and invitations were cabled to him. A great popular movement was started to present him with a handsome residence as a gift of a grateful nation to its hero. No sooner had the movement started than subscriptions came pouring in from all over the country, and among the first to contribute to this national testimonial was President McKinley.

Dewey's departure from Manila on May 20th, was a rousing ovation. As the *Olympia* got under way the *Oregon*, the *Baltimore* and the *Concord* fired the Admiral's salute, and at the first shot the bands on board started and the white-clad sailors swarmed on deck and gave cheer after cheer. And then came a short half-hour which, in noise at least, equalled the memorable day which first sent Dewey's name sounding around the world. Guns were fired seemingly from everywhere, bands played and men shouted themselves hoarse, little steamers, darting here and there in excitement, whistled their shrill farewells to the departing Admiral, and big steamers, standing stolidly in the harbor, blew their deep basses to swell the chorus. The whole of Manila had gone hero-mad, and through it all, the hero bowed his triumphant way, sorry to leave the scene of his new-won fame, yet glad to get home again to quiet and to rest.

His very leaving was a sign that peace was near for he had requested to be kept on duty until the war was over.

RENEWED HOPES OF THE INSURGENTS.

For a time it seemed almost as though the war were coming to a close, but the near approach of the rainy season made the Filipinos once more take heart, and their guerilla style of warfare became more aggressive. They knew that the suffering of the American soldiers during this rainy season would be greater than their own and that it would give them a chance to recuperate and gather together their more or less scattered forces.

Toward the latter end of May, the Philippine courts which had been closed ever since the American occupation were reopened with all of the Spanish system which did not conflict with the sovereignty of the United States. The Chief Justice of the Court was a native, and the Philippine members were all prominent lawyers of the islands.

General Otis in reply to Secretary Alger's inquiry as to how many troops he considered necessary to complete the conquest of the islands, stated, that with 30,000 troops the American control could be maintained. This once more started the agitation for another call for volunteers, but no steps were taken in that direction. General Otis already had within about 5,000 of the number he required and it was generally understood that if he asked to have his forces increased it would be done by forming skeleton regiments of the volunteers who were mustered out and filling them in with raw recruits.

THE DEFEAT OF PIO DEL PILAR.

During the first week of June a vigorous campaign was begun against General Pio del Pilar. The campaign had for its object the cutting of the insurgent forces in two and the establishment of an American line across the island. The rebel positions at Canita, Taytay and Antipolo were taken in turn. Part of Whalley's brigade under Colonel Truman advanced from Pasig and stormed Taytay, easily driving the rebel skirmish line back. The rebels after setting fire to the town fled to the hills.

General Hall's brigade, with a view to surrounding the enemy, swept down the valley toward Antipolo. Before the advance of the heavy American skirmish line the rebels were powerless. Antipolo was taken and Pio del Pilar's army fled to the mountains. Hall and Truman then joined their forces at Taytay, having thoroughly scoured the Antipolo and Manquina Valleys. Meanwhile, Colonel Whalley, with eight companies of Washington volunteers, embarked in native canoes and being towed by three gunboats, advanced on Morong and after some resistance captured the town, the rebels taking to their heels. The result of these movements is that the American forces gained complete control of Laguna de Bay and cut off the Filipinos from an important source of food supply. It also sent General Pio del Pilar into the mountains where he could do no harm. The next move in contemplation was the sweeping of the Morong Peninsula, where it was supposed a number of Filipinos were still entrenched.

THE HEAVIEST FIGHTING OF THE WAR.

On the 10th of June, a force of 4,500 men under Generals Lawton, Wheaton and Ovenshine, after some hard marching managed to clear the country between the Bay of Manila and Bay Lake, south of Manila. The fighting during this movement was bitter and the obstacles almost insurmountable.

Just south of Las Pinas occurred some of the heaviest fighting of the war. The Filipinos on this occasion showed better discipline and more stubborn bravery than at any other time, and it was only after the severest fighting and the concentrated fire of the gunboats on Bakoor that the rebels were eventually forced to abandon their position. The country through which the fighting was done was mainly made up of lagoons, mud and water fringed with bamboo. No sooner had the firing opened than it was seen that the Americans had the hardest task of the war before them. Finally after the severest kind of fighting, the Fourteenth Infantry swam the Zapote River and drove the rebels before them. The Filipinos still resisted desperately but they had been broken and soon retreated to the strongly fortified town of Imus.

General Otis cabled to Washington,—" Success Lawton's troops, Cavite Province, greater than reported yesterday. Enemy mumbering over 4,000 lost in killed, wounded and captured more than one-third. Have retreated south to Imus, their arsenal."

On June 20th, he sent the following dispatch :

" Wheaton at Imus. * * * Sent battalion south on reconnaissance direction of Perez Das Marinas yesterday morning. Battalion encountered enemy's forces 2,000, marching to attack Imus, successfully impeding its progress. Repulsed enemy with heavy loss, enemy leaving over 100 dead on the field, our loss five killed and twenty-three wounded. Wheaton * * * * is driving enemy beyond Perez Das Marinas, now in his possession. Wheaton's qualities for bold and successful attack unsurpassed."

Reports had for some time been circulated that General Luna was killed at the headquarters of Aguinaldo in an altercation with an officer and toward the latter end of June, the Filipino Junta in London, admitted that it had definite confirmation of the report.

About the same time the reports that another call for volunteers would be issued became stronger and it was known beyond doubt that the Cabinet had given the matter its serious attention on more than one occasion.

No formal call for volunteers was made, however ; it was simply announced that fifteen new regiments would be formed for special service. In a remarkably short time these regiments were completed and ten additional ones were recruited before the middle of September. Campaigning in the Philippines, though by no means a sinecure, so far as health and comfort were concerned, became a series of small victories, comparatively unimportant in themselves but serving to advance the American lines and to scatter the Philippine forces.

In the latter part of June, General Otis, yielding to the petitions of many of the merchants of the islands, opened a number of ports including, among others, San Fernando, on the west coast of Luzon, Aparri, on the north coast, Curimoa and all ports in the islands of Samar and Leyte, and shippers immediately began to send out their delayed cargoes of hemp.

The tropic weather soon began to tell seriously on the condition of the American troops. From the middle of May to the middle of July, no volunteer regiment had a sick list of less than 20 per cent., and most of them had more than one-fourth of their number unable to report for duty. The Nebraska Regiment, which was the worst sufferer, had less than two hundred sound men in its ranks during the first week of July. At this time, the American newspaper correspondents in the island, chafing under the restrictions of the censorship, issued a "round robin," setting forth their grievances, and presented it to General Otis, who promised greater liberality in the future. The "round robin" created quite a disturbance in Washington, though no official steps were taken in the matter.

During July, an important change was made in the rules governing practice before the courts, and the American system was, in many respects, substituted for the Spanish. The change abolished procurators and shifted all of their duties to the attorneys. It also required that members of the bar must be residents of the island, and that citizens of foreign governments be ineligible to practice at the bar. The new order gave the courts sole power to determine the qualifications of the attorneys—a power which, before that, had been in the hands of the bar association.

Minor battles were constantly being fought with victory always on the American side. About July 20th, Captain Byrne of the Sixteenth Infantry, with seventy men, routed the robber bands at Negros to the number of 450 men and killed 115 of them. On July

26th, Colomba, an important trading town on the south shore of Laguna de Bay, was captured by Brigadier-General Hall after two hours of sharp fighting. During this action, Captain McGrath of the Twenty-first Infantry and Lieutenant Batson swam the river under fire and procured a casco to ferry the troops across. Two or three days later, the insurgents attempted to re-take the town but were repulsed after an hour's hard fighting. During August, General MacArthur made decided advances which served to clear the country to the left, right and rear of the insurgents. On August 12th, General Young's forces occupied San Mateo after severe fighting and a brave charge over mud-covered fields.

General Bates' mission to Sulu accomplished his end about this time. On August 24th, General Otis cabled the War Department as follows:

"General Bates has returned. Mission was successful. Agreement made with Sultan and Datos whereby sovereignty United States over entire Jolo archipelago is acknowledged; its flag to fly on land and sea. United States to occupy and control all points deemed necessary. Introducing firearms prohibited. Sultan to assist in suppressing piracy. Agrees to deliver criminals accused of crime not committed by Moros against Moros. * * * Moros, Western Mindanao, friendly, ask permission to drive out insurgents."

In spite of the numerous defeats inflicted upon them, the insurgents still continued their campaign. It was impossible, on account of the weather and the bad condition of the roads, to carry on any very vigorous plan of action against them, although small fights were constantly occurring. After giving up San Fernando, they entrenched themselves about Angeles, in which position they made a stubborn resistance to the attack of Lieutenant-Colonel Smith's regiment and gave up only after four hours' hard fighting. In the province of Cavite, they were supposed to have been effectually scattered but succeeded in gathering together several thousand men and occupying a number of the smaller towns, from which it was almost impossible to drive them until weather conditions became more favorable.

After the San Fernando engagement, the insurgents tried to stop the northward advance of the Americans by threatening the railroad communication. A considerable force of General Pio del Pilar's men crossed the Rio Grande, and threatened Balinag, Juinguo and several other places whose garrisons were small, and other bands attempted to tear up the railroad tracks between Bigaa and Malolos. Reinforcements were sent from Manila, however, and, the garrisons from Balinag and Juinguo set out against Pio del Pilar's forces at the same time. The combined attack easily drove the insurgents away. The Filipinos were also easily repulsed when, in September, they attacked Santa Rita, Cuagua and San Antonio.

The offers of autonomy which the Americans had made to the Filipinos did not meet with a favorable answer. The reply adopted by the Filipino Congress repeated the arguments contained in the appeal to the powers for recognition and the claims that the Americans were the aggressors in the war and concluded:

"Notwithstanding the foregoing, we could have accepted your sovereignty and autonomy if we had not seen by the behavior of the Americans in the beginning that they were strongly opposed to us through race prejudice, and the high-handed methods of dealing with us made us fear for the future in your hands. Finally, we thank you for your offers of autonomy under sovereignty."

The Philippine Commissioners, having completed their work, were recalled by the President in time for them to reach Washington early in November, when the results of their investigations were to be laid before the President. The fact that General Otis did not return with them, but sent in his written report, effectually silenced the rumors that he was to be recalled from command.

During this time, changes were being made in the American forces in the islands. The volunteer regiments were all sent home by the middle of September and additional regiments had been sent out to take their places. The reception accorded the returning volunteers by their home cities was, in each case, an ovation. The cities were gaily decorated and everyone put on holiday attire to celebrate fittingly the return of the heroes. Nevada, Colorado, Washington, Wyoming, Utah, Nebraska, Pennsylvania,—every state that had a regiment in service, joined in the jubilations. The reception of the Tenth Pennsylvania, in Pittsburg, was attended by President McKinley and many of the most prominent men of the nation.

But all the patriotism, all the fire and enthusiasm of a hero-worshipping nation, burst forth in one great wave when Admiral Dewey reached New York. The route of the great parade in his honor was lined by countless thousands of cheering, shrieking, men and women; the whole country rose up to shout a greeting and a welcome to the man who had sent her fame ringing round the world on that memorable first of May. The arch that spanned the course of the parade was the best product of America's architectural genius, the loving cup and the sword presented as the nation's gifts were the richest products of the maker's art, nothing that could be done to honor the hero was left undone. Governor Roosevelt proclaimed September 29th and 30th public holidays, and throngs from every state in the Union rushed to New York to join the celebration. In Washington, Admiral Dewey was officially received by the President and escorted by a mounted escort of notables to the Capitol where Secretary Long presented him with the nation's sword. President McKinley concluded the ceremonies with a dinner to the hero at the White House. The same scenes were witnessed in Washington as had been seen in New York,—the same wild enthusiasm,—the crowds of shouting humanity pushing and surging to get a glimpse of the man who had given them an ideal of American manhood and American bravery. And through all the tumult, Admiral Dewey, cool, modest, retiring, bowed his way, thankful for the gratitude of the people, but more thankful for the rest that awaited him after it was all over.